COLLECTED WOR

BERNARD LONER(

VOLUME 5

UNDERSTANDING AND BEING

COLLECTED WORKS
OF BERNARD
LONERGAN

UNDERSTANDING
AND BEING

The Halifax Lectures on INSIGHT

Edited by Elizabeth A. Morelli
and Mark D. Morelli

Revised and Augmented by Frederick E. Crowe
with the collaboration of
Elizabeth A. Morelli, Mark D. Morelli,
Robert M. Doran, and Thomas V. Daly

Published for Lonergan Research Institute
of Regis College, Toronto
by University of Toronto Press
Toronto Buffalo London

Understanding and Being

Second edition, revised and augmented, of
Understanding and Being:
An Introduction and Companion to Insight,
edited by Elizabeth A. Morelli and Mark D. Morelli,
first published by The Edwin Mellen Press,
New York and Toronto, 1980.

ISBN 0-8020-3987-1 (cloth)
ISBN 0-8020-3989-8 (paper)

Canadian Cataloguing in Publication Data

Lonergan, Bernard J.F. (Bernard Joseph Francis), 1904–84
Collected works of Bernard Lonergan

Vol. 5, edited by Elizabeth A. Morelli and Mark D. Morelli, also issued
separately and originally published: New York : E. Mellen Press, 1980.
Partial contents: v. 5. Understanding and being.
Includes bibliographical references.
ISBN 0-8020-3987-1 (v. 5)
1. Theology – 20th century. 2. Catholic Church. I. Crowe,
Frederick E., 1915– II. Doran, Robert M., 1939– .
III. Lonergan Research Institute. IV. Title.
BX891.L595 1988   230   c88-093328-3

The Lonergan Research Institute
gratefully acknowledges the contribution of
M. JEANNE BELAIR
given in honor of her uncle
M. JOHN BELAIR, S.J.,
initiator of the Halifax lectures,
toward publication of this volume
of the Collected Works of Bernard Lonergan.

Contents

McNally Building, Saint Mary's University, Halifax, where the *Insight* seminar was held in 1958.

Editors' Preface

Our preface will say something (1) on the planning and course of the seminar which issued in this volume; (2) on the record of the seminar proceedings; (3) on the 1980 edition of *Understanding and Being*, and (4) on the relation of the present volume to that edition.

The Halifax seminar on *Insight*. Bernard Lonergan taught at the Gregorian University in Rome from 1953 to 1965, and from 1955 on returned each year to spend the summer in Canada or the United States.

During part of this time his brother and fellow Jesuit, Greg, was stationed in Halifax, and that simple fact stands at the source of the volume *Understanding and Being*. For from 1956 to 1958 (at least those years), Bernard would go to Halifax at the invitation of the President of Saint Mary's University, Fr Patrick Malone, to spend a good part of the summer with his brother's community; and it was through the enterprise of Fr M. Jack Belair, also on the staff of the University during those years, that he was persuaded to give these lectures.

A veteran sailor (he had crossed the Atlantic that way seven times), he traveled by sea for his first trip to Halifax in 1956, embarking at Naples on July 8, and landing on July 18. The next year, however, he was due to lecture at Boston College right after classes ended in Rome, so abandoning sea travel (permanently, it turned out), he flew to Boston, gave his two weeks of lectures (Mathematical Logic; Existentialism), and flew on to Halifax for the rest of the summer.

It was during this vacation that he agreed to lecture the following year on the book *Insight*, which had just appeared. And so next July he was back in Halifax, relaxing and preparing his lectures for the coming seminar: 'I have been working out the relations between 'Insight' and Kant's Critique of Pure Reason, and the rest of the time loafing.'[1]

The seminar opened on August 4th, with about 35 registrants, and others sitting in as auditors. They were a diverse mix (professors and teachers, students and professional people, lay and clerical vocations) and had diverse home bases (from St John's, Newfoundland, to Los Angeles, California). The atmosphere was familial: for example, Stan and Roberta Machnik, close friends of Bernard, motored from Montreal with their children; the latter were lodged in the university infirmary at night, found entertainment at Saint Mary's Boat Club during the lectures, and were put to bed early in the evenings, to allow both father and mother to attend all sessions.[2]

Lectures were held mornings, 10.00 to 12.00, Monday to Saturday the first week (Saturday included because the following Monday was a civic holiday – 'Natal' day in Halifax), and Tuesday to Friday the second week. Evening discussions, 8.00 to 10.00, were held on at least six days: Monday, Tuesday, and Thursday of the first week (there was none on Wednesday, and no record of any on Friday or Saturday); and Tuesday, Wednesday, and Thursday of the second week.

Record of the seminar proceedings. When Fr Stan Tillman, Professor of Philosophy at Xavier University, Cincinnati, arrived for the seminar with full taping equipment, the task of recording the proceedings was turned over to him, and it is his voice that is heard in the announcement as each tape begins.

This was the only recording made of the seminar proceedings. It is good quality, made on 7-inch reels (1800 ft, 1 1/2 hr at 3 3/4 ips), but of course there are unfortunate gaps: the first and last words of the lecture or discussion are often lacking, as is the first hour of the lecture of Wednesday, August 13, and only five of the evening discussions were recorded. The original reels have not survived, but copies were made (also on reels) and distributed immediately, through Alan White & Associates, Westmount, Montreal (we are not aware of copies made by anyone else). Further, cassettes were made from the reels, and copies made of the cassettes, but we have not documented that development.

1 Letter to F. Crowe, July 23, 1958. Extracts from Kant that Lonergan made at this time are extant in the Archives.
2 Letter of Stan Machnik to Fr R. Eric O'Connor, August 6, 1958.

Three sets of the copied reels were available to us for this edition: that of the Lonergan Research Institute (LRI); one from Fr W.A. Stewart (WAS) of Saint Mary's University, complete except for the first part of discussion 4; and one from Fr Daniel J. Shine (DJS), Boston College, complete except for lecture 10. Even though all three derive from the one original, there are several differences in the beginning and ending points, and some internal differences due to splicing, over-recording, and so on; for reader control we will note the more important of these.

For the morning lectures, however, there are further resources in two complete sets of fairly copious notes: one made by Fr Stewart (WAS), the other my own (FEC); for the first four lectures there are also some pages of notes made by Fr Tim Fallon, then a doctoral student in the University of Toronto. Unfortunately, except for the odd fragment, no notes seem to have been taken at the evening discussions.

Transcription was not begun till a dozen years later, when Fr Belair found willing secretaries (from the Adult Studies Department of the University) to tackle the job. But secretaries, even university secretaries, are not always experts on Lonergan's ideas, and this transcript, which anyway did not get beyond the first four lectures, has its full share of mistakes and question marks; still, it was a start on an enormous and valuable project.

It was around this time that Philip and Fiona McShane arrived in Toronto, set to work on the task anew, and produced an expertly done transcription of all ten lectures, and three of the five taped discussion periods. The aim of this transcript was a text that would reproduce Lonergan verbatim, 'warts' and all;[3] it was not meant to be an edited text, but it is an indispensable first step, it was used by the editors of 1980 and 1989 (though they did their independent work of transcription), and it remains in the Lonergan Archives as a valuable check on edited versions.

***Understanding and Being* 1980.** In the 1970s, when Lonergan was still at Regis College, Toronto, Elizabeth A. Morelli and Mark D. Morelli came to that city for doctoral studies in philosophy.[4] In 1973 they asked Fr Lonergan's permission to edit the lectures for possible publication; this he readily granted, but he gave instructions that they should 'rewrite' the lectures for the reading public, and encouraged them to value 'correct-

3 Letter of Philip McShane to F. Crowe, March 21, 1988.
4 Each in due course began a thesis project dealing with Lonergan's ideas; both theses were happily completed, and have been published by University Press of America.

ness' over verbatim reproduction of his words. This put a heavy responsibility on the young editors, involving them in 'the restructuring of sentences and paragraphs, the reordering of paragraphs within sections, the writing of portions missing from the tapes, the deletion of certain bald statements at Lonergan's direction, the introduction of section divisions, section headings, and chapter headings,' and so on. In this task they worked from a corrected transcription (of lectures and discussions) which they produced themselves, listening on some occasions 'as many as fifty times' till finally less audible portions of the tapes were deciphered.[5]

Only those who have been through similar work on Lonergan's lectures will realize the enormous labor this brief account merely suggests. The result, however, justified and rewarded the labor; Lonergan wrote the Morellis that he 'was very pleased with the smooth job you performed,'[6] and he reported to John Todd, 'I read through their transcription and found it excellent.'[7]

The editors gave their volume the title *Understanding and Being*, explaining in their Introduction[8] that chapters 1–5 correspond to the first part of *Insight* (hence, *Understanding*), and chapters 6–10 correspond to the second part which treats of metaphysics and its extension into other areas (hence, *Being*).

The present volume. The new edition of *Understanding and Being* had its own difficulties, for its appearance in the context of the Collected Works suggested some modification of editorial policy, but Lonergan's approval of the 1980 volume required us to ponder well any changes we might make. This was worked out at length by the Morellis and the Toronto section of the team – Robert M. Doran and myself, joined later by Thomas V. Daly – with frequent exchanges by letter or by telephone.

It remained our intention, of course, to respect Fr Lonergan's wish that the text not be a verbatim transcription, to respect also the text that he had approved for publication. Within those restrictions, we have tried to situate the volume in the context of the Collected Works, which is that of the total history of Lonergan's thought. From his first 'publication' in

5 From the Morelli correspondence with the Lonergan Research Institute, during 1988.
6 Letter of July 12, 1978.
7 Letter of September 16, 1978.
8 Elizabeth A. Morelli and Mark D. Morelli (eds.), *Understanding and Being: An Introduction and Companion to Insight* (New York and Toronto: The Edwin Mellen Press, 1980) x.

1928 to his last in 1983, Lonergan's work is the basis for study of a fascinating history, in which he not only developed his thought enormously, but communicated it in quite different manners for quite different readers or audiences. One has only to study *Verbum*, *Insight*, *Method*, and the papers of *A Third Collection* to realize the continually expanding dimensions of his thinking. But he worked too in a series of quite diverse settings: doing research on Thomas Aquinas for Thomist scholars, lecturing on theology in Latin for a largely clerical audience, writing for the university world in *Insight* and *Method*, speaking to specialists in his carefully crafted congress papers, adopting a teaching style in his occasional lectures and summer institutes, and conversing quite informally in interviews he gave – the context changes, and his style changes with the context.

We think we have been able to set our text in this ongoing history, without running counter to the wishes Lonergan expressed in 1973. The text remains that which was so competently edited in 1980. The changes introduced into that text are the minor points of style that situate the talks in Halifax in 1958, the work of a teacher teaching rather than of an author writing a book. A review of the 1980 edition remarked that 'it affords ... a suggestion of what it is like to be taught by [Lonergan] when he is in full form.'[9] So we have 'lecture' instead of 'chapter,' 'if you say' instead of 'if one says,' 'yesterday' instead of 'in the previous chapter'; and coming to particularities of space and time, we have reference to a 'harbor' instead of a 'river' bridge, to 'Sputnik' rather than to a 'satellite,' and so on.

In regard to other changes we have exercised greater freedom, and this under three headings: footnotes, editorial notes, discussion periods.

In the footnotes we have related the text closely to the state of the recording, noting when the sound starts and stops, when it is indistinct, when coffee breaks occur, when Lonergan speaks in an aside (at least, where that fact is more significant). This not only controls the editing but also helps interpret the text: for example, a summary takes on a slightly different meaning when it is given before or after a coffee break. We have tried to track down more of Lonergan's undocumented allusions, while distinguishing our bibliographic material from his (notes are regularly those of the editors, unless otherwise stated). Some of his sketchy documentation, based on imperfect or faulty memory, is included as revealing

9 Fred Lawrence, *Theology Today* 39 (1982–83) 478–79.

the background out of which he lectured. Cross-references from one part of the proceedings to another are also more numerous.

The editorial notes are a somewhat different matter. In contrast to the footnotes, which remain for the most part within the context of the seminar and the book *Insight*, they take as their context the total work of Lonergan: 'they would illuminate his meaning through data on his history, on the context in which he wrote [or spoke], on parallel or contrasting points made in his other writings [or lectures]' (*Collection* [Collected Works of Bernard Lonergan 4, 1988] 255). But they are in the nature of research notes rather than interpretation or history. Interpretation and history must surely follow: the lectures were given a year after the publication of *Insight*, when reviews had started to appear, and five years after Lonergan had written the book, when he had had time to reflect on his ideas and solidify or advance his position. One could undertake some very interesting studies of the relation of *Insight* to these lectures, and pointers to such studies creep into the notes, but that is not their specific purpose.

The other major difference in this edition is the inclusion in full of the evening discussions, so far as that was possible. Selections from all five discussion tapes were transcribed and edited by the Morellis and included in the 1980 edition. For the present edition, I transcribed the two tapes omitted by the McShanes – in the verbatim form they used, but for the most part in a preliminary draft; thanks to the suggestions and corrections sent me by the Morellis, I did not have to complete this task, so my text too, with its imperfections, remains in the Archives as a partial check on the edited text.

In the execution of our task, the tapes were played over and over again, as for the 1980 edition. Lonergan spoke with remarkable clarity (though his unusual cadence and intonation take some getting used to), but he frequently talked while working at the blackboard, and sometimes dropped his voice for an aside; in the evening discussions many of the questions and remarks from the floor were indistinct, and regularly there were interferences – laughter or coughing within the lecture room, airplanes flying overhead, and so on. There can therefore be no definitive transcription of the tapes; both the Morellis and the Toronto team found new clarity as they listened again, and future listeners will no doubt further improve our work.

Similarly with the editing: Lonergan spoke in a freewheeling manner, with frequent false starts, digressions, asides, corrections, anacoluthons, faults of grammar, and so on. So there is no definitively right way to do it, but the 1980 edition pleased Lonergan, and that is the edition we present again, with the differences noted, and some few revisions that were agreed upon. The full text, in fact, went to the Morellis, lecture by lecture and discussion by discussion, for their input, and the final form is the work of the whole editing team.

As for the minutiae of editing, we followed closely the pattern set in volume 4 of the Collected Works, using the *Oxford American Dictionary* and *The Chicago Manual of Style* as guides. Latin and Greek phrases are left in the text (the Greek in roman transcription this time), and translations, except in certain lexicographical passages, are left for the back of the volume. For the frequent references to Aristotle and Thomas Aquinas, we have slightly adapted regular usage (Bekker numbers, of course, are given for Aristotle, and numbers of the Marietti editions for some Thomist references). We give scripture the way Lonergan did, but regularly add the text of the *Revised Standard Version*.

We thank those who responded to our request for memories of the seminar, its subsequent history, notes and tapes of the proceedings, or suggestions on this edition: M. John Belair, Stan and Roberta Machnik, Philip McShane, Patrick Malone, Daniel J. Shine, William Arthur Stewart, and Stan Tillman; Marcela Dayao for putting the whole text on computer; The Edwin Mellen Press for their gracious cooperation; Roderick Mac-Kenzie, William Mathews, Walter Principe, Giovanni Sala, Leo Serroul, Michael Vertin, and Geoffrey Williams, for advice on various minutiae of editing. Special thanks are due to Gregory H. Carruthers for his work on the Lexicon of Latin and Greek Words and Phrases, and for compiling the Index. Finally, the Trustees of the Lonergan Estate ask us to express their special thanks to Elizabeth A. Morelli and Mark D. Morelli for the generous transfer of the copyright.

Frederick E. Crowe
(for the team of editors)

UNDERSTANDING AND BEING

The Halifax Lectures on *Insight*

1

Self-appropriation and Insight[1]

1   Self-appropriation

By way of an introductory lecture we will try, What is self-appropriation? *Insight* may be described as a set of exercises in which, it is hoped, one attains self-appropriation. The question naturally arises, What does that mean, and why go to all the trouble? Unfortunately, the question is so fundamental that to answer it is in a way more difficult than to attain self-appropriation.

You may have heard this story about Columbus. When he was hailed before the grandees of Spain for some misdemeanor or crime, he alleged in his defense the greatness of his exploit in discovering America. They said to him, 'Well, there was nothing wonderful about that. All you had to do was get in a boat and travel west, and you were bound to hit it sometime.' To make his point Columbus asked, 'Which one of you can make an egg stand on its end?' All of them thought about it, and some tried it, but none succeeded. 'Well, can you?' they demanded. Columbus took the egg, gave it a little tap, and it stood on its end. 'Well, that's easy!' they said. 'It's easy when you know how,' Columbus replied.

More generally, it is much simpler to do things than to explain what you are trying to do, what the method is that you are employing in doing it, and how that method will give you the results. In other words, the simple matter of attaining self-appropriation can be complicated by an

1 Opening lecture, Monday, August 4, 1958.

enormous series of surrounding questions that are all more difficult than
the actual feat of attaining self-appropriation. For that reason I do not
start talking about the method of the book *Insight* until about chapter
14.[2] Prior to that there is a method, but it is pedagogical – the type of
method employed by a teacher who does not explain to his pupils what
he is trying to do but goes ahead and does it. He has a method, but they
are being cajoled. They have their attention held, one thing is given them
after another, and they get there. But if the teacher had to answer such
questions as 'What are we trying to do?' and 'How are we going to get
there?' he would never succeed in teaching anything. Questions about
method and questions about the possibility of knowledge are much more
difficult than the knowledge itself or the actual achievement.[a] Still,
because there is needed perhaps some framework for these lectures, I
will begin by discussing self-appropriation.

1.1 The Pursuit of the Unknown

First, then, seeking knowledge is seeking an unknown. If we knew what
we were looking for when we are seeking knowledge, we would not have
to look for it, we would have it already. If you want a motorcar, you know
exactly what you want, but when you want knowledge you cannot know
what you want.

Now this seeking of knowledge is a special kind of tendency. Aristotle
spoke about heavy bodies seeking the center of the earth. They had a
natural appetite to fall, but it was an unconscious appetite. In us, when
we are hungry we seek food, and when we are thirsty we seek drink, and
in that there is a conscious tendency, a conscious feeling. It is not merely
a tendency towards an object, it is a conscious tendency. But in seeking

2 Bernard Lonergan, *Insight: A Study of Human Understanding* (London:
   Longmans, Green and Co., 1957; 2nd ed., revised, 1958; paperback ed.,
   San Francisco: Harper & Row, 1978) 396–98. *Insight* was written during
   the years 1949–53. Parts of it were rewritten during 1954–55, in
   response to the publisher's critiques. It was published on April 1, 1957.
   Revisions for a second edition were done in April 1958, just a few months
   before the present lectures were delivered. A third and then a fourth
   edition, and several reprintings, followed without change, except that the
   fourth edition changed the pagination of the preface (with the result that
   all the index references to the preface are off by one page). The Collected Works edition (CWL 3) will incorporate some of this history; the
   rest can be studied in the Archives at the Lonergan Research Institute,
   Toronto.

knowledge, not only do we tend towards it, not only do we do so consciously, but we also do so intelligently. Moreover, we do so critically; we examine what we have been given and wonder if it is right, and we test it and control it. Furthermore, one can seek knowledge quite deliberately; one can travel all the way from California to Halifax to follow a course of lectures and discussions. Seeking knowledge may be not only conscious, intelligent, and rational, but also deliberate. Scientists seek knowledge, aim at something, seek an unknown, and yet they go about it methodically. They have a series of well-defined steps which they take. This deliberate, methodical seeking of an unknown that you find in science is quite different from the deliberateness and method, for example, of a construction company putting up a new building. They have blueprints; they know exactly what they want all along the line. But when you're seeking knowledge you're seeking an unknown.

There is a combination, then, of knowledge and ignorance: knowledge, in the sense that knowledge is sought consciously, intelligently, rationally, deliberately, methodically; and ignorance, because if you already knew you would not have to bother seeking. This combination indicates the existence of an ideal, the pursuit of an ideal. Moreover, it is a built-in ideal; it is based upon innate tendencies. Aristotle's *Metaphysics* begins with the statement, 'All men naturally desire to know.'[3] He goes on to add, 'particularly with their eyes,' but the point is that there is a natural tendency, a natural desire to know.[b]

The scholastics distinguished natural, acquired, and infused habits. Supernatural habits are said to be infused. Faith, hope, and charity do not come by nature, or by the efforts of nature, but by the grace of God. There are also acquired habits: you are not born knowing how to play the violin or with an innate tendency to typewrite so many words per minute; the habit has to be acquired. But besides infused and acquired habits there are also tendencies with which we start out and which we must have in order to start. If a child never asks questions, you cannot

---

3 Aristotle, *Metaphysics*, I, 1, 980a 21–26. Aristotle's text reads: 'All men by nature desire to know. An indication of this is the delight we take in our senses; for even apart from their usefulness they are loved for themselves; and above all others the sense of sight. For not only with a view to action, but even when we are not going to do anything, we prefer seeing (one might say) to everything else. The reason is that this, most of all the senses, makes us know and brings to light many differences between things.' Translation by W.D. Ross, in *The Basic Works of Aristotle*, ed. Richard McKeon (New York: Random House, 1941) 689.

teach him. You class him as retarded or lower than retarded. There has to be something with which to start, and that is this tendency towards the ideal.

The pursuit of knowledge, then, is the pursuit of an unknown, and the possibility of that pursuit is the existence of an ideal.

1.2 The Development of the Ideal of Knowledge

My second point is that this ideal is not conceptually explicit. It becomes explicit only through the pursuit of knowledge. I will illustrate that first from science and then from philosophy.

1.2.1 In Science

It is well known that Pythagoras proved the theorem that the square of the hypotenuse is equal in area to the sum of the squares of the other two sides of a right-angled triangle. But the Pythagoreans also made another famous discovery, that of the harmonic ratios. The harmonic ratios are the reciprocals of an arithmetical progression: thus $1/2$, $1/4$, $1/6$, ... are harmonic ratios because 2, 4, 6, ... form an arithmetical progression. The Pythagoreans discovered that the fractions corresponded to the tension or the length of strings on a musical instrument, and that discovery was a knockout – there is a connection between mathematics and the sounds that are harmonious! They discovered not only that the mathematics was very interesting in itself, but also that it had a relation to what is listened to, the music: it accounted for the harmony in music. You can see how the Pythagoreans obtained from that the notion that the whole of reality is made up of numbers. The ideal that the universe is to be explained by numbers came as a generalization of this discovery – that, at least, is a fair guess about the origin of this Pythagorean doctrine.

The discovery of the relation between numbers and sensible phenomena was developed by Archimedes. He made the famous statement, 'Give me a place to stand, and I will lift the earth' – he discovered the law of the lever. He wrote a treatise on floating bodies in which elementary principles of hydrostatics are worked out in the same way as geometry was worked out by Euclid.

Then in the modern world Galileo put forward the ideal that what you are seeking in knowledge is the mathematization of nature, the expression of nature through numbers. He discovered the law of falling bodies: when bodies fall in a vacuum the distance traversed is proportional to the square of the time elapsed. Such is the mathematical formula for the free fall of a body. Kepler discovered his law of planetary motion, that the planets move in ellipses, that the sun is at one of the foci of the ellipse, that the area covered by the radius vector is a function of the time. There are two foci; the radius vector is the line from a focus to the perimeter; the planet moves around the perimeter; the moving radius vector sweeps over equal areas in equal times; and the square of the period (the time taken by the planet to complete a circuit) is proportional to the cube of its average distance from the sun. All of these further discoveries are analogous to the Pythagorean discovery of harmonic ratios: Archimedes' law relating displacement and buoyancy; Galileo's law of falling bodies; Kepler's three laws of planetary motion. In each case there was formulated a mathematical expression verifiable in concrete data.

An enormous further step was taken by Newton in his *Mathematical Principles of Natural Philosophy*. He went from particular laws, such as those of Galileo and Kepler, to system. In other words, just as Euclid posited a set of definitions, axioms, and postulates from which followed a series of theorems and problems, so Newton proposed not just particular laws but a whole system. Just as Euclid demonstrated his theorems, so Newton proved that if a body moves in a field of central force with some velocity v, then that body will move in a conic section.[4] The geometry of conic sections was worked out by the Greeks; what Newton proved was that a body moving in a field of central force will move in a conic section. He did not merely establish a particular law, but from a set of axioms regarding laws of motion he deduced the movements of the planets. Kepler discovered the figure inductively by examining the data on the movements. Newton explained deductively why it had to be that figure, why it had to be an ellipse or some other conic section, after the fashion of Euclid deducing his theorems[c] from his definitions and axioms.

I have illustrated the development of an ideal of knowledge. What is the ideal? It is the mathematization of nature. It starts from particular laws; it moves towards a system; and its great achievement was Newtonian system. It lasted for a few hundred years, but it had been on the basis of Euclidean geometry. Einstein moved it to another basis, a more general geometry, and quantum mechanics has taken us right out of the field of

4 An explanation of conic sections followed – omitted here.

law and system. The fundamental ideal has become states and probabilities.

The ideal, then, not only develops; it changes. So one's ideal of knowledge, what one is seeking in knowledge, is something that is not conceptually explicit. It becomes explicit in the pursuit of knowledge.

This particular line of development starts from particular discoveries and moves to Newtonian system and beyond that to the system of relativity. When scientists still fail to obtain theories that satisfy all the data, they change the ideal itself from law and system to states and probabilities. They begin working towards a different ideal of what knowledge really would be if they reached it.

We may take another example, one that runs concomitantly. The scholastic definition of a science is 'certain knowledge of things through their causes.'[d] Certain knowledge of things expresses common sense. If through certain knowledge of things – for example, I know this is a brush – I work out all the causes, I have moved into science. This notion of science has an implication. If you are seeking certain knowledge of things through their causes, you start out from the thing, and you work to the discovery of the causes. When you have the causes, you want to check; so you work back from the causes until you can construct things out of them. The scholastics called the first part of this movement resolution into the causes, *resolutio in causas*, analysis. The second part of the movement was *compositio ex causis*, synthesis. From the ideal of science as knowledge of things by their causes we get the two ideas of analysis and synthesis: movement from the things to the causes, and then movement from the causes back to the things.

Moreover, Aristotle had a very precise idea about things and an equally precise idea about causes. What is a thing? A thing falls under the predicaments: substance, quantity, quality, relation, action, passion, place, time, posture, habit. A thing is what fits under the ten predicaments. What are causes? There are four: end, agent, matter, and form. The end moves the agent, the agent moves the matter, and from the matter being moved arises the form, which is the end as realized.[5]

Now what took place? We had an ideal: science is knowledge of things

5 For Aristotle on predicaments, see *Categories*, 4. (In the following chapters Aristotle treats the single categories in turn.) See also *Insight* 395, 497. On causes, see *Physics*, ii, 3, 194b 16 to 195a 26; *Metaphysics*, v, 2, 1013a 24 to 1013b 2.

through their causes. The ideal implied a double movement of analysis and synthesis – analysis to discover causes, and synthesis to move from causes to the things. What happened is that analysis and synthesis survived, but not the things and causes as understood by Aristotle.

This can be illustrated in two ways, first from Thomist Trinitarian theory and then from science.

Thomist Trinitarian theory is a clear instance of first an analytic movement and then a synthetic movement. In the New Testament what we are told regarding the Blessed Trinity is the mission of the Son and the mission of the Holy Ghost. After a series of Greek councils we arrive at three persons and one nature. There is nothing in the New Testament about persons or nature; these technical terms do not occur. Since the three persons are distinct, we find in the Cappadocian fathers the treatment of the properties of the distinct persons. Each person must have something proper to himself, otherwise he would be the same as the others. Further, both the Cappadocian fathers and Augustine had the idea that these properties must be relative. They cannot be something absolute, because God is simple; if these properties are to be reconciled with the simplicity of God, they have to be relative. Where do the relations come from? They come from the processions. Augustine explained the processions by a psychological analogy. He said they were something like the movement in the mind from understanding to conception, from judgment to willing. So first we have missions, then persons and nature, then properties, relations, processions.

What do we find in St Thomas' *Summa theologiae*, part 1, questions 27–43? Thomas does not start out from the missions; missions come at the end, in question 43. He is making the other movement, from causes to things, synthesis. He begins from a psychological analogy and moves to the processions, to the relations, to the persons, to the missions. The order of discovery is just the opposite of the order of doctrine.[e] In doctrine you start from principles and draw all the conclusions, but in discovery you discover one conclusion after another and gradually you move on to your principles.[6]

---

6 On St Thomas' procedure in the *Summa theologiae*, see Bernard Lonergan, *Verbum: Word and Idea in Aquinas*, ed. David B. Burrell (Notre Dame: University of Notre Dame Press, 1967) 206–15 (CWL 2); see also Lonergan's 'Theology and Understanding' (1954) in *Collection*, ed. Frederick E. Crowe and Robert M. Doran (Toronto: University of Toronto Press, 1988) 114–32 (CWL 4).

In Trinitarian theory, then, we have analysis and synthesis. We have the analytic movement up to St Thomas, and the synthetic movement in St Thomas' *Summa theologiae*. But we do not have things, and we do not have causes. God is not a thing in the sense of the Aristotelian predicaments, and the generation of the Son by the Father is not a matter of causality. The Son is not another God, and neither is the Holy Ghost. Things and causes vanish, but analysis and synthesis remain.

Now we may take a scientific illustration. There are over three hundred thousand compounds known to present-day chemistry, and those are not mixtures but compounds. Chemists explain all of these compounds by a periodic table of about one hundred elements. On the one hand, there is the composition of the compounds from the elements, sometimes in fact and sometimes just in theory (for compounds cannot always be synthesized). On the other hand, there is the analysis of the compounds into their elements. But these elements are not Aristotle's things. In a chemistry course you may be given an introductory definition of hydrogen – hydrogen is an odorless gas with various sensible properties – but you very soon forget that definition, and operate in terms of atomic weight, atomic number, and other properties implicit in the periodic table. The one hundred elements are defined by their relations to one another; they are not defined in terms of substance, quantity, quality, and so on, as these terms are taken in their ordinary meaning.

Thus we have what Whitehead called the bifurcation of nature.[7] Eddington distinguished two tables.[8] One of them was brown with a smooth surface on four solid legs and pretty hard to move around. The other was a pack of electrons that you could not even imagine. Which of the two tables is the real table? For the chemist the elements are atoms, and we do not see atoms; so he moves away from the field of things in the Aristotelian sense and from causes in the sense of end, agent, matter, and form. He thinks instead in terms of analysis and synthesis. The ideal of knowledge, then, develops in the pursuit of knowledge. The ideal becomes explicit through the pursuit.

7 Alfred North Whitehead, *The Concept of Nature* (Ann Arbor: The University of Michigan Press, 1957). The second chapter is entitled 'Theories of the Bifurcation of Nature.'
8 Sir Arthur Eddington, *The Nature of the Physical World* (Cambridge: The Cambridge University Press, 1928) xi–xv; also *New Pathways in Science* (Cambridge: The Cambridge University Press, 1947) 1.

1.2.2 In Philosophy

Our first point was that seeking knowledge is seeking an unknown, and this implies an ideal, a set of tendencies. But this ideal is not explicit; it becomes explicit in the process of seeking knowledge. That becoming explicit involves a change in the ideal. In Newton science achieves law and system, and that ideal is pursued up to Einstein. But there follows a phase in which what is sought is not law and system but states and probabilities. Similarly and concomitantly, science starts off with an ideal in terms of things and causes, and moves to a practice that is a matter of analysis and synthesis.

The question arises, What is going to happen next? Scientists have moved from law and system to states and probabilities. Is there going to be another change, and if so what will it be? They have moved from things and causes to analysis and synthesis. Will there be another change, and if so what will that be? Above all, what on earth can the philosopher be aiming at? If he is seeking knowledge, he is seeking the implementation of some ideal. What can that ideal be?

The ideal of pure reason resulted from the transference from mathematics to philosophy of the ideal of a set of fundamental, analytic, self-evident, necessary, universal propositions from which, by deduction, we reach equally necessary and universal conclusions. Philosophy became the product of the movement of pure reason from self-evident principles to absolutely certain conclusions. That was one ideal, and it was implemented by Spinoza, Leibniz, and Wolff.

Kant's *Critique of Pure Reason* is a critique of that ideal. He is criticizing an ideal of knowledge, and introducing into philosophy the same type of movement as we find in the movement of scientific ideals. Briefly, Kant's criticism is that in mathematics pure reason can arrive at satisfactory results because it can construct concepts, that is, because it can represent, as he puts it, in a pure a priori intuition, the concept itself; but that cannot be done in philosophy, and therefore philosophy cannot successfully follow the method of pure reason.

There we have an ideal in philosophy, a deductivist ideal proceeding from analytic propositions to universal and necessary conclusions, and also a criticism of that ideal. In fact, the ideal of pure reason is the Euclidean ideal. It is what in contemporary scholastic circles is called essentialism.[f]

However, there is a more general theorem that might be put by a

Hegelian, regarding the explicitation of ideals. It involves six terms: implicit, explicit, abstract, alien, mediation, reconciliation.

The transition from the implicit to the explicit may be illustrated by the ideal of temperance, as during the prohibition period. When you seek temperance, you are expressing a tendency towards the ideal. The ideal arouses a lot of enthusiasm. But that expression of man's capacity for the ideal is abstract; it does not express the whole of man's capacity and desire for the ideal. It does not deal with the whole concrete situation, and in that way it is an abstraction. Because it is an abstraction there is an opposition between the expressed, explicit ideal and the subject in whom the ideal is implicit. That opposition is alienation. The pursuit of temperance through prohibition gave rise to considerable alienation, and the laws of prohibition were repealed. While temperance is a fine ideal, still that particular means of bringing it about led to all sorts of abuses. The expression of the ideal, because it was just an abstraction, something inadequate to the subject in whom the ideal is implicit, was alien, and that alien aspect brings to light the opposition between the subject and the expression. Alienation mediates or draws forth from the subject a more adequate expression of his ideal. When that more adequate expression is thus mediated, we have reconciliation.

A Hegelian might argue that, since any expression of any ideal is bound to be abstract, it cannot be adequate to what is implicit in the subject. Law and system is one abstract expression; certain knowledge of things through their causes is another. Because they are abstract, these expressions really are alien. The more you use them, the more you will bring out the aspect of antithesis, alienation, opposition, and consequently you will call forth something else to correct it. So there is a movement from law and system to states and probabilities, from knowing things through their causes to analysis and synthesis. But analysis and synthesis, states and probabilities, are also abstract. In due course the inadequacy of those realizations will become apparent, and we will move on to something else.

Let us take another illustration from philosophy. In the nineteenth century there began to appear, and there may still exist, books on epistemology that took their starting point in the existence of knowledge. Universal scepticism is self-contradictory; because it is contradictory, knowledge exists. But just knowing that knowledge exists is knowing something very abstract. What kind of knowledge exists? What is the knowledge that exists? If you express the knowledge that exists abstractly, what will follow? You will have a mere abstraction, and it will give rise to alienation. It will give rise, for example, to what has been called the Catholic ghetto. Catholics have held on to this idea of knowledge, while the rest of the world pays little attention to it. Merely to assert the existence of knowledge without saying as fully as you can just what knowledge is, is to utter an abstraction, which gives rise to alienation. No solution is reached until that alienation is changed into a means by which something else is brought forth which is at least less abstract. However, the Hegelian difficulty probed rather deeply; it attacked *any* explicit ideal of knowledge.

1.3 The Problem

Perhaps I have given enough illustrations to enable us to conclude that there exists a problem. What have we seen? The pursuit of knowledge is the pursuit of an unknown. It is not only a conscious pursuit but an intelligent, rational, deliberate, and methodical pursuit. The pursuit of building a house with the aid of a set of blueprints is clearly deliberate and methodical. But how do you proceed methodically and deliberately to the attainment of something that you do not know, something which, if known, would not have to be pursued? We have to acknowledge, then, the existence in man of something like a natural ideal that moves towards knowledge. Moreover, this ideal is not explicitly conceived by nature. While the tendency is innate, while it belongs to man by nature, while it is not something acquired like facility on the violin or the piano or the typewriter, still the exact goal of this tendency is not explicitly conceived by nature. Man has to work out his conception of this goal, and he does so insofar as he actually pursues knowledge. In the working out, this ideal becomes concrete or explicit in a series of different forms in the sciences and in philosophy.

And therefore there exists a problem, first, because the ideal of pure reason has been criticized: on the one hand by Kant for his reasons, and on the other hand by most contemporary scholastics in their objections to what they call essentialism. That ideal is wrong, but what is the right one? If it is not pure reason, then philosophy is not a movement from self-evident, universal, necessary principles to equally certain conclusions. What is it? What are we trying to do? Next, there is the Hegelian difficulty, that any explicit ideal will be an abstraction and will be found to be inadequate; another will arise, and the new one will suffer from the same inadequacy.

The problem exists not only theoretically but also concretely. You cannot take a single step without presupposing or implicitly invoking some ideal of knowledge, and in many of the exercises throughout these lectures we will be adverting to this fact, that in all one's questions, in all one's efforts to know, one is presupposing some ideal of knowledge, more or less unconsciously perhaps.

1.4 Self-appropriation

The solution offered in *Insight* to this problem is self-appropriation. Self-appropriation is being introduced in terms of a problem. The ideal we seek in seeking the unknown, in trying to know, is conceptually implicit. There does not exist naturally, spontaneously, through the whole of history, a set of propositions, conceptions, and definitions that define the ideal of knowledge. But to say that conceptually it is implicit, that it is implicit with regard to statements, that these statements differ in different places and at different times – they are historically conditioned – is not to say that it is nonexistent. While the conception of the ideal is not by nature, still there is something by nature. The ideal of knowledge is myself as intelligent, as asking questions, as requiring intelligible answers. It is possible to get to these fundamental tendencies of which any conceived ideal is an expression, and if we can turn in upon these fundamental tendencies, then we are on the way to getting hold of matters of fact that are independent of the Hegelian objection. We are capable of getting hold of fundamental matters of fact in terms of which we can give a fairly definitive account of the cognitional ideal.

What you hear are words. If the words mean something, then there are concepts in the mind, acts of meaning. If you or I hold that the words mean something that is true, then there is judgment. It is in judgments, concepts, and words that you make your goal in knowledge explicit. The trick in self-appropriation is to move one step backwards, to move into the subject as intelligent – asking questions; as having insights – being able to form concepts; as weighing the evidence – being able to judge. We want to move in there where the ideal is functionally operative prior to its being made explicit in judgments, concepts, and words.[9] Moving in

---

9 The phrase 'move in there,' which occurs passim in this section, refers to a diagram to which Lonergan pointed on the blackboard. Notes taken show it as follows:

there is self-appropriation; moving in there is reaching what is prepredicative, preconceptual, pre-judicial. In what may resemble Heidegger's terminology, it is moving from ontology, which is the *logos*, the word about being, the judgment about being, to the ontic, which is what one is.

How do you move in there where the ideals are functionally operative in tendencies and achievements? What exactly happens when one is trying to achieve self-appropriation? Let us take the word 'presence.' It is an ambiguous word. First, you can say that the chairs are present in the room, but you cannot say that the chairs are present to the room or that the room is present to the chairs. The latter is a different, a second, sense of 'presence': being present to someone. It has a meaning with regard to animals. A dog walks along the street, sees another dog on the other side, and crosses over. The other dog is present to him, but not in the sense that the chairs are present in the room. Here we have presence to someone: I am present to you, and you are present to me; this presence is different from the presence of the chairs in the room. Moreover, there is a third meaning of 'presence': you could not be present to me unless I were somehow present to myself. If I were unconscious, you would not be present to me in the second sense. If you were unconscious, I would not be present to you in the second sense. So there is a third sense of presence: presence to oneself.[g] To sum up: there is a merely material sense of presence – the chairs are present in the room; there is a second sense – one person is present to the other; there is a third sense – a person has to be somehow present to himself for others to be present to him. In self-appropriation it is the third presence that is of interest. You are there, and your being there to yourself is the type of presence with which we are concerned.

Now what on earth do you do to get that presence of yourself to yourself? Do you crane your neck around and look into yourself to see if you are there? First of all, that cannot be done. You cannot turn yourself

---

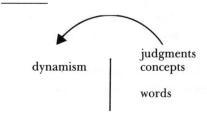

dynamism   judgments
concepts

words

inside out and take a look. In the second place, even if you could, it would be beside the point. Why is that? Because if you could, what you would arrive at would be, not the third type of presence, but only the second. You would be looking at yourself, you would have yourself 'out there' to be present to yourself. But we want the *you* that is present, to whom you would be present. What is important, in other words, is the looker, not the looked-at, even when the self is what is looked at. So it is not a matter of introspection in any spatial sense, in any sense of 'looking back into,' because what counts is not the presence of what is looked at, but the presence of the subject that looks, even when he is looking at himself.

That third presence is the fundamental presence. But simply as presence it is *empirical consciousness*. You can go a step higher, beyond empirical consciousness; you need not be just there. When you are teaching a class, for example, you can see from the looks on students' faces who is getting it and who is finding it rather dull. If it is clicking, if it means something to them, then there is not merely presence, empirical consciousness, but also *intelligent consciousness, intellectual consciousness*. They are catching on; they are understanding, or they are trying to understand; they are very puzzled or tense – intellectual consciousness. On this level, you are present to yourself as trying to understand, as saying 'I've got it!' and as conceiving and expressing. But beyond this second level, there is a third level on which you are present to yourself, *rational consciousness*. When you do understand, you think, 'After all, is that just another bright idea, or have I really got it properly?' On the level of rational consciousness, the level of reflection, the question is, Is it true or false? And when your judgments move on to action, you have, fourth, *rational self-consciousness*.[h] Then your rational reflection is about yourself. It is conscience in the ordinary sense – 'Am I doing right or wrong?' – where rational reflection is concerned with your own action.

What, then, is this business of moving in on oneself, self-appropriation? It is not a matter of looking back into yourself, because it is not what you look at but the looking[i] that counts. But it is not just the looking; it is not being entirely absorbed in the object; rather, it is adverting to the fact that, when you are absorbed in the object, you are also present to yourself. If you were not, it would not count. If there were no one there to see, there would be nothing present to the seer. That to whom other things are present, that which must be present to itself for other things to be present to it, is not merely there. He or she is intelligent, rational, rationally self-conscious.

So our concern in *Insight* is a series of exercises in which we move towards the functionally operative tendencies that ground the ideal of knowledge. The first part of *Insight* is primarily concerned with moving in there. In the second part we begin to draw conclusions, and that is where the arguable issues arise. But there is very little point to the argument unless one has been in there, because that is what we are trying to express, that is where the evidence lies, that is the point that has to be made.[10]

The book *Insight* is therefore a series of exercises in self-appropriation, in reaching the factual, functionally operative tendencies that express themselves successively in the series of ideals found in the sciences and in philosophy and, for that matter, in theology (and that is why I am interested). In fact, chapters 1 to 8 are concerned with understanding understanding, insight into insight. In those eight chapters there is a series of insights presented, and the point is not having all the insights – you do not have to have them all – but to notice when you have them, to advert to them, to move into self-appropriation. Chapters 9 and 10 are concerned with understanding judgment, the next level. Chapter 11 is affirming *your* understanding and *your* judgment.

That, roughly, is the technical side of the problem.

1.5 The Existential Element

Now there is a joker in this business of self-appropriation. We do not start out with a clean slate as we move towards self-appropriation. We already have our ideals of what knowledge is, and we want to do self-appropriation according to the ideal that is already operative in us – not merely in terms of the spontaneous, natural ideal, but in terms of some explicit ideal. I do not suppose that any of you will want to do self-appropriation by way of measurements and experiments, but many would say that our results cannot be really scientific unless we do it that way. Perhaps some of you will think that the thing to do is to define our

10 After coffee break Lonergan gave a resume of the preceding hour (the first paragraph following) before going on to §1.5, The Existential Element.

terms very clearly, establish our self-evident principles, and then proceed with deducing. And there can be other ideals besides these that govern one's procedure. Again, the results at which we arrive may not fit in with preexistent explicit ideals, and there will arise another conflict.

In other words, this business of self-appropriation is not a simple matter of moving in and finding the functionally operative tendencies that ground ideals. It is also a matter of pulling out the inadequate ideals that may be already existent and operative in us. There is a conflict, there is an existential element, there is a question of the subject, and it is a personal question that will not be the same for everyone. Everyone will have his own difficulties. There is an advantage, then, to having a seminar on the subject. It gives people a chance to talk these things out in the evening session, to talk them out with others. There is a set of concrete opportunities provided by the seminar that cannot be provided by any mere book. The more you talk with one another and throw things out, the more you probe, and the more you express yourself spontaneously, simply, and frankly, not holding back in fear of making mistakes, then the more quickly you arrive at the point where you get the thing cleared up.[j]

This matter may be illustrated in another way. We are aiming at an explicit ideal of knowledge based upon self-appropriation. But you know the Latin tag, *Qualis quisque est, talis finis videtur ei*,[11] the end seems to vary with each man. The kind of man one is determines what his ideals will be. The kind of ideal you have at the present time is a function of your past experience, your past study, your past teachers, your past courses in philosophy. Insofar as there is a struggle about agreeing with *Insight* or disagreeing with it, that struggle arises on a very fundamental existential level. It is akin to Heidegger's classification of men as authentic and inauthentic; in other words, there is a criticism of the subject. Something similar comes up in *Insight* – the existential problem.[12]

The problem can be illustrated from scholastic thought. I believe that the fact of insight is explicitly and with complete universality acknowledged by Aristotle and determinative in Aristotle's thought. I believe the same is true of St Thomas. But in an article published in 1933 in *Gregoria-*

---

11 Frequently quoted by Thomas Aquinas, e.g., *Summa theologiae*, 1, q. 83, a. 1, obj. 5. It came to him from Aristotle, *Ethics*, iii, 5, 1114b 1; in the Ross translation, 'the end appears to each man in a form answering to his character.'

12 See, for example, *Insight* xxviii, 385–86.

num by Fr Peter Hoenen on the knowledge of first principles, in which he was trying to draw attention to this matter, he reported that he could find only seven scholastics in the course of seven hundred years who adverted to the possibility.[13] Why is it, if I am right in saying that insight is fundamental in Aristotle and St Thomas, that in the course of seven hundred years only seven scholastics advert to the possibility, and only some of those accept it? It is this existential problem. It is the presence of a ready-made ideal of what knowledge must be, blocking self-appropriation.

The existential problem is a fundamental issue that arises in *Insight*, and those who have read the book will probably know about it. I certainly know about it; I certainly have experienced it in myself, or I would not have written the book.[14] But why is it that insight has been neglected? It is because, if you frankly acknowledge that intellect is intelligence, you discover that you have terrific problems in epistemology. It is much simpler to soft-pedal the fact that intellect is intelligence than to face out the solution to the epistemological problem. That, of course, is only my opinion on the matter, which I cannot force upon you; self-appropriation is something you do yourself.

1.6 Summary

So much, then, for the general question, What is self-appropriation, and why bother about it? We noted that this type of talk is really much more difficult than self-appropriation itself, because we are talking around the subject. To work out the theory of how to make the egg stand on its end is much harder than giving the egg a little tap, as Columbus did, and

13 Peter Hoenen, 'De origine primorum principiorum scientiae,' *Gregorianum* 14 (1933) 153–84. (But Hoenen does not say 'only seven scholastics,' and in fact the count is not wholly clear in his exposition.) There is an unedited English translation of this and other articles of Hoenen's, in the Lonergan Center of Milltown Park, Dublin. See also discussion 4 below, § 10, Intelligence in Contemporary Thomism, where Lonergan remarks that Hoenen still used Scotist language to set forth his very Thomist discovery. – Lonergan's use of 'possibility' here is explained by the terms in which Hoenen discussed the question: the 'possibility' that first principles arise through the immediate abstraction of the universal principle from phantasm.

14 We suggest this reading – the tape is not clear. Lonergan's remark, 'or I would not have read the book,' may have been a joke rather than a slip of the tongue.

having it stand there. In general, questions of method, questions of the possibility of knowledge, are in the second remove, and they are much more difficult, much more abstract, much more complicated, than the business of doing it. However, to have a framework for our lectures and our evening discussions, we put down a series of points that give some idea of what self-appropriation is. But note: this is only a framework; it is not a premise from which we are going to draw conclusions; it is an invitation to self-appropriation. What are you trying to do, how do you move towards it, and why do you bother about it?

Our first point was that seeking knowledge is seeking an unknown. Our second point was that the movement to that unknown is the movement towards an ideal that is not conceptually explicit. It becomes conceptually explicit as an axiomatic system, as observation in an experiment, and in many other ways in the course of pursuing knowledge. Thirdly, we provided illustrations from science of the development of the ideal. There is the movement from Pythagoras, through Archimedes, Galileo, Kepler, Newton, and Einstein. In that movement the ideal of law and system is worked out fully. When it is deserted one moves on to an ideal of states and probabilities. There is the ideal of certain knowledge of things through their causes, which implies analysis and synthesis. Analysis and synthesis survive, while things and causes in the Aristotelian sense are not operative in that scientific knowledge. A chemist does not bother his head about matter or form or end, but talks about agents and reagents, and so on. In other words, the ideal assumes explicit forms historically.

Fourthly, the philosophic problem arises when the ideal of pure reason, as developed by Spinoza, Leibniz, and more systematically in schoolbook fashion by Wolff, is criticized by Kant. Kant's *Critique of Pure Reason* is a critique of a particular ideal of knowledge. But then, fifthly, there is the general Hegelian objection, that any explicitly formulated ideal is going to be abstract. Because it is abstract it is going to come into conflict with the source of the ideal, and it will be consequently a source of further discoveries that change that explicit formulation.

The answer to that Hegelian objection is not easy; you cannot put it into a formula. But our approach, our way to get around it, is to move in on the concrete subject, where the tendencies that are expressed in the ideal are functionally operative. That turning in is a matter of consciousness, and we have distinguished three senses of the word 'presence.' The chairs are present in the room. We are present to one another. We are all present to ourselves. And as present to ourselves we are not looking at ourselves, we are not objects, we are subjects. It is the present subject that counts, and that present subject is not only present but also intelligent, reasonable, and, when he makes decisions, self-conscious.

Finally, there is a joker in the problem, the existential element. There are already existent ideals, and there are those who want self-appropriation spontaneously and naturally.[15] Spontaneously, naturally, your ideal of knowledge will govern your attempts at self-appropriation, and unless your ideal is perfectly correct before you start, it will prevent you from arriving. In other words, there is the need of some sort of a jump, a leap.

2   Illustrations of Insight

Now we shall move on to the exercises, beginning with exercises in the act of insight itself. In the book *Insight* there is, first of all, a lengthy description of Archimedes' discovery, and then we consider the insight behind the definition of the circle.[16] But here we will take a few other examples. There will be two things to note. First, there will be the example; secondly, there will be advertence to what is happening in oneself when the insight occurs.

2.1 Insight in Plato

In the *Meno*, one of the early dialogues of Plato, Socrates is interested in establishing his theory of anamnesis, recollection, memory.[17] The ideas are known by remembering them. We remember them because we were in some previous state. To prove the theory of anamnesis, Socrates summons a boy. The Greek word for a boy also means a slave, but here the idea is of a young person, totally uneducated, having no knowledge whatever of geometry. Socrates' purpose is to show that this slave boy can remember ideas from some preexistent state.

In the dust Socrates draws a square, *ABCD* (see figure 1). He then asks the boy to draw another square the area of which is exactly double that of the first. The boy says, 'That's easy.' He produces the side *AB*, so it is double its original length. Socrates says, 'Well, draw the whole square.' So the boy draws it, having to produce sides equal to the base all the way

15 The word 'self-appropriation' is editorial, for Lonergan's 'it.'
16 *Insight* 3–13.
17 Plato, *Meno* 80d–86c.

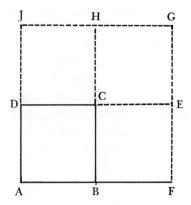

Figure 1

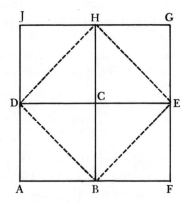

Figure 2

around. Socrates makes the observation that it seems more than double, that it seems to be four times the area. He adds the lines *CH* and *CE*, and we can see that each of the four squares is equal, that what the slave boy arrived at was a square four times as big as the original and not twice as big. Socrates then points out that the square wanted is not only double *ABCD* but also half *AFGJ*, and he asks the boy to find that square. Finally, the boy stumbles upon line *BD* (see figure 2), and he can come up with a square that is double the original one and half the bigger one. Triangle *ABD* is equal to *BCD*, *DHJ* is equal to *CDH*, *EGH* is equal to *CEH*, *BEF* is equal to *BCE*, so the square *BEHD* in the center is half the bigger square.[18]

18 Considerable editing was needed in this paragraph, as is generally true
    wherever diagrams are involved, since Lonergan's explanation was

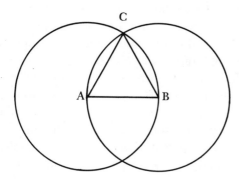

Figure 3

Now the boy does not know Pythagoras' discovery that the square of the diagonal is equal to the sum of the squares of the two sides, but he stumbles upon the answer through the diagram, through the concrete instance. By asking questions and without giving him the answers, Socrates brings the slave boy to the point where he finds the square that is double the original one. Socrates asks, 'How did he know? I didn't tell him; I just asked him questions. He must have had the idea from before.' Aristotle did not believe much in this remembering it from before, but he figured that the diagram[k] had something to do with it, and it has.

2.2 Insight in Euclid

Take another instance. Euclid's first proposition is to construct an equilateral triangle on a given base in a given plane. And you remember the solution – if you studied Euclid's construction and not some modern variation in which all the problems and theorems are changed. It is to take center A and radius AB and draw a circle (see figure 3). Take center B and radius BA, draw another circle. You get point C. Join CA and CB. Because AB and AC are both radii of the same circle, they are equal. Because BA and BC are both radii of the same circle, they are also equal. Things equal to the same thing are equal to one another. Therefore, all three sides are equal, and we have an equilateral triangle.

Now if you are familiar with geometry, you know that Euclid has

---

interwoven with drawing at the blackboard and pointing to the figures there.

slipped. He undertakes to solve his problems and prove his theorems in virtue of his definitions, axioms, and postulates. But there is one step here that is not covered by any of Euclid's definitions, axioms, or postulates, namely, that the two circles will intersect at point *C*. There is no way of proving *that* from the whole set of definitions, axioms, and postulates. But we are certain they must intersect. If we do not know that from Euclid's definitions, axioms, and postulates, how do we know? Euclidean geometry, as worked out at the present time, introduces different axioms to be able to handle this sort of thing. But what we can see immediately is that if we have two circles, and the distance between their centers is greater than the sum of their radii, they cannot intersect; again, if there are two circles and the distance between their centers is less than the difference between their radii, one may be inside the other. There is a third case between the case when they are outside one another and the case when one is inside the other. It is an intermediate case, in which the circles must intersect. One can find a formula that expresses when the circles in the same plane must intersect. The conditions for this third case can be laid down, but for centuries most people did Euclidean geometry without bothering about that. They just saw it in the diagram. They saw that it had to be so, that if you start with base *AB* and draw the circles with *AB* as the radius of both, you are bound to get intersecting circles. You see, then, in the concrete instance what is universally true. But you cannot see, imagine, a *must*. You understand that it *must*, and this understanding with respect to diagrams, with respect to images, is insight.

We may take a second example from Euclid. In the first book, proposition 16, Euclid proves the exterior angle to be greater than the interior opposite. Take the triangle *ABC* (see figure 4). Produce the side *BC* to *D*. *ACD* is the exterior angle which he wants to prove is greater than *BAC*, the interior opposite. His method is to bisect the side *AC* at *E*, join *BE*, produce *BE* so that *EF* is equal to it, and join *FC*. By bisection *AE* is equal to *EC*. By construction *BE* is equal to *EF*. Because vertically opposite angles are equal, these two triangles *ABE* and *CFE* are equal in all respects. Thus the angle *BAE* is equal to the angle *ECF*. But manifestly, the angle *ECD* is greater than the angle *ECF*. Therefore, the exterior angle is greater than the interior opposite.

What Euclid does not prove is that the line *FC* falls within the angle *ECD*. If it does not fall within the angle, you have no proof that one angle is bigger than the other. If the line produced from *F* were to fall elsewhere, the proof would not hold. This is another reason why modern geometers

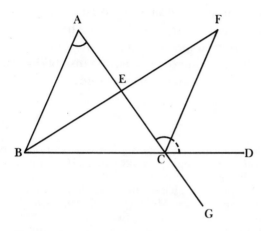

Figure 4

have an entirely different set of axioms. With the different set, they can do the proof in different ways. There is more than one set with which you can prove all of Euclid's propositions, but Euclid's propositions do not suffice by themselves as a rigorous deduction.

However, you can see by an imaginative experiment that the line *FC* has to fall within the angle. First, the size of the triangle makes no difference. Secondly, it makes no difference which side it is on; the whole construction can be put on the other side. But if you observe that construction, you can see that the line *FC* is bound to lie in the angle. You can see it in all possible cases by supposing you have rigid rods and by moving them in imagination, so that you make the two sides of the triangle take all possible positions[l] and make the rest of the figure follow according to the laws of the construction. You can see that no matter how you twist or turn those two lines, line *FC* always lies within that angle. You see what must be so in the image. But you don't imagine the *must*; you understand it. Imagination and sense present what is there. I can see a piece of yellow chalk, but I cannot see that there must be a piece of yellow chalk. One cannot see a *must*. You just see facts or the factual[m] or the empirical or the given. So we have here another example of an insight, a casual insight that existed for centuries before geometry textbooks made it explicit. Euclid says he is proving everything from his definitions, axioms, and postulates, but he really is not. He uses casual insights as he goes along.[19]

19 A lengthy passage on logic machines was eliminated from the text at this

I have drawn your attention to Euclid's use of casual insights. We see intellectually, we grasp, a *must* in the image, and if we get hold of all these insights, we can find an expression for them in a set of axioms.[20] To do geometry the way Euclid did it, you have to be having insights as you go along.[21] Because Euclid uses casual insights, he illustrates very clearly the occurrence of insight.[22]

point, as a result of the following communication from Lonergan: 'I no longer hold the opinion that a computer could replace Hilbert's work on a logically rigorous Euclidean geometry. Perhaps the contrary view could be eliminated from the typescript. That would preclude unnecessary controversy' (Letter to E. Morelli and M. Morelli, July 12, 1978). In a telephone conversation later that summer, Lonergan added this explanation: 'You need Hilbert to program the computer. Eliminate implication that a machine could do it, *without prior programming*. You have to get the theorems first; then the machine work is really superfluous' (from notes on the conversation, made by Mark Morelli).

As a consequence, several passages were eliminated from the transcript of the tapes, here and elsewhere in the lecture. With this caution on Lonergan's stated clarification, and because of the historical interest of this development, we reproduce the omitted passages in footnotes (see also notes 20, 22, 24, 25, 30 below). The omission here was transcribed as follows:

'Now just by way of a footnote: Supposing you work out a watertight set of definitions and axioms – and they've done it – then you do the whole of your geometry without having any insights: it has to be all up in the axioms. And if you do the whole of your geometry without any insights, a machine can do it. Thus you get the sentential calculus, the symbolic logic, which exhibits what can be done by a machine, by a digital computer, by an electronic computer. There are no insights occurring during the whole operation. You have to have an intelligent man to set the machine up, and he has to have all the insights before you start. It is not a matter of going so far in a problem and then sticking in an insight – "Well, we can get around that" – and going on. But it's a matter of setting down rigid axioms right from the start to cover all eventualities. Then the machine can do the whole of geometry for you, if you have everything up in the axioms. Of course, you have to know the geometry better than Euclid did to be able to draw up these axioms.'

20 Omitted (see note 19): 'and the machine can do the geometry and get all the right answers every crack, if there is nothing wrong with the machine. The machine does not have to be intelligent: it just has to follow directions.'

21 Here Lonergan gives another example of Euclid's casual insights; it has to do with the angle subtended at the center of a circle by an arc on the circumference. But the argument is not clear from the tape.

22 Omitted (see note 19): 'and symbolic logic, mathematical logic, illustrates doing the stuff without having any insights.'

2.3 A Note on Advertence

Our attention has been on the object, but when we were attending to the object something happened in us. *We* saw that it *must*. We have spoken of intellectual consciousness. It is wanting to see, it is trying to see, it is catching on. St Thomas says that whenever we try to understand anything, we form images, in which, as it were, we see the solution to the problem.[23] He is talking about insight. Beyond the level of sense – colors, sounds, odors, tastes, feelings – and beyond the level of imagination, there is this *must* and *can be* and *cannot be* that we grasp. Getting hold of that is the insight. It is that event that is our primary object of attention.

2.4 The Rise of Symbolic Logic

Why have mathematicians moved off into a symbolic logic?[24] It is because they have been stung, so to speak. They thought they had an insight, and they discovered that it was wrong. The insight in question regarded Euclid's parallel postulate (see figure 5). If a line *AB* cuts two straight lines *CD* and *EF* at the points *G* and *H*, in such a way that the two angles *BGD* and *AHF* are less than two right angles, then the lines *CD* and *EF* will intersect. The postulate has been put in different ways, but the implication is that, if the angles are exactly equal to two right angles, the lines are parallel, lines that never meet on either side no matter how far they are produced. Why is it that the insight is right with regard to the intersecting circles, and right with regard to the external angle, but wrong with regard to this? It is because this case involves an infinite phantasm, an infinite image, and we do not have infinite images. We have images that we can extend indefinitely. You can extend them according to the parallel law, and you get Euclidean geometry. But you need not extend them according to the parallel law. Space can keep getting roomier or tighter the further you move out; and then you get a different kind of space, in which the parallel law does not hold.

23 Thomas Aquinas, *Summa theologiae*, 1, q. 84, a. 7: 'hoc quilibet in seipso experiri potest, quod quando aliquis conatur aliquid intelligere, format aliqua phantasmata sibi per modum exemplorum, in quibus quasi inspiciat quod intelligere studet' – one of Lonergan's favorite passages in Aquinas.
24 Omitted (see note 19): 'in which the whole of the geometry is built up without having any insights.'

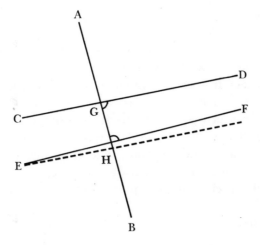

Figure 5

It was because of their suspicion about this case of what seemed to be just as good an insight as those regarding the intersecting circles and the external angle that mathematicians first discovered that you can have a completely coherent geometry, and hold that, even if the angles are both right angles, the two lines will intersect. You can also hold that you can have several straight lines through the same point, none of which intersects with another coplanar line: the hyperbolic. It can be proved quite simply that these other geometries are coherent, because if they are wrong, the Euclidean geometry of the surface of the ellipsoid, or the Euclidean geometry of the surface of the hyperboloid, has to be wrong. Euclid cannot be right and these geometries incoherent. That is the reason why the mathematicians are shy of insights. In this case they were satisfied that a mistake was made, and consequently they have moved off into symbolic logic, development[25] from acknowledged axioms, and this gives rise to further problems on the foundations of mathematics: What axioms are mathematical axioms? How do we know which axioms to take? Which ones give mathematics? Those are further questions.

---

25 Omitted (see note 19): 'the purely automatic development'.

2.5 Insight in Aristotle

Now let me take another illustration. I said that insight is acknowledged by Aristotle. When discussing the eclipse, Aristotle says the moon suffering an eclipse becomes darker and darker, and for us to explain the eclipse of the moon is rather difficult. But if you were on the moon you would see the earth cutting in between the sun and the moon and causing the shadow, and you would know why there had to be an eclipse. That is an instance of an insight. If you can see the earth cutting in between the sun and the moon, you know why the moon is thus darkened.

But there is another point to be noted here. Aristotle divides questions into four types: (1) What? What is it? (2) Is it? (3) Why is it so? (4) Is it so? 'Is it so?' and 'Is it?' are just factual questions, questions of existence. 'What is it?' and 'Why is it so?' are questions for intelligence, questions of some determination of what exists. Aristotle wanted to know the meaning of *what*. What are we looking for when we ask, 'What is it? *Quid sit?*' The answer, of course, is the *quidditas*! But what does *what* really mean? Aristotle's answer was not *quidditas*.[26] *Quidditas* is a technical term that was invented in the Middle Ages. Aristotle's answer was, *What* means *why*. How can *what* mean *why*? In some cases, he says, it is quite easy to see. You can change the *what* question into a *why* question. If you ask, for example, 'What is an eclipse?' you can say instead, 'Why is the moon thus darkened?' The reason why the moon is darkened in this way is what an eclipse is – namely, a blocking of the sun's light on the object that is eclipsed. The answer to the *why* question and the answer to the *what* question are the same.[27] However, Aristotle notes that there are some cases where you cannot break it up in this way. When you say, 'What is a man?' or 'What is a house?' how are 'man' and 'house' to be changed? If you can make 'eclipse' a darkening of the moon and ask, 'Why is the moon thus darkened?' you can change the *what* question into a *why* question. But how do you break 'man' up into two words, so that you can say, 'Why is this a man?' Aristotle did not tackle this problem in the

26 Lonergan was indulging in a bit of irony at this point, conveyed to the audience by tone of voice and demeanor, and acknowledged by their laughter. But *quidditas* is not itself a pejorative term; on the contrary, it is extremely significant, expressing our anticipation of a future insight – see lecture 3, §2, The Notion of Heuristic Structure, and *Insight* 509.
27 Aristotle, *Posterior Analytics*, II, 2; see also Lonergan, *Verbum* 12–16.

Posterior Analytics, but he does deal with it in the *Metaphysics*, book 7, chapter 17. His doctrine of matter and form arises out of this problem. When you ask, 'What is a man?' you mean, 'Why is *this* a man?' You have *this*, what you point to, the materials. You ask, 'Why is this a man?' The answer is the *soul*. It is the soul in this matter that makes it a man. If you had a different kind of soul, you wouldn't have a man. Soul is what you know by insight into the sensible data. Just as you have insight into sensible data, so there is form in matter. Aristotle's 'matter and form' distinction is tied right in with insight.

2.6 Insight in Kant

It was not only Aristotle who adverted to insight, and it was not only Plato who used it. Kant, in his Transcendental Doctrine of Method, where he is presenting the fruits of his labor, distinguishes between mathematics and philosophy.[28] Both use pure reason, but in mathematics you can construct your concepts while in philosophy you cannot. What does Kant mean by constructing concepts? He means exhibiting the concept in a pure intuition. He uses the triangle as an example. You can imagine a triangle that conforms exactly to your definition of a triangle. Because you can have an image that conforms exactly to your definition and represents it perfectly, it is possible to have synthetic a priori principles, and not only analytic principles, in mathematics. In an analytic principle there is a subject and a predicate, and the predicate expresses what belongs to the subject. But the synthetic principle is a universal and necessary proposition in which the predicate is not just part of the subject but goes beyond the subject. You can have synthetic principles in mathematics because in mathematics you can have this image, you can construct an a priori intuition. An a priori intuition of what? Of the concept of the subject. Because you have that construction, you can add on a predicate that is not contained merely in the idea of the subject.

Kant has made a very good point. What he is talking about, it seems to me, is materially the same sort of thing we were illustrating from Euclid. How do you know that the circles must intersect? If you attend just to the Euclidean definitions, axioms, and postulates, you can derive

---

28 Immanuel Kant, *Critique of Pure Reason* A713–27/B741–55. See the English translation by Norman Kemp Smith (New York: St Martin's Press, 1965) 576–87.

analytic propositions and necessary conclusions from those propositions. But it is only when you appeal to the image of the circles in the three cases – one inside the other, one totally outside, and the two intersecting – that you can define the conditions under which the two will intersect. In that case, because you can appeal to the image, you can have a synthetic a priori proposition.

Kant, Aristotle, and St Thomas all knew about insight. The difference between Kant, on the one hand, and Aristotle and Thomas, on the other, is this: Kant's a priori is independent of experience. The a priori is in intellect independently of experience; it is absolutely independent of experience. You have the concept, and when you have the concept you can exhibit it in an image; but Kant does not think of the image as *causing* the insight. In Aristotle and St Thomas, on the other hand, the insight and the concept are distinguished, and the phantasm, the image, causes the insight. In Kant there is no talk of the insight, but only of the concept, the image, and the concept governing the image. Kant's synthetic a priori presupposes that the insight already exists and that the concepts are already formed. Given those presuppositions, one controls one's images, but the images do not cause the insight. Kant cannot allow that and still retain his definition of the a priori as independent of what is given. While it is still more complex than this, this is the contrast simply put.[29]

2.7 Summary

I have illustrated insight in instances, from the problem of the *Meno*, from Euclid on the intersection of circles and the external angle. We have considered in terms of insight why there is symbolic logic in modern mathematics, the pure rigorous deduction that a machine might perhaps do.[30] The reason is the distrust of casual insights. First of all, if you have casual insights, you are kidding yourself if you continue to believe that you are deducing your geometry from the axioms. It does not really follow from the axioms. So it is inaccurate to use casual insights. And secondly, sometimes, as in the case of the parallel postulate, these insights can be wrong. There results a movement off into symbolic logic. And so you get an explanation of this mathematical movement in terms of insight.

29 For a fuller treatment of the a priori, see lecture 7 below, § 1, The Question of the A Priori.
30 Omitted (see note 19): 'in which you get all your insights at the start, and the machine can do the rest.'

On the other hand, I illustrated insight from Aristotle and Kant, though they deal with it in different ways. We noted the role of insight in Aristotle with regard to the problem of breaking the *what* question into the *why* question. Out of that problem there arises the matter-form distinction. The matter is *this*, what one points to, while the form is what is known by insight into the sensible data. We noted Kant's discussion of the possibility of synthetic a priori principles to illustrate his own advertence to insight.

So insight is a fundamental idea, both in mathematics and in philosophy.

Now the illustrations I have given are the meat as far as self-appropriation is concerned. What I said about them is just talk, building it up, going round it. What counts is noticing when you have the insights. What we want is self-appropriation.[31] This is what counts. Concepts are easy: we have them if we have words with meaning. But what counts is understanding, and this is what we must appropriate. That is the point of the illustration from Kant, one aspect at least of the Kantian problem. It is the point also of the other illustrations: we try to see what mathematicians understand – spatial images; or what physicists understand – for example, motion. We will come to a real problem when we ask what philosophers understand, since it is not mathematics, not physics, not any other similar field. Neither is it *ipsum esse*, as in the beatific vision. There does not seem to be an object for philosophical understanding. But that is a question we will deal with later.[32]

---

31 The longest-playing tape for this lecture (DJS) stops here; the WAS tape had stopped at 'problem of the *Meno*' (beginning of §2.7), and the LRI tape at 'can be wrong' (a few lines later). The rest of the lecture is filled in from notes taken (FEC and WAS).

32 See lecture 9, Metaphysical Analysis and Metaphysical Integration.

2

Elements of Understanding[1]

1   The Value of Self-appropriation

We have been discussing self-appropriation, and we wish now to take the question further. But let us preface our lecture with some reflections on the value of the self-appropriation we discussed yesterday.[2]

First of all, self-appropriation is advertence – advertence to oneself as experiencing, understanding, and judging. Secondly, it is understanding oneself as experiencing, understanding, and judging. Thirdly, it is affirming oneself as experiencing, understanding, and judging. The analysis of knowledge, then, yields the three elements: experience, understanding, judging.

In direct knowledge, the experienced is the sensible object of seeing, hearing, feeling, tasting, smelling, and movement. Understanding is with respect to that object; as St Thomas puts it, quoting Aristotle perpetually, phantasms, images, are to the understanding as colors are to sight. – With regard to experience, there is the object in potency and the object in act; for example, the bell as potentially sounding and as actually sounding. You have to have hearing in act to have actual sounding: without ears

---

1 The second lecture, Tuesday, August 5, 1958. Recording of the lecture began a little late, with Lonergan in midsentence speaking of the previous evening's discussion and asking for ideas on ways to improve the format of the discussions.
2 This sentence is editorial, inserted in clarification of what seems to be the lecture plan.

you have potential sounding, the movement of the bell, but you do not have hearing, and without hearing you do not have sounding. Similarly with regard to understanding, the intelligibility is not actually in the image, but potentially.[3] – Finally, in direct knowledge there is the third step, judging: Is it so?

Self-appropriation involves the same three steps, except that the experience is taken on the subjective side. We have spoken of the ambiguity of presence. For you to be present to me, I have to be already present to myself. Now I can be present to myself not merely as experiencing, as empirically conscious, but also as trying to understand, as actually understanding, as reflecting and about to judge, and as judging. The repetition of the same three steps with regard precisely to the levels of self-presence is what gives you self-appropriation, self-knowledge.

Consequently, we have a theory of knowledge that accounts for itself and thus solves a fundamental difficulty in theory of knowledge, the self-referential problem. People can work out a theory of knowledge and say what knowledge is, but the knowledge they describe may not be capable of providing that account of knowledge. The simplest case of this is Hume's theory of knowledge. Hume said that our knowledge consists in sense impressions which are put together by habit. Is that theory of knowledge a matter of sense impressions put together by habit? If it is, it is of no more value than the knowledge that Hume criticizes. In other words, there is the knowledge of the critic and the knowledge that he criticizes. If the knowledge that he criticizes is inadequate, where did he get his criticism? Is *it* knowledge? But in our account, we have exactly the same structure, the same type of acts occurring, in the knowledge as described and in the knowledge that does the describing or gives the account.

But why are we attempting self-appropriation? To use an expression borrowed from Kant last night,[4] if one is to be a philosopher, one cannot be just a plaster cast of a man.[5] To deal with philosophical questions, one needs a point of reference, a basis that is one's own. Your interest may

---

3 A remark here, 'However, that's by the way,' shows that the previous three sentences (enclosed here between dashes) are a digression. In fact, the topic touched on comes up for detailed treatment in lecture 7, § 1.3, The Notion of Being as Natural.

4 See discussion 1, § 6, Self-appropriation and Truth.

5 Immanuel Kant, *Critique of Pure Reason* A836/B864; Norman Kemp Smith 655–56.

quite legitimately be to find out what Lonergan thinks and what Lonergan says, but I am not offering you that, or what anyone else thinks or says, as a basis. If a person is to be a philosopher, his thinking as a whole cannot depend upon someone or something else. There has to be a basis within himself; he must have resources of his own to which he can appeal in the last resort. Kant put the issue this way: knowledge is either a matter of principles or a matter of data.[6] Thus people can learn a science that is a matter of principles, or their learning can be simply a matter of data. They can quote Wolff, for example, to meet every possible occasion, but if you dispute any of Wolff's definitions they are at a loss – they do not know what to say. In that case, Kant says, what you have is a plaster cast of a man. The value of self-appropriation, I think, is that it provides one with an ultimate basis of reference in terms of which one can proceed to deal satisfactorily with other questions.

2   The Nest of Related Terms

That basis, as expressed, involves a nest of related terms.

Self-appropriation on the level of experiencing oneself as experiencing, understanding, and judging is just the experiencing. On that level, you have no statement of what you are doing or of what you are trying to do; you are just having experiences. Experiencing is prior to inquiry, understanding, conception, reflecting, reflective insight, and judging. As yet you have no understanding of the basis, nor any concept of it. You are there, and you are adverting to the fact that you are there; you are intelligent and trying to understand, and you are adverting to that; you are reflecting and weighing the pros and cons preparatory to a judgment. But you are not yet judging; you are not yet understanding this buildup, and you are not affirming anything. You have the materials for it, but you haven't yet arrived at the second step. If one is to *say* anything about it, it must be presupposed that one has already arrived at least at the second step. Insofar as one is at the second step, one is on the level of the object of thought, the hypothesis. In *Insight*, up to the end of chapter 8, we are concerned with the nest of related terms made up of empirical presentations, inquiry, insight, conception. Chapters 9 and 10 deal with reflection, reflective understanding or reflective insight, and judgment. It is only when one moves on to that further level of judgment that one

6 Ibid.

is able to deal with true and false, real and imaginary, and so on. We move to that third level only in chapter 11 when we arrive at self-affirmation.[a] Our immediate concern, though, is not with the level of judgment, but with the nest of terms that pertain to the first and second levels; we want to get this first part clear.

These related terms refer to elements in knowledge that, on the whole, can be separated. In any case, they are distinct. First, one can have empirical presentations without inquiry. In a warmer climate one can lie on the beach and watch the clouds go by without any concern for anything whatever. Least of all does one have any intellectual concern. One is having the empirical presentations, but there is no desire to understand and no effort to understand. (One can have that even in the classroom!)

The second element, inquiry, is the element of intellectual alertness. One is trying to get hold of something; there is an effort to understand; you are not understanding anything yet, but you are puzzled. It is this element of inquiry, I think, that Aristotle refers to when he says that wonder is the beginning of all science and philosophy.[7] In the dream state, you are in a pattern of experience, but when you start to wonder about something, when you are trying to understand, you are moving into the intellectual pattern of experience. You are giving the flow of experience an orientation towards understanding. That wonder is the root of all questions. It is not itself the question formulated in words; it is not the question formulated in concepts in the mind; it is just the effort itself, without any formulation. At this point it is not understanding that we are trying to understand, but the effort to understand.

Thirdly, inquiry heads for insight. The insight is the click, the grasp, what is added to your knowledge when you see the *must* in the data. For example, in the problem of constructing the equilateral triangle, you see that the two circles must intersect. If one is center A and radius AB, and the other is center B and radius BA, and they are both in the same plane, they are bound to intersect. You see it, you know, you have caught on to something. Similarly, with regard to the external angle, although there is an element in Euclid's proof that does not depend upon his definitions, axioms, and postulates, you can see in the imaginative data that the line has to fall within the angle. You grasp the necessity, and that grasp is the insight.

But insight is not yet conception. What is the general statement of the

7 Aristotle, *Metaphysics*, 1, 2, 982b 12–18, 983a 12–18.

conditions when two coplanar circles must intersect?[8] You have to take time out to think out a general formula that adequately expresses the insight. The insight is into *this particular case*, and you can see that in any other drawing exactly similar to this one the circles would be bound to intersect. But you have to do some further thinking if you want a conception, an expression, a general formulation, of that insight. Let us move on to that further thought.

Take one circle with radius R_1 and another circle with radius R_2, and let the distance between their centers be S. Now let us start with R_1+R_2 less than S, but move the circles towards one another.[b] As long as R_1+R_2 remains less than S, the two circles are not going to intersect – they will be quite outside one another (see figure 6). But when R_1+R_2 is exactly equal to S, the two circles are brought into contact so that they touch at one point (see figure 7). Now if we continue gradually to make R_1+R_2 greater than S, then for a while the circles are cutting (see figure 8); but if we make S much smaller, one circle can be pulled inside the other, with the two circles touching for a moment (see figure 9) and later neither touching nor intersecting (see figure 10).[9]

Thus by taking the two circles, proceeding systematically through the various possibilities, and noting the formula in each case, we can come, I think, to a general statement of when two coplanar circles will have to intersect: when the distance between the centers is less than the sum of the radii but greater than the difference between the radii, the two circles will intersect.

8 Lonergan said before putting this question, 'You remember that yesterday I had difficulty in formulating the conditions under which the two coplanar circles must intersect. I started to say something, and I was wrong.' In fact he stumbled a bit in this second attempt also, and thus illustrated in his own effort the difficulty of going from insight to formulation.

9 From this point forward it is impossible to follow the tape as Lonergan works out his argument at the blackboard. But the process is clear: he would envisage the five cases diagrammed in figures 6 to 10, in order to arrive at the two conditions needed for the intersection of the circles. We have therefore given his stated method of procedure (with some editing), but have omitted the complexities of his argument (which may be deduced from the five diagrams with their formulae). The next paragraph in the text (again edited) picks up his lecture at the point where he reached his conclusion.

It should be noted that some copies of the 1980 edition were printed with an error in figure 9. Possibly some copies had an error also in the formulae of figure 8.

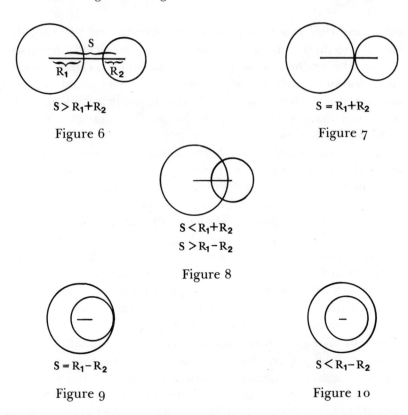

$$S > R_1 + R_2$$

Figure 6

$$S = R_1 + R_2$$

Figure 7

$$S < R_1 + R_2$$
$$S > R_1 - R_2$$

Figure 8

$$S = R_1 - R_2$$

Figure 9

$$S < R_1 - R_2$$

Figure 10

Now from the trouble we had in figuring that out, you can see that the general conception, the general formulation, is not the same as the insight into the particular case. To get the general formulation one has to imagine the whole series of cases: the circles outside one another, one circle being pulled into the other, one circle already inside the other. Among those, there are cases in which the circles intersect and, again, cases in which they do not intersect.

3   The Difference between Insight and Conception

The difference between insight into the particular case, which, as we saw, is going to hold whenever we construct an equilateral triangle, and the more general formulation that covers all possible cases of circles intersecting is of considerable importance for distinguishing between the scientific expression of an insight and, for example, the artistic expression of an insight. An artist has insights, but he does not express them in general formulae, in terms of R_1, R_2, and S. He does not express them in any abstract terms, where 'abstract' refers to scientific or philosophic terms. He expresses himself in poetry, in painting, in the plastic and visual arts, and in other manners. Artistic expression does not move off into this abstract field of general formulation. The artist gives a concrete expression to the insight into particular situations or data. In short, I think there is an insight in art, but the artist does not attempt this type of conception. The artist's expression of his insight is his work of art, whatever the work of art may be.

In the history of Socrates we find a second illustration of the difference between insight into the particular case and the general formulation. Socrates went around Athens asking people, 'What is it to be a brave man? What is it to be a temperate man? What is it to be a wise man? What is it to be a just man?' The Athenians felt they had a very good idea of who was brave, temperate, just, or wise, and who was not, but they could not answer Socrates' questions. Socrates would make monkeys of them every time. How was it, then, that they did know what it is to be brave, temperate, just, and wise, and yet invariably Socrates was able to show them that they really knew nothing about the subjects at all?

The Athenians had insights that dealt with particular cases, but they did not pursue the scientific ideals of definition of terms and of general formulation. Socrates' questions, on the other hand, tended to be of the type, What is the general formula that covers all cases of bravery, temperance, justice, or wisdom? That is the same sort of question as, What is the general formula that covers all cases of circles intersecting? The Athenians had never thought of that sort of thing, and even today the commonsense people of any city have never thought of it. Men of common sense know perfectly well, in any particular case, whether a fellow is brave or cowardly, and they will acknowledge a series of intermediate cases where they would not use the words or would not know what words to use. In particular instances, they have perfectly clear ideas, just as when we constructed the equilateral triangle it was clear to us that the circles would intersect. But to go on to give a general account, a general formula, that covers all cases of bravery and settles all disputed or borderline instances is quite another matter, and it involves the introduction of a scientific ideal.

According to Aristotle, what Socrates did was to introduce universal definitions. To introduce universal definitions is to introduce a scientific ideal. It is an element in the explicit formulation of the ideal of scientific knowledge as it was attacked by Husserl in his *Crisis of European Sciences and Transcendental Phenomenology*.[10] Husserl says, as regards the traditional notions, that part of our trouble is the fact that the ideal of science on which the Greeks started is one that depends upon Athenian common sense. The ideal has shifted a bit, but it is still in terms of their fundamental language. The possibility of Husserl's criticism lies in the fact that the Athenians worked out the meaning of the terms that existed in their language before they were scientific. What is *sophia*? What is *epistêmê*? What is *synesis*?[11] Similarly, we can have the simple insight needed in the case of the equilateral triangle before asking for a general statement of the conditions of the two circles intersecting. That type of question requires further insights that are not necessary for doing Euclidean geometry.

4   The Content of the Insight

We have been illustrating the difference between insight and conception. Now we want to get a more accurate notion of the exact content of the insight. What does the insight add to the empirical presentations?

In *Insight* we consider in detail the definition of a circle.[12] We start with the cartwheel and draw the radii. We see that if any of the radii are unequal, there are bound to be either bumps or dents in the perimeter. If one radius is a little too long, we have to bring the perimeter out, and if one is a little too short, we have to bring the perimeter in. However, if one considers that the radii are infinite in number and that they are all exactly the same length, then the circle is bound to be perfectly round. That is the insight. What the insight grasps is necessity and impossibility – the necessity of the circle being perfectly round if the radii are equal, and the impossibility of the circle being perfectly round if any radii are unequal.

When we say that the insight grasps necessity and impossibility, we are *saying*. If one is saying, one is conceiving. If one is conceiving and saying,

10 Edmund Husserl, *Die Krisis der europäischen Wissenschaften und die transzendentale Phänomenologie: Eine Einleitung in die phänomenologische Philosophie*, herausgegeben von Walter Biemel (The Hague: Martinus Nijhoff, 1954; 2nd printing, 1962); trans. David Carr, *The Crisis of European Sciences and Transcendental Phenomenology* (Evanston: Northwestern University Press, 1970).
11 In an aside Lonergan distinguished Husserl's criticism from the answer to it, but indicated he would not deal with that answer at this time.[c]
12 *Insight* 7–13.

one has already gone beyond the insight. Consequently, we have to be careful of what is called the psychological fallacy. The psychologist is always going to use concepts and judgments when he talks, but what he is talking about may be in a stage prior to conception and judgment. The fallacy is this: if the psychologist is using concepts and judgments, then what he is talking about is a matter of concepts and judgments. But that does not follow, for you have to use concepts and judgments to discuss anything, but everything is not simply concepts and judgments. There is no tendency, for example, to think of chairs conceiving and judging, even though we use concepts and judgments when talking about chairs; there is no danger of the fallacy there. But there is very much a danger of the fallacy when we talk about our own minds. Consequently, when I say that by insight we grasp necessity of the curve being perfectly round if the radii are all equal, and impossibility of it being perfectly round if any are unequal, I am speaking, I am using concepts. Insight is prior to concepts, even to the ones I use here. I am giving an expression of the insight. I think the expression is accurate, but the insight does not consist in that expression; it does not consist in the concepts that govern that expression. The insight consists in the basis from which I can have those concepts and that expression.

Now notice that the curve is perfectly round. That is a sensible presentation. We are not talking about abstract roundness but about the roundness of *this* curve. We are not talking about the abstract radius – there is only one abstract radius – but about *these* radii multiplied, taken in a group indefinitely large, an infinity of them. We are talking about particular radii and a particular case of perfect or ideal roundness. What the insight grasps in this sensible presentation is necessity and impossibility. It adds to what is merely presented. If the radii are equal, the curve has to be perfectly round – necessity. If any of these radii are unequal, then the curve cannot be perfectly round – impossibility. The sensible elements, then, are radii and an ideal roundness. The nexus between the two, a necesary nexus between the two, is what insight grasps. In this case it grasps a necessary relation.

5   Conception and Abstraction

Once insight grasps that necessary relation, it is possible to go on to the definition of a circle. But when one goes on to that definition, there is always the trick, as in the case of the intersection of the two circles. One has to think of the general case, and attention to the general case may not be had automatically. One can say that a circle is a locus of points equidistant from a center. That expresses the insight, but as yet one has not given the general case of all the necessary conditions. That definition is perfectly satisfactory for the outlined map of Africa on a globe. All points on the coast of Africa are approximately equidistant from the center of the earth, and all that we said was 'a locus of points equidistant from a center.' The definition of a circle is a locus of *coplanar* points equidistant from a center. There is the same sort of trick in any definition. The definition wants to state in the general case what is necessary and sufficient to have the insight. When we defined a circle omitting 'coplanar,' we omitted a necessary condition for having the insight. We can see that we have not given all of the conditions – the outlined map of Africa certainly does not resemble anything perfectly round.[13]

Conception, then, expresses generally what is essential to having the insight, and that is a matter of abstraction. You pick out from these particular radii and this particular case of perfect roundness everything that is necessary, and nothing that is not necessary, to have the same insight again. In other words, you select what is essential and omit what is incidental; you select what is relevant and omit what is irrelevant; you select what is significant and omit what is negligible. You can see that the word 'essential' has a very precise meaning. It means 'essential to having the insight,' that is, essential gnoseologically. What the essences of things are is a further matter, but as far as cognitional analysis goes, conception is the selection from the data, the empirical presentation, the image, of what is essential to having the insight. There is also the inessential. It makes no difference if the background is green or white or black. It makes no difference what the color of the chalk is or how big the circle is. But there has to be a center, a perimeter, and equal radii of any size, in any position, and the center, the perimeter, and the radii have to be in the same plane.

A circle is a locus of coplanar points equidistant from a center, and every one of the points in the locus has to be the same distance from the center. It is true that this definition need not be taken as absolutely first. For example, one has to have a system of measurement to know which radii are equal. In other words, there can always be prior questions,

13 Lonergan's humorous remark on the map he had drawn: 'It doesn't resemble Africa very much either.'

but the geometers went on for twenty centuries before discovering that Euclidean geometry was metric, that there were metric presuppositions involved. So we need not attempt to answer all questions; we are understanding as much about the matter as the geometers did for twenty centuries. The fact that there are always further acts of understanding is something we will have to take into account, but we do not need to have all the previous acts of understanding in every illustration. If we did that, we would never get anywhere. We have to pick out what is essential to the insight we want.

6   The Difference between Empirical Data and Concept

I have given one example of a conception, a selection from data of what is essential to having the insight. It is also a definition.[14] This brings to light the difference between the conception and the empirical data. Euclid's center is a point, and I cannot imagine a point. The Euclidean point has position but no magnitude; any image of position without magnitude is not an image at all. No matter how small we make a dot, it is still not a point, it still has some magnitude. If we eliminate all size from the dot, there is no mark at all. Similarly with regard to the line: the Euclidean line has length without breadth or thickness. No matter how finely pointed the pencil used to draw it, the line will always have some thickness. Even if we only imagine it, it still has some breadth. If we eliminate all breadth, we eliminate the drawing of the line. The concept steps beyond the level of what can be presented empirically. The circle that satisfies the definition is not anything we can imagine; it can only be conceived. The selection from the data of what is essential to the insight leaves behind elements that are necessary for having any empirical presentation at all, or at least it can do so. It does so in this case of the point and the plane curve, because the point has position without magnitude, and the line of the plane curve has length without breadth or thickness.

In this connection, Aristotle in his *Metaphysics* (book 7, chapter 10) distinguished between parts of the matter and parts of the form. It is the same distinction we made with respect to the image in the example of the circle. In the circle, parts of the matter are the color of the background, the color of the line, the size of the circle, the size of the dot used

---

14 The relation of concept to definition came up in discussion 2 that same evening; see § 1, Insight and Its Conceptual Expression.

to represent the point, the thickness of the line used to represent the real line which has no thickness at all. These are all parts of the matter. Parts of the form are the elements that have to be there to have the insight: radii, center, perimeter, and equality.

The Aristotelian distinction between parts of the matter and parts of the form offers, I think, a fundamental clue to what the phenomenologist is after. The phenomenologist does not want to describe absolutely everything. He gives a selective description, a description of what is significant or, as he himself says, of what is essential, of what is relevant. That description, the presentation of data that communicates to us what is essential, is a selection of the parts of the form that are in the matter. It is not discussion on the level of conception, where one tries to give a general formula that covers all possible cases. The phenomenologist presents us with a concrete situation, and in that concrete situation he picks out the parts of the form from the viewpoint of certain insights. It is a concrete mode of communicating insights. I do not say, of course, that this formulation of phenomenology is that of any phenomenologist, but I think it is a good clue to understanding what phenomenologists are doing.[d]

This account of phenomenology ties in with what seemed to be recognized at a meeting of phenomenologists at Louvain in 1951. The meeting included outstanding phenomenologists from Germany, France, Belgium, and Holland. Their conclusion, or something that some of them claimed and the others probably recognized, was that one does not settle any epistemological, metaphysical, or philosophical questions by phenomenology. What I have said is consistent with this. Epistemological, metaphysical, and philosophical questions arise on a level that we have not dealt with yet, while phenomenology as engaged in phenomenological description is not even talking on the level of conception.[15]

There is an early notion of phenomenology in Hegel.[16] There is a series of developing ideas on what phenomenology is in Husserl's writings, and a transposition of Husserl's notion in Heidegger. One finds a movement out into descriptive psychology in the work of Buytendijk, for example. Buytendijk gives a phenomenological description of two people meeting,

15 H.L. Van Breda, ed., *Problèmes actuels de la phénoménologie* (Bruges: Desclée de Brouwer, 1952). The bibliographic data were given by Lonergan, with some account of Van Breda's work on Husserl.

16 This and the following paragraph have been relocated; on the tape they precede the previous paragraph.

an encounter, in which he briefly presents the parts of the form in a meeting, what is significant in a meeting.[17] A similar transference of Heidegger's type of phenomenology to depth psychology is made by Ludwig Binswanger. His phenomenology of dreams is an existentialist interpretation of depth psychology.[18]

There is, then, a considerable movement at the present time with respect to describing the concrete by selecting the parts of the form that are in it from the viewpoint of certain insights. Phenomenologists are communicating insight through the concrete, and not through the general conception that selects what is essential and is found in every case. Phenomenology is talking to the Athenians the way the Athenians could understand, not in the way Socrates did, for which he was put to death.

7   Nominal, Explanatory, and Implicit Definition

In *Insight* a distinction is made of three types of definition: nominal, explanatory, and implicit.[19] Nominal definition supposes insight into the use of words. For example, you can nominally define a circle as a perfectly round plane curve, and you can go on to use the word 'circle' correctly in the light of that definition. Again, you can define a straight line as a line that lies evenly between its extremes; and that gives you a good rule for using the words 'straight line.'

An explanatory definition adds a further element which, if not added in the definition, would have to be added by way of a postulate. Euclid defined the straight line as a line that lies evenly between its extremes, but he had to add the postulate, All right angles are equal. He defined the circle as the locus of coplanar points equidistant from a center, and consequently he did not have to add the postulate, All radii of the same circle are equal. You can put your postulates in the definitions or separate from them. If they are separate, the definitions are merely nominal; if they are in the definitions, the definitions are explanatory.

---

17 F.J.J. Buytendijk, *Phénoménologie de la rencontre*, translated into French by Jean Knapp (Bruges: Desclée de Brouwer, 1952). Lonergan referred also to other works of Buytendijk.

18 Ludwig Binswanger, *Being-in-the-World*, trans. Jacob Needleman (New York: Basic Books, 1963) 222–48. In the lecture Lonergan could not remember Binswanger's name, but spoke of 'a German writing about 1937.' See also discussion 5 below, §3, Archetypes.

19 *Insight* 10–13.

Finally, the postulational element of the explanatory definition can be used alone, and then the definition is implicit. Implicit definition is of far greater generality. In Hilbert's *Foundations of Geometry*, points and straight lines are defined by the postulate, A straight line is determined by two and only two points.[20] Two points and a straight line are set in correlation; if we have two points, that will determine what we mean by a straight line, and if we have a straight line, that will determine what is meant by a point. The only thing that is settled is the relation between the two points and a straight line.

By 'point' Hilbert does not mean position without magnitude, something that you approximate by a dot, nor does he mean by 'line' something with length but without breadth or thickness. That is one case of his definition, but his definition is satisfied equally directly if by a straight line you mean $ax + by + c = 0$, and if by two points you mean (a,b) and (c,d), where a, b, c, and d are any constants, and x and y are variables. These are the formulae for a straight line and a point in Cartesian geometry. In doing analytic geometry, Descartes and geometers in general interpreted these formulae in terms of Euclidean points and lines. But Hilbert's implicit definitions apply just as directly to these mathematical formulae as they do to represented dots and lengths.

Implicit definition, then, prescinds from the matter; it gets entirely away from the matter. It is just the expression of the relational element, and it picks out what is of scientific significance, introducing us to complete generality. To use explanatory definitions which presuppose nominal definitions is to tie down your science to what you were thinking about at the start. If you use implicit definitions, you have thrown yourself open to all possible isomorphic cases. In other words, where the same implicit definition holds with regard to materially distinct things, you have an isomorphism. For example, with regard to points and lines in the Euclidean sense and points and lines in the mathematical sense, there is no similarity between the dot and the ordered pair of numbers, but every relation that holds between points and lines in the one sense holds between points and lines in the other sense. When you base your geometry on implicit definitions, you are dealing purely with relations; you have

20 D. Hilbert, *The Foundations of Geometry*, trans. E.J. Townsend (La Salle, Ill.: Open Court, 1947). What is now the 'sole authorized' English edition, translated from the tenth German edition by Leo Unger, was published by Open Court in 1971, 3rd printing, 1987; in this edition, see p. 3.

moved on to a further stage of abstraction. Implicit definitions are simply relational structures, and the terms of the relations are left indeterminate. When definitions are implicit, the concrete meaning can be anything that will satisfy them.

8   The Definitions of the Related Terms

To bring the discussion full circle, then, what kind of definitions do we have of empirical presentations, inquiry, insight, and conception? First of all, we can define them by their internal relations. Empirical presentations are what are presupposed by inquiry. If one's mind is a perfect blank, one cannot ask questions. There has to be something given to wonder about, some interruption in the blank, if one is to be able to ask, What? Why? How often? or Is it so? Empirical presentations, then, are the material presupposed by inquiry; they are the material into which you have insights; and they are that from which you abstract the parts of the form, omitting parts of the matter, when you have a general conception. Similarly, what is inquiry? It is what arises upon empirical presentations and leads on to insight and conception. Insight is what answers inquiry about empirical presentations and what grounds conception. Conception has its relations as well. It expresses the insight that satisfies the inquiry into empirical presentations. We have, then, a nest of terms related to one another.

Insofar as you have no self-appropriation whatever, the four terms stand as do Hilbert's points and lines in their implicit definition. There is a purely relational structure; the four terms are defined by their relations to one another, the way 'point' and 'line' are defined by Hilbert, and there is no material realization that is relevant. Thus the four terms – empirical presentations, inquiry, insight, and conception – could have a whole series of quite different meanings so long as the definitions remain merely implicit, and the definitions have to remain merely implicit if you have no self-appropriation at all. But in the measure that you have some degree of self-appropriation, the four terms take on a meaning from your experience of yourself; and the greater the degree of self-appropriation you have, the more meaning the terms take on, and the fuller, the richer, the wider are the implications.

These terms, then, have a fixed element – their mutual relations – and a variable element that increases with self-appropriation. So they are analogous – something fixed and something variable – and consequently they are open. We are not tying ourselves down to some sense of 'inquiry' that can be strictly formulated. Inquiry is what stands in certain relations to insight and conception, and that matrix of relations is the matrix that expresses one's own self-appropriation.[21]

Now that set of relations between empirical presentations – either data or images – and inquiry, insight, and conception can be taken beyond implicit definitions, where the terms are simply related to one another, to the fullest enrichment one could wish from self-appropriation and all of its implications. A set of basic analogous terms whose meaning develops with the development of the person indicates[22] the fruit of self-appropriation, the basis that makes the difference between the plaster cast of a man and the philosopher.

9   The Expression and Object of Insight in Aristotle

What I have been saying may be tied up with a few remarks on Aristotle's *syllogismos epistêmonikos*, his explanatory syllogism. Aristotle's syllogistic is concerned with valid inferences, but it is not concerned solely with valid inferences.[23] Aristotle used his syllogism as an expression or way of communicating insights.

In the old type of logic book that was based on Aristotle, one can find the fundamental example of an explanatory syllogism. The example states: if the moon has phases, then it is a sphere; the moon goes through phases; therefore, it is a sphere. It also states: if the moon is a sphere, then it will have phases; the moon is a sphere; therefore, it will have phases. The phases of the moon are the reason why we know that the moon is a sphere, the *causa cognoscendi*, and the fact that the moon is a sphere is the ontological reason for the moon having phases, the *causa essendi*. In the first case, the subject is the moon, the middle term is phases, and the predicate is sphere. In the second case, the subject is the moon, the middle term is sphere, and the predicate is phases. This example exhibits the relation of the three terms – subject, middle, and predicate –

---

21 Coffee break was taken here. On resuming the lecture, Lonergan began with practical suggestions – omitted here – for the format of the evening discussions.

22 The change from 'provides' (p. 55 of the 1980 edition) to 'indicates' is made on the basis of an annotation in Lonergan's own copy.

23 On syllogism as it relates to valid inference, see lecture 5, §8, The General Form of Reflective Understanding.

where what from one standpoint is the predicate is from a different standpoint the middle term. When phases is the middle term, we have the *causa cognoscendi*, the reason why we know. But when the sphere is the middle term, we have the *causa essendi*, the reason why the thing is so.

Syllogism is a vehicle for expressing an insight. What is the insight in question? Suppose the moon were a flat disc that reflects light from the sun. Then you will see the whole disc illuminated if you are anywhere within the 180-degree angle on that side of the disc. If you are on the other side of the disc, you will not see anything at all. In either case, you would not see the series of phases normally seen in the moon on successive nights. To account for that series of phases in the one object that is reflecting light, there has to be a spherical object. That is an argument that shows why the moon must be a sphere. Why must it? Because it goes through the phases. That is the reason you know that the moon is a sphere. On the other hand, the phases do not make the moon into a sphere or change the disc into a sphere; they are just the reason why you know. On the ontological side, the sphere is the *causa essendi*, the ground of there being phases.

Because syllogism is a means of communicating insights, Aristotle preferred syllogisms in the first figure and had a doctrine of syllogism that is not simply a matter of valid conclusions.ᵉ Aristotle's doctrine of the explanatory syllogism shows that he is trying to do in his logic something that the symbolic logician is trying to avoid. The symbolic logician wants a logical process that moves along without any casual insights. He wants to avoid anything like the inadequacy of the proof of the external angle or of the solution to the problem of constructing an equilateral triangle. The distrust that arose over the case of the parallel axiom underlies his desire to have things worked out in a rigorous fashion.²⁴ He does not want any insights cropping up after he has laid down his definitions, axioms, and postulates. His conclusions depend simply upon these.²⁵

24 Omitted here: 'in such a rigorous fashion that a machine could, in principle, do the logic of it.' See note 19 to lecture 1.
25 Omitted here: 'conclusions depend simply upon these, with no further additions. To make sure you have no further additions, you adopt a logical procedure that in principle could be done by a machine. This is logic designed to avoid insight. It is quite different from Aristotle's understanding of syllogism as an instrument for communicating insight.' See note 19 to lecture 1.

In *Insight* I offer an example of explanatory syllogism as a means of communicating insight. I present a syllogism with regard to special relativity:

> If the mathematician's insights into principles and laws do not vary because of a constant velocity or a transformation of axes, then the expressions should remain invariant under these transformations.
> But his insights do not vary.
> Therefore his expressions should remain invariant.[26]

That syllogism attempts to communicate the insight behind special relativity. Syllogism, then, is not merely a matter of valid conclusions, which is the single aspect that is attended to in symbolic logic; it can also be a matter of communicating insight.

Moreover, while in the case of Aristotle's syllogism regarding the moon there are three terms – subject, middle, and predicate – Aristotle holds that the answer to all questions is a matter of finding the middle term. It must be found not only when there are three terms but even in the case of the simple question, What is the moon? In other words, he proceeds to the limit. When there are both substance and accidents, a sphere and phases, then it is quite easy to find the three terms and to line them up so that one has the *causa cognoscendi* and the *causa essendi*. Then too, one can switch them around and make the *causa cognoscendi* the predicate. But Aristotle proceeds a step below that; he wants to account for our knowledge of the basic term, the subject, as well.

Aristotle accounts for our knowledge of the subject in the same way, except that he moves from the subject down to matter. I mentioned that the question, What is a house? is answered, has its meaning explained, by saying why these bricks, stones, and pieces of wood are a house. It is because they are put together in a certain way, and that answer is the fruit of an insight. The second element, over and above the matter, that makes the bricks, stones, and wood a house, is designated by Aristotle by a whole series of expressions: *eidos* (*species*, species), *morphê* (*forma*, form),

26 This is a different rendition of the syllogism found on p. 24 of *Insight*; but Lonergan was not quoting formally from the book – he concluded with the remark, 'However, I just mention that incidentally.'

aition tou einai (*causa essendi*, the cause of being), *to ti ên einai* (*quod quid erat esse*, the essence, what a thing was to be).

In the *Physics* Aristotle enumerates his four causes as end, agent, matter, and definition (*to ti estin, quod quid est*). But in his other enumerations, presumably later, the fourth cause is not the definition (*to ti estin*), but the form (*to ti ên einai*).[27] What is the difference between *to ti ên einai* and *to ti estin*, between the form and the definition? It is the difference, with which we have already dealt, between the content of the insight and the conception, the general definition. Aristotle moved back as best he could – and it is marvelous that he did as well as he did – from conception to insight, by talking about their objects: *to ti ên einai*, the form; *to ti estin*, the definition; and also *ousia* (essence). This can be found in the *Metaphysics*, book 7. In book 8 Aristotle says that the *ousia* is form with matter too, but in book 7 he is dealing with the question, What is the *ousia* of a thing? Finally, in chapter 17 of book 7, after wandering in all directions, after meeting all considerations,[28] he comes to deal with the question, What is a man? What does it mean to ask, 'What is a man?' He says that *ti estin* means *dioti*, or why is it, or *propter quid*; that *quid* means *propter quid*; and that *what* means *why*.[29] But how can one ask, 'Why is a man?' That does not seem to make much sense; but one can make it make sense by asking, 'Why is *this* a man?' just as 'Why are these bricks and stones a house?' This is a man because of the form, because of the *eidos, morphê, aition tou einai, to ti ên einai, ousia*. A whole set of terms comes tumbling out.

Aristotle, I suggest, is trying to pin down the object of insight; so not only does he talk about subject, middle, and predicate, but also about one's knowledge of the subject. He accounts for one's knowledge of the subject in the same way, but by a trick. For subject one substitutes the matter; for middle, the form; and when one has the form added to the matter, one has a being. It is the *aition tou einai*. If you add on the form, you add on the cause of being, the cause of a thing's being something.[f] If it is neither a man nor a house nor any other thing, it is just prime matter. So the form is the *aition tou einai*. The *to ti ên einai* is what you understand before you are able to formulate it; it is the form, *intelligibile in sensibilibus* (the intelligible in the sensible).[30]

27 References to *Physics* and *Metaphysics*: see lecture 1, note 5.
28 In an aside: 'It's a beautiful piece of work, that seventh book.'
29 See lecture 1, §2.5, Insight in Aristotle, where the example is an eclipse.
30 Lonergan has been running through the list of terms (presumably written on the blackboard). At this point he comes to *eidos*, and makes the

I think that what Aristotle was trying to express ties in with what I have been saying. But his expression was under quite different conditions. The reflective, introspective type of psychology and talk about self-appropriation were not yet possible.

10 · The Notion of System

Let us move on to the notion of system. So far we have been concentrating on particular insights, and most of our illustrations have been geometrical: the insight by which you define the circle; the insight by which you see when circles must intersect; the insight that you add over and above the axioms in order to prove that the external angle is greater than the interior opposite. But in Euclid we do not simply have stray insights such as the ones we have been illustrating. What we have is a fundamental cluster of related insights and a set of definitions, axioms, and postulates from which follow solutions to problems – and definitions are proofs of theorems, demonstrations of theorems. The whole thing holds together.

The difference between stray insights and clusters of related insights may be discovered through a consideration of what occurred prior to and with Newton. Prior to Newton, Archimedes studied floating bodies, Galileo worked out the free fall of a body, and Kepler worked out the laws of planetary motion. But Newton set down laws of motion and proceeded to demonstrate that if a body moves in a field of central force its trajectory is a conic section. He set out with a minimal cluster of insights, definitions, postulates, and axioms, and proceeded to account for the laws that had previously been empirically established, bringing them into a single explanatory unity.

A single insight yields a conception, a definition, an object of thought; but from a cluster of insights, you build up a system of definitions, axioms, postulates, and deductions. We have to note that a system is quite an achievement; systems are not numerous. There are Euclid's geometry and subsequent developments in geometry, Newton's mechanics and dynamics and the building upon Newton, and the Mendeleev table in chemistry. System, then, is the expression of a cluster of insights.

---

incidental remark, '*Eidos* also means species in the logical sense.' He then repeats his earlier remarks on *ousia*, 'Identification of the form with *ousia* occurs in book 7; but in book 8 Aristotle goes on to say that *ousia* in material things is form and matter.'

By way of contrast, St Thomas' *Summa theologiae* and his *Summa contra Gentiles* are not simply systems. While those works do hold together, his method is not that of setting down definitions, axioms, and postulates, and then deducing. In fact, that is just what he does not do.

Moreover, St Thomas does not have the concerns of a systematic thinker. As an example, let us take the term *actio* which I have investigated at some length.[31] In Scotus' *Quodlibeta* there is a passage in which he says that *actio* is used in fifteen different senses, and he lists all fifteen.[32] When he uses *actio* he uses it in one of these senses. He has the concern of the logician, the concern of the man who wants a perfectly general conception and statement of his idea and of all the different ways in which that idea can be thought about and expressed. But what do we find in St Thomas? On one page he says, *Actio dicitur dupliciter*, and he gives two meanings of *actio*. But on the next page we find, *Actio dicitur tripliciter*, and he gives three more meanings which do not correspond to the first two. If we turn the page again, we find, *Actio dicitur dupliciter*, and still more meanings.[33] St Thomas does not have that concern of the logician who is out to say definitively just what has to be said; his is an entirely different type of thinking. What is his method? It is a series of questions and answers, not the formulation of a cluster of insights. It is something more closely related to the process of presentations, inquiry, insight, conception, and

---

31 Bernard Lonergan, *Grace and Freedom: Operative Grace in the Thought of St. Thomas Aquinas*, ed. J. Patout Burns (London: Darton, Longman & Todd, 1971) 63–91, 131–33 (CWL 1); *Verbum* 119–24.

32 The detailed Index to Scotus' *Quaestiones Quodlibetales* (St. Bonaventure, N.Y.: The Franciscan Institute, 1950, photomechanically reprinted from the L. Wadding edition) gives several references to *actio*, but we have not found the list of fifteen uses to which Lonergan refers.

33 Lonergan's papers include some card indices, among which is a card with the heading 'Duplex actio.' This lists over thirty relevant loca: for example, 'duplex operatio' (*Summa contra Gentiles*, 2, c. 1, §3) and 'triplex operatio' (ibid. 3, c. 22, §2: it was Lonergan's practice to number the paragraphs in the Leonine manual edition of the *Summa contra Gentiles*). The latter locus lists three uses, but does not use 'triplex.' If we go directly to Aquinas, we find that there is a statement in *Summa theologiae*, 1, q. 76, a. 1: 'Attribuitur ... aliqua actio alicui tripliciter,' and there are frequent references to 'duplex actio,' but we have not found the sequence of 'dupliciter' and 'tripliciter' which Lonergan describes. The *Verbum* Index, under *Actio*, gives one reference to a threefold division (besides several to a twofold), but that does not seem relevant to the present question; what is relevant is Lonergan's remark on the 'fluidity of terminology' in Aquinas: *Verbum* 122 (and see the whole section on 'Duplex Actio,' pp. 119–24).

sufficient conception to deal with the question at hand. People have to work out just what the Thomist synthesis is and determine what the exact meanings of the Thomist terms are. St Thomas has not done it for us.

Finally, system is not a complete method. While you can build up a system from clusters of insights, definitions, axioms, and postulates, you also encounter further questions. The mere fact that you have the system opens the way to raising further questions that cannot be answered in terms of the system. It turns up difficulties that lead you to the point of adding more insights to the basic cluster, and consequently of giving different meanings to the definitions and of augmenting the axioms and postulates. In this manner one reaches a further system.

11   Higher Viewpoints

I call the transition to a further system a transition to a higher viewpoint, and I illustrate it in *Insight* by a process from very elementary arithmetic to algebra.[34] We start off with 1 and 2; 2 is one more than 1, and 3 is one more than 2. All of the definitions are in terms of the operation of addition. We move on to an analogous expansion. Invert addition, and you have subtraction; take addition a number of times, and you have multiplication; take multiplication a number of times, and you have powers. Then take the inverse of those operations. When you follow this out generally, you encounter difficulties, and further questions arise. We have questions about negative numbers; for example, what is the meaning of adding negative numbers or multiplying something by a negative number? Even the meaning of 'one' and 'equals' becomes a bit obscure as, for example, in the illustration in *Insight*: Let x equal $0.\bar{9}$, where $0.\bar{9}$ means $9/10 + 9/100 + 9/1000$, etc.; then $10x$ equals $9.\bar{9}$, where $9.\bar{9}$ means $9 + 9/10 + 9/100 + 9/1000$, etc.; hence $9x$ equals 9; therefore, x equals 1. But this does not seem to be the original meaning of 'equals': $1 = 0.\bar{9}$.[35]

Not only can we move from one system to a subsequent system, from arithmetic to algebra, for example; but this movement keeps on recurring. There is the movement from Euclidean geometry to Gauss and Lobachevski and then on to the more general geometry, and in general

---

34 *Insight* 13–17.
35 Lonergan adds, 'That's just incidental. I mention that series because multiplying by 10 sometimes causes difficulty.'

the mathematician acknowledges the possibility of indefinite progress. We can always move on to further systems, and the fact should not surprise us. Putting it ontologically, any finite essence is contingent, and insofar as one's cluster of insights is knowledge of essence, it is knowledge not of what must be but of what might be, and there is room for other things that might be. In other words, objectively a finite essence is not what must be but simply what can be. Consequently, a system that is an understanding of finite essences is not knowledge of something that must be, but knowledge of what can be. If knowledge develops, if one's knowledge gradually approaches a full understanding of essences, then in its systematic procedure it will move through a series of systems before one accounts for absolutely everything.

12   The Significance of Symbolism

Let us take another illustration in connection with higher viewpoints. Higher viewpoints are usually expressed symbolically, and there is something worth noting about symbolism: the symbols fulfil a function that is in some respects similar to that of the geometrical diagrams.

We will take the square root of 1764 as an illustration. To take the square root, we divide off the last two numbers, and we go on dividing them off by pairs; we draw a line down the left side; the nearest to the square root of 17 is 4; 4 multipled by 4 equals 16; subtract 16 from 17 and bring down 64; double 4 and get 8; 8 will go into 16 twice, so we write down 2 beside 8; multiply 82 by 2 and we get 164. We see, then, that the square root of 1764 is 42.

Why does it work? How would you take the square root of MDCCLXIV, which is exactly the same number in different notation? The routine of taking square roots is commonly taught without telling people why it works. Why should it work? It is the expansion of the algebraic formula

$$(a+b+c+d+ \ \dots \ )^2 = a^2 + (2a+b)b$$
$$+ (2a + 2b + c)c + (2a + 2b + 2c + d)d + \ \dots$$

You may say that you divide the numbers off by twos in the routine procedure because you are squaring the first number. But let us take the simplest case, and then we can generalize. Let a be the number in the tens and b the number in the units, of the number that is the square root of 1764. Then a is 40 because it is in the tens, and b is 2; a^2 is 1600 and

$2a$ is 80. So we have $(40+2)^2 = 1600 + (80+2)2$. That is the reason why it works. This formula has been transposed into a routine, and the routine covers up the intelligibility of the formula.

In general, the discovery of an apt symbolism greatly simplifies mathematics and makes possible enormous developments. Both Newton and Leibniz are said to have discovered the calculus, but they represented the same thing by different symbols. Newton wrote $\dot{y}$ to denote what Leibniz represented by dy/dx. The second formula immediately suggests all sorts of developments which are not suggested by the other; it admits developments of the symbolism itself which are not at all possible in the other representation. The apt symbolism is an enormously important element in the advance of mathematics, because, where in elementary geometry one gets insight into one's constructions, in mathematics one gets insight into the structure of one's symbols. Because one can get insight into the structure of one's symbols, the mathematician goes on with the business of higher viewpoints in a way no one else does.

13   Inverse Insight

So far we have been talking about insights in which you catch on to something, for example, why the routine for taking the square root works. The routine works because it is a mechanization of an algebraic identity. Now we have to consider the inverse case where you understand that there is nothing to be understood. The inverse case is also extremely important in building up a science, because if you understand that something is *not to be understood* a series of problems is eliminated.

For example, when a body is in movement we look for a cause to account for it. Newton's first law of motion is to the effect that if a body is at rest or in uniform motion, moving with a uniform velocity, then it remains in that state as long as there is no cause intervening. That is a matter of understanding that constant velocity does not require a cause; it is like rest. All problems of explaining constant velocities are eliminated; bodies just keep on going, and we do not have to explain why. As a consequence, the science of mechanics concentrates simply upon the far more general case of accelerations, changes in velocity. There are no problems connected with velocity; all of the problems are on the level of acceleration. There are no problems of causes of rest, and if constant velocity is considered to be the same sort of thing, then the same sort of answer is to be given: the body is moving, and it keeps on doing so as long as no cause intervenes. There results the possibility of having a far more compact science of mechanics than would be possible if one had to have causes for constant velocity. Constant velocity, then, is one instance of the inverse insight, and in general, whenever an inverse insight comes in, an enormous sweep is given to science, and a new addition of some significance is made to it.

Let us take another example of inverse insight, the square root of 2. Aristotle says that most people are surprised when they are told that there is no number equal to the length of the diagonal, or that the diagonal is incommensurable with the side of the square. But if the geometer were told that there was a diagonal that could be commensurable with the side, he would be still more astounded.[36] The Greeks knew about irrational surds, but they put it in terms of incommensurability.

You expect the square root of 2 to be some number in the elementary sense: there is some improper fraction m/n, where m and n are integers, such that m/n is equal to the square root of 2. But you can demonstrate that it cannot be a number in that sense. If m and n are integers, it is possible to remove from them all of their common factors. Let us say that, with all of their common factors removed, we have p/q. Square both sides and we have $2 = p^2/q^2$. But if all of the common factors have been removed from p and q, all of the common factors have been removed from p^2 and q^2. Therefore, it is impossible to say that q^2 goes into p^2 twice. There cannot be some improper fraction m/n, where m and n are integers, such that m/n is equal to the square root of 2. There must be some other type of answer. Thus irrationals were introduced as a type of number that is not the same as an improper fraction. This inverse insight is the limitation theorem in mathematics; it is the 'what cannot be done' that opens up a new field.

The idea of inverse insight arises in a much more general way, and in a way in which there is no surprise, in connection with the idea of what St Thomas called the *conditiones materiae*, the *materia individualis*, what is spoken of with regard to abstraction. If one asks why this point is different from that point, one may answer that they differ because of the distance between them. Take a third point that is equidistant from the other two. Why does this one differ from the other two? One may answer that it is because of these distances. Why do the three distances differ? One may answer that it is because they are pointing in different directions. But

36 *Metaphysics*, 1, 2, 983a 12–21.

suppose they were pointing in the same direction; then what would be the difference between them?[37] They are in different places. Why are they in different places? Because they are between different points. We have gone around in a circle. We can never arrive at any explanation; the places are just different. We cannot have an insight into everything. There has to be a part in the empirical presentations that is *just given* and that does not correspond to any insight.[38]

That is the fundamental inverse insight that makes scientific collaboration and scientific generalization possible. It makes scientific collaboration possible, because the work done in this place at this time is relevant to knowledge of what will occur at this other place at this other time. The results here do not depend upon the time and place, but upon something at this time and at this place. Similarly, the results there do not depend upon that time and that place, but upon something at that time and at that place. If that were not true, we would need a different science for every time and every place. Space and time are the *conditiones materiae*. There is something in the empirical presentations that just remains on that level and has no corresponding insight – an empirical residue. Again, there is in the limit no explanation of the difference between this instance and that instance. The difference is just a brute given; it is a fundamental datum.

37 This somewhat obscure line of argument is clarified in *Insight* 27: 'why are equal and parallel distances different distances?'
38 The was reel runs out here. The lri and djs reels take us to the end of the next paragraph, presumably the end of the lecture, with Lonergan concluding, 'I have taken longer than I intended over that.'

3

The Dynamic Aspect of Knowing[1]

At present we are dealing with the set of fundamental terms: presentations, inquiry, insight, and conception. In lectures 5 and 6 we will have occasion to deal with further terms: reflection, reflective insight, and judgment. All of these terms can be defined by their relations to one another; they can all be implicitly defined. Presentations are what one inquires about and has insights into, so as to be able to formulate what is essential, significant, relevant, in the presentations. Similarly, the other terms can be defined by their relations to the rest.

But while each term can be defined by its relations to the others, we are not simply dealing with a purely axiomatic formulation. The precise meaning of the terms and relations is had by each of you in the measure that you achieve self-appropriation, that you are present to yourself as having presentations, as inquiring, as catching on and getting the point, as conceiving. The wealth of meaning, the precision, the fulness of the terms, increases in each of you with your degree of self-appropriation, and that work of self-appropriation can be done by no one else for you.

Throughout the last two lectures we have been making the gestures and uttering the sounds that facilitate the process of catching on to just what is meant by presentation, inquiry, insight, and conception. But as a matter of fact what we are dealing with is not just a set of static elements

---

1 The third lecture, Wednesday, August 6, 1958. Recording started with Lonergan in midsentence at 'set of fundamental terms.' It had been announced that there would be no discussion that evening.

but a process. It is always process *in us*; our knowing is always dynamic; we are always moving on to the next step. The pursuit of knowledge is the pursuit of an unknown. It is guided by an ideal, and the ideal changes and becomes more precise in the course of the pursuit. Consequently, what we have to do now is grasp that dynamic aspect, and grasp it in a reflective fashion. We have to perform the activities and go through the routines that will bring to explicit consciousness the dynamic aspect of the process of knowing. We do not want to endow these terms simply with the static meaning they may have as a result of merely implicit definitions; we do not want the mere suggestion of their dynamic aspect that is had from an implicit consciousness of their meaning. We want to bring the dynamic aspect of these terms to explicit consciousness.

1   A Comparison of Scientific and Mathematical Understanding

We begin with a comparison of a scientific and a mathematical insight. If we imagine a cartwheel and seek to explain why it is round, we do not want to know the final cause, that is, why we want a round wheel. We do not want to go into the sociology of wheelwrights to find out why they specialize in making wheels. We do not want to study the technology of their tools or the sources of their materials. We want the explanation of why the cartwheel is round; we want an immanent intelligibility, an intelligibility that may be had in the wheel itself. What we arrive at is the definition of the circle. In similar fashion, when Galileo discovered the law of falling bodies, he was not asking why it is that bodies fall or why they should not stay put. He was not inquiring into final causes, nor was he asking about material causes. While there had been an opinion that bodies fell according to their weights – the heavier bodies fall faster – he ruled out that view experimentally. And he was not concerned with the efficient causes of the fall. He wanted the immanent law of the fall, and he found it by correlating the distance and the time. Anything that falls, falls a certain distance, and it does so in a certain length of time. Galileo discovered that there was a proportion between the distance traversed and the time squared.

If we compare the insight that is formulated by a proportion between the distance and the time squared with the definition of the circle, we find certain similarities and certain differences. In the first place, there is similarity insofar as one starts from sensible data in both cases. Why is a cartwheel round? What is a free fall? Secondly, in both cases one is not concerned with final causes, efficient causes, or material causes. One is concerned with an immanent intelligibility in the thing, event, or process. Thirdly, as we noted earlier, the circle is defined in terms of points and a line, and points and lines cannot be imagined. Anything one imagines has some magnitude, and a point is just position without magnitude. A line has length without breadth or thickness, and anything one imagines has to have some breadth or one has no image whatever. What one discovers is in a field of concepts, of things that are just supposed. 'Let us suppose' that there are points, things with position and no magnitude; 'let us suppose' that there are lengths without breadth or thickness. Such things are conceptual. Something similar happens with regard to discovering the law of the free fall: the law holds only in a vacuum, and we cannot attain a perfect vacuum. The free fall and the circle are equally out of this world. Finally, both the law of the free fall and the definition of the circle can be expressed in formulae, the formula for the definition of the circle being $x^2 + y^2 = a^2$, where a is the radius.

While there are those similarities, still there are differences. Discovering the definition of the circle does not involve any field work. You do not have to go around studying different instances of the cartwheel and other wheels, checking whether the definition really explains all of them. In geometry it is sufficient if you understand what you imagine. But when you are studying the free fall of bodies, it is not sufficient simply to understand an imagined free fall. What you have to understand is the way bodies actually do fall, and consequently Galileo has been said to have climbed up and down the tower of Pisa and let bodies fall directly, and he had to build his inclined planes and let bodies slide down the planes in order to obtain his series of data and his set of measurements.

Further, in the case of the geometrical insight, the data are continuous. You can have an infinity of points by drawing a straight or a curved line. But in scientific work the data are never continuous. In other words, you cannot have an infinity of measurements in scientific work. You *can* take measurements: when the time is 1 the distance traversed is x, when the time is 2 the distance is y, when the time is 3 the distance is z, and when the time is 4 the distance is up off the graph. You can interpolate: you can ask where the body is at one-half second, at one and one-half seconds, at two and one-half seconds, and you can find the distances in those cases. You can break it down as much as you please, but you never arrive at an infinity of measurements of distance and time. After a sufficiently large number of measurements has been obtained, you can draw a free-hand curve, but to do so is simply to anticipate what there would be if there were a law that covered all possible instances. When you draw a free-hand curve or write down the formula $s :: t^2$ (the distance is proportional to the square of the time), you are going beyond what you know by actual measurements. This formula will hold for all possible values of s and t. In short, you go off into infinity as soon as you write down a formula or draw a free-hand curve. So, when dealing with imaginary objects such as the circle, the presentation can be continuous, but in empirical science there is always some finite number of measurements, and arriving at a formula that expresses the numerical continuum or drawing a free-hand curve is going beyond what is really known. You are expressing an anticipation of intelligibility in the data, namely, that they will conform to some law.

Moreover, no matter how many points you have, it is always possible to have the mathematicians devise some other curve that will cover all of those points equally well. The possibility of some other law is not excluded. You can test the free-hand curve that corresponds to $s :: t^2$ for some point, and find that it is wrong. Another formula can be found that will take care of that point, but it will correspond to a different curve. In other words, we said yesterday that, if the radii of the circle are all equal, the curve *must* be absolutely round; but in this case we are saying that, if the data are such and such, then *possibly* the law is: s is proportional to t squared. It is hypothetical. In science the insight grasps possibility, whereas geometrical insight usually aims at necessity.

Again, in geometry one's imagination adjusts to one's concepts. You may have been a bit surprised when I said that one cannot imagine a point, that no matter how small you make the dot it still is not a point because it has some magnitude. Why would you be surprised? Your imagination adjusts itself to your concepts. You were trying to imagine, as though you really were imagining what your concepts were expressing. But in science you do not have that adjustment. The sensible data remain what they are. No matter how beautiful the theory, it does not change the data, although it may modify your approach to the data, and de facto in some sense it should, as we will see.

Finally, the development of geometry or of mathematics has an internal circuit. Definitions, axioms, and postulates are set up, and deductions are made. More and more problems and theorems are found simply by returning to imagination – or by developing the symbolism, which is another instance of the image, the object of insight. The circuit of presentations, inquiry, insight, and conception swings back through more figures or more symbols to further presentations. On the other hand, in the development of science there is an external circuit. The scientist's conception is a hypothesis. He says, 'Let us suppose that the distance traversed is proportional to the time squared.' He starts drawing the conclusions from that hypothesis, but he does not simply say, 'Therefore, this is so.' He tests each one of the conclusions under all possible circumstances, and by that further testing either he confirms the law which he proposed as a hypothesis or he finds further data that lead him to correct it or to move on to the discovery of further laws. In mathematics the circuit – presentations, inquiry, insight, conception – is immanent; it is sufficient to draw the figures and write down the symbols. But the circuit in science involves dealing with things; it involves, as we will put it later, a canon of operations.[2]

2   The Notion of Heuristic Structure

The comparison of mathematical and scientific insights does not answer the question with which we began. We just drew attention to elementary differences in order to set in motion our four basic terms. We want now to grasp the dynamic aspect of the process, and that process as formulated, as brought to explicit consciousness, is a heuristic structure. 'Heuristic' is from the Greek word *heurisko*: I find. In Greek, the ending *-ikon* denotes the principle.[3] So a heuristic is a principle of discovering.

To illustrate heuristic structure in *Insight*, I take a simple example from algebra.[4] When after three o'clock will the minute hand first exactly cover the hour hand? At once the algebraist says, 'Let x be the number of minutes after three o'clock.' At x minutes after three o'clock the minute hand will have moved through x minutes. Then he infers that, while the minute hand moves over x minutes, the hour hand moves over $x/12$ minutes. The minute hand goes through sixty minutes as the hour hand goes through five minutes. The ratio is 12 to 1. Next, by advertence to

2 See §7 below, Canons of Empirical Method.
3 Lonergan added some remarks on Greek usage: 'The *kinetikon* is what moves, the *kineton* is what is moved.' We might add that the famous 'eureka,' which figured so prominently at the beginning of *Insight*, is also a form of the Greek *heurisko*: where 'heuristic' is a principle of discovery, '[h]eureka' means 'I have found it.'
4 *Insight* 36.

the diagram of the face of a clock, he sees at once that at three o'clock the hour hand has a fifteen-minute start. Thus $x = x/12 + 15$. Solve the equation, and you will find out exactly when after three o'clock the one hand covers the other.

Now we have to reflect on that process. What happened? The pursuit of knowledge is the pursuit of an unknown. We have given the unknown a name x. In doing that we are making the process explicit; we are making our cognitional elements explicit in their dynamic aspects. We have given a name to the goal, a name that does not determine anything: let x be the unknown, the number of minutes after three o'clock. Next we wrote down everything we knew about x. When the minute hand goes through x minutes, the hour hand goes through $x/12$ minutes, and the hour hand has a fifteen-minute start. We arrived at an equation, and from our habits in doing mathematics we know how to solve the equation. Upon solving the equation we have our answer. That is an analogy, an illustration of a heuristic process. By making explicit the fact that you are heading towards some unknown, you make things more precise.

What is the unknown? Is that procedure in algebra unique, or has it other instances? We talk about the nature of life, the nature of light, the nature of energy, the nature of man, and so on. We can talk about all of those things even though we do not know what their natures are. What do we mean by 'nature'? By the nature of light we mean what we will know when we understand light. In other words, 'nature' is the name of the unknown towards which inquiry is heading. Just as the algebraist writes down x, so in common speech we use the 'nature of ...' The 'nature of ...' is the name for what we either know or do not know,[5] that is, for what we would know if we understood a given set of data. When you ask, 'What?' you ask about the 'nature of ...' The question, What is it? may be made more explicit: What is the 'nature of ...'?

The heuristic element in our knowing is quite explicit in Aristotle. He speaks of the *to ti estin* and the *to ti ên einai*. In medieval philosophy there is the concern with *quidditas*. Quiddity is what you know when you know what it is, when you understand it. It is, if you wish, a dummy term – you do not know yet – but still it is not a useless dummy. It is an extremely

5 There is question here whether to write 'neither ... nor' or 'either ... or.' We chose the latter, the words Lonergan actually used; but the former, suggesting Plato's paradox of inquiry – neither knowing nor not knowing – may convey better his intended sense.

significant dummy, because it expresses your inquiry, your anticipation of a future insight. Just as in the algebraic problem, by studying certain properties of the x we really did find out what the x is, so by making explicit our talk of the 'nature of ...' we will be on our way to discovering what the nature is.

3   Heuristic Procedure in Science

How do we go about finding the 'nature of ...'? In dealing with the algebraic problem we began by noting everything that had some relation to our unknown. When we know the nature of our x, we will have had an insight, we will have understood. Whenever we understand, there is this property at least to what is understood, namely, that similars are similarly understood. Just as we could write down about the hour hand that it moves $x/12$ minutes when the minute hand moves through x, so here we can write down that similars are similarly understood. This simplifies enormously the problem of understanding things. If the physicists or the chemists required a different explanation for every hydrogen atom, it would be very difficult for them to find them all because hydrogen is supposed to make up about fifty-five per cent of the universe; but they need only one, from the cognitional viewpoint, because similars are similarly understood. One cannot have a different insight if the presentations are similar in all respects. A number of other conclusions can be drawn from this point that similars are similarly understood; the 'nature of ...' is some sort of universal.

Now we can put a further question. What do we mean by 'similar'? This brings us again to what Whitehead called the bifurcation of nature, which is really the bifurcation of understanding. We found this bifurcation exemplified in Eddington's description of the two tables[6] – one solid and round with a smooth surface, and the other a collection of electrons that is not even imaginable. Accordingly, by 'similar' one may mean 'similar to me,' as when one says, 'It looks similar,' and in that case, the sense data, the color, shape, sound, feel, and so on, are similar, and similarity means similarity in relation to observers, to us. But by 'similar' one can also mean similarity of things in their relations to one another. Things can be similar insofar as they are found in the same place, are of the same size, change size at the same rate, and so on.

6 See notes 7 and 8 in lecture 1.

The second type of similarity is the point to measurement. When Galileo made his measurements, he came up with a series of measurements of distance with corresponding measurements of time, and he found a similarity in the law relating the distance and the time. Here similarity is rather complex. Distance and time are related to one another by a certain proportion. When the distance is 1, the time is 1; when the distance is 2, the time is 4; and so on: $s = t^2$. What turns out to be common to all cases of the free fall is the relation $s = gt^2/2$. If one prescinds from interferences, this relation is found in every instance, and the similarity exists in the relation of the aspects of the free fall. In other words, all the relations to us of a free fall are forgotten. You forget about what happens when something freely falling hits you, or what you would lose if you dropped your watch or your glasses. Just as in the case of the circle we related the equality of the radii and the appearance of roundness, so here we are relating distance and time. By a rather complex dealing with distance and time, we arrive at something that is similar in every case of a free fall. That step by means of which we arrive, through measurement, at the relations of things to one another is the fundamental step in the whole of the development of science from Galileo to the present day. Modern science employs the procedure of withdrawing from relations of things to us, considering the relations of things to one another, and attending to the similarities there, in order to determine the 'nature of ...'

That step gives rise to difficulties, however, for it presents us with a world we find extremely odd and strange. Difference in temperature is not difference in the feeling of heat. The temperature of this piece of tin is the same as the temperature of the blackboard, but this piece of tin feels colder. Temperature is not defined in terms of the relations of things to us, but in terms of the relations things have among themselves. Similarly, mass is not weight. Weight is mass multiplied by the acceleration of gravity. Mass is not given in the simple fashion in which weight is given. Yet temperature and mass are fundamental concepts in physics. How do you arrive at them? You arrive at them through making and correlating measurements. From the correlation of measurements, you arrive at formulae, and in the formulae you get constants – the constants of mass, for example.

The fundamental concepts in your science are reached through the correlations of measurements. You step away from the relations of things to us to arrive at the relations of things to one another. You arrive at those relations of things to one another through measurement. The measurement relates two objects with one another; for example, the length of one's ruler and the object one is measuring are related in a measurement of length. Next, you compare measurements with one another – for example, the measurement of time with the measurement of distance – and you proceed from a series of discrete points to a freely drawn curve or a formula. By making the formula not merely a proportion but an equality, you introduce a constant such as mass. While it is not quite that simple, you can see the general build-up.

People may ask, 'Is this scientific world the real world?' You cannot say it is unreal simply because it is not related to your senses. But let us leave the question at this point, because questions of reality will be taken up later in these lectures.[7]

Now not only does the scientist refer to the 'nature of ...,' proceed on the principle that similars are similarly understood, and seek similarities in the relations of things to one another, and in seeking such similarities in the relations of things to one another arrive at such formulae as the law of falling bodies, Kepler's law of the movement of the planets, and so on. There is also another aspect of his procedure. Besides the movement upwards from the data towards the determination of the formula, there is also a downward movement that is operative in the sciences, and that downward movement is partly illustrated by the anticipation of a 'nature of ...'[8] Again, the idea that similars are similarly understood, and the idea that the relevant similarities in science are not similarities of things in their relations to us but rather in their relations to one another, pertain to the downward movement on the data.

Let us review the movement upwards from the data. Galileo had to let bodies fall and measure the distance they traversed in given times, and that appeal to concrete data was essential to his procedure. Moreover, once you have an array of measurements, the simplest method is to chart them on a graph – time along the base and distance up the side – and then to draw a curve. There is a whole set of techniques for what is called curve fitting, namely, finding a curve that goes through all of the points. But curve fitting does not tell us much; what we want is a formula which

---

7 Lecture 7, §2, The Notion of Objectivity, and lecture 8, A Definition of Metaphysics.
8 On the scissors-like action of natural science, see *Insight* 312–13, 461, 522–23, 577.

will enable us to put the whole thing into mathematics, and which will take it beyond the visual stage of a graph. We want to put it into a formula that can be mathematically manipulated. That is the movement upwards from the data: bodies fall, and one makes measurements, one correlates the measurements, one fits them onto some sort of a curve, one finds the formula from the curve. This is the strictly empirical side of the process, and it is guided by one's anticipation of the 'nature of ...' and by the notion that similars are similarly understood and that the relevant similarity is a similarity of things in their relations to one another. While the process is guided by these anticipations, still it develops up from the data.

Now the physicist uses further tricks that expand these anticipations of intelligibility. He not only has in the back of his mind, probably not in explicit consciousness, the fact that he is seeking the 'nature of ...' according to a rule that similars are similarly understood and that the relevant similarity lies in the relations of things to one another, but he goes further and adds differential equations to his anticipation. There is an example of a differential equation in *Insight*.[9] It is an equation that can be reached under the most general suppositions. It is simply mathematical, quite independent of any determinate set of data. It is not arrived at by any process of observation and experiment. The mathematician can provide the physicist with a sufficient number of such differential equations, and they function as anticipations of the formulae that are to be discovered. The general formula for a wave motion can be very briefly written down:

$$\partial^2 y / \partial t^2 = a^2 (\partial^2 y / \partial x^2).$$

What is to be noted is that this equation can be obtained from simply general considerations. Further, an equation of this type has a whole series of possible solutions, and the law the physicist is seeking will be one of those solutions. The differential equation, then, is an anticipation of the possible laws relevant to the formulation of a given thing that one is trying to understand. It provides a determination from above downwards on the possible formulae that are to be obtained. Anticipations of invariance operate similarly. They have a certain amount of concrete justification, but largely they have a purely theoretical basis, and yet they determine or limit the field of possible laws. They provide an anticipation of what the possible laws can be.

9 Ibid. 38–39.

The point is simply that the scientist is not a passive sensitive receptor. He is out to know something; he names his unknown; and he can determine the properties of the unknown, simply because he is going to know it by understanding: it will be a case of 'Similars are similarly understood.' He has learned to focus on a certain type of similarity, namely, the similarities that reside in the relations of things to one another, and he thereby gets away from the relations of things to us.

That type of general anticipation which guides the investigation, which represents the dynamic aspect in this structure of presentation, inquiry, insight, and conception, is prolonged in general mathematical operations such as the general equation for a wave motion that covers an indefinite number of possible particular types of waves. The generality of that equation can be illustrated. It is equal to any function whatever of x plus or minus at; in other words, to any algebraic function of x plus or minus at, any trigonometrical function of it, and so on. They all solve that differential equation, and so saying that it is a wave motion does not impose much of a restriction upon one's possible laws. Still, the existence of differential equations of that type provides a determinant from above upon the possible laws that can be found. There are many questions to be asked about that, but the discussion would presuppose so much detailed knowledge that we cannot fruitfully pursue it.

We have been attempting, then, to grasp the dynamic aspect of that process of presentation, inquiry, insight, and conception. We are trying to see that process in movement. The movement is brought to explicit consciousness when the mathematician says, 'Let x be the required number of minutes,' and when the scientist says, 'I am looking for the "nature of ..." ' When the scientist finds the 'nature of ...' he will be understanding. If he is understanding, then similars will be understood the same way, and the relevant similarities are similarities of things in their relations to one another, not similarities of things in their relations to us. That general formulation of a heuristic structure that has determinants coming from below upwards and determinants coming from above downwards gives us a general idea of the dynamic aspect of inquiry and of this cognitional process.

4   The Limitation of Classical Procedure

Procedures of this type lead to just one kind of science, classical science. As a result of proceeding in this fashion, one obtains scientific knowledge of the type associated with Galileo, Newton, Maxwell,[10] and Einstein, who were great physicists and great contributors to the field of physics. Similarly, it is the type of science associated in the main with chemistry – and so on. However, this type of science has limitations, and it is important to grasp what those limitations are if we are to gain some understanding of the attention that is now being given to statistical science. We will take a few moments to find out what those limitations are.

The treatment of the limitations of classical procedure is found in *Insight* in the section on concrete inferences from classical laws,[11] and the point to that section can be put very briefly. The scientist is concerned with solving a problem, but by 'problem' one can understand either of two things. There is, first, a kind of problem which is encountered in concrete operations when one wants to do something, for example, when one wants to put up a sputnik.[12] In that case, all the data relating to the problem are determined concretely. Now it is especially relevant to this type of problem that there is an insight that goes beyond all that is contained in the science as a system. Let us suppose that one knows all of the laws of physics and all of the ways in which they can be combined. To apply those laws to any concrete case one still has to have an insight into this concrete situation, an insight that enables one to select these laws rather than those, an insight that grasps what one has to measure in this situation to be able to apply the laws to it. One must have an understanding of the concrete situation to be able to apply even perfect knowledge of physics to it.

There is a second type of problem, the kind of problem encountered in the manuals and textbooks. It is a problem of a different sort. It is an ideal problem. For example, Newton's theorem that the trajectory of a body moving in a central field of force is a conic section is a conclusion that can be deduced from Newton's principles and axioms. It is the solution to a problem in an ideal case. There is not simply a central field of force; there is another mass in the field from which the force comes,

10 Lonergan here and rather regularly referred to 'Clerk Maxwell' as if the name were hyphenated – which is the way it sometimes appeared in *Insight*.
11 *Insight* 46–53. The tape gave us some difficulty here, and we edited this and the following paragraph without full clarity on Lonergan's argument. Fortunately, pp. 46–47 of *Insight* cover the same ground. See also discussion 4 below, §8, Probability and Determinism.
12 The first sputnik had been launched in the year preceding these lectures, on October 4.

normally at least, and that other mass will involve a further complication of the problem. Newton's theorem meets an *ideal* problem, and the problem itself is set by an insight. While in the concrete problem one has to have an insight into the situation to know which laws to use, in this case from one's knowledge of the laws one conceives ideal situations in which the laws will work beautifully. Proceeding in this way, one can obtain a very nice solution. One has the theorem that the trajectory of a body in a field of central force is a conic section; one has the knowledge of just what happens in a simple harmonic oscillator; and so on. In other words, one can conceive ideal cases in the light of the laws, and in such ideal cases one can know just what is going to happen all along the line.

Full knowledge of all classical laws makes possible the invention or construction of a large series of ideal cases to which actual events can be taken as approximations, and so we can have scientific predictions. But the mere fact that it is possible to set up ideal cases from a complete knowledge of laws, and to predict what is going to happen all along the line in those ideal cases, suggests that it is also possible to have a perverse type of mentality, a mentality which invents situations in which things cannot be worked out so neatly.

Let us consider, for example, the break in a game of pool. There are fifteen balls in a triangular shape and a cue ball anywhere along the line at the other end of the table. What happens at the break at pool? The cue ball can be shot from any of an infinity of positions from the middle of the line to the left, and from another infinity of positions to the right. Further, it can travel with any of an infinity of mass velocities, and it can hit the triangular configuration of balls at a variety of points. Moreover, the balls of the configuration can be grouped with many different degrees of tightness. When all of this is determined in any particular case, you can figure out exactly what is going to happen, but that would be extremely difficult. It would be difficult, not only because of the question of how tightly the balls fit together, but also because there are interferences. Balls bounce against the bands and come back, and they move at slightly different speeds. The speed and direction of the cue ball will determine whether the balls collide or not, and whether or not they do collide determines later movements. The whole thing would have to be followed through step by step.

What would be the general solution to the problem of what happens at the break at pool? There is no general solution. The problem involves an indefinite series of cases. You can have casuistry on it. It is something entirely different from the trajectory of a body moving in a central field of force, or from the simple harmonic oscillator. It is different from any other process one can construct that is governed by a concrete insight linking knowledge of the laws with ideal situations, and that involves finding ideal situations in which the laws enable one to predict everything. Just as there is that case, so there is the opposite case in which intelligence is working at the perverse goal of finding a concrete situation such that full knowledge of the laws does not enable one to predict in the general case exactly what is going to happen.

That possibility reveals a limitation to classical procedure. In other words, that possibility exists even if we presuppose full knowledge of classical laws. The perverse fellow, equally knowledgeable, can find something that will not satisfy, just as the other fellow can find ideal situations that do satisfy. The existence of such a limitation is an example of an inverse insight, in a sense.[13] One understands that there can be a case which does not submit to an ideal solution, that there can be a case that is designed to evade subsumption under any ideal solution. It is not just one problem, but a series of problems set by a concrete situation. With the break at pool there is the problem of the strike, the problem of rebounding balls, the problem of what happens next, and so on. This limitation to full knowledge of classical laws provides an example of a case in which one understands that there is no concrete insight to be had that will give one an ideal solution. Because of that, we have the 'hole in the fence,' as it were, the vacuum, through which another type of approach to deal with that kind of problem can be introduced; namely, statistical method.

5   Probability Theory

I do not attempt to offer a theory of probability in *Insight*, but a heuristic structure that heads toward the determination of a theory of probability.[14] Perhaps I should give a few words of explanation for that procedure.

13 Lonergan hesitated here: 'it's an inverse insight. Well, no, not exactly. Yes, it is, in a sense.' The final qualification reflects a similar view in *Insight*: 'the occurrence of something like an inverse insight ... at least one can speak of a devaluated inverse insight that divides classical and statistical anticipations' (54–55).
14 Ibid. 53–68. The parallel to this opening sentence is found on p. 66: 'our

There exists a mathematical calculus of probabilities, and the essence of the calculus is that, given probabilities P_1, P_2, P_3, one can deduce other probabilities P_x, P_y, P_z. That is the calculus of probabilities. It presupposes certain proper fractions, given as probabilities, and deduces other probabilities from them. That set of procedures can be cast in an axiomatic form and made into a mathematics.

However, the theory in its present state does not seem to be entirely satisfactory. There are two types of case, the a priori case and the a posteriori case. The a priori case is fairly simple but not relevant to empirical science. Suppose you want to know the probability of casting a seven or having a run of n heads. In that case, because of a full knowledge of the operations involved, you can work out a priori what the probabilities are going to be. However, if you want to know the probability[15] of the number of deaths per thousand of population in a given area, there is no a priori method for determining such a frequency. You have to deal with what people do; you have to approach the problem empirically. One a posteriori definition of probability that is given is that the probability (or the relative actual frequency, some fraction) is equal to the limit, as n approaches infinity, of the ratio of n_i (the number of cases that occur) to some total number of cases (n):

$$p = \lim_{n \to \infty} (n_i / n)$$

Some sort of definition of that type is needed if you are going to have an a posteriori notion of probability that will be suitable for empirical work. There are theoretical difficulties with that notion, and they are presented by Lindsay and Margenau in their *Foundations of Physics*.[16] Further, there

purpose has been not to work out definitive foundations for statistical science but to grasp in some fashion the statistical heuristic structure.'

15 Lonergan's actual phrase here was 'the probability of the frequency of the number of deaths.'

16 Robert Bruce Lindsay and Henry Margenau, *Foundations of Physics*, rev. ed. (New York: Dover Publications, 1957) 165–67 (page reference given by Lonergan). Thomas V. Daly contributes the following clarification: Lonergan is here using the notation of Lindsay and Margenau (161, 163), with p substituted for their $w(i)$. This notation does not correspond to that used by Lonergan when he comes in §6, The Notion of Probability, to his own definition: 'a probability is an ideal proper fraction from which actual relative frequencies diverge but do not do so systemati-

is the difficulty involved in introducing the notion of infinity. The empirical scientist never reaches an infinity of cases; and if infinity is involved in the very notion of probability, then one may at least raise the question whether it is ever possible either to establish or to refute any given probability.

Again, certain forms of the theory of probability may not involve any intelligibility whatever. Albertson, in his review of *Insight,* quotes Bohm to the effect that, if you presuppose probability, you have no intelligibility at all.[17] I do not know whether Bohm is right or not, but I do not see that it is *impossible* that he is right. The set of data comes under probability if certain conditions are fulfilled. If those conditions are simply the exclusion of intelligibility – as they are, namely, the exclusion of law (and that is generally the idea of the probability aggregate) – and if you affirm that there is a probability and this only at infinity, do you imply any intelligibility in the probability aggregate at all? It is not too clear that you do, and so the conclusion that to assert probability in the actual universe is to deny intelligibility may be true, given the notion of probability implicit in that set of assumptions. In other words, that conclusion has been drawn, whether it is correct or not. I do not see that it *need be* incorrect – I am explaining the reasons why I have a rather remote approach to probability.

Further, is the calculus of probabilities, as it presently exists, in the situation in which Euclidean geometry was before the series of geometries was developed? In other words, is there possibly a series of calculi of probabilities? Does the calculus of probabilities as it exists at the present time actually have the status that Euclidean geometry was supposed to have before the other geometries were introduced? The absence of contact with empirical problems in probability suggests to me that there may be that possibility, but I do not know. However, if you want to talk

---

cally.' Thè notation which he uses for that definition, as copied from the blackboard by both FEC and WAS, corresponds to the notation used in *Insight* 58. Here (in §5) i is the index for types of event, so that n_1, n_2, n_3, ... (which add up to n) correspond to the p_i, q_i, r_i, ... used in §6; but, in that §6, the index i indicates an occasion on which a count of n items is taken, so that p_1, p_2, p_3, ... are the numbers of just one type of event, as counted on different occasions.

17 James Albertson, s.j., *The Modern Schoolman* 35 (1957–58) 236–44, at 44. The views of Albertson and Bohm came up again, in the evening discussions; see discussion 4, §1, Immanent and Projected Intelligibility, and §2, Probability Theory and the Existence of God.

about probability in an empirical sense, you have to go beyond stating a fraction – so many times on so many occasions – as simply a proportion.

We can illustrate the matter from an a priori case of probability. In tossing a coin and selecting the sequence of tosses at random under the required conditions, a run of n heads has a probability of $1/2^n$. When does that probability begin to exist? If you approach the question simply mathematically, it always exists. Anything that is mathematically true is always so. But how many tosses must you have before the probability $1/2^n$ exists? If you have simply one toss, it is impossible to have a run of n heads. If you have n tosses, it is possible to have a run of n heads, but is it probable? If you have $n \times 2^n$ tosses, then a run of n heads fits in with the distribution, with the possibilities. One run of n heads is one of the possible combinations out of 2^n possible different combinations that you can have. In other words, it would seem that, at that point, a run of n heads becomes probable, but you cannot say at that point that, if I do not get a run of n heads, therefore the probability is falsified. How many tosses must you have before that probability would be falsified?

I think these questions are relevant if one is to have an empirical theory of probability. An empirical theory would have to provide a statement of the number of occasions necessary for the probability to exist – for the probability, in other words, not to be merely a possibility but for that predicted event to be truly probable – and a statement of a larger number where, if what is probable does not occur within that range, then there is reason for saying that that probability is wrong. That is, an empirical notion of probability raises questions of existence, of possible verification and possible refutation, that do not arise within the limits of a purely mathematical theory.

Now difficulties with the theory[18] of probability originate from a number of sources, some of which are recognized and some of which are my own; but for those reasons I did not attempt in *Insight* to do more than set up a framework in which the notion of probability may, with the advance of science, be more fully developed. Again, when I speak in *Insight* of probabilities, of statistics, I do not envisage quantum mechanics. There are cases in which probability arises, and it is towards understanding such cases that my theory is developed. I did not attend to quantum mechanics, first of all, because I do not know enough about it. In the second place, though, there is the fact that Heitler, for example, in the

18 Lonergan's actual phrase for 'theory' was 'the calculus up to the theory.'

introduction to his *Quantum Theory of Radiation*, says that the theory gets such excellent results that it practically has to be right; however, we have to use mathematical procedures that are quite unacceptable; and while it may be possible to have a purely mathematical solution to these difficulties, still it seems desirable that there be further clarifications of certain fundamental concepts.[19] In other words, as often happens in the sciences, the results are running ahead of the finished theory. Any attempt to work out an adequate theory, or to illustrate the nature of science and the nature of theory from quantum mechanics, did not seem to me to be opportune for these two reasons, the first more cogent perhaps than the second.

6   The Notion of Probability

What is the approach to probability that we have in *Insight*? First, we set up our inverse insight: there is a limitation to what can be known through classical laws. In other words, if there were the ideal, full knowledge of classical laws – and that does not mean the knowledge attained at the present time – still one would be able to predict in general only in the way that one can predict the eclipses of the moon and the transit of Venus. That type of prediction could be generally possible only insofar as there are schemes of recurrence – that is, what corresponds in the actual world to a systematic insight. By a scheme of recurrence we mean this: any law that you find has conditions, but you may have such a conjunction of laws that they fulfil one another's conditions, so that the process goes on indefinitely. That is the fundamental element, it seems, in the possibility of these long-term, fully accurate (within the ordinary limitations of observation) predictions.

When what exists is an example of the perverse type of intelligence that knows all of the laws and figures out a case in which this long-term prediction cannot be done, in that case of complexity that does not conform to any sort of scheme of recurrence, the calculation of every element in the particular is theoretically possible, but de facto the information necessary to make the calculations is lacking. You can go from one situation to the next, deduce it, and from the next go on to a third, but you have to go through the whole series. You cannot just jump from

19 Walter Heitler, *The Quantum Theory of Radiation*, 3rd ed. (Oxford: The Clarendon Press, 1954) xii.

any one to any other the way you can in certain determinate predictable processes. Working it out in one case provides very little help in working it out in the similar cases. The whole job has to be done over again. In short, there is indefinite complexity. What the scientist wants in any case is a general solution, and so in cases of such complexity he moves on to probability.

Statistics is concerned with cases where indeterminacy is not presupposed.[a] The mechanics of tossing a coin or of casting dice is an entirely determinate process. There is no reason why the mathematician, given the initial position, momentum, and twist of the die and the full information on the surface where it is going to fall, should not be able to calculate with perfect accuracy what the result in each case will be. There is not necessarily presupposed any indeterminacy in any single process. However, there is a coincidental aggregate, an element that is not subject to law in the *sequence* of tossing a coin or casting dice or dealing cards, and so forth. That element of lack of law, lack of scheme of recurrence, lack of system, appears in the fact that before the dice are thrown you rattle the box, before dealing the cards you shuffle them, and so on. In other words, there is no intelligible systematic link between the successive occasions. You have different hands in cards because the deck is shuffled before dealing; you have a coincidental aggregate in the sequence of casting dice because, in each case, before casting them you rattle the box. You do something to make the next throw independent of the previous one, in order to eliminate any regular law linking the successive cases. When there is that element of coincidental aggregates, you have excluded the element of scheme of recurrence that makes possible the long-term, systematic, accurate predictions, and you have the case of probability.

First, then, we have the existence of a limitation on classical procedure. Secondly, while accurate prediction could theoretically be had if sufficient information were available in each case, still a general determination, a general answer that requires the sequence of cases, cannot be had from classical law. In that case, we have an objective field for probability; knowledge of probability in that case is not simply a cloak for ignorance. There is something that cannot be done by classical laws, namely, they cannot provide a general account of what happens where some scheme of recurrence is not operative, where the successive instances are not linked according to any rule or law, where they are not directly linked to one another.

The case of the probability aggregate sets the question, What is a probability? To answer that question we offer a general definition that is not sufficient, however, to form the base of a calculus of probabilities or distributions. It is a very simple definition.[20] Suppose you have arrived at a set of fractions, p_i/n_i, q_i/n_i, r_i/n_i, ... where we have types of event that are indicated by the differences of p, q, and r, sequences in which n observations are made and you have different series of n's (there are N n's, as it were, N occasions on which you observe n sets of events), and they distribute. The relative actual frequency for one type of event is p_i/n_i: some number of the total gives you that fraction. Another number of the total gives you q_i/n_i, and so on. And on a series of occasions you get your different values for i.

Then if, on that supposition, you can find ideal fractions, p/n, q/n, r/n (the ones without a subscript), that are fixed fractions for all occasions, while these others, p_i/n_i, q_i/n_i, are fractions arrived at empirically, on the first, second, third, fourth, fifth, sixth investigations, and if the difference between the ideal fractions and the series of actual results is a set of random numbers not subject to any law, then p/n, q/n, r/n will be the probabilities of events.[21] So a probability is an ideal proper fraction from which actual relative frequencies diverge but do not do so systematically. The difference between the probability and the actual relative frequency, in other words, is random. These differences are not subject to any law.

With that general, very remote, and insufficient determination of the notion of probability, we take two steps. First, we try to understand the case of the a priori probability, and then we set up the general structure within which an empirical notion of probability can be developed with further work in the field.

A priori probability: The first step is simply to ask what is meant when one says that the probability of heads is one-half. There are three steps in the answer given. The first is that the number of possible manners in which a coin may be tossed is indefinitely great. In other words, there are all sorts of exact positions in which the toss might start, all sorts of momenta – direct momentum and angular momentum – that the coin

---

20 Lonergan stopped his explanation after a few sentences, and said, 'Let's start again.' The rest of this paragraph adheres closely to his second attempt.

21 Lonergan indicated at this point that a full explanation should take account of the determination of the notion of state. See the index of *Insight* under State.

might have, all sorts of surfaces on which it may fall. But for every time you get heads, you might have had tails, had you just turned the coin over before starting. So half of the total set of possibilities gives you heads, and the other half gives you tails. That is the first point – the possibilities divide into two equal groups.

The second element is this: either the sequence of tosses is guided by some law or it is not. In other words, there is the relation between the initial position, the initial momentum and the initial angular momentum, in case one as compared with case two, as compared with case three, and so on. Either one can discern some law in that sequence or one cannot. If there is some law, then it is not a question of probability. For example, if a man comes into your room every morning and tosses a coin twenty times and every time he gets heads, you might be surprised for the first few times; but if he kept on doing that every day for ten years you would eventually ask him how he does it. He has some control over the sequence, and it would not be a case of probability. The first point, then, is theoretical: the possibilities are divided into two equal groups. The second point is that concretely the successive throws are random. They are not related according to some law; there is no law governing what is going to happen the next time if this happens this time. That is the random character of the sequence, the coincidental aggregate.

When these two points are combined, we arrive at the notion of probability. Either the number of times you get heads out of the total number of tosses oscillates at random about one-half, because that is the number of possibilities, or else there is some systematic factor present favoring one side rather than the other. If there is some systematic factor favoring one side rather than the other, then we do not have a case of probability; de facto, the second condition has not been observed – this excludes systematic favoring of anything, and consequently it excludes systematic favoring of one half of the possibilities instead of the other. So when you say that the probability of tossing heads is one-half, you also mean to say that you do not have a case of probability if there is any systematic favoring of one possibility rather than the other. Thus you can set to the data this disjunction: either these data oscillate at random about one-half, or there is systematic favoring of one possibility. If there is systematic favoring you are not dealing with the probability aggregate; statistical methods do not provide the relevant explanation. In such a case, the relevant explanation is obtained by asking the fellow how he does it – there is a systematic factor at work. On the other hand, if there is no systematic factor at work, then the result of tossing the coin should be such that the number of heads you get out of the total number of tosses will oscillate at random about a center, namely, one-half.

General structure: Now if that is the meaning of probability in the a priori case, it is relevant within the context of the heuristic structure we have set up. The classical heuristic structure, which arrives at laws, takes care of one alternative. Either the data being examined come under law or they do not. In other words, either law can account for them entirely the way it accounts for the movements of the planets as long as outside interference with the planetary system is excluded; or, on the other hand, there is some point where law is not in control, namely, on this concrete level where we have no scheme of recurrence.[22] If there is some point where law is not in control, then there is an absence of system, and that absence of system provides a premise for affirming probability. In other words, if the actual relative frequencies do not oscillate about the probability at random, then there is some systematic factor at work, and we have to shift back to the classical case. That general idea, I think, will suffice. At the end of chapter 2 of *Insight*, I discuss the development of a heuristic structure using that idea. A parallel is drawn with the heuristic structure of classical work, and an analogous procedure is set up for statistical work. We are using an insufficient idea of probability, but at least it is an idea concerned not with purely mathematical theory but with the occurrence of events – *verifiable* probability.

Our aim this morning has been to set in explicit conscious motion our four basic terms: presentations, inquiry, insight, and conception. We did so by indicating the nature of heuristic structure. I hope I threw some light on it with what I attempted to say in chapter 2 of *Insight*. The pursuit of knowledge is the pursuit of an unknown, but you can use that fact to help you arrive at knowing it, and you do so insofar as you anticipate acts of understanding. When you understand, you have something that holds equally well in all similar cases, and the relevant similarities are similarities in the relations of things to one another. In that way, one can build up the classical heuristic structure, and as a second step, by picking out a limitation in that classical heuristic structure, one can go on to statistical structure.

22 There is a marginal notation on Lonergan's own copy of the 1980 edition, correcting 'the scheme of recurrence' to 'no scheme of recurrence.'

7   Canons of Empirical Method

The third chapter of *Insight*, which we can treat rather briefly, presents an answer in dynamic terms to the question, What is science? People ask what science is, and often they want to be given a definition in terms of genus and species. Moreover, genus and species are usually thought of in terms of similarity, and indeed similarity to us. There is overlooked in that sort of answer the fact that science has not yet arrived at its goal, that it is in process, moving towards a goal. We are on our way, and what we have achieved so far is pretty good. While we do not say that it is never going to be corrected in any respect, still any future advance will have to take into account everything we do have and explain things just as well as we are explaining them at present, and something more. Otherwise, we will not budge, we will stay where we are. In other words, there is a dynamic aspect.

Just as in the whole of dynamics it is the differential coefficient that counts, not the differential equation, so an answer to the question, What is science? is best had, not by a series of statements about some static entity, as though science were some static entity, but by a set of canons, a set of rules that guide what the scientist is doing. You are probably familiar with Einstein's answer to the person who asked him how a theorist of knowledge is to take advantage or make use of the physicist. Einstein's answer was, 'Pay no attention to what they say, watch what they do.'[23] The reason for the answer, of course, is that although the physicist is competent in his own field, when he starts to explain why things are proceeding this way or that, he is usually employing a rather inadequate theory of knowledge to express himself. When you pay attention to what he says, you are giving the authority of a physicist to an inadequate theory of knowledge.

'Watch what they do!' The canons of empirical method express what scientists do in terms of the analysis of knowledge we have been setting forth. Let us briefly consider the canons of selection and operations, the first two of the canons presented in *Insight*.[24]

The first canon is a canon of selection. Namely, the number of possible

23 See Albert Einstein, *Essays in Science* (New York: Philosophical Library, 1934) 12.
24 *Insight* 71–76. For the other canons (relevance, parsimony, complete explanation, statistical residues), see the rest of the same chapter.[b]

hypotheses and theories is indefinitely large, and to have a theory all one has to do is define terms, make postulates, and carry out deductions. What does the scientist do with regard to that infinity? He has a canon of selection. The scientist pays no attention whatever to any theory that does not imply precise, exact, sensible consequences.[c] That is the first elimination. There is a second elimination: the scientist rejects all theories that have sensible consequences but which, unfortunately, are not verified. So the canon of selection involves selection out of the field of possible theories and hypotheses. It restricts the scientist's attention, first of all, to theories that are relevant, that have a direct bearing on things that can be sensed. Secondly, it provides an automatic principle of ending all debates and all disputes. There can be, even at the present time, disputes and questions in scientific theory, but as soon as a theory is presented, either it has sensible consequences or it is not a scientific theory. If it has sensible consequences, a way will be found to determine whether those sensible consequences are such as the theory predicts, and it is by checking results that the theory is eliminated. That is an extremely useful way of settling questions, and it is a way we attempted to use, in a different mode, when we set up our theory of metaphysics.[25]

According to the canon of selection, scientific theories must have sensible consequences, and that raises a question: What are sensible data? The one relevant point to be made is that one must not presuppose that the scientific observer is a scientific observer by passivity, inertness, lack of training, lack of formation, lack of direction along a given line. Sensible data may be defined as the contents of acts of seeing, hearing, touching, tasting, smelling. But such contents do not occur in a cognitional vacuum. To observe scientifically requires training. It requires the development of conceptual categories, and so on. If there were small bugs on the table, you or I would have little more to say than that there are some bugs; but the entomologist, trained in scientific observation, would have a hundred things to say about them. To observe scientifically is not just a matter of having better eyes; it is to bring sensible data within a new context.[26] Insofar as his observation is detached and disinterested, rather than

---

25 See lecture 8 below, § 1, The Underlying Problem, and § 2, Positions and Counterpositions; also *Insight* 385–90.
26 The DJS reel takes us to this point; the LRI reel stops a few lines earlier, and the WAS reel stops toward the end of the preceding paragraph. The text has been completed from notes taken at the lecture.

dominated by ordinary desires and aversions, the scientist's percepts move into coincidence with the sensible data.

Secondly, the scientist's trained approach to sensible data is not merely informed but also controlled and guided. We have seen how presentations give rise, through inquiry and insight, to the formulation of hypotheses and laws, and how there is also a downward influence of theory on the presentations. This downward influence, based on scientific laws, consists of a set of premises and rules that guide the scientist's activities on the data. The new data uncovered through operations generate further questions, further insights, and so lead to the discovery of new laws, or to the confirmation or rejection of the existing laws.

There is, then, a canon of operations that results in an enormous systematic enlargement of the field of observation, of carefully controlled observation. It is a means of cumulative verification: 'Galileo's law is verified' means that it has seemed to work for four hundred years. It is a principle of construction: we know best what we make. It is a principle of analysis: we construct nature in thought even when we cannot do so actually. It is a check on theories and their ramifications. It heads for system, a related set of laws: the law of falling bodies leads to the law of air resistance, and so on. It heads, too, for a higher viewpoint: while the mathematician advances to higher viewpoints solely by the construction of symbolic images, in which he might grasp the rules of a more comprehensive systematization, the empirical scientist advances to higher viewpoints more fundamentally, by the expansiveness, the constant verifying, constructiveness, analyses, and systematizing tendencies of the canon of operations.

4

Common Sense[1]

So far we have been outlining a specialization in the pursuit of knowledge – a pursuit of knowledge for its own sake – and most of the examples have been taken from science and mathematics. But there is a type of knowledge that differs from mathematics and science,[2] not insofar as they have practical applications, but in their pure state. I wish to recall, then, the general characteristics of the specialized pursuit of knowledge, because it is only by contrast with that specialized knowledge that one can form any adequate, precise notion of the far more common type of knowledge that we name common sense.

1   Specialized Knowledge and Common Sense

Aristotle credits Socrates with the introduction of universal definitions. That pursuit of universality in definition is a fundamental characteristic throughout the whole of mathematics and science. Traditionally, necessity is connected with universality; but that notion of necessity is more doubtful at the present time. Necessity is no longer stressed so much because, clearly, all of the sciences proceed by hypothesis and verification; they do not arrive at what is necessarily so, but only at what de facto is true. That is the most they hope to attain. Mathematicians have discovered that

---

1 The fourth lecture, Thursday, August 7, 1958.
2 The tape recording picks up the lecture at this point. The opening sentence is reconstructed from notes taken at the lecture.

they are in exactly the same boat. They can deduce their conclusions with rigorous necessity from their initial primitive propositions, but they cannot affirm that their primitive propositions are necessary. In other words, the formulation they have found for their primitive propositions may admit higher viewpoints; whether that difficulty can be overcome is a further, rather complicated question. I believe there is some possibility of overcoming it; but at present certainly it has not been overcome by contemporary mathematics.

The pursuit of the universal is not confined to definitions – to knowing, for example, exactly when two coplanar circles will intersect as something over and above seeing that in this case or in this type of case they must intersect. Universal definitions are wanted because universal propositions are wanted, and universal propositions are wanted with the degree of accuracy that allows them to bear the weight of deduction. In other words, the mathematician and, ideally, the scientist too do not want to make any general affirmations or negations that are simply approximations to 'You know what I mean.' Mathematicians want to state things in such a way that they can go ahead and draw all of the strictly logical conclusions that are possible and find that every one of them is true. The scientist, to achieve this, has to introduce a technical vocabulary, invent a language of his own, use terms that do not occur in ordinary speech. The mathematician goes even further – he simply uses symbols.

Finally, the viewpoint at which science arrives is that things are to be considered, not in their relations to us, but in their relations to one another; historically, modern science arrived at this viewpoint from Galileo on. In any science there is a preliminary stage in which the science is descriptive, in which it is simply cataloguing the sensible qualities of things. A good example of this is botany, at least the older classification, in which different elements in the flower are selected, and classifications are based upon genera and species and subspecies according to the presence or absence of sensible qualities that are easily determined. However, no science that becomes explanatory remains at that level; it moves on to another level on which one deals with things in their relations to one another. The chemist will begin with things as described in terms of their sensible qualities, but he moves on to construct a periodic table in which about a hundred elements are mainly determined by their relations to one another within the table – by their atomic numbers, atomic weights, affinities, valences, and so on. The objects are defined in their relations to one another, and these objects, insofar as they are so determined, bear no immediate relation to us, to our sensible apprehensions; yet they form the basis from which more than three hundred thousand compounds can at least in principle be composed.

The scientist builds up a world that is entirely different from the world of common sense, and he does so because of his pursuit of an ideal in which knowledge is universal, in which it is so exactly formulated that any strictly logical deductions from his statements will also be found to be true. To achieve this he uses a technical language. And he does not consider things primarily in their relations to us. He considers those relations to us just as a steppingstone, a tool, a way of approaching objects, while his scientific knowledge is of things in their relations to one another.

Now much more primitive and common and, at least chronologically, much more fundamental is a type of knowledge that does not result from such a specialization of the desire to know. In this more common case, which we will call common sense, the desire to know is simply a part of the desire to live, and knowledge is a part of living. Knowledge is an important part of living; it has a fundamental role within living; it is in no way thought little of. Still, knowledge is not pursued for its own sake, it does not become an end in itself. It is simply one part in the total end which is living, living as a man. In this case, knowledge is not specialized away from the practical. If one seeks knowledge simply for the sake of having knowledge, it will have practical applications; but those practical applications are somebody else's business – the applied scientist, the engineer, the medical doctor, and so on. There are plenty of people to attend to those practical applications. The mathematician and the scientist are concerned with knowledge itself, and they specialize in that work, while others specialize in the application of theoretical knowledge to practical living. However, everyone has to do his own living; everyone has to deal constantly with concrete, particular things, persons, situations; and there is a knowledge adapted to that purpose. It is a knowledge that arises within the global context of living, and that context, as it were, determines the limits of this knowledge.

Common sense can be described negatively by noting that there is no methodical exploitation of universality. Universal definitions have to be introduced into human civilization and culture. Socrates tried to introduce them into the minds of the general public; but he did not take the precaution of collecting together into a lyceum or an academy the people who might be interested in that sort of thing. He taught in the market-

87 Lecture 4

place, and the marketplace reacted in the long run rather violently against him – the people eliminated him. Human society does not spontaneously accept the drive towards the universal. It is not concerned with the universal definition of bravery or truth or justice. While we want people to be truthful, brave, and just, that is just part of human living.

Not only does the idea of universal definition have to be developed and communicated by such a technique as is employed in a Platonic dialogue, but the notion of a logical system also has to be developed and introduced. That development and introduction, on the theoretical side, was done by Aristotle. The superb concrete illustration, of course, is Greek geometry. In the Great Books series put out by Mortimer Adler, there is a volume in which you can sample the chief fruits of Greek geometry: the thirteen books of Euclid, a series of treatises by Archimedes, a series of treatises by Apollonius of Perga on conics, and finally the work of an arithmetician, Nicomachus of Gerasa.[3] In the works of the Greek geometers there is represented concretely the idea of setting down at the start certain definitions, axioms, and postulates and common notions, proceeding rigorously step by step to the proof, whole series of proofs, books of theorems, and only incidentally to the solution of problems of how to do things. The ideal of logical system, an organized knowledge, is a possibility that man has to discover and realize. It was realized first of all in the geometrical field; but one finds it again in Newton with regard to mechanics and dynamics.

Common sense relates things to one another; it is not merely the relating of each individual thing to oneself. The whole of the technical art involving the use of tools and instruments flourished before any great introduction of science into practical living. In this commonsense use of tools things are related to one another, but those relations, if one examines them, are found to rest ultimately upon the relations of things to us, and they do so in a way that the scientific relations of things to one another do not. We always start from relations of things to us, from what some present-day analysts of science call epistemic relations; but science advances to the point where it principally is concerned with what are

---

3 Robert Maynard Hutchins, ed., *Great Books of the Western World* (Chicago: Encyclopaedia Britannica Inc., 1952). Mortimer Adler was the associate editor, but editor-in-chief of the accompanying *Syntopicon*. Lonergan is referring to Vol. 11.

called formal relations, that is, relations that hold between things them-selves considered apart from us, and the things are then defined by those relations they have to one another.

In commonsense knowledge, then, there is an absence of any systematic exploitation of universality through universal definition and deductive system. There is no attempt to conceive things simply in their relations to one another; that is something that has to be discovered. Further, there is no technical language, because technical language simply means language invented for the purposes of the specialized knowledge that arises in the pursuit of knowledge for its own sake.

2   Common Sense as Intellectual

What is the character of this common, everyday, general knowledge? It is something that is very difficult to get hold of with precision. I offer an analysis in chapter 6 of *Insight*, but an analysis of common sense is convinc-ing in the measure that one can be, in a description, suggestive, allusive, evocative, bringing to people's minds something of their own experience, something of their familiarity with ordinary human affairs.

Briefly, common sense is intelligent; it involves insight. Intelligent people are not confined to universities; we find them everywhere, in every walk of life, on every level of culture, in every type of human activity. – We also find stupidity, and that is a great consolation inasmuch as we find people who are even less intelligent than ourselves. – This intelligence arises from a flow of questions. It arises from the same intellec-tual alertness, intellectual curiosity, that is at the root of science. People want to know *why*. However, they do not want the answer to that question to be, 'Well now, you go to a university and study this subject for four years, and then you will have a fairly good grasp of the rudiments of it.' They want the answer to be something that can be given to them right away. They do not want to take the detour of specialized knowledge; rather, they want the answers given in a manner that will do away with the detour; they want a shortcut.

Because there is no exploitation of the ideal of universality, common-sense understanding is not built up in the same way as mathematical or scientific knowledge. Commonsense understanding understands similars in the same way, just as scientific understanding does, but it does not go on to pursue universality for its own sake by seeking a universal definition. In commonsense understanding there is, first of all, a flow of questions, and secondly, a clustering of insights. People catch on to one thing and then another, building up habitual clusters of insights into the problems of their concrete living. For example, a child has to have insights to learn to talk, to use language. There is a build-up of a cluster of insights, but the cluster is not aimed at arriving at universal definitions and universal propositions that will bear the weight of systematic and rigorous deduction. The cluster is aimed at guiding concrete action, and it is expressed, not in rigorous fashion, but by communication.

Human communication is a process that stands on a series of levels. Suppose you are seated in your room working and someone comes in. There is a change in you by the mere fact that someone has entered, and the change differs with the person who enters. There is an intersubjectivity that is basically on the sensitive level, and it is perhaps most intense in mother and child. There is a sensitive basis for communication by the mere fact of the presence of another, and still more so by the presence of another who is known and is the object of affection, and so on. The communication that arises on that base takes place through signs, through the human body. The cluster of insights is not any disembodied thing that rests upon technical language aiming at universality and at the satisfaction of the logical requirements of the possibility of a deductive system. It is immanent in this sensitive being. Man is an animal who also understands, and his understanding is the accidental form, as it were, of his physical appearance. It is said that anyone over thirty is responsible for his face, and that is one way of putting it. In other words, one communicates, one is already in communication, by virtue of the fact that one is understanding; and what communication aims at is the communication of that understanding.

Common sense, then, does not desire to communicate in any technical fashion. It sizes up the other person, sizes up how much he understands, what he understands, what he does not understand, and makes the signs that seem likely to enable him to understand, to catch on, to see things the same way. The signs made, the words used, are limited simply to that. Very often one's attitude will be, 'You don't understand.' One need not say it: one can just not answer a question, but go on to something else. There is a variety of ways in which one person communicates to another whether and what he understands. If you think the other person is interested, you are much more prepared to communicate, and you do so with far greater ease. On the other hand, if you feel that the other is hostile and cold, you are very much on the defensive.

There is, then, the flow of questions that is witnessed in a child of a certain age, and it frequently gets cut off very quickly. There is the clustering of insights. Besides these, there is communication and interaction. Many of our fundamental insights into human living arise in the process of interaction: watching other people do things, seeing if we can do them ourselves, not succeeding, watching more carefully the next time, and trying again in emulation. The whole of man's psychology is integrated in the developing of these basic clusters of insights, and in their testing and communication through the development of ordinary language.

Now what is the general character of these clusters of insights? I have said that their build-up is not guided by the ideal of universality, by the exigencies of the possibility of a rigorous deductive system. What, then, does guide it?

Commonsense knowledge consists in a set of clusters of insights such that by entering into, by taking a look at, any given situation that ordinarily arises in one's life, one is able to decide that no further insights are needed, or that one or two more are needed, to be able to deal with the situation. Where the scientist or the mathematician wants as many insights as are necessary in order to arrive at a set of definitions and principles that will enable him to deal universally with all possible situations of a defined type, the man of common sense wants a nucleus such that with the minimum of further insights he will be able to deal with any concrete situations that arise in his living.

Let me illustrate. A man who had been teaching elementary Latin for about twenty years once said to me, 'There is nothing that can happen in that class that hasn't happened before, and I know exactly what to do. I've lost interest in it. There are no more problems.' The cluster of insights necessary for dealing with concrete situations of a given type had been fully acquired; he knew just what to do in any given situation. However, if he were to change the situation by moving somewhere else, so that not only one or two new people enter the situation, but a completely new staff in a different locality where the students have a different mentality and different interests, new problems would arise. Again, if he were to leave teaching for another field, new problems would arise. When that happens, the previous cluster of insights is less relevant, and it has to be complemented by new insights into the way the new people react, into their interests, and, especially if the job is changed, into what has to be done in the new types of situations that keep arising.

Again, if one returns to a job one originally had and attempts to carry on in exactly the same fashion as before, without adverting to the possibility that things are different now, that there is a difference of mentality, one may very easily come a cropper. In other words, common sense is a matter of concrete insight into concrete situations. It builds up into a nucleus, and that nucleus is such that with minimal additions a person is ready to deal with any of the situations that arise in his life.

Because common sense is so specialized, there are diversities of common sense. The sciences are separated from one another because they deal with different objects. Physics differs from chemistry because it deals with different objects; biology differs from both because it has still further objects. But common sense in one man does not differ from the common sense in the next in that fashion. Women have a different type of common sense from men, because they deal with different types of situations. Their concerns lie in a different field. People from the country differ from those in the city. People of one social class have a different common sense from those of another. People in one nation are strange to people from another. If you go to Europe, you may find people odd, and they may find you odd, because there are different specializations of common sense. Common sense is not the same thing everywhere. I went to England to study from 1926 to 1930, and I found that everything there moved about four times more slowly than in Canada. Then I went to Rome to study theology, and I discovered that there everything moved about four times more slowly than in England. The difference, of course, is not merely temporal; it involves a total difference in attitude towards living and towards how things are to be done, what is the right thing to do, and so on.

The notion of specializations of common sense makes it clear how there can be complete incomprehension between people where classes become stratified. One thing that struck me in England was that I simply could not understand what the natives of Oxfordshire were saying. The first time I tried to buy a ticket in the underground in London, I could not understand what 'aightpence' was. There is stratification of the population in Europe generally, more pronounced in some countries than in others, but a thing totally novel to people from Canada and the United States. When there is such stratification, incomprehension can exist not only between classes within a country, which is one of the fundamental social problems at the present time, but also between nations. The more diverse the whole cultural background is, the greater that incomprehension.

Common sense, then, consists of a basic nucleus of insights that enables a person to deal successfully with personal and material situations of the sort that arise in his ordinary living, according to the standards of the culture and the class to which he belongs. It follows that where the scientist or the mathematician wants to lay down universal principles that hold in all applications, common sense deals with proverbs. What are proverbs? They are general rules that usually one will find worth while paying attention to. The truth of a proverb is not a premise from which you can deduce conclusions that are going to be found to be true in absolutely every case, so that, if one exception is found, the proverb is no good at all. If you interpret the proverb as though it were a mathematical, scientific, or philosophic principle – something that has to be true in absolutely every case or else it is simply false and of no use whatever – you miss the point of the proverb. It is a piece of advice that is relevant to the processes of knowing. For example, 'Look before you leap' is the proverb that governs the point that usually you have to complete your habitual nucleus of insights if you want to deal in exactly the right fashion with a situation that is a bit novel, a bit strange, not the sort of thing to which you are accustomed. And it is a good bit of advice: it hits off exactly the point that the nucleus has to be completed as soon as the situation ceases to be within the ordinary routine. The same may be said of all proverbs.

Again, common sense communicates its wisdom in fables, allegories, and so on. St Jerome says that the Orientals love to string similes together the way one puts pearls on a cord.[4] The mode of generality of commonsense communication is the story, the fable, the allegory, through which those who want to understand, those who want to become wise, can have insights that will complete their outlooks on life. In other words, there is a special methodology to common sense, a special set of criteria, and all of the criteria are different from the explicitly formulated criteria of the specialization of knowledge illustrated by mathematics, science, and philosophy.

Again, you cannot simply subsume commonsense procedures under logical categories. In logic we speak of the argument from analogy, and it is a very difficult argument to express. What is the commonsense argument from analogy? Common sense does not need two identical situations that it can proceed to understand in exactly the same fashion.

---

4 We have not been able to locate this reference.

That is simply a case of 'Similars are similarly understood.' Rather, the commonsense use of analogy is simply the use of the nucleus with regard to what is common in the two situations, and the differentiation of the nucleus in different ways, adding different acts of understanding with regard to the differences in the situations. This is the sort of thing that you can do quite easily, but it is not the sort of thing that you can formulate logically with ease. If you want to express anything that approximates to the flexible use of analogy that appears in common sense, you have to have recourse to the fact that really the man of common sense is understanding that the two situations are different. While there is something similar in the way he understands both, there are also differences in his understanding. He adds one insight to deal with one situation and another insight to deal with another, and he does both without thinking about it. Common sense has no theory of common sense. To obtain a theory of common sense we had to begin from the specialized type of knowledge, and then contrast that with commonsense procedures.

So much, then, for common sense as intellectual.

3   Common Sense and the Role of Philosophy

Now we will introduce a problem.[a] We began by speaking of self-appropriation, and that was fine because we all have ourselves. Then we went on to geometrical insights, and that was not too bad because they were fairly simple geometrical insights. But yesterday we started talking about science and heuristic structures, classical and statistical heuristic structures, and the canons of scientific method. There is an obvious difficulty: what has all that to do with my self-appropriation, if I am neither a mathematician nor a scientist and I have no ambition, desire, or perhaps even possibility, of becoming either? There seems to be an evident contradiction. We began by talking about self-appropriation; then we went on to something that in many cases has nothing to do with *my* self. There is a real difficulty here; it is not simply the logical type of difficulty that is solved by making a distinction.

The difficulty, however, is not all on one side. We are in a dilemma. So let us look at the difficulty on the other side. Suppose we wanted to base our philosophy on the knowledge that results from the desire to live, that is, on commonsense knowledge. On this side we encounter a difficulty with an objective and a subjective aspect. We will begin with the objective aspect.[5]

We have distinguished two kinds of knowledge. First, there is a knowledge that results from an explicit, methodical effort to arrive at knowledge for its own sake without paying any attention to the practical utility that may arise from it. Such knowledge does have practical utility, but the practical utility appears in some concrete fashion perhaps one, two, three, or four centuries later. The mathematician, the pure scientist, and the philosopher are concerned with knowledge insofar as it arises as the result of an explicit, reflective, consciously methodical, deliberate effort to arrive at knowledge. The operative criterion as they proceed is not practical utility, what use it will be or what good it will be. If for every theorem Euclid proved, he also had to prove to his listeners what the good of it would be, he would not have gotten far, and he would have needed different answers for every group of students. Euclid had to disregard questions of practical utility; he had to go right ahead and do his job, and then perhaps persuade others to think it worth while to go to all the trouble of learning. And similarly with all knowledge of this specialized type that results from the pure desire to know. Secondly, there is a type of knowledge with a different methodology and, one might almost say, a different type of technical logic. That type is common sense, and we all have it. It has its differentiations from class to class, from culture to culture, from job to job; but there is enough of it that is common to everyone.[b]

Now let us suppose that we wanted to base our philosophy, or at least our fundamental epistemology and metaphysics, simply upon common-sense knowledge, the knowledge that results from the desire to live. Suppose we forget about this specialized knowledge. That proposal could be entertained, but, as we have said, it is only one side of a dilemma, and, objectively, two difficulties arise on that side.

The first difficulty, given the supposition, is that there is a fundamental incoherence in an effort to develop a scientific pursuit.[c] The philosopher, no less than the scientist, has to tell the pupil who asks, 'What is the good of it?' to wait, to do the work for the time being; he has the same difficulty that Euclid would have had. The philosopher is engaged in a pursuit of knowledge in a speculative fashion, not in the quasi speculative but really quite practical fashion of common sense.[d] If we appeal simply to common-

5   For the subjective aspect, see §4, Philosophy and Self-development.

sense knowledge in doing philosophy, then we are involved in some sort of incoherence. What we are doing can have no guidance in its specific form from the merely commonsense knowledge to which we wish to appeal. If common sense has a different structure and procedures of its own, if it has its own mode of communication and so on, we will not find in common sense the directives necessary to constitute philosophy as a speculative type of knowledge, a speculative discipline.[6]

Moreover, the attempt to base a philosophy simply upon common sense is not only incoherent in the abstract. If we claim to be Aristotelians or Thomists, then we are misinterpreting our sources, because Aristotle certainly was not simply a man of common sense and St Thomas was certainly not simply a commonsense man. They are two outstanding instances of people who were not simply men of common sense. Moreover, Aristotle was not simply a philosopher. He thought out an extremely brilliant physical theory that remained in vigor for about fifteen hundred years – and that's more than any subsequent physical theory has had time to do! One may object that the competition was less keen then, and that may be true enough, but it remains that Aristotle was a man of extremely great speculative capacity. True, there is some probability to the view that the *Corpus Aristotelicum* was the product not of Aristotle alone but of the Lyceum. Whatever may be the precise origin, there is no doubt at all that there is an enormous amount of knowledge for its own sake, and that this is the fundamental ideal operative in the *Corpus Aristotelicum*. Again, if one is familiar with the state of theology before St Thomas began to write, one can see that what he did with it was a matter of taking a heap of stones and building a cathedral. The interest in knowledge for its own sake was dominant in his thinking. If we appeal, then, simply to common sense in doing our philosophy, we appeal to a guide that will not be sufficient insofar as philosophy is de facto not mere common sense. We already have all of the philosophies contained in common sense simply by having the common sense, and there is no need for the further explicitation.

First, then, common sense will not provide us with a guide for constructing philosophy in its proper character as a speculative discipline. In the second place, we can say we want to follow Aristotle or St Thomas, but if we are following them we are not following a merely commonsense ideal; they were extremely scientific people. In following Aristotle or St Thomas

6 On commonsense method in philosophy, see *Insight* 416–21.

we will be appealing to science, but to science as it existed in the year 400 B.C. or 300 B.C. or 1250 A.D.; while there is science in Aristotle and science in Thomas, it is not our science. Moreover, it often happens that those who take this attitude do not know the science in Aristotle; they are not aware of what the world system thought out by Aristotle consists in, what its basis is, what it implies.

On this side of the dilemma, then, there is the objective difficulty of incoherence, an abstract incoherence and a concrete incoherence. But there is also the second objective difficulty that we have mentioned.

One may think of philosophy as not merely another specialization – another hole or series of holes in which we dig and outside which we very carefully put the things we find – but as having something to do with going around and seeing what is coming out of all the holes.[7] If one's philosophy is to fulfil any integrating function, it has to be cognizant not merely of commonsense knowledge but of scientific knowledge as well. Scientific knowledge has to be taken into account. If it is not, and in the measure that it is not, philosophy is refusing the responsibility that belongs to its office. If philosophy is an integrating discipline, then it has to integrate. It cannot insist on being a specialty based upon common sense.

Again, if I may speak as a theologian, the fundamental theological problem at the present time is a problem of integration.[e] St Thomas is credited with integrating theology with philosophy, and Aristotelian science had already been integrated with Aristotelian philosophy. It is a hierarchical straight line; reconciling theology with philosophy automatically implied an integration with science. But if philosophy swings over to dependence upon common sense and does not integrate science, then theology is not going to be able to use that type of philosophy for an integration of the natural sciences.

Moreover, there have developed in recent centuries the empirical human sciences, and they cannot be classed with the natural sciences. However, as the human sciences are actually carried out at the present time, to a large extent they can be so classed. Many human scientists are trying to ride the bandwagon of the physicists and chemists, and a science of man is pursued as though man were just another electron or another atom. As long as human science is of that type, as long as it is carried out

---

7 See lecture 8, §3, Metaphysics as Synthesis, where Lonergan mentions in this connection Thor Heyerdahl, author of *Kon-Tiki*.

in that manner, we shall have creeping socialism. For if the scientific knowledge of man is in terms of the types of knowledge that are possible of electrons and atoms, then there is no question of developing a science of man that can speak to man. Rather, we simply develop scientists who are consultants to government, thereby giving government more power to control man. If philosophy is not attempting an integration of the sciences in the proper sense, then it cannot exert an influence upon the human sciences.

Further, the human sciences, insofar as they are empirical sciences, insofar as they deal with man as he is in this concrete world, are not capable of complete subsumption under a merely philosophic viewpoint. Insofar as man in this world suffers from original sin and receives God's grace and either accepts or refuses it, there are fundamental truths about man that cannot be subsumed under a philosophy considered as knowledge natural to man, knowledge attained by reason. Those truths have to be subsumed under a theology. Now it is in these empirical human sciences that there arise problems of integration not only in human living but within theology itself. The whole of anthropology, the whole history of literatures, and consequently the literary history of the Bible, the whole of patristic study and conciliar study, and all of the particular human studies that enter into theology, cannot be assimilated by theology unless synthesis is found, unless integration is found.

So we have a dilemma. On the one hand, self-appropriation for us does not seem to be a matter of paying attention to mathematics or empirical science, because that is *not me*. On the other hand, unless our interest in philosophy extends not only to knowledge of the commonsense type but also to knowledge of the scientific type, our philosophy, and even more our theology, will be incapable of performing an integrating role.

The problem is a problem in the field of knowledge. I do not wish to present a practical problem. While in one sense it is a practical problem, in another it is not.[8] The topic that came up in discussion[9] was, Do we

8 On commonsense practicality, see *Insight*, chapter 6, 178 and passim; chapter 7, 207–209 and passim; chapter 10, 293. On insight as the key to practicality, ibid. xiii–xv.
9 Lonergan seems here to be referring to discussions that came up during the coffee break, which followed the preceding paragraph. If so, we have here a clue to the structure of the lecture. The previous paragraph was a summing up, to conclude the first part of the lecture. It was meant to be followed by the paragraph that starts the second part of the lecture, taking up the subjective aspect of this side of the dilemma. The

have to start introducing scientific stuff right away into our philosophy classes? I am not dealing with that level yet. What I am arguing for, what I am dealing with, is the existence of a general question of orientation. I have set a dilemma: if we are content with the self we already have and content to appropriate that, we will find it much simpler to base our philosophy upon commonsense knowledge and to prescind from science, perhaps even adding the rationalization that science really does not know the really real but only phenomena; but on the other hand, if our philosophy is to be a principle of integration in the different scientific departments, if it is to be a tool for theology in dealing with its problem of providing the element of religious integration that is a part of the issues raised by empirical human science, then we have a problem. To put it more concretely, we go to great expense to have Catholic universities, but if our professors cannot be anything more than specialists in physics, specialists in chemistry, specialists in biology, specialists in history, if they can search and search for philosophic and theological aids to give them the orientation that would be specifically Catholic in their fields, and still not find them because neither philosophy nor theology is doing its job of integrating, then we have a problem.

4   Philosophy and Self-development

The problem, we said, is twofold. It has its objective side, and the objective side is the minor side. I think a philosopher does need some grasp of the general orientation of the scientific mind; he has to be able to understand the type of thinking the scientist does; he has to know something about heuristic structures and higher viewpoints. At least that is a minimal requirement. I do not think he needs detailed knowledge in the various scientific fields or an ability to discuss them in detail. Again, I do not think philosophy is based upon science any more than it is based upon common sense.[10] Its basis is self-appropriation, appropriation of the self that one actually is.

But besides the objective side of the problem, which comes most into view when one talks about integration, there is the subjective side of the

_____

present paragraph is, therefore, an insert between the two parts of the lecture, arising out of the coffee-break discussion, and interrupting somewhat the rather careful transition Lonergan had prepared.

10 *Insight* 398–401, 423–30.

problem, and that is the fundamental side. That is the real block. According to the French existentialists, *L'homme se définit par une exigence,*[11] man is defined, not by some static essence that he has at first, but by an exigence, by a requirement to become intelligent and rational or whatever the ideal formulated by the particular existentialist may be. Quite clearly, there is a point to that. Everyone has his own personal development, and that development is not exclusively in the moral field. We are familiar with development in the moral field; it is that which is most easily apprehended. But development is not restricted solely to the moral field. There is also a development on the purely intellectual side. Self-appropriation is a function of the self that is appropriated, and development in the self is a prerequisite for having something to appropriate that will be adequate to the task of integration in philosophy and, from my viewpoint, still more importantly in theology.

We make ourselves. It is not only that knowledge is an ideal and that its precise nature is something that has to be discovered in the pursuit of knowledge itself; but we ourselves are selves that develop. We develop in response to situations, outside influences, but we also develop from within. That development from within is the fundamental problem: becoming aware, explicitly conscious, of what intelligence is; becoming explicitly conscious of what judgment is; and seeing the philosophic implications of what intelligence and judgment are.

This point regarding self-development can be illustrated by a reflection that occurred to me in reading Bronislaw Malinowski's *Magic, Science, and Religion.*[12] In that work Malinowski presented a study of intelligence in the Trobriand Islanders, and his thesis was to the effect that, as far as the practical affairs of everyday life went, the Trobriand Islanders were just as intelligent and reasonable as you or I. They knew about preparing the ground, planting the seed, pulling out the weeds, reaping the harvest, and keeping enough to have seed for the next season. They were perfectly

11 The phrase '*L'homme se définit* ...' occurs in *Insight* (625) without a reference. It occurs also in the notes of Lonergan's lectures on existentialism (p. 5 of the mimeographed set put out by Thomas More Institute,. Montreal, in the section On Being Oneself [CWL 18]), again without a reference. The idea is found passim in various existentialists, but we have not located the specific words Lonergan uses.

12 Bronislaw Malinowski, *Magic, Science, and Religion, and Other Essays* (New York: The Free Press, 1948, reprinted Westport, Conn.: Greenwood Press, 1984) 17–36. As was often the case, Lonergan gave much of the bibliographical data from memory, with uncertainty about some details.

intelligent and reasonable in everything regarding the practical affairs that they had under their control; they were intelligent and reasonable in everything that was part of their living. But that field of practical living was surrounded by an enormous structure of myth and magic, and in that they seemed to belong to an entirely different race. Myth and magic, of course, also entered into their practical affairs. Whenever there was an eventuality that they could not control, a coming storm or something similar, the magic entered in to perform its important functions; and on other occasions it had supplementary functions. However, it did not interfere in any way with doing the things that were necessary.

Now in our civilization, there has been a very marked tendency – it is not a universal rule or a necessary law – for scientific thinking to be positivist, pragmatist, antimetaphysical. One can discern a dichotomy (in a much more cultivated form, of course) existing in this mentality which is similar to the dichotomy in the mentality of the Trobriand Islanders. On the one hand, the Islanders were perfectly intelligent and rational where concrete results depended upon what they did; on the other hand, there was a field of myth and magic. Similarly, the scientist is completely intelligent and rational; he wants anything he does or thinks to have a justification in its sensible consequences. His conception of science is a development of the intelligent and rational department of primitive living. But instead of myth and magic on the other side, he has antimyth and antimagic – a blank. He knows nothing about these things; he is an agnostic; and for a great part of his life he does not worry about it.

But while the person who is a scientist or a mathematician does not suffer too much from that blank, the general population does suffer. For example, when I was a student of philosophy we had a course in education,[13] and the educational system in Germany seemed to me to be the most thorough and marvelous that one could devise. All types of needs were met. The standards in the classical *Gymnasium*[f] seemed to me from Canada fantastic. One obtained one's *matura*[14] in Greek when one had read all of the dramatists, most of Thucydides and Plato, and so forth. That was all just an ordinary part of the requirements for entering a university. Similar standards were maintained in the *Realgymnasia*, the

13 The *Catalogus Provinciae Angliae Societatis Iesu* lists Fr Henry Irwin as Lecturer in Pedagogy at Heythrop College for the three years in which Lonergan studied philosophy there (1926–29).
14 What in the English-speaking world was called matriculation.

Volksschule, and all along the line. But then the country was taken over by Hitler. If a vacuum exists in the popular mind, a terrific irrational national convulsion can result. This is one of the main problems of our time. We cannot be content merely to make more cultivated and more civilized the intelligent and rational part of Trobriand living, while maintaining a surrounding no man's land which used to be inhabited by myth and magic but which is now empty – we do not admit, Here be strange beasts;[15] we simply do not bother about it. The real problem of human development is the problem of occupying this territory, this blank, with intelligence and reasonableness, just as we have occupied the territory that can be controlled by sensible consequences.

I have spoken of a type of evasion that is associated with what may be called roughly the scientific mentality in recent centuries. However, I think there can be a similar evasion if the philosopher concentrates on commonsense knowledge and asks himself abstract questions such as, 'Does knowledge exist? Is there any knowledge at all?' rather than the question, 'Is there knowledge of this very accurately determined, specific character?'[g] In other words, you can ask in general the questions, 'Does knowledge exist? Do we know anything at all? Is scepticism wrong?' and you can answer that scepticism is wrong, and conclude that you are all set. On the other hand, you can ask, 'What is knowledge?' and proceed to give an extremely lengthy account, in considerable detail and with considerable sweep, of just what you mean by knowing, just what the conditions are under which it arises, just what the conditions are under which it develops. Then you can ask whether *that* knowledge exists. What happens in the first case, when you put the extremely abstract question? You create a little world, within which you have complete certitude, and you are quite right in having that; knowledge does exist, there is no doubt about it whatever. But the territory you are occupying is very small, and you lose your power of influencing and integrating other fields: the problem of integration is ignored.[h]

What is to be done about this? That is a further question, and still more practical questions are still more remote; but I think that this fundamental issue has to be faced. Unless we ask for a rather full account of knowledge,

15 'Here be strange beasts' is a stock phrase, as appears from the fact that there are books in print under such titles as *Here Be Dragons, Here Be Monsters*, etc. The reference is surely to early maps, on which the map-maker would inscribe, over unknown areas, such phrases as the one Lonergan quoted.

and then ask whether that type of knowledge exists, what we are doing is affirming something that is very abstract; because it is abstract, it will be found alien. The philosophy department becomes just another department, and it is alien to everyone else; it is alien to the students – they are not interested in it; and it is alien to the specialists in other fields. That alienation becomes mediation, it becomes a source of correcting the situation, insofar as we confront the problem intelligently and attempt to meet it deliberately. In other words, the issue *is* practical in a fundamental sense of self-development, of development of the self that is to be appropriated.

I have been asked, What hope is there of communicating a philosophy of self-appropriation? The hope is simply this: there is a possibility of communicating a philosophy of self-appropriation insofar as you can interest people in self-development, in intellectual self-development. Self-appropriation can be hindered by total absorption in the object, as in the specialized sciences. It can be hindered because philosophy does not attempt to be a general view of what is going on in all of the departments of knowledge, and consequently tends to be content with what is abstract and what is alien both from ordinary living and from other departments. I am not talking about the possibility of having a true philosophy. I believe that, if you work from common sense alone, you can arrive at a very large number of propositions that are absolutely true and extremely important, but I am raising the question of philosophy on the level of our times.[i] I am raising the question of a philosophy that is capable of performing an integrating function with regard to knowledge in general, that is concerned with the intellectual and rational development of the student of philosophy, a personal development concerned with the man that is defined by a requirement. One may say I am concerned with the *bene esse* of philosophy, not with its *esse*, not with its existence, but with its fruitfulness.

The matter may be put differently. Georges van Riet published a lengthy doctoral thesis – some 665 pages – at the University of Louvain in 1946 entitled *L'épistémologie thomiste*.[16] It consists in a review of the epistemological doctrines and theorems that have been presented by Thomist philosophers since the time of Balmes early in the nineteenth

---

16 Georges van Riet, *L'épistémologie thomiste: Recherches sur le problème de la connaissance dans l'école thomiste contemporaine* (Louvain: Editions de l'Institut Supérieur de Philosophie, 1946).

century. Van Riet divides the philosophers into classes. First, there are those whose epistemology is fundamentally a matter of confrontation; and there are subdivisions under this heading. Secondly, there are those who hold an epistemology that is based upon understanding, comprehension, intelligence; and there are subdivisions here too. Finally, he has a category of epistemologies that are based upon judgment, and he divides them into two main classes: those that depend upon general judgments, and those that depend upon the act of judgment itself. As you can see from the spread of opinions, there does not exist a scholastic epistemology that is some settled doctrine. There would not be that spread of opinions occupying all possibilities – experience, understanding, and judgment, a series of variations – if there were a well-known solution that is generally accepted. The solution is just not there, and to think it is there is my idea of a myth.

We have a problem. It is not a problem of the existence of knowledge, but a problem of the existence of some detailed account of knowledge. That is where the problem lies. It is not a problem of existence but of fruitful existence. It was this idea that was in the back of my mind in writing *Insight*.[17]

5   The Notion of the Thing

The matter that we have been considering from different angles appears again when we take up the notion of the thing. The notion of the thing has its objective difficulty and its subjective difficulty.

Objectively, I contend in *Insight* that you have a thing when you have a unity-identity-whole which insight grasps, some identical unity that is comprehensive of a whole in individual data. This distinguishes the thing from the scientific law. The account of both classical and statistical method that was adumbrated yesterday and worked out in slightly more detail in *Insight* was concerned throughout with relations between the properties or the qualities of things – relations between masses, within electromagnetic phenomena or heat, and so on. In that presentation, nothing was said about things. The fundamental difference between the thing and the

17   '... in writing *Insight*' is an editorial addition, its validity shown by such passages as the paragraph on pages xiv–xv of the book: 'No problem is at once more delicate and more profound.' It is possible, however, that in this lecture Lonergan was simply referring to what was in the back of his mind as he dealt with the problem here.

scientific law is that in knowing a law, such as the law of inverse squares or the law of the free fall of a body, your knowledge is relational; moreover, it is knowing things in their relations to one another; it is based upon general characteristics; it is not considering data as individual. On the other hand, in knowing a thing, insight is not concerned with data as of a kind, but with these data, and in these data it discovers an intelligible unity. The unity is not instantaneous; it is a unity of data in their temporal succession, a unity not just within space but within space and time. It is an identity; it is what you mean by 'the same' or, at least, it is connected with that notion. However, the expression 'unity-identity-whole' is not an adequate account of the notion of the thing, because we have not yet treated judgment and the notion of being. What is said about the thing in chapter 8 of *Insight* is not complete. Chapter 8 aims at a characterization of the notion of the thing as a unity-identity-whole discerned in individual data.[18]

The unity-identity-whole can be differentiated in two ways. It can be differentiated by its relations to us, by its colors, shape, the sounds it emits, the feel it has, and by more complex relations, but relations ultimately in which the point of reference is the percipient subject. On the other hand, it can be differentiated by relations among the things themselves, by their relations to one another. From these terms, insofar as things are differentiated by their relations to one another, one obtains the elements and compounds of chemistry. Again, one obtains the individuals in the biological species insofar as they are understood phylogenetically and ontogenetically, that is, in terms of a biological theory as opposed to practical dealings with plants, animals, and men.

Consequently, the notion of the thing is a bridge between commonsense knowledge and scientific knowledge on the objective side. We have commonsense knowledge of the thing in terms of its relations to us, and those are the relations that are picked out by the practical activity of everyday living. A fundamental characteristic of being a man of common sense is being able to drop the curtain cutting off theoretical questions, being able to limit one's questions. Questions go on indefinitely; any answer gives rise to further questions; but the man of common sense cuts off those further questions where they cease to be of any practical importance. For

18 A metaphysical account is presented in chapter 15 of *Insight*, after the treatment of judgment and the notion of being; see especially § 3, Explanatory Genera and Species.

example, if a person were to hear the expression of my interest in knowing something about science, and respond by saying, 'Well now, that means that the chemistry department has to get its appropriation,' he would be taking a commonsense attitude toward what I have been saying, and he would be cutting off what I am interested in at the moment. The commonsense account of things in their relations to us has all the characteristics of common sense already presented. We move away from commonsense interest when we begin to move into scientific observation and description. We are not yet on the explanatory level where things are related to one another, as they are in Newton's theory of dynamics or Einstein's theory of relativity or in the periodic table of elements; but on the other hand, our interests are not the practical, concrete interests of the desire to live that provides the limit to the questions that common sense will bother considering. The field of questions is broader, and the interest that guides scientific observation and description is some implicit or more or less explicit view preparing the way for knowledge that will be in terms of the relations of things to one another. Finally, when things are known in their relations to one another, there emerges a hierarchy of genera and species, and it is indicated and discussed in chapter 8 of *Insight*.

This account of the notion of the thing is just one aspect of the matter, the objective aspect. But there is also the subjective aspect.

We are born animals, and we develop as animals much more rapidly than we do as intelligent and reasonable beings. We say that children have reached the age of reason when they are seven years old; we say that a person is a minor until he is twenty-one, and a person is a rather developed biological specimen before he reaches twenty-one. There is a development of man as an animal, and on top of that a further development of man as intelligent and reasonable, and there is a lag between the two. While the lag exists, still it does not mean that we are inefficient, that we are not able to live in a manner appropriate to our age all along the line.

The notion of the thing can be brought into explicit consciousness when a person has a good idea of what an insight is, what common sense is, what science is, and how the different sciences may be related to one another. However, we do not start off with that notion of the thing in kindergarten, and we may not notice any change in our notion of the thing since we were in kindergarten. In other words, besides the objective side of the notion of the thing, we have a functionally operative notion or way of reacting, a knowledge of how to use the words and how to react to things, according to the differences of age all along the line. In fact, we attend much more to things than to qualities, and that is something that really one does not notice. We have to have our attention drawn to it, as it were, the first time at least. What is first is the thing.

What is the thing? It is a highly ambiguous notion. Toward the beginning of chapter 6 of *Insight*, there is a series of descriptions of patterns of experience. They are very schematic. They attempt to indicate, in the abstract manner that alone is possible, different possible types of patterns of experience. Man is never just an animal, although there may be some question about that in the very early months of life.[j] Intelligence is present, and there is the possibility, as it were, of a continuum of experience. To attempt to isolate distinct patterns in that continuum, to say that at such a time one is in this pattern and at another time one is not, is extremely difficult. All that such descriptions can do is provide suggestions, arrows, pointing to possible points of reference which in different combinations may give one some approximation to what the pattern of experience at any given moment in any given individual may be.

However, at the root, the lowest possible base, of this subjective attitude, which is really a spectrum of attitudes, there is simply the response of extroverted consciousness to an external central force which I name the 'already out there now real.' I explain this in terms of the reactions of a kitten to a saucer of milk and to a picture of a saucer of milk.[19] It is something that can be conceived simply in terms of a biological pattern of experience. Because the consciousness is practical, and because practical consciousness is concerned with dealing with situations, and because the situation is already there to be dealt with, we have the 'already.' The consciousness is extroverted, its focus is 'out.' Because the consciousness is in a body, it is 'out there'; the body is always in one place, and 'there' is what is 'out.' Consciousness has memories, and it has anticipations, but it is active in the 'now.' It can be deceived by appearances in a very momentary way perhaps; the kitten might be deceived by an extremely realistic picture of a saucer of milk, but then it would not be 'real' milk because, when the kitten tried it, it would not obtain the ordinary satisfactions it obtains when it tries a saucer of 'real' milk.

This notion of the 'real' object, which can be accounted for in terms of

19 *Insight* 250–52.

the most elementary type of consciousness, is something that, unless adverted to, can be confused with philosophic problems surrounding the notion of the thing, the notion of reality, and the notion of being. When I say that the apprehension of the thing, or the global attitude towards things that I characterized as the 'already out there now real,' is philosophically irrelevant, I do not mean that it is mistaken. Animals are not mistaken; they survive beautifully. Insofar as men are guided by that attitude, the errors that arise are, on the whole, negligible. To conceive this notion as giving rise to some problem that is philosophic seems to me to be simply a mistake. In other words, we do have this notion of the thing, and as far as it goes, it is a perfectly satisfactory and functional and successful notion and attitude; there is nothing whatever to be said against it. However, it is not a philosophic notion.

Idealism is distinguished into the Berkeleian type and the later German type. The earlier Berkeleian type gives rise to the problem expressed in the questions, Are there really objects out there? Or, is *esse percipi*? Is it all in my perceiving? To my way of thinking, that is not a philosophic problem. It is something that is settled on the same level as that on which it arises. If one's already-out-there-now-real reactions and global apprehensions function successfully, that is all there is to be said about them. They do not arise from asking questions and answering them, and if a person lacks a sense of reality in that sense, raising questions and answering them is not going to give it to him. If a person does have a sense of reality in that sense, questions and answers are not going to weaken it. Raising and answering questions are intellectual operations on a different level. All problems of intellectual knowledge are problems that arise in the form of questions and are settled in the form of answers, and the sense of the 'already out there now real' finds answers rather meaningless, rather 'unreal.' We have a sense of reality, and that sense of reality runs concomitantly with the being that we know in true judgment. When a judgment is true, normally the sense of reality is satisfied. But philosophic issues lie upon the level of judgment, on the level of questions that admit intelligent and rational answers. They do not lie on this lower level, and philosophic considerations do not seem to be capable of doing anything significant about changing the lower-level sense of reality. However, that raises a lot of questions.

There, then, you have the subjective side of the problem of the notion of the thing, namely, that we have a whole gamut of apprehensions of the thing, and not all of them are equally relevant to raising and settling philosophic questions.[20]

To sum up this whole section: the objective aspect of the difficulty of the notion of the thing regards bringing the notion of the thing into explicit consciousness as a unity-identity-whole grasped by insight into data as individual. On the other hand, there is the subjective aspect of the difficulty of the notion, rooted in the fact that, before we develop in intelligence and reasonableness, we develop as animals. Unless we sharply distinguish between the thing and the 'already out there now real' which can be accounted for in terms of the most elementary type of consciousness, we risk confusing them in our philosophic thought.

20 The lecture ends here, as is shown by Lonergan's concluding words, 'I thank you,' heard on both the WAS and the DJS reels; the LRI reel stopped two lines earlier at 'gamut.' The whole last paragraph in our text is editorial.

5

Judgment[1]

Today we have to add on the end product of the process we have been discussing – the judgment or assent.[2] Newman's *A Grammar of Assent* is a classic upon the act of judgment, and it becomes rather rich on the antecedent process of reflection involved in judgments that are particular and concrete. Newman names this antecedent process of reflection the illative sense.[3]

Judgments may be characterized in a series of fashions. I have said that presentations are what inquiry is about, and inquiry is what arises upon presentations; inquiry leads to insights, and insights are into presentations.[4] Then, when we have the insights we formulate generally what is

1 The fifth lecture, Friday, August 8, 1958.
2 The tape begins at 'end product,' but notes taken (both sets) show there was no extensive loss.
3 John Henry Cardinal Newman, *An Essay in Aid of a Grammar of Assent* (first publication, London, 1870), chapter 9. See our editorial note *b* to chapter 1, *Collection* (CWL 4) 257.
4 Here and passim in the lectures, especially the fifth, Lonergan kept referring to a diagram he had put on the blackboard. Both sets of notes show it with nine arrows disposed as follows:

necessary in the presentations to have the insights, and so we have an expression of what is relevant, to the point, essential. Presentations, inquiry, insight, and conception were defined by their internal relations. Similarly, the new elements that are now being added are also definable by their internal relations.

1 Judgment and Propositions

When one reaches the expression or conception of an insight, one can utter in words a definition which may be nominal, explanatory, or implicit; one can present a whole hypothesis; one can present a whole theory. But is it true? Is it so? That is a question that need not be answered yet. In writing *Insight* I said what I thought was true, but in reading *Insight* a person does not say after every sentence, 'It is true.' One has to come to make one's own judgment on the matter. The eight hundred pages of propositions are just objects of thought until such time as one sees reason to agree with them. Consequently, definitions, propositions, hypotheses, theories, even if they are spread out over hundreds of pages, may be simply objects of thought. It depends on who is reading them, who is uttering them. If I say, 'Kant said so and so,' it does not mean that that is what I think. It is the old distinction of the medieval theologians, *non asserendo sed recitando*. When they dislike something Augustine said, they say he said it *recitando, non asserendo*.

In other words, there is no sure criterion to be had from words whether one is expressing merely an object of thought or an object of affirmation. 'It is a rainy day.' If the assertion is in quotes, I am taking no responsibility for it; it is the sort of thing one might consider. On the other hand, it may be something that I really agree with; it may express exactly what I am absolutely certain of, or what I think is probably so, or what I am inclined to agree with. In that case we are moved from the second level, the level of understanding, to the third, the level of judgment. The act of judgment is the act that adds assent to a proposition, that changes a proposition from the expression of an object of thought, the expression

---

It corresponds closely to the schema on p. 274 of *Insight*, except that the up and down of the levels is reversed, and there is a change in the wording for the experiential level. The terms for that level are now: sensation, perception, (free) images. For the second and third levels, they are the same as in *Insight*, with minor variations: inquiry, insight, conception; and reflection, reflective understanding, judgment.

of some bright idea that comes into your mind, into an object of affirmation. An object of thought may or may not be true; and this is not confined to definitions, and the use of the verb 'is' is not excluded. There can be in eight hundred pages all sorts of affirmations and negations, but for you as yet they are just objects of thought, something you are willing to consider perhaps, but whether you agree with them or not you do not yet know. You may agree with certain parts and not with others. It is when one agrees, when one assents, that the proposition then becomes an object of affirmation.

One characteristic, then, of the act of judgment is that it transforms a proposition from an object of thought into an object of knowledge. The level of thinking heads for objects of thought; but the level of judgment heads for objects of knowledge.

2   Judgment and Questioning

There is a second way of characterizing the judgment. Just as insight is related to presentations, inquiry, and conception, so judgment is related to what goes on before it in the process. Questions on the second level are questions for intelligence: What? Why? How often? But questions on this third level are questions for reflection: Is it? Is it so? Whether this or that? The answers on the third level are of the type yes or no. It is or it is not. There are two basic alternatives. Those answers can also be modal: they can be qualified in as many ways as one pleases – possibly, probably, certainly, I don't know, we'll see. However, they are all of the basic type, it is and it is not.

There is a fundamental difference between the question raised on the second level and that raised on the third. If one asks, 'What is the logarithm of the square root of minus one?' it makes no sense to say yes or no. The question, What? is a question on the second level, and it asks for some sort of explanation, tentative or definitive. The answers, yes and no, are on a third level, and consequently you get nonsense if you say yes or no to the questions, What? and Why? 'Why are you here?' 'Yes.' It does not make sense. There are two fundamental types of questions: questions asking for explanation, that is, questions for intelligence; and on the other hand, questions for reflection. The judgment is an answer to a question for reflection.

So we relate judgment, on the one hand, to propositions, and as related to propositions it makes the difference between an object of thought and an object of knowledge. On the other hand, we relate judgment to questions, and it answers the questions, Is it? Whether it is so? It does not answer the questions, What? Why? How often? In chapters 1 through 8 of *Insight* we are on the second level, and we are considering questions for intelligence. In chapters 9 and 10 we are on a third level, dealing with questions for reflection, Is it? Whether it is so?

3   The Act of Reflective Understanding

Judgments are also related to the process of weighing the evidence. That is an extremely metaphorical description. The judge weighs the evidence; the jury weighs the evidence and pronounces the defendant guilty or not guilty. How do you marshal and weigh the evidence? Have you ever seen anyone do it? The expressions are obviously metaphorical, and the whole of chapter 10 is devoted to an attempt to make explicitly conscious exactly what occurs at that moment.

However, there is something that can be said right away about the relation between judgment and the act of grasping the sufficiency of the evidence for saying yes or for saying no; namely, if you do not grasp the sufficiency of the evidence and nevertheless say, 'It is' or 'It is not,' you are just guessing, you do not know, you are making a rash judgment. On the other hand, if you do grasp the sufficiency of the evidence, and you want to hem and haw, you are being silly. It is clear as day that it is or that it is not, and your hesitation about judging is irrational. In other words, *at that moment* a man's rationality is being activated. He has the sufficiency of the evidence, and it is up to him to judge; and if he does not judge he is introducing a contradiction within himself. He is rational, he is a reasonable being, and yet he is defaulting on his rationality if he grasps the sufficiency of the evidence and does not judge. Again, he is defaulting on his rationality when he does not have sufficient evidence and nevertheless does judge.

That process, incidentally, from reflective understanding to the act of judgment, is the psychological analogy. In other words, you can say that the act of judgment is caused by the act that grasps the sufficiency of the evidence; there is an aspect of causality there. But there is also a purely rational process, the rational dependence of the judgment on the sufficiency of the evidence. You have 'cause' there, but you also have 'because,' and not 'because' just as a word, but 'because' as rational consciousness, a consciousness that is obligated by its own rationality to judge. That is the rational necessity of judging. Judging, then, in the third place, is the fruit of the actual rationality of consciousness, and that aspect of judgment provides Augustinian and Thomist Trinitarian theory with its psychological analogy: the procession of the Son from the Father is not a matter of causing; it is a matter of the 'because' that occurs within a spiritual being.[a]

4   Judgment and the Person Judging

We have related judgments to propositions: they transform propositions from objects of thought into objects of knowing. We have related them to questions: they answer the questions, Is it? Whether it is so? and not the questions, What? Why? and How often? They answer questions for reflection, not questions for intelligence. They proceed rationally from a grasp of the sufficiency of the evidence. But there is a fourth aspect to the judgment. So far I have been talking about events as if there were nobody there; but there is *someone* who senses, imagines, inquires, understands, formulates his understanding, asks whether it is so, grasps the sufficiency of the evidence, and makes the judgment.

A distinction is made between *quo* and *quod*.[b] There is the person *who* understands, and there is the intellect *by which*, the act *by which*, he understands. And from that aspect, as related to the person, the judgment is a personal commitment. One of de La Rochefoucauld's witty remarks was to the effect that everyone complains about his memory but no one about his judgment. The reason is that we are not responsible for our memory; we feel no embarrassment if we cannot remember a name or a word or when something happened, and so on. Memory is not completely under our control. But the judgment is a personal act, a personal commitment. You do not have to say yes or no; you can say, 'I don't know.' You do not have to say, 'It certainly is so'; you can say, 'It probably is so' or 'It possibly is so.' All the alternatives relevant to human weakness, ignorance, and tardiness are provided for, and it is your rationality that is involved in picking out the right one. Judgment is something that is entirely yours; it is an element in personal commitment in an extremely pure state. Because it is so personal, so much an expression of one's own reasonableness apart from any constraint, because all alternatives are provided for, it is entirely one's own responsibility. Because it is entirely one's own responsibility, one does not complain about one's bad judgments; one is responsible for them.

5 Judgment in Itself

We have picked out four aspects of the judgment, relating it around the map: first of all, to propositions; then to questions; then to the reflective act of understanding; and finally to the person judging. We will now consider the judgment in itself.

Plato spoke of the conjunction and the separation of the Ideas, and Aristotle, following Plato, speaks of judgment as a conjunction or a separation or division. The same type of expression is found in St Thomas quite frequently enough. However, from the Thomist viewpoint the relevant composition is composition of essence with existence on the objective side. The act of judgment is not an act of synthesis, but an act in which one *posits* synthesis. A theory, a hypothesis, a proposition, a definition, already contains a synthesis. Judgment does not add further synthesis; it simply posits the synthesis that is the object of thought.[5]

As we have noted, your object of thought could be the contents of a whole book that is full of 'is' and 'is not': in every sentence there is one, perhaps several; for you, however, they are merely objects of consideration. If the study of grammar or language dominates your cognitional theory, you will try to associate judgment with the occurrence of the word 'is' and if you do, you will get into difficulties of various types. The judgment posits synthesis. It is true that its significant sign, so to speak, is the 'Yes,' the 'is,' the 'It is so,' 'Est, est,' and 'Non, non' – let your speech be 'Est, est,' 'It is,' 'Yes, yes,' and 'Nay, nay.'[c] But it remains that words are not used exclusively to express judgments, but also to report what other people said. Again, they are used to express mere theories, hypotheses, what you think might be so, what you have not made up your mind about yet. The judgment is the act in which you posit the synthesis, which as composition is the work of intelligence. In the general case, what are synthesized are the empirical presentations either of external experience or of the internal experience you are after in your search for self-appropriation.

Since judgment is positing synthesis, we can distinguish in the judgment between its proper content and its borrowed content. The proper content is the positing, the 'Yes,' the 'No,' 'It is,' 'It is not.' The borrowed

---

5 On judgment as synthesis, see *Verbum* 48–59; as positing synthesis, ibid. 59–66, and *Insight* 366.

content is the object of thought which is reached by conception on the second level. Judgment transforms the object of thought into an object of knowledge, and it does so by its proper content, by the 'It is'; but what it transforms – as it were, its matter – is the synthesis provided on the lower level of questions for intelligence, insight, and conception. Besides the explicit content of the synthesis and its positing – one borrowed, one proper – there is the implicit content. When I say, 'It is,' I also mean, 'It is true that it is.' Truth is the implicit content of every judgment. The implicit content can be made explicit; but it is really included in the simple statement, 'It is.'

6   The Context of Judgment

We have been considering a judgment; but there are all sorts of judgments, and they are related. You make a judgment because you grasp the sufficiency of the evidence. But your grasping the sufficiency of the evidence can depend upon past judgments; as soon as someone disputes the judgment, you begin invoking those past judgments to justify your present judgment. Again, you invoke them to limit, qualify, clarify, and explain just what you mean when you make this judgment. A judgment occurs within a context of other judgments, within a context of some determinate development of intelligence, and this contextual aspect of judgment is fundamental. We know our worlds not by one judgment but by an accumulation of judgments, as the fruit of a long series of judgments, and the meaning of any judgment is dependent upon a retinue of other connected judgments that explain it, give its presuppositions, exhibit its consequences, exhibit all the other complementary things that, in some extremely delicate fashion, qualify and elucidate the particular judgment we are making.

This context of other judgments can be considered logically. In that case we are concerned with the coherence of all the judgments we have made. Logical consideration makes each judgment compatible with all the others. The pursuit of the logical ideal usually results in correcting some of the judgments we have already made, or at least in making those previous judgments more accurate. In other words, besides the logical endeavor to obtain coherence in one's judgments, there is also the dialectical tendency to upset one's present position and bring about a more fundamental advance.

7 Rational Consciousness

A number of different aspects of the judgment have been presented, but the meat of the question really lies in what I have called the act of reflective understanding, the reflective insight that answers the question, Is it so? and leads to the judgment, It is, or It is not.

The act of reflective understanding occurs within rational consciousness, within the field determined by rational consciousness. Logicians acknowledge a principle of excluded middle: either it is or it is not; there is nothing in between. At the present time among mathematicians there is some dispute about the use of that principle. The intuitionists do not want to admit it into mathematics, while others insist upon admitting it. You can see where their difficulty lies. We can put questions that are not answered by either yes or no. Sometimes we want to change the question, when it is a tricky question of the type, 'Have you stopped beating your wife yet?' We do not want to answer either yes or no, because both answers have awkward implications. In other words, besides the choice between 'It is' and 'It is not,' we have the right to draw distinctions, to reformulate the question. I think that to insist that in any case, for any formulation, the principle of excluded middle can be applied is mistaken.

The scholastics always reserved the right to distinguish, and that is an illustration of the point that in the long run excluded middle is ultimately valid, but we do not have to accept the formulation of the question that anyone cares to put to us. We can recast the question in our own terms; we can say, 'I don't think we have yet arrived at the point where that question can be put satisfactorily.' Note, then, that questions are more important, generally, than answers. If the question has been put the right way, it is usually fairly easy to see whether the answer is yes or no. The problem is to find the right questions and the right series of questions.

Again, rational consciousness, besides imposing the alternative which leads to the law of excluded middle, also – and this definitively – posits, *means*, the principle of noncontradiction. You cannot make both the judgment, It is, and the judgment, It is not; it is either/or, not both; you cannot say yes and no with regard to exactly the same object – that is, not under the limitations of excluded middle.

In the third place, there is to the judgment an element of absoluteness. If it is true that on this day at this hour and moment I am talking to you, then eternally it could never have been and never will be true that I am not on this day at this hour and moment talking to you. There is an element of the absolute that appears in the truth of the judgment. But if we regard truth as a quality of the judgment, then since human judgments are not eternal, there is no human eternal truth. Whatever we may say about that, still there is an element of the absolute in the judgment that is illustrated by the statement, If Caesar did cross the Rubicon at such and such a time, then eternally no one could say that he would not and be truthful, and no one could say that he did not and be truthful.

Finally, the judgment makes the transition to an objective world. Let us suppose two spheres of exactly the same size. One of them is an aluminum shell, and the other is solid lead. You are seated at a table, and there is a curtain between your face and your arm. Your arm is flat on the table, your hand is open, and you can neither move it nor see it. In the first instance, someone places the lead sphere on the palm of your hand; and in the second instance, he places on your hand the aluminum shell, not all by itself, but with a spring above it that gives you exactly the same pressure that you would feel from the lead sphere. Then it is true of one sphere that it is heavy, and it is true of the other that it is light; but the pressure on the palm of your hand in both cases is exactly the same, and the feel is exactly the same. You can say, 'I feel pressure'; you can say, 'It appears to be heavy'; but you cannot say, 'It *is* heavy' or 'It *is* light.' The appearances are deceptive. How do you make the step? When do you come to the point where you have objective knowledge, when you can say, 'It is heavy'? It is in the judgment, insofar as you can introduce other data that settle the issue. If you are allowed to take either of the spheres successively into your hand, all by itself, and put your whole hand around it, then you can determine that there is no spring attached. Or you can move your hand quickly; when you move the lead sphere you will encounter considerable resistance, and when you move the aluminum sphere you will encounter hardly any. Then you will know which one is the heavy one, and you will be able to say, 'This *is* heavy.' That point is reached in the judgment.

The 'It is' has a connotation of objectivity. (We will consider objectivity later on.[6]) On the first level we have sensations, perceptions, and images. On the second level we understand, and understanding yields objects of thought – 'It may be heavy, and it may be light; if I could only get my hand around it and move it quickly, I would know which it is.' Then one performs the experiment, makes the judgment, and says, 'This *is* heavy.'

6 See lecture 7, §2, The Notion of Objectivity.

When one says that, one does not mean 'It *feels* heavy' or 'There is pressure on my hand.' One is talking about *it*. There is an element of objectivity entering in.

These four points characterize the whole process of rational consciousness. The process begins with the question, Is it or is it not? It includes the principle of excluded middle, provided the question is fairly put – either it is or it is not, either one or the other. It includes the principle of noncontradiction – it cannot be both. It involves an element of the absolute, the ground of what we mean when we speak of the eternality of truth. Finally, it involves an element of objectivity. When we judge we go beyond all question of feelings and appearances, and we say, 'It *is* so' or 'It is *not* so.'

8   The General Form of Reflective Understanding

Now we have to pull away the metaphors and take a step back from this business of weighing the evidence, weighing the pros and cons. Where are the scales on which we weigh the evidence? What do we mean by weighing the evidence? We introduce the term 'unconditioned,' and consider two cases: the formally unconditioned and the virtually unconditioned. The formally unconditioned is unconditioned in the sense that it has no conditions whatever. The only thing we could say is formally unconditioned, then, is God, absolute necessity. The virtually unconditioned has conditions, but they are fulfilled; it is *virtually* unconditioned. We can see in that notion something that ties in with the absoluteness of truth, with the absoluteness, It is heavy, that constitutes the objective element when we go beyond feeling heaviness, feeling weight, appearances, to what *is*. We will consider a series of cases of the virtually unconditioned, different types of judgments, and show that the virtually unconditioned in each case supplies the object grasped in the reflective act of understanding.

First, however, let us consider the general form of the grasp of the virtually unconditioned. The general form of the grasp of the virtually unconditioned[d] may be put syllogistically: If *A*, then *B*; but *A*; therefore *B*, where *A* and *B* severally represent one or more propositions. In the major, *B* is presented as a conditioned: If *A*, then *B*. In the minor, the condition is fulfilled: *A*. We have the conclusion because the combination of major and minor exhibits *B* as virtually unconditioned.

Note that this analysis of syllogism directs attention to the conclusion, and to the conclusion as virtually unconditioned. You may ask right away, 'How do we know the major? How do we know the minor?' Those are further questions. The point to the syllogism is that it exhibits B as virtually unconditioned, as a conditioned with its conditions fulfilled.

What is the function of syllogism? Is the function of syllogism a matter of writing down a formula that exhibits what happens in mental chemistry, the way the chemical formula represents what happens in chemical processes? The function of writing out syllogisms, or clarifying your thought to the point where you are able to put your assertions as conclusions from other premises, is that it puts into form the object of reflective understanding. Reflective understanding is aided by the syllogistic form of exposition because the syllogism exhibits the conclusion, the prospective judgment, the conditioned, as a virtually unconditioned.[e] You have the question, Is B true? Is the proposition or set of propositions under consideration true? The act of reflective understanding grasps that the proposition or set of propositions is virtually unconditioned; because of that grasp you have a grasp of an absolute, and you say, 'Affirm B; B is true.'

Now note particularly that this analysis considers the syllogism as an expression relevant to the third level of consciousness, the level of rationality. Before, when we were discussing insight, I said that Aristotle used the syllogism as a means for communicating insights on the second level, the level of intelligence, and I used the example of the phases of the moon. The phases are the *causa cognoscendi* of the sphericity of the moon; we know the moon is a sphere because it goes through these phases. If it were just a disc the whole circle would always be illuminated; because it has a spherical surface, we see its phases. The phases are the middle term; the moon, the subject; sphericity, the predicate. In that case, syllogism expresses an insight. But syllogism is relevant to the third level, as exhibiting the virtually unconditioned. Syllogism is an expression of the idea of validity; the idea of the virtually unconditioned connects judgment with the absolute.

We have, then, a general formula for what metaphorically we described as weighing the evidence, marshaling the pros and cons of the question. When do you have the evidence weighed? You have it weighed when you reach a virtually unconditioned. Rational consciousness knows beforehand the content of the judgment. Before you make the judgment, 'John is here,' you ask whether John is here; you have an object of thought. You raise the question, 'Is John here?' You grasp the virtually uncondi- tioned and say, 'He is here.' That is the process of judgment as a general scheme.

However, this is just a scheme. Moreover, it is a scheme that raises a very obvious further question: How do we know that this specific judgment is true? If it is by a further syllogism that we prove it, then we go off to infinity. How do we ever make *any* judgments? The answer to the question is that, in the case of syllogisms, the minor premise *A*, one or several propositions, is a set of judgments; we are already on the third level. But the fulfilment of the conditions need not be a set of judgments; it can be a set of experiences on the lower levels. Again, the major premise, If *A*, then *B*, insofar as we have a syllogism, is a judgment; but it is not necessary for reflective understanding that it be a judgment. It can be a structure immanent in one's thinking. So one can have the types of judgment necessary to arrive at the premises for syllogistic process.

In other words, if *A* and *B*, as representing the conditions and condi- tioned in a virtually unconditioned, must always be judgments, then we are driven back to an infinity of prior judgments before we can have *one*. There has to be an infinity, because every final judgment, every judgment *B*, depends upon other judgments. If, however, we can find *A* and the major premise, If *A*, then *B*, within the prior process of knowing, and reflective understanding capable of using *A* and *B* as they exist in this prior state, then we can get the judgment. I attempt to illustrate this first of all in concrete judgments of fact, and secondly in judgments on the correctness of insights. Logically, judgments on the correctness of insights should precede; but practically it is better to proceed the other way.

9   Concrete Judgments of Fact

The concrete judgment of fact may be illustrated by the simplest exam- ple – I indicated it last night.[7] A man leaves his home in the morning, and everything is spic and span. When he returns in the evening, the windows are broken, there is water on the floor, and smoke in the air. He makes the judgment, 'Something happened.'

How does he arrive at this judgment? First, he has two sets of sensible

7 See discussion 3, §1, Common Sense.

data, or one present set of sensible data and a set of memories of what his home was like when he left in the morning. On the empirical level, then – your A, the fulfilment of the conditions – there are his present perceptions and his memories of the state of his home when he left in the morning. Secondly, on the intellectual level, he has a grasp of the notion of thing. It is the same home; it is the same set of things that was in one state in the morning and is in another state in the evening. When the same set of things at different times is in different states, something has happened.

We can put this syllogistically. If the same set of things is in different states at different times, then in the intervening time something has happened; but this same set of things was in one state this morning and now is in another state; therefore, something has happened. The syllogism is quite simple. But the man does not use any syllogism to conclude that something has happened; it is obvious. Is he irrational when he says it is obvious? Not at all. He has the minor premise in his present perception and in his memories of the prior state; he has the unity, this same set of things, 'my home.' What he calls 'my home' was in one state according to his memories and is in another according to his present perceptions; and that is what is meant by the words, Something happened. Consequently, he has in his presentations and memories the fulfilment of the conditions for saying that something has happened, and in the meaning of these words, Something happened,[f] he has the link between those conditions and the judgment, Something did happen.

Again, this illustration from concrete judgments of fact is an illustration that avoids difficulties by several devices. The situation chosen is a familiar one; there is no difficulty about supposing that a man knows his own home. We obviate an enormous number of difficulties by presupposing a situation quite familiar to the person making the judgment; for then a quite definite problem arises due to an obvious change. However, essentially the same analysis is applicable where the relevant experiences are the experiences of a lifetime, where the relevant intellectual structure is as complex as you please, where the knowledge involved is that of a specialist or expert. In neither case do you have explicit syllogizing: but you will have the fulfilment of conditions on the level of experience; links between conditions and conditioned – a conjunction of the two (major premise) – on the level of intelligence; and a grasp in the two of the virtually unconditioned on the level of rational consciousness.

10 Judgments on the Correctness of Insights

A further question may be raised. How do you know that the insight is correct? How do you test the insights? The answer, very briefly, is that one can distinguish between vulnerable and invulnerable insights.

A vulnerable insight is really an insight; you have really caught on to something. But there are further questions that arise. Those further questions are such that the insight you have at present will be complemented and qualified and perhaps corrected to some extent by future insights. Your insight is just the beginning of a cluster of insights. As with the person who is studying a new science and doing fairly well at it, but who is not ready yet to write the exam, your insights are vulnerable. They are in need of being complemented by further insights that will enable you to hit things off accurately with regard to all of the new questions that can be put.

There is also a stage where insights move on to be invulnerable, in the sense that de facto there are no further relevant questions that might complement or change the given insight. The invulnerable insight hits things right off, and there is no doubt about it, no possibility of any further questions that will change things. If the man, when he arrived home, had said, 'There's been a fire here' instead of 'Something happened,' his insight would have been more vulnerable. It is just possible that someone was playing a practical joke, and had simulated all of the signs of a fire. That is the sort of thing you may discount; but you discount it from your knowledge of the situation and the sorts of things that will happen in a situation. If this had taken place in a boarding school, for example, you could not be so sure there had been a fire. It depends upon your judgment of the situation.

In other words, you move into a new situation; you find things a bit strange; you are not sure of yourself; you catch on, getting to know people, coming to know what you can say and do. Insights cluster, and you reach a point of familiarity; you are at home. You reach a point where everything that happens is fixed more or less within the same scheme. If anything really new turns up, you know enough about the general situation to know that this is exceptional, that you have to look for some special reason for it. Insights head towards a limit. When you reach that limit, you have the invulnerable insight, that is, you have reached a point where further questions de facto do not arise. There can be further questions, but they are not relevant. The man comes home and says, 'Something happened.' He is perfectly satisfied that something has happened. He moves on to a new question, 'Where is my wife?' But the first question is settled.

It is not easy to settle by a general rule when we have reached invulnerable insight. There is no formula for producing men of good judgment. Some people are temperamentally rash, and some are temperamentally hesitant. The rash are nearly always sure and definite, the hesitant nearly always slow to make up their minds and rarely are they certain. (True, there are some things that even the hesitant do not doubt, and some that even the rash will find doubtful.)

Again, psychic disturbances can eclipse judgment, for the level of judgment is a much more delicate level, one on which the balance of control is more difficult. And one reaches in psychosis the impossibility of judging. One uses here what are called 'reality tests' – really, tests of the possibility of judging.[8]

In short, a man may be rich, over rich, in insights, but the control needed for judgment may be lacking. One needs for judgment a fuller control of all faculties than one needs for insight. The control of judgment requires the poise of consciousness and the control over sensitive presentations and images that can be disturbed in the human makeup. If that control is disturbed, judgment is disturbed. St Thomas says that we can syllogize in our dreams, but when we wake up we find that we have made some mistake. Syllogizing in one's sleep is on the level of insight, but finding the mistake upon waking up is on the level of judgment. While insights are not excluded by the fact that one is dreaming, the intellectual element is not dominant at all; the dream is disconnected, and lower factors have control.[g] The possibility of insight is there, but the possibility of sound judgment is for the most part excluded, because sound judgment means control of *all* the relevant factors, and 'relevant' means 'relevant to the prospective judgment.' What is relevant to the judgment, Something happened, is much less than what is relevant to the judgment, There has been a fire, or the judgment, They have been having a good time. Those are further judgments that require much more in the way of evidence. When one cannot make a certain judgment that is more

8 The two preceding paragraphs and the first words of the following paragraph are supplied from notes (both FEC and WAS). There had been a coffee break, and afterward recording started late, at 'rich, over rich.'

complex, one can make a certain judgment that is more qualified. If the man is not certain on coming home that there has been a fire, he can be certain that something has happened. In other words, besides the alternatives of 'is' and 'is not,' 'certainly,' 'probably,' and 'possibly,' there is also an indefinite number of alternatives that can be introduced by qualifying the judgment, paring it down, making it still less and less that you are asserting. The more you qualify the judgment, the easier it is to arrive at the point where your insights are invulnerable, where there are no further questions relevant to making a prospective judgment.

Note that the condition of the invulnerable insight is stated objectively. The point is not that no further relevant questions occur to *me*, but that there *are* no further relevant questions. It may happen that no further relevant questions occur to me because I am not giving them a chance to arise, because I am a scatterbrain, because I did not think long enough about it. Again, it may be that further questions arise that seem relevant to me, but I do not have good enough judgment to judge whether they are relevant or not, to say, 'That's just silly.' The scrupulous person is the person who cannot say, 'That's silly, forget it.' He needs someone else to tell him.[9] Good judgment is a personal commitment; people complain about their memory but not about their judgment. Judgment is a personal commitment that involves one's own rationality. It is a contingent event; it usually depends upon an extremely large number of factors. But it is something that does happen; we do judge; there are things we are absolutely certain about, things that it would be silly to have any doubts about no matter how hesitant we may be. Our rationality reaches a point where, with regard to some judgment, sufficiently qualified, we are satisfied that there are no further relevant questions that will occur. We need not be satisfied that there are no further relevant questions that absolutely could occur; we are not dealing with judgments of absolute necessity when we are dealing with judgments on the correctness of our insights. Insights are correct *as a matter of fact*, and the fact is that there are no further relevant questions. It is not a question of possibility, 'Could there be some further relevant questions?' The question of possibility does not bear upon the judgment that de facto these insights have reached the point of invulnerability.[h]

---

9 Lonergan added, 'He also needs someone to tell him to obey' – standard practice in counseling scrupulous persons.

11   Probable Judgments

We have considered concrete judgments of fact and judgments on the validity, the correctness, of concrete insights. By combining these two one can account for all of the judgments of common sense. Common sense deals with the concrete and particular. First, its judgments are judgments that de facto I am understanding this situation correctly enough to make this qualified judgment about it; or, secondly, they are judgments that emphasize the factual elements: I have in my present sensitive experience and in my memories of the past a sufficiency of fulfilling conditions, A (where the major 'If A, then B' regards the correctness of insights), to say that B is not merely a conditioned linked to conditions, but that the conditions as well are fulfilled.

However, we will be told by the scientist that his judgments are only probable. Why is it that the scientific judgment, which is made with such an elaborate apparatus of methods, directives, experimentation, and precautions, is a probable judgment, while the judgments of common sense can be certain? The reason is this. The scientist works out, for example, the law of a free fall: the law of a free fall is a constant acceleration. He verifies that law not merely by dropping weights off the summit of the tower of Pisa or by sliding weights down inclined planes, but through four centuries of scientific work during which the law is assumed and any defects that are found in the results are not traceable to the law; it involves an enormous amount of indirect verification. Why is it that the scientist does not arrive at the virtually unconditioned? Why does he say his laws are probable?

The law of the free fall is practically certain, so close to sensible data that it is very difficult to conceive a possibility of things being thought of otherwise. However, insofar as this law is understood on the assumptions of a Euclidean space, it has to be revised when special relativity is introduced and space is no longer strictly Euclidean. In other words, assumptions that lie on a remote level may be changed, and then the law will not be used in exactly the same sense as before. In general, where measurements are involved and the law is very close to the measurements, one can be *almost certain*; but the higher one ascends in the scientific superstructure, the greater the possibility that some element in the theory that at the present time is assumed as basic may later lose its basic position. In mechanics and dynamics, the concept of mass is fundamental; in relativity, mass does not have exactly the same properties as it has in

Newtonian mechanics. Insofar as special relativity is said to have been sufficiently established, that is, to be still more probable than Newtonian mechanics, there is a change in that fundamental notion. Is there any way of proving that in any future mechanics mass will have the fundamental position that it has at the present time? This is the sort of question the scientist does not raise; he finds it simpler to say that he will consider that sort of question when the need for considering it arises. But he does not exclude the possibility, and insofar as such possibilities are not excluded, the scientist will in general say that his theory is probable.

In other words, the virtually unconditioned really does involve an absolute. Positively, the scientist can say that if the theory or the hypothesis is true, then it conforms to the data. But he cannot establish the alternative, namely, that there is no other theory that would cover all the data we have at present and account for further data that at the present are not accounted for. His argument, then, is really a matter of affirming the consequent; and the hypothetical argument in which one affirms the consequent is not logically valid. The scientist does not reach the virtually unconditioned. The scientific argument from verification is generally of the following type: If A, then B; but B; therefore A. If the theory, A, is true, then we have all these things that we account for; but we have all these things accounted for; therefore, the theory is a fairly good account of them. This is not a logically valid argument; but it is an approach towards having A established. When you establish 'If A, and *only* if A, then B,' then you can say, 'B, therefore A.' But in general, scientific theory is not that type of thing, and consequently the scientist says that his theory is probable; he is satisfied to keep on explaining as many of the data as he can, moving on to more and more satisfactory theories and hypotheses.

12   Analytic Propositions and Principles

There remains a third class of judgments that illustrates the virtually unconditioned in another way: analytic propositions and principles. I distinguish between the two. If you define any A as what has a relation R to B, that is, if by definition A is what has a relation R to B, then you can say, 'If there is an A there is a relation R to B.' That is an analytic proposition. What do I mean? I mean that it is a virtually unconditioned in virtue of the definition of A, namely, A is what has a relation R to B. The definitions supply the fulfilling conditions; the link between the definitions and this proposition is provided by the rules of syntax, the meaning of this collocation of words.[i] If one accepts the definition, then one must say, 'If there is an A there is a relation R to B.' The link between the conditions and the conditioned is given by rules of syntax, the way in which words combine to make complete sense. We have here, then, an example of a virtually unconditioned. The proposition 'If there is an A there is a relation R to B' is conditioned; it is true under certain circumstances or conditions. What are the conditions? The conditions to be fulfilled are fulfilled by a definition: A is defined as what has a relation R to B. The link between that fulfilled condition and the proposition consists in rules of syntax, rules that govern the way words combine to make sense. There we have an analytic proposition, that is, a proposition which is virtually unconditioned in virtue of definitions and rules of syntax.

One can affirm an analytic proposition within the sense defined. It will be noted, consequently, that analytic propositions are an indefinitely large group; we can have as many of them as we please; we can have as many of them as we can have different meanings assignable to A, R, and B. The only limit on the meanings is that R always has to be a relation, and A and B have to be terms of relations. To obtain another indefinitely large set, we just define another basic set of terms and make up more analytic propositions. There is an unlimited supply. Analyticity is simply the structure of the judgment: If A, then B; A; therefore B. The judgment, as resting upon a virtually unconditioned, is resting upon that structure; and that structure, as a structure, is something that can be satisfied by rules of syntax and definitions made ad hoc. Do we have any significant knowledge from that procedure? Not yet. This indefinitely large group of possible analytic propositions is just a set of possible ways of talking. It is not the set of ways in which anyone actually does talk; it is what would be true if someone were to talk in a certain manner; it is not a significant part within the field of knowledge. Rather, it is something that is true about our modes of speech and conventions in modes of speech.

From analytic propositions one can move on to analytic principles. Suppose that there are concrete judgments of fact of the type 'Something happened,' but in which one says, 'A exists in the sense defined,' or 'There exists an A with the relation R to B,' as matters of concrete fact.[10] Then one is transforming the analytic proposition into an analytic principle. In other words, an analytic proposition becomes an analytic principle in the measure that the defined terms in their defined sense occur in concrete judgments of fact.

Let us take an illustration from the ontological argument for the existence of God. Necessary existence exists necessarily. This is at least an analytic proposition; you are saying no more in the predicate than you have in the subject; you are just repeating what is in the subject. Does it involve any significant knowledge about the necessary existence? Insofar as it is an analytic proposition, it does not; it merely results necessarily from the way the terms are defined and from the rules that govern the way the terms are combined. However, if you can say that there exists a necessary existence, that there is something that exists necessarily, then you transform the analytic proposition into an analytic principle. In other words, the ontological argument is valid if God exists.[j]

In general, then, the point to the distinction between the analytic proposition and the analytic principle is, first of all, that it provides a way of dealing with the problems raised in symbolic logic, which is concerned with propositions that are tautologous, propositions that simply rest upon the way terms are defined and the laws by which terms are connected together. Tautologous propositions can be handled in that fashion. But when we speak of analytic principles we mean more than merely tautologous propositions. What effects the transition? It is the occurrence in concrete judgments of fact of the terms in the sense defined. For example, every contingent being has a cause. You can define contingency in such a way that it is necessary to say that a contingent being has a cause. But even though, by definitions of terms and rules of grammar, that proposition can be made into a tautologous proposition, an analytic proposition, still if you have a way of showing that some things that exist

---

10 The sequence here is somewhat obscure: Lonergan seems to have telescoped his thought. Notes (FEC) have the sentence: 'But if we add a concrete judgment, A exists, the analytic proposition is transformed into an analytic principle.' Possibly the sequence is as follows: 'Suppose there is an analytic proposition, A is defined as what has a relation R to B; but suppose there is also a concrete judgment of fact of the type, Something happened, in which one says, A exists in the sense defined, then one is transforming ...'

are contingent in the sense defined, you are going beyond the level of the merely analytic proposition. It is insofar as you show that there do exist contingent beings that you transform analytic propositions into analytic principles.[11]

The matter can be put in another manner. We hear a good deal about essentialism and existentialism. You can say that when you arrive at objects of thought you are thinking about essences, and when you make judgments you know existence. But when the linguistic apparatus is taken into consideration, you find that it has laws of its own that enable you, by definition and laws of syntax, to construct analytic propositions, the type of proposition such that, if you use the language, you have to talk this way – in other words, analytic propositions arise from the language itself. To move from the merely linguistic or merely essential or the mere object of thought, you need concrete judgments of fact.

I divide analytic principles into three classes. First, there are those in which the verifying judgments, so to speak, the concrete judgments of fact that transform analytic propositions into analytic principles, are affirmed simply. That is the philosophic case. Secondly, there are those in which the concrete judgments of fact that effect the transformation are affirmed provisionally. That is what occurs in the empirical sciences. Finally, there is the third case for mathematics, and I speak of these as serially analytic principles.

Let us consider the analytic principle in empirical science. The laws that are well established in a science function analytically; they function as first principles. When Boyle's law is established, it is assumed in order to establish Charles's law: it is more or less an assumption that is simply posited. In later developments, that is still more the case. Earlier laws are assumed; they function analytically; they function in the same way as analytic principles. However, they do so provisionally. Nothing will prevent me from qualifying both Boyle's law and Charles's law by van der Waals's formula for more specific cases. Consequently, when the analytic propositions – for example, there is a certain relation between pressure, volume, and temperature – have their verifying components, their existential components, in probable judgments, we have provisional analytic principles.

---

11 Slight changes in the text here are based on notations Lonergan made in his copy of the 1980 edition.

In the case of mathematics, I speak of serially analytic principles. There is no doubt that one can make concrete judgments of fact that involve 1, 2, 3, 4, up to any small number, and there is no doubt that concrete judgments of fact including numbers of the order of 10^{30} do not occur. If someone does happen to make a concrete judgment of fact that involves exactly that number, we can add 1 onto it and ask him to make the judgment about that. In other words, part of the number series does occur in concrete judgments of fact, but there is an enormous stretch of it that does not. Again, there may not exist absolutely level planes, but there are approximations to them. Just as there is a process to infinity in mathematics, so there is also a process of idealization. The mathematician turns analytic propositions into serially analytic principles insofar as in concrete judgments of fact some part of the theory or some approximation to what he is thinking about can be illustrated.

I should note that this account of the mathematical judgment of existence is not commonly proposed or considered by theorists on the foundations of mathematics. There are different schools on this issue. However, I do think there is some difference between significant mathematical propositions and the mere formation of what is linguistically necessary. You can be a symbolic logician or a mathematical logician without doing anything that is significantly mathematical. While that is a proposition that certainly would not be accepted by members of the Bourbaki school[12] – the reference is to N. Bourbaki, and the names I know best in that group of mathematicians are those in Paris[k] (Dieudonné and Cartan, I believe[13]) – this idea on mathematical judgment seems to me necessary.

12 A group, of limited and changing membership, of (mainly) French mathematicians who used the name Nicolas Bourbaki as a collective pseudonym in publishing a large treatise on advanced mathematics using an axiomatic approach similar to that of David Hilbert. This work, planned in six books arranged in logical rather than chronological order, has been published in installments under the general title, N. Bourbaki, *Eléments de mathématique* (Paris: Hermann, 1939–). Many members of the group have also published extensively in their own names. See R.P. Boas, Jr, 'Bourbaki, Nicolas,' in Charles Gillespie, ed., *Dictionary of Scientific Biography* (New York: Charles Scribner's Sons, 1970), Vol. 2, pp. 351–53. See discussion 1, §1, Mathematics and Logic.

13 The reference is almost certainly to Jean Alexandre Dieudonné and Henri Paul Cartan, though Lonergan (in uncertain voice and with an indication that he was not sure of the name) had said Carton for the

But if you ask the mathematicians for an authoritative view on what
mathematical existence is, you will not get this idea. They may, of course,
come round to it – I don't exclude that!

13 Self-appropriation

So much for a general account of what is meant by a judgment and the
conditions of a judgment. Our first efforts at self-appropriation stopped
at the second level, the level of intelligence. Today we have added a
further, much more delicate, and much more significant level, the level
of judgment.

Judgment has been characterized by its relation to propositions, its
relation to questions, its relation to reflective understanding, and its
relation to the person who commits himself by making the judgment. We
then considered judgment as positing synthesis, as a further level added
on to the synthesis reached in conception. The whole thing hangs
together. Just as earlier we had a set of terms defined by their internal
relations – presentations, inquiry, insight, and conception – so now we
can add on all of the elements of the further level of judgment, defining
judgment by its internal relations.

What we have been doing is determining the knowing subject by
implicit definitions; and the meaning of those implicit definitions is given
a positive content by one's own self-appropriation, insofar as I am aware
of myself as experiencing, inquiring intelligently, and judging rationally.
The fulness of my self-appropriation is the measure of the meaning, the
significance, that I can give to a merely postulational definition of that
set of terms by their internal relations. In other words, self-appropriation
is the experiential element that is expressed in the set of relations defined
by this set of terms; and the judgment of self-affirmation, treated in
chapter 11 of *Insight*, is the judgment relevant to self-appropriation. If
you think of the knowing in this judgment 'I am a knower' as our knowing
external objects, we must then add that this knowing, on all its levels, is
something that enters into my presence to myself. In the first sense of

latter. See, for instance, Jean Dieudonné, *Panorama des mathématiques
pures: Le choix bourbachique* (Paris: Gauthier-Villars, 1977), trans. I.G.
Macdonald, *A Panorama of Pure Mathematics as Seen by N. Bourbaki* (New
York: Academic Press, 1982); and Henri Paul Cartan, *Oeuvres*, 3 vols.,
eds. R. Remmert and J.-P. Serre (Berlin: Springer, 1979).

presence, the chairs are present in the room. In the second sense, you are present to me. But in the third sense, I have to be present to myself for anyone to be present to me. In self-appropriation, it is this third presence with which we are concerned.

Now this third presence of myself to me is given, but it is not known.[14] The whole set of definitions in these lectures could be only a relational structure. Self-appropriation gives it meaning, but as a hypothetical construct. Chapter 11 of *Insight* will add affirmation, will determine the hypothesis as fact, will make my presence to myself known.

14 Clear sound (LRI and DJS reels) stops with Lonergan in midsentence at 'not known'; a few words follow that may be, 'better, it's not.' The WAS reel had stopped early in the preceding paragraph, at 'by implicit definitions.' Our concluding sentences are added from notes taken (FEC).

6

Knowing and Being[1]

1   Self-affirmation

We have set up an idea of what goes on when we are using our intelligence and reasonableness. As yet, however, that idea is just a hypothesis, an object of thought. We have spoken of a flow of sense experiences, perceptions, and images; of a flow of questions for intelligence – What? Why? How? – and of insights that provide a basic element in the answer to these questions.[2]

We should note a fundamental paradox connected with insight. When you say *what* precisely, you are going beyond the insight to conception. What you are saying is more explicit than what is had in the insight as such. If you do not go beyond the insight to say what you have in it, you omit insight from your consideration. In other words, to express the insight you need to conceive, define, think, suppose, consider, and when you are that far you are beyond the stage of having the insight. But still,

---

1 The sixth lecture, Saturday, August 9, 1958.
2 Lonergan again illustrated this flow of activities by the diagram of nine arrows. See note 4 to lecture 5. There may be several names for describing any of the nine activities (see note 3 below for an example), but there is no confusion of level with level (see the beginning of § 1.1, Verification of a Set of Events), and no confusion of activity with activity within a given level. That is, the nine activities are quite distinct, though doubly interrelated: from level to level, and within each level.

you can draw attention to the insight, and explain just what its importance is, only by going on.

This is a basic case of the type of problem set by the psychological fallacy. The psychologist has to use his intelligence and reasonableness, concepts and judgments, to describe what is going on within us. But concepts and judgments are not the only things going on within us. He could be talking of something else; he could be using concepts and judgments to describe something that is not conceptual or judicial. When you are talking about physics you are using concepts and judgments; but no one supposes that atoms have concepts and judgments; and consequently, you do not ascribe concepts and judgments to atoms. But doing that can be quite difficult to avoid when you are talking about human beings.

We have to move now beyond the stage of hypothesis to a judgment regarding cognitional process.

1.1 Verification of a Set of Events

We have a first level, then, of sensation, perception, and images; a second level of inquiry, insight, and formulation;[3] and a third level of reflection, grasping the unconditioned, and judging. That is a theory about what goes on when we know. Are there any knowers in precisely that sense of knowing? We have the question, but how can we answer it? Each one has to answer it for himself. To say that there is a knower in that sense, that is, that there is a unity-identity-whole that senses, perceives, imagines, inquires, understands, conceives, reflects, grasps the unconditioned, and judges, is to make a judgment.

To make a judgment you have to grasp the unconditioned: not the formally unconditioned that has no conditions at all, but the virtually unconditioned. The virtually unconditioned is a conditioned with its conditions fulfilled. The link between the conditioned and the conditions is made by our definition of knowing. We mean by a knower a unity-identity-whole that performs those nine activities. That is our conception,

---

3 Here Lonergan repeats the terms just used to describe the activity of formulation: 'to conceive, define, think, suppose, consider.' All these terms pertain to the second level of cognitional process, but also they pertain to a specific moment of the process on that level: what in science is called formulation, but in Trinitarian theology is called 'uttering an inner word' (see our editorial note *d* to this lecture).

and there is a knower in that sense if that conception of the knower can be verified, that is, if you can assign experiences such that the propositions involved in that complex notion of a knower have their conditions fulfilled.

Note with regard to that fulfilment: If we wish to verify that pressure by volume equals 64, $PV=64$, we say, 'When V is 1, 2, 4, 8, 16, 32, 64, then P will be 64, 32, 16, 8, 4, 2, 1'; and then we set up an apparatus and see whether we obtain those numbers. But we do not see that the pressure is 64 when the volume is 1, and that the pressure is 32 when the volume is 2. Those are statements, judgments. What we *can* see, by taking a look, is a measuring rod set against the dimensions of the volume. Similarly, we can see the position of the needle on a dial. That is what we see, but the steps subsequent to that are steps involving intelligence and judgment. Those further steps enable us to make the statements: when the volume is 1, the pressure is 64; when the volume is 2, the pressure is 32; and so on. Consequently, verifying this conception is not another set of conceptions; it is something prior to conception, something much more primitive than conception.

Having the materials in which we verify is the point to our beginning by insisting upon self-appropriation. In the measure that one has achieved self-appropriation, one is capable of verifying in oneself that one is a unity-identity-whole that senses, perceives, imagines, inquires, understands, formulates, reflects, grasps the unconditioned, and judges. But there is a difference between verifying in the one case and verifying in the other. In the first case, one uses one's external senses, and one simply sees the position of the needle on a dial; one sees the way a measuring rod is set beside the dimensions of a container. That is all that one sees; one does not even see that expression of it. The expression is simply a description of what one happens to be looking at. But here, instead of looking out at something, one has to deal with one's presence to oneself. The chairs are present in the room; we are present to one another; and for us to be present to one another, we have to be present to ourselves. For anyone to be present to me I must not be unconscious. In the case of verifying oneself as a knower, trying to look at something is simply turning things upside down. What counts is the looker, not the looked-at.

The verification is of a set of events. One has to attend to the contents of the events sufficiently to be able to distinguish between them. I spoke of sensing, perceiving, imagining, inquiring, and so forth – a series of different types of events. But we do not have to go into detail about the exact objects of the events. What we are verifying are events of a certain type. In general, there is no difficulty about the first level. Unless we are blind, we see; unless we are deaf, we hear; unless we are like the animals that cannot form free images, we imagine. It is fairly easy to be present to oneself when one is sensing.

On the second level we inquire. Now, for example, we are trying to understand something about knowledge and philosophy. We have a desire to understand, and we do occasionally catch on to something. It takes time. We get some things right away; others we have to puzzle out. It may be years after one started studying philosophy that one finally gets the point about something. We do not have control over our insights, but we do understand, at times at least, and when we understand we know what it is to have a concept. When I was talking about the concept of the point as distinct from the image of a point, it was not as if I were talking to you about mystical experience. Mystical experience does not lie, perhaps, within the experience of all of us, but knowing what is meant by position without magnitude does occur within our experience. Even though we cannot imagine anything whatever that is just position without magnitude – we need something to mark the position, and that will always have some magnitude – the concept of the point has a meaning for us.

Again, you have listened patiently to all of these lectures, yet you do not swallow it all right down, you wonder whether it is true. You are not satisfied with a mere theory about knowledge; you want to know if that is what really goes on. If you ask the question, Am I a knower in that sense? you are asking the question for critical reflection. If you did not have critical reflection, you would not know what was going on here this morning. Critical reflection heads for a grasp of the unconditioned. You want to have this thing tied right down, nailed right down, before you are going to accept it. And if that isn't achieved, you say, 'Well, it may be all right – I don't know.' You have to reach the unconditioned, something that contains an element of an absolute, before you are able to say, 'It is so. I am a knower at least in that sense.' And note that the sense in question is not attained by taking a look at something. It is knowing in the sense that the judgment, I am a knower, occurs.

There may be further questions with regard to objects and the relation between subject and object, but we are not raising those questions yet. There may be a question whether this subject that I am knowing is just phenomenal or really real. We are not raising that question yet.[4] We have to find out that we are knowers in some sense before we can fruitfully go on to these further questions, before we can determine whether they have any meaning or are just mistaken.

Not only do we have these single acts; our consciousness, what is present in the third sense of presence, is not exactly the same on the three levels. On the first level it is simple empirical consciousness. Somebody is at home; there is not only a seen, but also a seer. But the somebody at home on the second level is intelligent, manifesting his intelligence. He is not simply the percipient of a series of images, clouds sailing through the windy sky. He is asking *why*. He wants to understand something, he achieves a certain measure of understanding, and he formulates that understanding. Moreover, he formulates it in order to check, in order to see whether he does really have it, and that brings him up to another level where his rationality comes into play. He wants to know whether it really is so, whether it is correct, and by that he means the attaining of something absolute, something such that when he says, 'It is,' he means that it is impossible for anyone at any time to say, 'It is not,' and be right.

1.2 The Unity of the Subject as Given

While we have isolated three types of acts on three levels, we have also been talking about the knower, the subject. Is *that* given? It is given that there is sensing, perceiving, imagining, inquiring, understanding, conceiving, reflecting, grasping the unconditioned, and judging. But is there any one thing there, where by 'thing' is meant a unity-identity-whole that senses, perceives, imagines, inquires, and so on?

A first clarification of this issue is to say that the very nature of these acts is such that there has to be a unity. Inquiry is about empirical presentations. There must be one and the same that is inquiring and is perceiving, is that to which presentations are made. If we have perceptions and empirical presentations by themselves, and inquiry completely separate, the inquiry will not be about the presentations. For inquiry to

4 In the second part of this lecture, and again, more explicitly, in lecture 7, §2, The Notion of Objectivity, Lonergan introduces the question of the really real, approaching it in a carefully defined set of steps: the linguistic, cognitional, metaphysical, and critical issues. See our editorial note *c* to lecture 6.

be about the presentations, we have to have a unity. For the insight to be into the presentations, it must be one and the same that has the perceptions and has the insights. For conception to pick out what is essential to the insight in the presentations, it must be one and the same that is conceiving and understanding and perceiving. For reflection to be about the correctness of the conception, we have to have a unity. When the link between the conditions and the conditioned is grasped by understanding, and the fulfilment of the conditions is given on the perceptual level, or in consciousness which regards all three levels, the grasp of the unconditioned must be combined with the other acts in a single subject. For the judgment to proceed rationally from the grasp of the unconditioned, it must be one and the same that grasps the unconditioned and judges. The judgment is not simply a proper content; it depends upon all the rest; it says yes to what has been processed through the successive activities. On the side of the object, therefore, the single activities are all tied together.

That would be a proof that to have a knower of that type one has to postulate some unity. One at least must postulate a transcendental ego that performs all of these activities, even if it is not given in consciousness. Even if one's consciousness is simply of the single acts and there is no consciousness of one subject of the series of acts, still one has to postulate such a subject, the transcendental ego, the condition of the possibility of knowing.

But, next, is that subject simply a postulate or is it given in the process? I can compare my seeing with your seeing, and the seeing is similar in the two cases. It is the same type of activity. If I see the wall and you see the wall, the same sort of thing is going on in you as in me. If I compare my seeing and my hearing, the two types of activity are quite different. Seeing is of colors and shapes; hearing is of sound. I can see without hearing, and I can hear with my eyes closed. They are quite different types of activity. Nevertheless, they are very closely connected together, because they are both mine, my seeing and my hearing, and we know much more about the 'mine' than we do about the seeing and hearing. I am there, seeing and hearing, and the 'I' that is there defines a field of consciousness within which I segregate different elements and call one element 'seeing' and the other 'hearing.'

Consciousness of the subject is much more easily reached in introspection than consciousness of the different types of act. We were self-conscious before we started this course, but only through considerable labor have we perhaps been able to get a clearer notion of what insight is, to pick out this act from the series and see its differences from the others, to pick out reflective understanding from the rest and see its relations to the others, the way it grounds judgment, and so forth. Knowing the different types of act, separating and distinguishing one from the other, and seeing their relations to one another, is quite a trick; but being the fellow that makes the judgment and understands whatever he understands – we are pretty well aware of him. That unity is given; it is not merely a postulate; it is a verification of the transcendental ego, of what would have to be postulated if we did not have the consciousness of this identity that perceives and inquires and understands. They are *my* perceiving, *my* inquiring, *my* understanding, long before the perceiving, inquiring, and understanding are distinguished from one another. The unity of the subject is given prior to any thinking about it.

1.3 Self-affirmation

I have been talking about the unity of the subject, but to speak of unity is to use a concept, and to say that there is a unity is to make a judgment. The unity that is given is neither a concept nor a judgment about myself. It is given in this presence of the third type. What is present is not nonintelligent; it is both intelligent and rational. But that description of what is present involves understanding something about it and making judgments. That in which we verify is the self that is appropriated through self-presence. The self is appropriated in the sense that we conceive it and judge it, but that very conceiving and judging enables us to find it; and, fundamentally, we can find it insofar as we ask questions.

There is no doubt that we would have to go to great pains if we wanted to keep our eyes closed all the time and see nothing, and we would have to go to great expense if we wanted a soundproof room in order not to be disturbed by any noises.[5] But there is no doubt either about our intelligence. We can think of playing the stupid fellow, letting on that we do not understand. Sometimes it is a useful device to say, 'What do you mean? I don't get it.' But we want to do that with a slight suggestion that we are not as stupid as we seem. We want to be intelligent about our acts

---

5 The 'soundproof room' is not an idly chosen example. The lectures and especially the evening discussion periods suffered considerably from various blasts of noise, such as airplanes passing overhead. See also discussion 1, note 29; cf. *Insight* 182.

of stupidity, and similarly with regard to our rationality. You may play the fool, but you want to give a hint that you are a wise man when you are doing it. Your rationality is yourself, and it is yourself at an extremely intimate level; you cannot break away from it.

In self-presence, then, we have the materials in which we can verify this idea of the knower. Each one has to make the judgment for himself. If a person has no experiences, he will not be able to say that he is a knower insofar as knowing involves that element. If he has lots of experiences but understands nothing at all and never wants to know *why* about anything, maybe he lacks the second level. If he works out endless theories and never bothers to ask whether they are right, maybe he lacks the third level. Each one has to answer this question for himself, 'In that sense, am I a knower?'

The question has a second part. Is there an 'I'? Is the unity that perceives, understands, and judges merely a postulate, or are my insights into *my* sensible presentations, and is the rationality of my judgment dependent upon *my* insights and *my* experience? Is there the one subject, not in the sense of finding the concepts 'one' and 'subject' in oneself, but in the sense of finding in oneself somebody at home, presence of the third type, that is intelligent and rational and performs activities that are described in this fashion?

First of all, then, the unity is given. It is on the empirical level, where the empirical level does not mean sense, perception, and imagination, but presence in the third sense. The process of conceiving the knower as characterized by this set of activities is a process from internal experience to a conception of oneself. It is an objectification of oneself. It is thinking oneself. When I consider the possibility that I am a knower, I, as performing all these activities, am on one side, and I consider a conceptual object on the other side, namely, 'a knower in this sense.' I am both subject and object. As intelligently conceiving, I am the subject; and as intelligently conceived, I am the object. Similarly, on the third level, as rationally reflecting, grasping the unconditioned, and judging, I am the subject; but as affirmed in the judgment 'I am a knower,' I am part of the object. So self-knowledge – the process from being present to oneself, and finding typical activities in that self, to understanding how these activities are combined, and from that combination working out a theory of what it is to be a knower – is an objectification of oneself.

This can be applied, incidentally, to the problem in contemporary theology of the consciousness of Christ. Who is the 'I' that says 'I am'? If your theology is purely metaphysical, you have great difficulty arriving at the subject. Your metaphysics will just be about the object. But the question is about the subject.[a]

That is the general process. As I have said, each one has to make the judgment for himself. Each one has to come to his own conclusion and decide whether he knows anything about experience, intelligence, and reasonableness from his own personal experience. If he finds no reasonableness in himself, of course, we need not bother too much about what he has to say. If he finds no intelligence in himself, we need bother still less, for he will just be talking gibberish. There are a lot of tricks connected with this self-knowing. If a person is not a knower, then he is fairly well excluding himself from ordinary discussion. In other words, while it is a contingent fact that I am a knower, still de facto I am, and if I talk as though I were not, I am involved in contradiction. The contradiction is between what explicitly I say and what implicitly I am. As Aristotle said it, What do you do with the sceptic? You get him to talk.[6] He cannot talk absolute nonsense; otherwise he would not be putting forth good arguments for his position. If he does not talk absolute nonsense, you can bring out what implicitly he is by showing him the signs of what he is, revealed in his talking.

1.4 The Nature of the Account

It may be asked, Is this a descriptive account of the knower, or is it an explanatory account? Our distinction between description and explanation was between the type of knowledge that appeals ultimately to the relations of things to us and the type of knowledge that involves relations of things to one another. It is clear that this is an explanatory account, insofar as it isolates fundamental elements, distinctive steps in the cognitional process, which are definable by their relations to one another. The definition constitutes a closed network of relations. That closed network of relations is not, however, simply an abstract formalism; it has its meaning from our self-appropriation.

Again, while the account is explanatory, it is not hypothetical in the sense in which explanatory science is hypothetical. Each of the elements is directly verifiable. The physicist will deal with ultimates such as mass,

---

6 Aristotle, *Metaphysics*, IV, 4, 1005b 35 to 1006a 28. See also discussion 5 below, the end of § 9, Isomorphism and Objectivity.

temperature, and the electromagnetic field vectors, and he will probably agree that there may be more perfect, future theories in which such concepts will not have the fundamental role that they have in classical physics. They are hypothetically posited, because once they are posited one obtains the maximum of conclusions that one can verify. But one cannot verify that they are fundamental concepts. Whether they ultimately are fundamental can only be determined in terms of an ultimate theory, and it is very difficult to say that the ultimate theory has already been reached.

On the other hand, in our account of the knower the subject is not something hypothetical. The subject is the 'I' that says, 'I am a knower.' Insight is not simply a hypothesis. A behaviorist or a certain type of linguistic analyst may say that intelligence, insight, has a meaning insofar as there are modes of external behavior that show a man to be intelligent. If that were the only evidence, insight would be a hypothetical entity used to account for that type of behavior. But if, in your presence to yourself within your own consciousness, you are aware that there occur jumps, that periods of darkness are followed by periods of increasing light, catching on, understanding things and seeing how they hold together, then insight is not simply a hypothetical entity but something that is verified in your experience.

This account of the knower is explanatory insofar as the elements it contains are intelligibly related to one another. As such the account necessarily implies the unity of the subject that inquires about his experience, has insight into sensible data, and so on. There is an intelligible unity-identity-whole implicit in this set of terms. Moreover, each different type of act is related to the others. We have a relational structure in which the different types of event are intelligibly connected. There is also a necessity of a concrete unity-identity-whole, because the insight has to be into experiences of the one having the insight. One and the same – to omit words like 'person'[b] and so on – has to inquire and have the experiences; I cannot wonder about your experience; there has to be some communication of your experience; it has to become my experience somehow before I can inquire into it.

Is this account, then, descriptive or explanatory? It has the advantages of both, one may say. It has all the advantages of the concreteness of the descriptive type insofar as the elements and the unity are verifiable in consciousness. It has all the advantages of the explanatory type insofar as the different elements are of their very nature interdependently linked together in the process.

1.5 The Impossibility of Revision

There is a further point to be noticed.

In general one may say that any scientific conclusion can be improved on. All one has to do is come across further data that do not fit in with contemporary theory, and find a better theory that accounts both for the data at present explained and the new data. Then the new theory is put forth, and the old one is set aside. It is the process of revision. There is a theory, new data, and then a new theory which satisfies not only the data accounted for by the old theory, but also the further data that have been turned up by new investigation. Now this new theory may be all very well for the present; there may be nothing better to offer; but those who take this theory as a starting point and examine things a little further will reach a much more accurate account, and then this theory will be set aside as antiquated.

Now to our further point, another interesting property of our account of self-knowledge. Let us suppose that there occurs a revision. The revision will be based upon further data. The further data may be given either by external sense or by internal consciousness, by the subject present to himself; so to have a reviser there must be external sense or internal consciousness. Unless we have that we cannot get further data; we cannot have any data at all. Moreover, if there is to be a new theory, we hope it is something intelligent. If it is intelligent, it will result from insight. Again, we hope we will be able to express it. It is not enough to say, 'I have a wonderful insight into what knowledge really is, but I can't tell you what it is.' We hope we will be able to conceive it. Moreover, it will have to be not simply a theory but a verified theory. When the new theory is proposed we will want to know whether it is right, or if it is better than the old one; so there will have to be critical reflection in the new theory. Again, if we are going to accept the new theory we will want to grasp the unconditioned; so there will have to be the grasp of the unconditioned. On that grasp of the unconditioned will depend the judgment, otherwise we would be unreasonable. So the possibility of a revision presupposes this analysis.

Whatever the difficulties are, the possibility of a revision is excluded.

It is true that things can be said more accurately and more fully. There are all sorts of further questions that can be raised apropos of things said in *Insight*. But if it is true that this is a structure that excludes the possibility of a revision, in the sense that any future revision in any concrete sense of 'revision' would presuppose knowing to be precisely a structure of this type, we have arrived at a fundamental invariant pattern. Any future advance in self-knowledge may fill out this pattern with further details, may enrich it with all sorts of conclusions; but to be a revision it has to preserve this pattern.

1.6 Self-affirmation and Judgment of Fact

Another aspect of the affirmation 'I am a knower in the sense defined' is that a knower in that sense is involved in any concrete judgment of fact. If you know any fact at all, you have to have this process.

Because fact is concrete, it involves experience. What is apart from all experience is not fact in the ordinary sense of the word. One needs the experiential element either of external sense or of consciousness. Again, fact is not some indistinct, indeterminate something. When we talk about facts we do not mean something vague and imprecise; we mean something that has been pinned down. If a witness offers a fact which is very vague, the jury thinks the witness does not know much about the facts. Facts are clear and precise, and to obtain that clarity and precision we have to go beyond the level of mere experience and achieve some insight and some conception. All precision comes through intelligence and conception. Moreover, a fact has an element of the absolute: if it is a fact, that is all there is to it. There is something absolute to a fact, and so we use the phrase 'the unconditioned.'[7]

What we mean by fact is what is known through experience, understanding, and judging. Fact is not simply sensible presentation; it is not simply seeing my hand outstretched with something across it. It is conceiving it as a hand, conceiving what is across it as a piece of chalk, and saying, 'That is really so; the chalk is on his hand.' While there is a good deal of confused thinking and talking about facts as though they were already clear-cut just by taking a look, merely through sense experience, de facto you cannot have the precision of what is called a fact without conception,

7 Lonergan referred here to a fuller exposition in *Insight*, presumably pp. 281–83, 'Concrete Judgments of Fact'; see also pp. 331–32.

and you cannot have the absoluteness of fact without judgment. To put it more simply, any judgment presupposes the unconditioned or it is not absolute. The unconditioned presupposes a conception; otherwise you do not have a conditioned, something determinate about which to make your judgment. This conditioned inherent in the conception results from insight and inquiry, and you have to have something to have insight into and to inquire about; so you need experience.

2   The Notion of Being

When we turn to the notion of being,[8] there arises the question of the object of knowledge. So far we have been talking about knowing, but the natural question is, Knowing what? If we put the question that way we are using 'object' in its linguistic or grammatical sense, as the object of the transitive verb 'to know.' But you can also speak of objects in a cognitional or criteriological sense, and then you ask, 'Is the knowing objective?' We deal with the different meanings of the word 'objectivity' and with the question in what sense this type of knowing has objectivity, in chapter 13 of *Insight*.

One can speak of objects metaphysically, and then one distinguishes three types of objects: the agent object, the terminal object, and the final object. The agent object is illustrated by seeing. What one sees is colors, and the colors are part of the causative process in producing the seeing. If I see red and there is no red there to be seen, then something is wrong. The object of seeing is part of the agent, the efficient cause, that produces the act of external sense. If there are no sounds and you hear sounds, there is something wrong; and similarly with regard to all the external senses.

Secondly, there is the terminal object. When one says one imagines something, one means first of all that there is not something outside one that is causing the image; one is causing the image oneself; one is producing the image. The image is a term immanently produced by the imagination. The image that is formed in imagination is a terminal object; it is something that is produced by imagining.

---

8 Coffee break intervened before the second part of the lecture, and again the recorder was slightly late getting started. The first clear words are 'the notion of being'; it is possible Lonergan began with a reference to chapter 12 of *Insight*, and its title.

There is also a final object. We form images to have some sort of apprehension of what is possible. When we think, 'Will I do this? Well, I can see *him* doing that,' and he is not doing it yet, we are just imagining him doing it. But there is a finality to that imagining, and that is a final object. We have the Latin tag – actually, it comes from Aristotle – *motus in imaginem est idem ac motus in imaginatum*.[9] Imagining both produces an image and wants to represent some object, what is imagined. There is a distinction between the image and what is imagined. We do not produce in ourselves what is imagined, otherwise we could produce in ourselves anything sensible. But we form the image within ourselves to move to the final object.

Finally, we can speak of objects in a critical sense. Is this type of knowing a knowing of what is real? We are using 'knowing' in a very determinate sense, as the combination of experiencing, understanding, and judging. When you reach the judgment, you have a closed unit that is expressed in a determinate proposition. Through the judgment you know something. As in the imagination, so in judgment we can speak of a terminal and a final object. The terminal object which you produce in yourself is the concept and the judgment, and through that concept and judgment there is a finality, a final object. But is that final object, known through the concept and the judgment – is that really what is real? That is the critical question, and it begins to arise in chapter 14 of *Insight*. Metaphysical analysis presupposes an answer to both this critical question and the cognitional question of objectivity (chapter 13). But we can throw in the above analysis on the way; it may provide a certain amount of clarification, since we hope to get to metaphysics later on. Now, however, we consider for a start an object in the linguistic sense. What do you know from this type of process? What is the object of the transitive verb 'to know' that we use for the activity 'knowing'? That is the present question.[c]

2.1 The Range of Knowing

One can divide objects into two classes, limited and unlimited. Sight sees only colors; there is no seeing without seeing colors, including black and white. Sight has no cognizance of sound, but there are sounds; therefore,

9 For an example of Thomist usage, see *Summa theologiae*, 2–2, q. 81, a. 3, ad 3m; Thomas (ibid., 3, q. 8, a. 3, ad 3m) refers us to Aristotle's *Librum de memoria et reminiscentia* (see chapter 1, 450b 27).

the object of sight is a limited object. Hearing is hearing only sounds; you do not hear colors. Hearing has a limited object. You can imagine only what is sensible; imagination has a limited object. What about the process of knowing? Has it a limited or an unlimited object?

If the object of knowing were unlimited, it might be unlimited in either of two senses: in the sense that what you can actually know, knowing as it is actually achieved, is unlimited; or in the sense that the effort to know does not stop at any finite limit. We have no experience of anyone whose actual achievement in knowing is unlimited in the first sense. We may talk of the Seven Sages of Greece or of any other master of knowledge, but we have never met a man who knew absolutely everything about everything. There is no past instance by which we can show that the actual achievement of our knowing was unlimited. Indeed, we can provide arguments that show that the actual achievement of our knowing, as long as our knowing is simply a process of the type specified, is going to be limited. We will consider that in a moment. But is our capacity to know, the range of our knowing, unlimited in the second sense? Is there no line at which we stop? Has our capacity to know, our desire to know, our range of possible vision, a horizon beyond which there is no question of our knowing? Or is there no horizon? In the sense of radical potency, radical teleology, radical finality, I think it can be shown that our knowing is unlimited.

We may ask the question, Might there not be something so totally different from our categories of knowing that it could not possibly fall within the range of knowing of this type? At least we raise the question, and the range of our knowing has its fundamental basis in asking questions. Is there an a priori limit to the questions we can ask, to the sort of thing we can desire to know? We can ask if there is anything beyond our total range. If we ask that, we have already asked a question about existence with regard to what lies beyond any hypothetical range one might like to set. Our range of interest extends beyond any finite limit that one cares to set. The mere fact that we make a hypothesis about a finite limit, any finite limit, to the range of possible questions reveals the unrestricted character of our knowing. I am not referring to questions that we hope to answer, or that can involve answers within the field of actual achievement. I am talking about a radical limitation to our mind. Is there a radical limitation to our mind, such that the question cannot even arise? There is not such a limit if we ask whether there are objects beyond the natural range; when we put that question our interest already transcends any hypothetical range. If this is so, then the range of our intellect, the radical range and not the range of what will fall within actual achievement at any future date, is unlimited. The range of our radical capacity, the range of our desire to know, then, is unrestricted. The object is everything about everything.

You can continue to ask further questions about any particular thing until you understand absolutely every aspect and every relation in which the thing is involved. What is true of any particular thing is true of all of them. You can keep on asking questions. To brush questions aside in principle – here it is not a matter of saying it would not be practical for me to pay attention to further questions now, because I have no hope in my lifetime of arriving at the answers; that is not brushing questions aside in principle, but giving a reason for not attending to these questions – but just to brush questions aside in principle is to run counter to the nature of one's intellect. It is an obscurantism. The radical meaning of obscurantism is implicitly or explicitly holding the thesis that the range of our knowledge, the range of our desire to know, is limited.

2.2 The Notion of Being

The cognitional name for the object that includes absolutely everything, every aspect of everything, is being. When St Thomas wants to prove that the object of our intellect is *ens*, he adduces the Aristotelian account of intellect, the *potens omnia facere et fieri*, able to make and become all things, a potential omnipotence, and he says that because it is *omnia*, it is *ens*, being.[10] Being does not lie within any restricted genus. While it can be divided up into beings of different kinds, being itself is not some limited kind. It corresponds to the negation of a finite limit, to everything about everything. Being, then, is a final object, the term of an unrestricted tendency, desire, effort to know. We work towards it. As through imagination we have an immanently produced object, an image, and through the image have a representation of what is imagined, so through understanding and judgment we have immanently produced objects, what is conceived and what is affirmed, through which we know what is, being. And that being can be considered in either of two ways, distributively or collectively. Distributively, one talks about beings; collectively, one talks about the totality of everything that is.

10 Thomas Aquinas, *Summa theologiae*, 1, q. 79, a. 7 c.

We have been determining the final object of our intellect from very general considerations. We now have to attempt to pin things down more precisely. If being is the object towards which our intellectual knowledge tends, then to know is to know being; being is the object of the transitive verb 'to know.' We have a fundamental identity: intellectual knowing of the type we have described and explained is identical with knowing being. One may have critical difficulties at once and say, 'That being is being in quite a different sense from what I understand; that isn't the being that really is.' Such critical difficulties are considered in chapter 14 of *Insight*, where we turn to metaphysics.[11] For the time being, we will use 'being' as the everything towards which our intellectual apparatus in principle tends. After we find out something more about it, we can raise the question whether that being which is known in that fashion is reality, or whether reality, as it is for some people, is something we know all about without any use of experience, understanding, and judgment.

We have spoken of being as final object. We set up an object that is unlimited, not in the sense of actual achievement, but in the sense that there is no a priori barrier to the questions you might ask. It is never intelligent or reasonable to brush aside questions without any reason whatever. If your intellect were something that was confined within a finite range, then there could possibly be questions that you could brush aside without any reason whatever, and so a certain measure of radical obscurantism would be justified. But if no obscurantism whatever is justified, then in principle there is no finite limit to our knowing. What the effort to know heads to is unrestricted, and because it is unrestricted we name it being. There is some association, then, between being, which is not within any genus and includes all genera, and the unrestricted objective of our knowing.

2.3 Intelligent and Rational Finality

We said that being is a final object. We must now consider more closely the finality involved. Traditionally, one speaks of finality or teleology, but one may use more popular terms such as drive, tendency, appetite, or desire.

A fundamental distinction is made between unconscious and conscious

11 See also lecture 8, A Definition of Metaphysics, in the present volume.

finality. According to Aristotle, any object has a finality to be at the center of the earth, and that is why objects fall. But if objects have that finality, at least it is a nonconscious finality; it is not something that is in consciousness. A second type of finality is conscious. To be hungry is to have a finality for food, to tend towards food, to be orientated towards eating. It is not an unconscious but a conscious finality, and the hungrier you are, the more conscious it is. People who had been in the German concentration camps prior to and during the last war said that their hunger practically excluded the possibility of any image except food; their attention was fixed on food. Again, some ascribe the fact that there is so much hunger in Russia to a deliberate policy: if the people do not have enough to eat, then they will be thinking about food and nothing else; they will not be up to anything more mischievous than that. There is, then, not only unconscious finality but also conscious finality.

The finality of which we are speaking is not unconscious, and it is not the type of consciousness illustrated by hunger. It is a finality of intellectual and rational consciousness. Intellectual and rational consciousness has a finality to the unlimited objective, to being. The finality is in what is present to itself when it is intellectually alert or critically reflective. To wonder is to manifest the finality of an intelligent subject, and to be critically reflective is to manifest the finality of a rational subject. We move from a level of sense presentations, perception, and images to a level of insight and conception, inasmuch as we are intellectually alert, inasmuch as we have not only verbal questions or questions conceptually expressed, but also that root of questioning that is intellectual curiosity, wanting to understand something. We move from the level of conception to critical reflective consciousness inasmuch as we are the root that is manifested in such questions as, Is it so? All efforts to understand and all understanding, all efforts to conceive and all conceiving, depend upon the wonder expressed in the questions, What? Why? and How often? All efforts to grasp the virtually unconditioned and actually grasping the unconditioned, all efforts to judge and actual judging, depend upon the desire that is expressed in such questions as, Is it really so? With wonder we have the finality that sets the process going, the finality that lifts us above the level of merely empirical consciousness to the level of intellectual consciousness; and then emerges the finality that lifts us above intellectual consciousness to rational consciousness. We are dealing, then, with a finality, a teleology, that is not unconscious but conscious, and not just empirically conscious but intellectually and rationally conscious.[12]

2.4 Finality and the Contents of Knowing

Intelligent and rational finality underpins all contents in our knowing; it penetrates them all; and it goes beyond them all.

First, it underpins all contents in our knowing. Unless you inquire you do not give insight a chance to arise. It is insofar as you are wondering about the data, trying to understand them, that you are in the pattern of experience within which insights arise. It is insofar as the experience ceases being merely experience and becomes an object for inquiry that there is illumination of the phantasm as a result of the basic activity of the *intellectus agens*. Further, this desire to understand underpins the understanding; and when you have understood, it underpins the conception. In the conception you want to pin down accurately what you grasped in the insight. The desire to understand heading to its full fruition requires that you say *what* exactly, that you formulate exactly what you would hold as a result of understanding things in that fashion. When you reach conception, again, the presence of a fundamental finality or teleology of intellect reveals itself in a further question. It is not enough to conceive; you want to know whether it is really so. The finality will not be satisfied with anything less than an absolute, an unconditioned. If you are to judge, the finality requires of you a grasp of the unconditioned, and if you have grasped the unconditioned it obliges you to judge; it is your rationality. All of these activities are underpinned by that finality.

Not only does this drive towards being, this intellectually and rationally conscious finality towards being, underpin all the contents and activities, it also penetrates them. When you are trying to understand, you are trying to understand being. When you are trying to conceive, you are trying to conceive being. When you do understand and conceive, what you understand and conceive is being, because that is what you are

---

12 Throughout this paragraph Lonergan made constant reference to the nine-arrowed diagram he had drawn on the blackboard (see note 2 above), but with special emphasis on the two arrows that represent the two basic questions, what *Insight* called questions for intelligence and questions for reflection.

tending towards.[13] Our understanding is a component in a knowing, and knowing is knowing being. We have decided to call the object of the transitive verb 'to know' being, because it is unlimited. The content of any particular act heads toward knowing being, and when you obtain the final increment, when you make the judgment, then you know some aspect of some being.

The matter may be illustrated by a consideration of the standard question, What is subsistence? There is a whole series of scholastic opinions on it. Usually in textbooks on metaphysics, the first chapter is on substance and everything is plain sailing; but the last chapter is on subsistence, and it is all disputed questions. Yet it is approximately the same question in both cases. The question is put by Cajetan in terms of the difference betwen humanity and man.[14] When you have an insight, you are given certain data, and you ask, 'Why are these data a man?' You grasp form, soul, and then you form the concept. You combine these data with this intelligible unity as you utter a concept.[d] What is the concept that you utter, humanity or man? What do you know by combining matter and form? What do you know where matter is particular, insofar as you are not forming a universal concept but a particular concept, even when you are dealing with the question of subsistence? Is it just matter and form, or is it matter and form as a differentiation of being? If it is just matter and form, what you conceive as a result of grasping soul in these data is humanity; but if it is this matter and form as a determination of being, it is a man. Humanity, *id quo est*, is abstract; man, *id quod est*, is concrete. Humanity is a principle limiting the being to being a man.

What is it that you conceive? If you attend only to the sensible presentation and the insight, then what you conceive is humanity, a compound of matter and form. But if you consider the finality of intellect towards being, what you are trying to conceive is being, and matter and form are a determination of that being, and you conceive a man. De facto, we form concrete terms before abstract ones because of the finality of intellect towards being. We have the content 'being' from the desire to know, and

13 The paragraph 'This finality ...' (fourth after the present one) is found at this point on the tapes; but its editorial relocation agrees better with Lonergan's announced sequence: 'finality underpins all contents ... penetrates them all ... goes beyond them all.'

14 Cajetan, *In IIIm*, q. 4, a. 2, vi. Our reference is to volume 12 of the Leonine edition of the *Summa theologiae*, where Cajetan's commentary is published.

the determination of the content from the intelligible form in the sensible matter. According to Cajetan's theory of subsistence, 'man' adds to 'humanity' a mode. On the present analysis, 'man' means a being. You do not know a being until you make a judgment, but you are thinking about being on the level of intelligence.

The notion of being, then, not only underpins all contents, it penetrates them. Because your understanding is a component in the process heading towards knowing, and knowing is identical with knowing being, your understanding is a determination of being, and you form the concept 'man.' On the level of intelligence you are just thinking a man. You do not know that a man is until you make a judgment. You think man, though, and not just humanity. In cognitional process there are not merely data of sense and the form grasped in insight, but also finality, the intellectually and rationally conscious finality of intellect towards being. Because of the finality, this humanity is thought as part of a whole, as the matter and form of something that is compounded not merely of matter and form but also of existence. This illustrates the penetration of all contents by being. Your questions are questions about being: What is it? Is it so? Your questions have their root in this fundamental finality.

This finality also goes beyond all contents. Any degree of understanding gives rise to further questions, to further understanding, and when you reach the further understanding you ask whether it is so. Affirming 'It is so' will itself give rise to further questions. When you grasp the unconditioned, you want to move to the level of knowing being. When you affirm, 'It is so,' you have reached it, but you have not entirely reached it. You know only some little aspect of being in any true judgment. You reach judgment only to raise further questions; there is no limit to further questions. For example, you may pin down your whole account of knowing, but others can easily go on to ask, 'What about this? And what about this?' You will have to think things out more precisely, more fully, to be able to deal with those further questions. When you arrive at judgment you complete one step in order to have one total increment, but that total increment is almost an infinitesimal. Because being is unlimited, you start over again, find a further aspect, add it on, and so on. Knowledge is something that gradually accumulates through our living. Because judgment is contextual, each new judgment has to fit into the set of judgments that is already determined.

So this intelligent and rational finality underpins, penetrates, and goes beyond all contents.

Further, it is the core of meaning. There has been a great deal of discussion in this century on the meaning of meaning. What is it to mean? Whenever you mean, you are thinking or you are knowing. Thinking is a stage; you think in order to know. Knowing is knowing being. Thinking, then, is in order to know being, and at the level of thinking, you are thinking about being. The object of all meaning is being. It may be true that the only beings that are, are the sensibly given that you can point to, but that is a particular philosophical theory, not a general analysis of meaning. The core of all meaning is being. However, determining what beings there are to be meant in a serious fashion requires answers to particular questions.

2.5 Finality as a Structured Notion

Further, this finality is a structured notion. To know is to know being, but knowing is structured. Knowing is a matter of experience, understanding, and judgment. Consequently, knowing being involves a structure by identity. Insofar as knowing develops on three stages, it is inevitable that the known involves a combination of three contents. If knowing is experiencing *and* understanding *and* judging, and if all three are required to have the known, then the known will involve a content from the experiencing, a content from the understanding, and a content from the judging, all combined into a single object.

This combination of all three contents in a single object is what is classically termed the proportionate object of our intellect – potency, form, and act. Potency, form, and act are constituents of a single concrete being in the same way as experiencing, understanding, and judging are constituents of a single increment in knowing. Because the knowing involves three acts, and each act has its own content, there will be in the proportionate known three different types of content corresponding to the differences in the three types of act. To establish theorems about that is a subsequent task, but this illustrates the fact that if knowing is structured, then what is known about being is going to be structured.

Again, if being is the object of the verb 'to know,' and our knowing is by inquiry and insight, reflection and judgment, then to say that something is a being is also to say that it is intelligible. The intelligible is what you can know by understanding and judging. You may mean by 'being' the 'really real' that is known without any experience or understanding or judgment; but if being is the object of knowing in the sense we have developed, then that being has to be intelligible – it has to be what you know insofar as you understand correctly. And if being is intelligible, it immediately divides into two types: first, the being that is totally intelligible in itself independent of anything else, the formally unconditioned, the *ens per essentiam*; secondly, a being whose intelligibility does depend upon something else, whose intelligibility is the intelligibility of the virtually unconditioned, the *ens per participationem*.

So we have arrived at a notion of being that is unrestricted, that includes everything about everything, that is not within any genus. It underpins, goes before, penetrates, runs into, coincides with, and goes beyond any particular act of knowing and any particular content of knowing which we may have. It is the core of all meaning,[15] and it is a structured notion.

We have here used our analysis of knowledge to develop a theory of being. At the present time it is just a *theory*, a hypothesis, an object of thought. But there are many theories. Parmenides, Plato, Aristotle, Scotus, Henry of Ghent, Hegel – all had theories on the matter. For Scotus, to take one example, being was some minimal content; for Hegel, being was again some minimal content, but without the Scotist idea of apprehension as taking a look. Which, then, is the right notion of being?

For Aquinas, the highest intellectual habit is wisdom. It is wisdom that selects the terms that determine the principles which determine everything in our knowledge. But how do we acquire wisdom? We cannot use principles here, for wisdom is their source. Aquinas would derive wisdom from two sources: (1) from Aristotelian metaphysics, and (2) from the Holy Ghost. In this lecture we have been developing a systematic propaideutic to wisdom. We begin with the notion of being. One's choice of the notion of being is going to determine everything else. So we have to have the right notion of being to acquire wisdom, but also we have to have wisdom to settle what the right notion of being is.[e]

---

15 All three of our tapes end somewhere in this paragraph. The rest of the text is reconstructed from notes taken during the lecture.

7

The A Priori and Objectivity[1]

1   The Question of the A Priori

Last week we worked out an account of cognitional process, and by positing an object of the verb 'to know' we worked out a notion of being.[2] Being is what you desire to know when you inquire; it is what you are trying to conceive when you conceive; and it is what you know when you affirm it. Now this notion of being was worked out without any mention whatever of any being. It is a notion of being that is completely compatible with an idealism that would assert that there is just one being, the one being that is the Absolute Idea. Again, the notion of being is quite compatible with an objective fact, that there is nothing whatever intelligible in data – it is just a kaleidoscope.[a] It is compatible with a world in which there are no substances except the subject, the unity-identity-whole that experiences, understands, and judges; it does not necessitate – that idea we've given you – that there exist any substances. And so on and so forth.

The notion of being that we have worked out seems to have been developed with complete independence of any being, and that naturally gives rise to the following questions: Is our notion of being simply an a

1 The seventh lecture, Tuesday, August 12, 1958.
2 Recording started at the word 'week' of our first line (DJS reel). Notes taken indicate there was no significant loss. 'Last week' – because there were six lectures the first week, Monday to Saturday, and four the second, Tuesday to Friday.

priori category that is imposed upon data? Is our position Kantian? If our position is not Kantian, how does it differ from the Kantian position? There is a whole series of questions connected with our approach to the notion of being.[3]

1.1 The Notion of the A Priori

'The a priori' is a term used in three contexts. First, it is used with regard to reasoning or inference. An a priori inference is from the cause to the effect; an a posteriori inference is from the effect to the cause; an *a simultaneo* inference is from the mere concept of the thing. You cannot have an a priori proof of the existence of God because God has no cause. Any argument for God's existence in terms of cause and effect has to be from the effect to the cause, an a posteriori argument. The Anselmian or Cartesian or Leibnizian arguments for the existence of God, which do not appeal to effects, are from the concept, and they are named *a simultaneo*. That is a fundamental use of a priori that antedates Kant.

Kant spoke of the a priori particularly with regard to propositions or judgments. His notion of an a priori proposition or judgment is that it is absolutely independent of experience. One can say that, if a man undermines his house, he should have known a priori that it would cave in, but that is simply a relative a priori. He would have to know beforehand from experience that heavy bodies fall. While he did not know beforehand from experience that *his* house was going to fall, yet he could have known; it was from other experiences that he knew that heavy bodies fall. If we want an absolutely a priori proposition, we want a proposition that is not only independent of this particular experience, but of experiences generally.[4]

Kant assigns absolutely a priori propositions two characteristics, necessity and universality. Strict necessity is never given in experience; experience is simply a fact. Again, strict universality is never given; you do not obtain a general law merely from observation. You can say, 'It usually happens,' but you cannot say, 'It always happens,' because you are not

3 Lonergan added a remark on 'the series of questions': 'I think they were bothering some of you[b] right from the start, and we have to get down and do something about it.'
4 Kant, *Critique of Pure Reason*, A1–2/B1–6; Norman Kemp Smith 41–45.

present on all occasions, particularly on future occasions. So strict necessity and strict universality – either one or the other – are taken as criteria of a priori propositions.

Kant further divides a priori propositions into analytic and synthetic. In the analytic proposition the predicate states what is implicitly contained in the notion of the subject. In a synthetic proposition the predicate goes beyond the subject.[5] As far as I know, no one seems to dispute that analytic propositions are a priori, insofar as they are universal and necessary. It is not experience as such that gives universality; it is not experience as such that gives necessity. With regard to a priori synthetic propositions, there are some scholastics who admit that they exist, but perhaps the majority deny that there are any – that is the general scholastic position. Josef de Vries, however – to give a single example – holds that the principle of contradiction and the principle of causality are extensive.[6] He does not say a priori synthetic but extensive. 'A cannot be not-A' is an extensive proposition. Not-A is not part of the content of A; to say 'Not-A' is to go outside the content of A. With regard to the principle of causality, if you say, for example, that a contingent being lacks intelligibility in itself, you are remaining within the content of the subject; but if you go on to say that a contingent being must be caused by some other being, you are going outside of the subject.

A third sense of the a priori was also introduced by Kant with regard to intuitions and concepts. Kant holds that there are a priori intuitions, a priori concepts, and also a priori ideas.[7] He reaches an a priori intuition by removing from intuition all of its contingent elements. If you are looking at a body and you remove the color, shape, hardness, its impenetrability, and so on, you are left with empty space; you don't remove that: it is intrinsic to having an intuition. So the space is a priori. Similarly, with regard to the concept, by a process of removal you are finally left with something that you do not obtain from experience, and Kant calls that a priori.

So much for the notion of the a priori.

5 Ibid. A6–7/B10–11; Norman Kemp Smith 48–49.
6 Josef de Vries, *Denken und Sein* (Freiburg im Breisgau: Herder & Company, 1937) 114. The bibliographical data were given by Lonergan.
7 The phrase 'and also a priori ideas' was added in the tone of an afterthought, and Lonergan did not go on to expand the notion, though he did deal with intuitions and concepts.

1.2 The Central Issue

Now the real issue is, How much of knowing is from the subject, and how much is from the object? That is the fundamental question of fact. We can examine our knowing and distinguish its different elements or parts or components and pick out those that come from the subject and those that come from the object – that is a question of fact. But there is also the question of significance: depending upon your notion of what knowing ought to be or must be, you can attach an enormous or a negligible significance to the question.

Knowing can be conceived as intrinsically or essentially a matter of confrontation, of taking a look, seeing what is there, intuition. Since knowing, on this account, is what comes from the look, anything that comes from the subject is not knowing at all; and if it comes from the subject, that just means it is not knowing. Knowing is what is given in the look, and what is known is what is out there to be looked at and seen when one looks. One may go further and distinguish between sensible looks (looks through one's senses) and spiritual looks (looks with one's intellect, interior and spiritual x-rays that penetrate the essence of things and see the essence that is there).

On the other hand, if knowing is conceived not as looking but as an ontological perfection of the subject, then you might say that the more knowing there is in the subject that comes from himself the better off he is. The premise that knowing is essentially a matter of looking is denied by this view. A fellow who knows something is better off than a fellow who is ignorant; an intelligent person is better off than a stupid one, and he is more likely to know something. Knowing is a perfection of the subject that knows. It may be that knowing, in some cases, includes knowing something else, but that is incidental. Looking is not the essence of knowing. We have knowing when we have experience, understanding, and grasp of the unconditioned, and those terms say nothing about looking. When we examined the subject, we found experiences, acts of understanding and formulation, grasp of the unconditioned and judgment. Our account of knowing was simply of perfections in the subject.

If you conceive knowing as a perfection, then the question of the a priori, of what comes from the subject and what comes from the object, is of minor moment. You are not upset: 'This comes from the subject?

Well and good. He has the perfection by nature. This comes from the object? Well, he had to be helped by the object to arrive at knowing.' It is only on the assumption that knowing is intrinsically a 'looking at' that the question of the a priori has any great significance. We have, then, really two questions, a question of fact and a question of significance. It is the question of significance that concerns us, and the notion one has of what knowing is makes the question of the a priori of either major or minor significance.

We are concerned in particular with the notion of being. We worked out a theory of knowing in chapters 1 to 10 of *Insight*, affirmed the fact of knowing in chapter 11, and in chapter 12 we wrote down the identity: knowing is knowing being. From that identity we worked out our notion of being. We put an object after the verb, and we said that object was being. But knowing is natural to us; therefore, knowing being is natural to us.

Our account certainly involves a dependence of knowing on the subject. But it is not simply our account. We know because it *is* natural to us. Plants do not know, because it is *not* natural to them to know. Animals have sense knowledge, but not intellectual knowledge. But we know. Why? We have a different nature. Again, at least in Thomist philosophy and theology, different types and modes of knowledge are distinguished: there is the knowledge of man in this life, the knowledge of the separated soul after death, the knowledge of the angels, and the knowledge of God. A different account of the knowledge is worked out in each case, because one account states what is natural to man in this life, and other accounts state what is or would be natural or possible in a separated soul, or in an angel, or in God.

The question, then: Since knowing is something natural, if you identify knowing with knowing being – and it is rather difficult not to, because otherwise it is knowing nothing; it is not really a free choice – then you are set with some sort of problem. We will take the problem, first of all, in traditional scholastic terms, and secondly in terms of the Kantian definition of the a priori,[8] that which is absolutely independent of experience. And, in answer to the problem, we will work out in just what sense our notion of being is from the subject, a priori.

8 See below, §§ 1.4 to 1.7.

1.3 The Notion of Being as Natural

First, in ordinary scholastic terms the distinction is between what is known by nature and what is known by acquisition. Besides natural knowing and knowing by acquisition, there is also infused knowing, the infused intellectual habits – faith, prudence, and wisdom, the gifts of the Holy Ghost of which theologians speak, and so on. There is also bestowed knowing, the beatific vision. All of these distinctions are traditionally made with regard to man. With regard to God, the scholastic theory is that God by his nature knows himself, everything that is possible, and everything that is actual. He does this with no dependence whatever on the object; the object entirely depends on him, and it is a case of knowing. In Thomist theory, the angels know themselves continuously by nature, and they know God by knowing themselves as in an image, continuously and habitually, that is, when they please. The angels have connatural species by which they know other things. There is no theory whatever, either in divine knowledge or for that matter in angelic knowledge, of a knowing that is not simply natural; even the species, while infused, are connatural. In man, there is no actual knowledge by nature. We are born ignorant. Nature gives us nothing in act.ᶜ However, we have by nature the potency to know; all our cognitional faculties are from nature in the broad sense. While in modern philosophy nature is contrasted with spirit, in scholastic philosophy nature is a more general term; it is whatever you know when you understand. That is the terminology I have been using. So, when you understand man, you understand him to have by nature the capacity to know.

Consequently, while by nature we have knowing in potency, it is by acquisition that we move to knowing in act. Our potency to know, our capacity to know, is from nature, but any actual knowing involves some influence from the object. So, while it is by nature that we have sight and are able to see, still it is not without colored objects, without light, that we actually do see anything. When your eyes are closed and you press your eyeballs, you actuate the sense of sight, and you do see colors. An object is needed to effect the transition from the potency to see to the act of seeing. Again, sight sees nothing but the colored, the luminous; by nature it is restricted to that. The potency determines the range of possible objects attained by ocular vision. Similarly, by nature hearing is confined to a determinate range of sound, of possible objects; but actually hearing a sound requires an activity from an object. Then, with regard to intellect, the sensible object and the activity of the agent intellect are needed. So, in traditional theory, with regard to intellectual knowledge, we have by nature the agent intellect that uses our sensible knowledge to produce acts of understanding. The capacity to understand, the agent intellect, the sensitive potencies, and correlations among these three are from nature; but an actuation of the process requires, first, the actual perceptions and the formation of images, and then the intervention of inquiry at that occasion. When inquiry has intervened, we begin to have acts of understanding.

Moreover, in intellect the habits of science in general are all acquired. The human intellect, at the start, is like a blackboard on which nothing is written. It is only gradually that we acquire the sciences. Still, there is a reference to something known by nature in Aristotle, namely, the principle of contradiction, and in St Thomas the *habitus principiorum* is described not as an acquired habit but as a natural habit. You do not have to teach people the principle of contradiction; they know that by nature; it is natural knowledge. Further, as these principles all regard being, St Thomas also affirms that being is naturally known. Just as sense – sight, for example – is a potency that by nature is determined to a certain range of possible objects, so also intellect has by nature a determinate range. It is *potens omnia facere et fieri*; its range is everything. According to St Thomas, because its range is everything, its range is being.

St Thomas also speaks of a natural desire to know God by his essence. He develops the idea through about thirty-eight chapters in the *Summa contra Gentiles*. The argument throughout the long section on the finality of human life stands upon the natural desire to have the beatific vision, to know God by his essence, and that idea remains fundamental in the *pars prima* and the *prima secundae* of the *Summa theologiae*. A desire to know God by his essence is something natural. It is not something acquired, produced in us, something we get out of objects.[9]

According to traditional scholastic theory, there is in man a set of potencies with determinate ranges, and there is even a natural habit in intellect itself that regards the first principles of being and by implication makes the notion of being itself natural. In the doctrine found in St Thomas there is the equation between knowing and knowing being:

9 Thomas Aquinas, *Summa contra Gentiles*, 3, cc. 25–63; *Summa theologiae*, 1, q. 12; 1–2, q. 3, a. 8. See also Bernard Lonergan, 'The Natural Desire to See God' (1949), in *Collection* (CWL 4) 81–91.

knowing is natural; therefore, knowing being is natural. Being is somehow a priori? The answer to that problem is that traditionally being is
said to be known by nature; it is natural knowledge.

This is not the type of theory of knowledge that says knowing must be
identified with looking, that if there is anything from the subject at all it
is not knowing. If we acknowledge a natural habit, if we acknowledge
that there are not only acquired habits in the intellect, but that there is
also a natural habit of first principles on which absolutely everything else
depends, then we are not free to jump to the conclusion that knowing
must be looking, and so we have no reason to be upset if knowing is said
to be knowing being. Knowing is natural, and therefore knowing being
is natural. Knowing being is natural insofar as we have natural potencies
and some natural habits. The whole of our knowing is not by acquisition,
by the action of objects on us; part of it is had from nature. We have some
resemblance to God, who is completely independent of all objects, and
to the angels, who are largely independent of objects.

1.4 Inquiry and Experience

We have discussed the question of the a priori in terms of traditional
categories. While we do not find St Thomas or the scholastics generally
talking about the a priori in the Kantian sense, still they have their own
way of talking about such things, that is, by making a distinction between
what is known naturally and what is known by acquisition. However,
the distinction between what is known naturally and what is known by
acquisition is not exactly the Kantian distinction between the a priori
and the a posteriori. The a priori is what is absolutely independent of
experience. So we can put our question again. To what extent is our
intending being, conceiving being, knowing being, absolutely independent of experience? In what sense, then, is our knowledge of being a
priori?

We have to distinguish the series of stages in which our knowing comes
into action.[10] There is a flow of sensations, perceptions, and images.
There is wondering: What? Why? How often? There is insight into the
presentations of this flow, into the sensible presentations or into the

---

10 Reference again to the figure used repeatedly of the nine arrows, with
the remark, 'We have done so by a triple level of arrows. Each arrow
represents a flow.'

presentations of one's own consciousness, and there are the formulations, conceptions, suppositions that result from the insight. Then there is another type of question, the critical attitude with respect to the formulation: Is that right? Finally, there is grasping the unconditioned and judging.

The fundamental moment in the notion of being lies in the capacity to wonder and reflect, and that as potency we have from nature. If a person naturally does not have the capacity to wonder, to be surprised by what he sees or hears or feels, to ask why, to ask what's happening, what's up, then there is no remedy; there is nothing we can do. We cannot endow people with intelligence. Intelligence fundamentally is this capacity to ask questions, and this capacity is entirely from nature. It was from this capacity that we drew an essential moment in showing that knowing is knowing being, or what precisely is meant by being. We said that we can ask questions indefinitely; no matter what we may try to think up that lies outside the range of our possible knowledge, still we wonder whether it is, whether there is anything beyond. We ask questions even with regard to the beyond. Because our questions are about being, and the range of our capacity for asking questions is unlimited, being is absolutely universal and absolutely concrete, the object towards which knowing moves.

So we have something from nature that provides us with a clue as to what the object of our knowing is, namely, absolute universality and concreteness. What our knowing aims at is knowing everything about everything. On the level of potency, this is from nature, and it is independent of experience. We must have it to be able to ask questions, to wonder, to set the process going. However, the occurrence of actual wonder, actual inquiry, is not absolutely independent of experience. We cannot wonder or inquire without having something about which to wonder or inquire; and it is the flow of sensations, perceptions, and images that provides the materials about which one wonders or inquires. So actual wondering has at least an occasion, an object, supplied from experience. The experience provides the material about which inquiry actually occurs. The potency is from nature; the exercise involves experience.

1.5 Understanding and Experience

There is a difference between the dependence of the exercise of inquiry upon experience and the dependence of the insight upon experience. One might say that the experience provides materials about which one inquires; it provides the materials on which agent intellect operates. On the other hand, the insight depends upon the experience as upon an object; it is an insight into the presentation. As St Thomas puts it in the *Quaestio disputata De anima*, about article 16 (you can get the reference in my *verbum* articles[11]), images are not simply an occasion for insight, as Plato held; they are not simply a disposition, as Avicenna held, but they are the object. The images present to our intellects, to our understanding, their object. And he quotes the familiar phrase from Aristotle that images stand to understanding as colors stand to sight. The image is an object with respect to the insight: it is the object in the same sense as the color is the object of seeing. Just as inquiry, then, requires the experiential flow to have the materials about which it inquires, in a more fundamental sense the insight's dependence is more manifest because the flow is not simply an occasion for the insight or a disposition for the insight.[12]

There is a point to notice about the intelligibility of the image. Qua image, it is simply potential intelligibility, it is not actually intelligible; qua understood, it is the intelligible in act, identical with the act of understanding. Color as seen is not on the wall actually, it is there potentially; color as seen is identical with the act of seeing. Not that the intelligibility grasped is only in the act of understanding: it is potentially in the image[d] from the fact that the image causes it.

When we move to conception or formulation, the matter is more complex, since we form concepts in many ways. There are three cases: abstract essence, 'humanity'; particularized essence, 'this instance of humanity'; and the universal or particular thing, 'man' or 'this man.' While this does not exhaust the list of possible modes of conception, it does provide us with a sufficient basis.

By your insight into the image you are able to formulate the conditions, the elements in the image, necessary to having the insight. If you see in this circle that the curve must be perfectly round if all of the radii are

11 *Verbum* 28, note 132, refers to *De anima* 15, and this is surely what Lonergan had in mind, for he quotes Thomas as saying in that article: 'non per accidens tamquam excitantes ut Plato posuit; neque disponentes tantum sicut posuit Avicenna; sed ut repraesentantes animae intellectivae proprium obiectum ut dicit Philosophus in III de Anima.'

12 Lonergan at this point gave a brief explanation of Avicenna's position: 'According to Avicenna, the agent intellect is a separated being that, when we have the phantasm, impresses the species, the metaphysical condition, the metaphysical limitation of the act of understanding, upon our intellect. In that sense the flow of images is a disposition.'

equal, if that is what insight grasps in the image, then you can proceed to the definition of a circle, which is something like a definition of man. But you can proceed in more abstract fashion. You can select simply what is grasped by insight, namely, necessity and the conditions for that necessity, and then you have an abstract essence. Implicit definitions are of this sort. You select the determining relations, the postulational elements in the definition, with respect to whatever common matter you may need, and you have an abstract essence. It is not inevitable that every time this act occurs there results a universal, because what is operative is not a sausage machine from which one can get only sausages, but an intelligent and rational consciousness. When you have the insight, you can express it from the viewpoint of abstraction, picking out the abstract essence. You can also express the intelligibility grasped in this particular image with all of its determinations, and you have a particularized essence.

When, however, you simply pick out, in scholastic terms, the common matter and the form, 'humanity,' or the individual matter and form, 'this instance of humanity,' you are in a way prescinding from the intention of being that lies at the root of inquiry. The intention of being comes to light when, instead of speaking of 'humanity' and 'this instance of humanity,' you speak of 'man' and 'this man.' It is not by another type of insight that you get 'man,' as though by one type of insight you get 'humanity' and by another 'man.' But you get the abstract essence 'humanity,' when you hold down the influence of the intention of being, this heading towards being, and you get 'man' when you include it, when you let it have free play. Your inquiry is your *intentio entis*, your intention of what you are heading for; and your *intentio entis* can find in 'this instance of humanity' as conceived, as thought, what can be, at least what can be thought as existing. It is the sort of thing that could be. If it were a contradictory notion, you would say it could not be.

When the content of the insight into the phantasm is formulated in a conception, the conception may simply express form and common matter, and then you have 'humanity' or 'circularity.' It may express individual matter and form, and then you have 'this instance of humanity' or 'this instance of circularity.' Or, you can go further, and in the form and individual matter understand the full potentiality of being, and then you make the step from the *id quo* to the *id quod*. It is insofar as the source of the inquiry is teleological, insofar as it is aiming at the universe of existence (if there is any such thing), that one steps up from particularized essence to particular thing or particular existence. That stepping up is not automatic; it is not the operation of a machine. It is intelligent. Intelligence grasps the potentiality of being, of an existence, in the particularized[13] essence, and that effects the step from the *id quo* to the *id quod*.

If you think simply of the insight and the experiential data, then what you formulate is just how much of the data is necessary for having the insight, and you get abstract essence. Recalling the example of the circle, you have to have a plane surface, a curve, and equality of all radii; but you need not have *this* plane, *this* curve, and radii of *this* size, because that is irrelevant. If you consider the process, as starting from insight into phantasm, as heading towards conception, as concerned with picking out the essential, you get abstract essence – humanity, or circularity, so to speak – form and common matter. If you think of this process as serving a different end, if you have grasped the abstract essence and you want to consider this instance of it, then, since what is operating is an intelligent consciousness, you can pick out the data that de facto fall under the present insight, and you get a particularized essence, this instance of humanity. But insofar as this wonder, this inquiry, represents a fundamental finality, intelligence grasps, when it goes on to the particularized essence, the potentiality of being.[14] The particularized essence is a constituent condition of what can be.

We are dealing with[15] the emergence of the concept of being. We have an inquiry, a natural finality, a teleology, which unfolds in cognitional process. It is dormant when one is not intellectually alert, intellectually curious, when one is living in a Humean world of experiences, sense impressions. The sense impressions, the flow of sensations, perceptions, and images, can be an occasion on which the finality becomes inquiry. Through the insight and its expression, the finality becomes operative as

13 Lonergan said 'abstract essence' – perhaps a slip of the tongue. The force of his argument seems to call for 'particularized[e] essence.'
14 Lonergan seemed to correct himself here, starting to say 'intelligence grasps in the abstract essence' and changing to 'when it goes on to the particularized essence.' Abstract essence also is potentially being, but the particularized essence is, as the scholastics would say, in *potentia proxima*. See, in the preceding paragraph of our text, 'the full potentiality of being'; the 'full' is editorial, but includes what the scholastics would mean by proximate potency to the real.
15 Coffee break intervened here, and recording of the second part of the lecture began only with 'the emergence.' Notes taken show that nothing of significance was lost.

a requirement, a criterion. The insight and the experience together can give you either an abstract essence or a particularized essence, depending on your point of view; but insofar as that essence satisfies the requirements of intelligence with respect to its finality, insofar as it meets the criterion of intrinsic intelligibility, you move from essence to being, from the *id quo* to the *id quod*.

1.6 Judgment and Experience

When St Thomas discusses the habit of first principles, he gives a great deal of attention to the fact that the whole is greater than the part, and that that is fundamental in all cognitional theory.[f] But he does not explain what he means. At least I found no text in which he did explain it. What *might* be the relevance of the whole being greater than the part, as something fundamental in all cognitional process, is the transition from the *id quo* to the *id quod*, from the abstract essence 'humanity' to 'man,' to what can be, in the sense of the thought of what can be. The teleology that becomes inquiry, on the one hand, causes the step from essence to being, from the *id quo* to the *id quod*, from 'humanity' to 'man'; but, at the same time, it operates by way of a criterion, an exigence, a requirement. Not just anything it conceives can be raised up in that way; only that which satisfies a demand for intelligibility, which can be thought as being, which is intrinsically intelligible, can be raised up in that way. Insofar as the conception is an object of thought, insofar as it is what can be thought as being, there arises the question, Is it? Inquiry sets off another exigence, the question for reflection, Is that so? Raising that question, it also imposes another criterion, another exigence. You can say, 'It is,' if and only if you have grasped the virtually unconditioned, if and only if you can reach an absolute. On the other hand, if you do reach an absolute, a virtually unconditioned, then you cannot be rational and not affirm that this object of thought is.

Now insofar as there is a requirement, a criterion of the virtually unconditioned, there is operative something that we have from nature; but insofar as we grasp the virtually unconditioned, we are dependent. We are certainly not knowing something, grasping something, that is absolutely independent of experience. You cannot have the fulfilment of the conditions for a virtually unconditioned without the experiential level, without the experience either of outer sense or of inner consciousness. Again, you cannot have the virtually unconditioned without grasping a link between conditioned and conditions, and you get that on the level of intelligence. But you cannot have the level of intelligence without inquiry into the data, and without having the data, not merely as occasion or disposition, but as object for the insight. So the act of grasping the virtually unconditioned is in no sense absolutely independent of experience. On the other hand, the requirement that you have to have the virtually unconditioned if you are to judge, and that if you have the virtually unconditioned you cannot be rational and not judge – not without doing violence to your own rational consciousness – that is had from nature.

1.7 Summary

Briefly, then, the intention of being functions as a finality. It is radically from nature, and it functions in knowledge as a finality, a guide, a criterion, a requirement. It is absolutely transparent; it is not an a priori that determines what you will know, but it demands, it initiates, the process of knowing, guides the process, and sets criteria by which one carries out the process correctly or incorrectly. It sets the process going as inquiry, and it guides it by a requirement of intelligibility through which one effects the transition from essence to being, from *essentia* to *ens*. Once that transition is effected, you get your question, Is it? *An sit?* That question is not only asking for an answer; it is also setting up a criterion, a requirement, and an exigence. If you grasp the virtually unconditioned, you can answer, 'Yes,' and if you grasp it, you cannot be rational and not answer, 'Yes.'

The whole known essence and existence of the thing as affirmed in judgment depend upon experience in a series of different ways. They also depend upon intelligence and reasonableness, but the intelligence actuates the intelligibility of the experience, and the reasonableness sets up the criteria by which the cognitional process develops from experience to affirmation. To put the question in terms of independence, Is your knowing being independent of experience absolutely? The answer is simply, No, it is not absolutely independent. On the other hand, Is there anything in your knowing of being that comes from nature? Yes, there is, but that which we have by nature is a perfect transparence. It does not prejudge any issue. It does not give you the intelligibility that you can conceive not merely as essence but as being, and it does not give you the virtually unconditioned; but it sets the criteria that move you through the different stages of knowledge. As inquiry, it leads to the insight. The content of the insight can be conceived in a variety of ways; but if you reach the intelligibility of essence, you move on, in terms of the finality of intellect, to being, to the existent. Insofar as you are moving on, recognizing what is grasped, what is set forth in the concept, not merely as an object of thought but also as the thought about a being, there then arises the question for reflection, Does it exist? Is it?

A question has been raised of the a priori, and the answer is very complex. The a posteriori and the a priori, experiencing and not experiencing, however, are not the fundamental categories in which a satisfactory answer to the question is obtained. The fundamental categories are what we know by nature and what we know by acquisition.

2   The Notion of Objectivity

In chapter 13 of *Insight* we go on to the notion of objectivity. You will notice that, while we have developed a notion of being and discussed in what sense it is a priori and in what sense it is not, in what sense it is dependent on experience and in what sense it is not, still we have not yet bothered about beings. We have just been discussing structures and procedures. But how does one get to an object?

The first question is, What do we mean by an object? We began by distinguishing different senses of the term.[16] There is a linguistic sense, the object of the transitive verb 'to know,' and we said that the object of intellect in that sense is being. There is a cognitional sense. What are the phenomena, as it were, with which we are concerned on the psychological side of knowing an object? What is an object in that sense? There is a metaphysical sense. We spoke of moving object, agent object, such as the external sensible object; we spoke of terminal object, the immanently produced image, concept, judgment; we spoke of final object, what you know through the image, what is imagined, what is conceived, the 'what

16 Lonergan said, 'We began by distinguishing senses of objectivity.' But the four senses set forth in lecture 6, at the beginning of §2, The Notion of Being, and summarized again here, are four senses of 'object' distinct from, though related to, the four senses of 'objectivity' about to be set forth now. It is possible that Lonergan made a slip of the tongue here, but it is also possible that he was using 'objectivity' in two senses; we thought it wise to bypass the question in the text, and so substituted 'senses of the term.'

is' reached through judgment. Then there is the critical question, namely, Is what you know through a true judgment really what is real? We have been dealing with the first, the linguistic, and we move on to the second, the cognitional,[17] and there we distinguish four senses of objectivity.[18]

2.1 The Principal Notion of Objectivity

First, there is a principal notion. It is defined in terms of a pattern of judgments. A, B, and C are objects, distinct objects. If it is true that we are defining 'object' in terms of truth, in terms of judgment, then we want a set of judgments to define what we mean by distinct objects, facts. A is; B is; C is; A is not B nor C; B is not C nor A, and so on. If you have a set of affirmative and negative judgments in that pattern, then A, B, and C are distinct objects. By an object we mean what you know through a set of true judgments. If you have just one, then you have one object; if you have a series, and no one is any of the others, you have a set of distinct objects. That is the principal notion of the object, defined through your true judgment in which you know, It is. 'It is' stands for the fulfilment of the virtually unconditioned; A, B, and C stand for intelligibilities that have been promoted to thought of being.

Besides the term 'object' just now defined, in chapter 11 of *Insight* we determined what was meant by being a knower. Any object that is a knower is a subject, and so we have a definition of 'subject': if it is true of A, or B, or C that A is a knower, or B is a knower, or C is a knower, in the sense employed in chapter 11 – a unity-identity-whole that senses, perceives, imagines, inquires, understands, conceives, reflects, grasps the virtually unconditioned, and judges – then A is a subject, or B is a subject, or C is a subject.

Note that this definition of subject and object does not say whether

---

17 The tape of this sentence gives us, 'We've been dealing with *that*; now we move to the *second*.' On paper, 'that' seems to refer to 'the critical question,' which Lonergan has just discussed. But there is a distinct sound of chalk tapping on the board to designate 'that'; both sets of notes show that 'that' refers to the first item in Lonergan's list of four, the linguistic; and the sense of the argument requires this interpretation. For these three reasons we edit as shown, 'We have been dealing with the first, the linguistic, and we move on to the second, the cognitional.'

18 Lonergan certainly said 'object objectivity'; it is impossible to determine from the sound whether he was correcting himself or meant to combine the two words.

there are subjects or objects. It states what you mean by subject and object. Moreover, it shows where the bridge comes in. We have been describing knowledge as something going on within the subject. How does the subject know anything besides himself, if what we have been describing is simply a process going on within the subject? Well, the subject, this process, can yield judgment, a series of judgments. We have accounted for the possibility of judgment. What happens when you judge? Experiences, understanding, grasp of the unconditioned, according to the requirements of the process. The process will terminate in judgment. If your judgments fall into the pattern we have described, then insofar as those judgments are acts of knowing, you are knowing objects and subjects according to the fulfilment of the conditions. In other words, there is no problem of a bridge. If you can reach the judgment, you are there. An object means no more than that A is. If I am A, and A is, and B is, and A is not B, then we have a subject: I am a knower (established in chapter 11); and we have an object: something that A knows, that I know, that is not myself, that is not the subject. Through true propositions, you can arrive at an objective world. That is the principal notion of objectivity.

2.2 Absolute Objectivity

Where is that objective world at which we arrive? Is it the world around us, each of us being a center of his own universe, that we look out and see? That is not the problem of objectivity we are solving. We move to the objective world represented by the series of judgments insofar as there is an absolute objectivity.

The principal notion of objectivity is concerned with a multiplicity of objects, some of which are subjects. It involves a multiplicity of true judgments falling within a certain pattern. But absolute objectivity is found in each judgment by itself. The virtually unconditioned is an unconditioned, and an unconditioned is an absolute. An unconditioned is not dependent, qua unconditioned, on anything. Not depending on anything, it is not dependent on the subject. The process of knowing, when you grasp the unconditioned and affirm it, moves beyond subjectivity by the mere fact that you reach an unconditioned. You step in, through the judgment, into an absolute realm. There is nothing outside being that can take a look at it and have being as its object. If it is outside being, it is nothing. You move through judgment, through the unconditioned, to an absolute realm, and in that realm you find not only objects but also yourself.

The bridge between subject and object is through absolute objectivity positing an absolute realm within which real distinctions occur. What are distinct objects? *A* is, *B* is; *A* is not *B*; consequently, there are two. If that is true, then in this absolute realm there are two. If one of them is a knower and the other is not, then one is the subject and the other is not a subject but just an object. When you say, 'I am,' when you make that true judgment, you know yourself as in that absolute realm, as posited absolutely. That judgment does not give you a *sense* of yourself; you have to have that sense to be able to make the judgment properly – to go through the argument of chapter 11. You have to be familiar with your own experience and intelligence and reasonableness. But that familiarity is just the experiential side. When you know yourself through the judgment, you know yourself as objectified. If the subject is not objectified, the subject qua subject is not known in that absolute realm. It is the subject qua objectified, qua affirmed, that is known in the absolute realm. Once that is reached, you proceed by the principal notion of objectivity to divide up the absolute realm into many objects, none of which is the other, if the relevant set of judgments occurs.

2.3 Normative Objectivity

There is a third sense of objectivity, normative objectivity. In this sense, objectivity is opposed to subjectivity. We may say of a person's opinions that they are 'merely subjective.' What is opposed to the merely subjective? Is it what you look out and see? That is the popular opinion on the matter. They say, 'He is reading into the text.' That is subjectivity for them, because for them the text is not just a matter of black letters on a white background in a certain spatial order; the thought of St Thomas or Kant is out there in the text to be looked at. Some people read things from their minds into the text; they are not objective; they are merely subjective. That is one sense of subjectivity.

There is another way of conceiving subjectivity. This process has a guide in the pure desire to know, in its finality. That finality as such withdraws a man from other concerns; it gives the detachment, the disinterestedness, of the inquirer, of the one who is concerned to know what is. Objectivity is yielding to the dominance of that finality; it is not allowing desires and fears to interfere with it. Insofar as your desires and fears are interfering with this process, you have subjectivity in the sense that is opposed to objectivity. Again, inquiry, the demand for intelligibility, the demand for the unconditioned, are norms immanent within this cognitional process itself. Insofar as one is meeting those requirements, one is objective. Insofar as one's desires or fears or any other factor in one's makeup are interfering with the execution of this process according to its own immanent norms, one's judgments will be merely subjective.

2.4 Experiential Objectivity

There is a final, experiential sense of objectivity. Here we come closest to knowing as a look. You can have a theory of knowledge in terms of the look; the whole business may be based upon the analogy of what is supposed to be reached by this type of objectivity. In other words, inquiry and insight presuppose something that is given. You have to have something given to have something to inquire about; you have to have something experienced to have materials into which you have the insight; you have to have something experienced to have the materials from which you abstract, or which you add on to an abstract essence; you have to have experience to have the fulfilment of the conditions in the virtually unconditioned. There is not only the intellectual process that operates upon a given; there has to be the given, too.

This is very relevant to objectivity, because besides the given there is the merely imagined. We do not have control over the given; but we can imagine pretty well what we please. If this process were simply a matter of understanding what we imagine, none of us would ever make mistakes. Insight is infallible with respect to what one is imagining. However, what one is imagining may not be the same as what there is to be sensed, what can be sensed, what is given. Insight is *per se* infallible and *per accidens* makes mistakes. It is infallible[g] because it is insight into what we imagine, and it is *per accidens* mistaken insofar as what we imagine may be very different from what is to be seen or heard or tasted or smelt or felt.

Experiential objectivity, then, is the given as opposed to what is produced ad libitum, what is produced at will. It is the given that will fulfil conditions for the virtually unconditioned. But it is not formally the fulfilling condition. It fulfils conditions insofar as there is an intellectual structure that is raised, and insofar as what is given fits in. As given, it is merely given; but as within the context of the activities of intelligence and reasonableness, it becomes condition and fulfilling condition.

There remains a third element here. We have distinguished the given from what is freely produced, and this is not always a watertight distinction. There are such things as illusions and hallucinations[h] in pathological states. Insofar as one is in such a state, what otherwise would be said to be produced freely is not produced freely. A man who had been in an asylum recovered and wrote a philosophical article to the effect that what he saw was very real to him.[19] In such a state, with regard to one's sense of reality, all of the requirements are met. How does one distinguish between the given and the freely produced? Is it in virtue of some immanent quality that we are to look for in our experiences in the normal state, and in virtue of some other quality that will shoot up a label that says, 'This is a hallucination'? That might be very convenient, but things do not work out that way. How do we know we are not crazy, listening to talk about being and objectivity? How is this problem to be handled?

It is handled as one handles any other problem, by intelligence and reasonableness. The freely produced or what is produced by psychological aberration is a perfect counterfeit of what is given. Still, it is given not for normal living but for the science of abnormal psychology. From that given, you arrive at a true account of abnormal psychology. It is not a suitable given for doing physics, doing chemistry, doing biology, doing normal psychology, doing philosophy, or settling the practical affairs of one's ordinary life. How do you distinguish between the two? It is a matter of understanding and forming concepts and making judgments.

Of course, it is also true that a person in a pathological state cannot spot what is wrong in his case. However, while the person in the pathological state cannot spot what is wrong, those who are not in that state can spot what is wrong with him. He does not have the freedom of control of the sensitive processes that permit correct judgment. You cannot settle this question of the difference between the given and the abnormally produced by saying that when you are normal you are able to take a look to see what is there, and when you are not normal you look and see what is not there. In either case, all you have is the look, and to know whether you are normal or abnormal you would have to have a super-look in which you would look not merely at your looking but at what it was looking at. The difficulty would recur with regard to the super-look. Some super-looks might be normal and others abnormal. There is no

19 John Custance, 'Philosophical Reflections of a Lunatic,' *The Hibbert Journal* 51 (1952–53) 165–69.

solution on the side of the look. The solution has to be on the side of inquiry, intelligence, working out the characteristics of abnormal and normal states, and making the judgment that when these characteristics arise the man is out of his head, and he will not be held responsible for what he says and does.

2.5 The Problem of Objectivity

That is just the *notion* of objectivity. It defines terms, it gives a meaning to the word 'objectivity' on the cognitional side. But it is not a meaning of objectivity that settles whether or not there are any objects, whether or not there is a real world, or whether or not what we know by this process corresponds to what we all know very well really is. It is just a set of 'ifs' and definitions. If there is a set of true judgments to the effect that *A* is, and *B* is, and *C* is, and one is not the other, then there is a set of objects. If it is true that each is a knower, then there is a set of subjects. But whether it is true or not is not handled by the principal notion of objectivity. Again, if one reaches the virtually unconditioned, there is at least one case of absolute objectivity; but that definition of absolute objectivity does not settle whether or not such a case arises. We settled one case in chapter 11 of *Insight*. It is very easy, if people have common sense, to settle others. But the notion of absolute objectivity as such does not exclude relativism. A relativist could admit that notion of absolute objectivity, but he would say we never actually reach it; we never reach the virtually unconditioned. It is only when we understand everything about everything that we really get hold of the unconditioned. There are always further questions in any particular judgment we may happen to make, and they can change intrinsically the content of the judgments we make. We never really reach a virtually unconditioned.

Again, this notion of normative objectivity is *one* way of conceiving normative objectivity. But, as we illustrated, there are other ways of conceiving it. Which way is right? Are we right in saying that normative objectivity is meeting the exigences of the pure desire to know? Or would it be more correct to say that normative objectivity is paying attention to the object, seeing what is out there to be seen?

Finally, we have given an account of experiential objectivity. But others might claim that it is just a travesty of the notion of objectivity, that there is where the whole of knowledge lies – taking a look at the object; it is not merely an experience, it is seeing what is there, it is an intuition.

In other words, besides the notion of objectivity, there is a problem of objectivity, and something must be said about it. We have set up conceptions, but we have to face the fact that there is a problem.

Of course, it is not a problem that exists merely between all scholastics, on one side, and the rest of the world, on the other, who have the misfortune of not agreeing with the scholastics. Van Riet offers an objective and detached review of scholastic opinions on epistemology from Balmes in the early part of the nineteenth century to about 1945. He compares Joseph de Tonquédec and Joseph Maréchal.[20] De Tonquédec is a Parisian, Maréchal is a Belgian, both are Jesuits, and they hold completely different views on the question of objectivity. De Tonquédec works out a complete theory of knowledge in terms of seeing, confronting. His approach is entirely in terms of objectivity in the sense of taking a look, and he has a bit of difficulty handling judgment. Knowing is looking, and that position dominates his entire exposition and investigation. In Maréchal, however, we have just the opposite. For Maréchal, finality is the dominant notion. So the problem of objectivity is not just a problem that exists between scholastics, on the one hand, and the rest of the world, on the other. It is part of contemporary scholasticism. It has been consciously present for at least one hundred and fifty years, and it has been operative for about eight hundred.[i] Not only are there these two neatly opposed positions, but van Riet exposes all sorts of intermediate positions.

There is, then, a problem of objectivity, and the problem has different aspects. The *first* of these is the question of the starting point. We began from cognitional process, and we have reached a point where a notion of objectivity has been defined entirely on the basis of a study of cognitional process. As we shall see, we can proceed to a metaphysics of the object in general, of the knower, and of knowing. When we have reached that point, we will be able to give an account of knowing by positing being in terms of our metaphysics, conceiving the knower as a being, reformulating everything that has been said in terms of beings that are known and beings that know. All of the activities can be spoken of in terms of being, potency, form, and act. It is just a matter of changing the language. So one may begin from knowing, arrive at objectivity, work out the metaphysics of objects and of knowing, and then repeat the whole account of knowing in metaphysical terms.

20 Georges van Riet, *L'épistémologie* ... 263–338.

The point is to complete the circle. One way to complete the circle is to begin from knowing. But one can begin with the metaphysics of the object, proceed to the metaphysical structure of the knower and to the metaphysics of knowing, and move on to complement the metaphysics of knowing with the further psychological determinations that can be had from consciousness. From those psychological determinations one can move on to objectivity and arrive at a metaphysics. One will be completing the same circle, except that one will be starting at a different point. One can begin from what is prior *quoad nos*, what is first for us, or one can begin from what is prior *quoad se*, what is first in reality. As long as one completes the circle, the same thing will be said, but it will be said at different points along the line.

In principle, it makes no difference where one chooses to start.[j] What is important is going around the circle. You can complete the circle in various ways. You can complete it with a very sketchy account of knowing and a very sketchy account of metaphysics. Your theory of knowledge may be substantially correct, but it may be anything but complete. Your account of metaphysics may be substantially correct, but it may leave many questions unanswered. You can complete a small circle, or you can complete the circle in a bigger way, with far greater determination in your theory of knowledge and with far greater determination in your theory of metaphysics. De facto, what happens is that you move from the small circle to the big one. You first do the circle in a small way, and then you do it in a bigger way. First you get the general idea of the whole way around on one level, then you go the whole way around on a higher level. The more significant the developments are, the higher up you move. Human understanding is potential, and any developed cluster of insights on knowledge and metaphysics is expressed in a set of terms and relations. The more you understand, the more complex are the relations, and the fuller are the terms. Insofar as there is any progress, if we keep on understanding more and more, if not individually then at least collectively, then these circles keep expanding. They move up a pole, as it were, with smaller circles at the bottom and bigger circles at the top.[k]

The problem of the starting point, then, is not a material problem, a serious problem. What counts is completing the circle correctly. Start where you please, start where it best meets the exigences of your audience or your reader. Again, what counts is getting things right and being more and more complete in what you have to say. What counts is not being the type that asks only, Do we know or do we not? and that answers, We know! – for them all is finished – and not being the type that asks only, Is there something real? and that simply answers, There is! Again, all is finished.[21]

The *second* aspect of the problem of objectivity regards the directive notion of knowing.[22] This is the basic issue. What is your dominant supposition? Is knowing, with de Tonquédec, a looking? Or is it, with Maréchal, basically a perfection?

Different answers here will determine different criticisms of Kant. Thus de Tonquédec holds that what is wrong with Kant is his ideal of pure reason and the categories of understanding; Kant should be content with intuition, and put more stress on it. Maréchal, however, criticizes Kant for putting too much stress on intuition and not enough on judgment.[23] My own position is that for Kant you have knowing when intuition operates in such a way that you have concepts. But he does not recognize judgment and grasp of the unconditioned; he does not make the unconditioned a key point. The fundamental opposition is illustrated by Kant's position, and it is here that the basic issue comes to light. Kant's judgment that in knowledge we reach only phenomena is coherent if judgment is basic. That is, he can assert that this particular judgment is true and make it fundamental if the truth of judgment is fundamental. But, for Kant, judgment is not fundamental. Consequently, Kant's position does not square with his theory.

What is the fascination of the view of knowing as looking? Is it merely a mistake? Not entirely. There is involved another factor, the subject himself. We saw that self-appropriation involves development of the self which is to be appropriated, and the same problem recurs here. A pragmatic attitude is a way of human living, living by results, by what people say, and so on. There may be an implicit appeal to the virtually unconditioned, but it is 'by the way'; it is inconsequential; it is not our actual way

21 The LRI tape stopped at this point, the WAS reel a few lines before (at 'what counts is getting things right'), and the DJS reel early in the preceding paragraph (at 'You can complete the circle in various ways'). The rest of this lecture is reconstructed from notes taken.

22 The phrase 'directive notion of knowing' is from the FEC notes; the WAS notes have 'dominant direction of knowing.'

23 Maréchal's critique of Kant is found in his 5-volume work, *Le point de départ de la métaphysique* (Louvain: Museum Lessianum, 1922, 1923, 1923, 1947, 1926): see Cahier 5, *Le Thomisme devant la Philosophie critique*, 1926. On Maréchal see also discussion 1, §13, Objectivity, and discussion 4, §6, Maréchal, Kant, and Lonergan.

of living. There is a contradiction within the subject. There is a dynamic of events in human development; it is animal, intelligent, and rational. Consequently, the weight that can be carried by the rational part of man is a variable, but we are always living. To meet the problem, one must shift one's basis. The shift from animal to intelligent level occurs philosophically as the shift from sensism and related positions to essentialism.[24] The shift from intelligent to rational level occurs philosophically as the shift from essentialism to existentialism in our sense, that is, to a position which makes truth dominant and operative in a fundamental way in one's philosophy. *Qualis unusquisque est, talis et finis videtur ei:*[25] as one is more consciously oriented in terms of truth, one will seek that higher level. Consequently, the problem is not just a matter of opposition over the basic issue of knowing as looking or as a perfection. Far more fundamental and far more difficult is the existential problem of the subject, the shift which is the development of the self which is to be appropriated.

There is, finally, a *third* aspect to the problem of objectivity, the cognitional problem of fact. What is true? What do we know? The conversion, on the intellectual side, is effected by the study of facts. Whether one adverts to it or not, the finality of the subject is operative; but through the study of facts one can bring the subject to a fruitful advertence to the conflict between what he holds as theory and what he does in actual knowing and practice.

24 Here we follow the notes of was. fec notes have 'relativism.' Both would fit the meaning; see *Insight* xxviii, for a reference to idealism, immanentism, relativism, in one who acknowledges understanding but does not acknowledge judgment.
25 A slight change from the Latin quotation in lecture 1. See note 11 there.

8

A Definition of Metaphysics[1]

The lecture this morning is on chapter 14 of *Insight*.[2]

We began these lectures with science as pursuit of an ideal, where the ideal shifts in virtue of the pursuit – first, from knowledge through causes to analysis and synthesis; then to law and system; and then to states and probabilities. So we suggested self-appropriation as a means of going to the root of the ideal and its developments. Our hope was to find a fixed structure in virtue of which we could orientate ourselves.

Now if science moves from pursuing a knowledge of things by ultimate causes, first to analysis and synthesis, and from analysis and synthesis to law and system, and from law and system to states and probabilities, then one may ask, 'What is philosophy? Is philosophy any of these? Or is it some new form of knowledge?' Thus self-appropriation may be seen as a way of orientating philosophical inquiry as well.

1   The Underlying Problem

A further fact is to be noted. The self to be appropriated is a self that develops. Essences, if given, are subject to development, and so is the

---

1 The eighth lecture, Wednesday, August 13, 1958.
2 The first hour of this lecture (§ 1, the Underlying Problem, and § 2, Positions and Counterpositions) was not recorded, but has been reconstructed from the notes of FEC and WAS. § 3 returns to the tape recording.

self. It is not some static essence; there are differences in the self. And so the question arises, Which self do we choose to appropriate?

A general view of the developing self, and a general form of choosing which self to develop, have become a preoccupation with the existentialist philosophers. Thus for Heidegger, a fundamental category is *Sorge* correlated with *Welt*. *Dasein* is being-in-the-world, and this being-in-the-world is a function of one's concern.[3] And what we find in existentialist philosophy we find also in depth psychology; thus Harry Stack Sullivan speaks of the 'selective inattention' which neurotics display for their not-world, for what is 'not real for me': that is, what lies beyond their horizon, what is not their concern, what is not real for them.[4]

Inasmuch, however, as we began from scientific considerations, we acknowledge a pure desire to know correlated with a universe of being. On the subjective side there is a desire to know by correct understanding in true judgment, and the objective of this desire is a universe of being whose reality corresponds to the totality of true judgments – knowing everything about everything.

Now this universe of being is not identical with 'my world' – Heidegger's *Welt*. My world is centered on me, and as I move out from that center in a series of concentric circles, my concern steadily decreases. If you think of a bus driver, a mechanic, a miner, and ask what his world is, well, it is his family, his relatives, his work, and so on. It is a world settled by concern, he is that concern, and about concerns beyond that world he does not care. He is the center of his world. It is the real for him. He is concerned with events in Lebanon only when they threaten to upset that world.[5]

3 Martin Heidegger, *Sein und Zeit* (Tübingen: Max Niemeyer, 1927) 180–230; trans. John Macquarrie and Edward Robinson, *Being and Time* (New York: Harper & Row, 1962) 225–73.
4 Harry Stack Sullivan, *The Interpersonal Theory of Psychiatry* (New York: W.W. Norton & Company, 1953). There is a much fuller treatment of selective inattention in Sullivan's *Clinical Studies in Psychiatry*, ed. Helen Swick Perry, Mary Ladd Garvel, and Martha Gibson (New York: W.W. Norton & Company, 1956) 38–76; we have no evidence, however, that Lonergan read the latter book, whereas the former one is mentioned in three footnotes in *Insight*.
5 The allusion is surely to the turbulence of 1958, when there was a rebellion in Lebanon. In May the Sixth Fleet of the United States carried out maneuvers in the Mediterranean, and in July, just before these lectures, Eisenhower dispatched thousands of marines to Lebanon at

This results normally in a tension between one's own world and what is beyond one's horizon. Everyone has his own world, and the universe of being is apt to seem very unreal in comparison. The night of sense of the mystics is the destruction of one's *Welt*, but our aim is not to destroy it, or to bring it into coincidence with the universe of being, or to transpose it into that universe, but rather to highlight the idea of the real, and so to remove the conflict.

The trouble, then, lies with the notion of the real. Is the real to be identified with the universe of being, or is it to be settled by my autobiography? The real for me may well be my *Welt* – my autobiography – and then the not-real is what I'm not concerned about. But the pure desire to know can also become a dominant *Sorge*, and then, though there will not be a complete elimination of merely personal concern, still this world of one's concern will move into coincidence with the universe of being.[6]

How does one promote such development? It is a matter of the development of understanding and judgment, and there are no surefire recipes, nor is there any set of rules that will guarantee that anyone's world will move towards the universe of being. To insist on any such recipe is to miss the fundamental point: the subject in his development, and the spontaneous limits of psychological development.

There are indeed means to advance, but they may hinder and distort development as well as promote it. One can do something to speed up the process, but there is danger of imbalance.

A religious background, for one example, is a great help in bringing one's *Welt* into harmony with the universe of being. It enables one to accept a reality that is not seen or felt – immortality, soul, God, and so on – giving reality to what otherwise would not be 'real for me.' But while it confers an inestimable aid in the process of development, it can in the concrete work out as a hindrance: namely, if religion does not keep pace with other development. Thus the faith of a child requires development

---

the request of the country's president. It is a different incident that is referred to in § 3 below, Metaphysics as Synthesis; see note 16.

6 The phrase 'move into coincidence with the universe of being' occurs verbatim in both sets of notes. Verbally, it contradicts the statements of the preceding paragraph, but the FEC notes underline the word 'move' and the WAS notes later have 'will move towards the universe of being'; the emphasis, then, is not on static coincidence, but on a process of becoming.[a]

into the theology of an adult. If development remains childish – on the level of 'Sister told me' – this can be dangerous in the life of the cultured adult, who will decide, not only that such faith is outmoded, but also that religion itself is childish. At best, religion will cease to have much influence in adult life. History gives us material to ponder in this connection: The church in Europe lost the workers in the nineteenth century; but would the church have lost the workers in the nineteenth century if she had not lost the intellectuals in the eighteenth?

Again, for a second example, a philosophic tradition can accelerate the development, but equally the tradition may result in limiting one's philosophic development. One cannot get along without a tradition: it assigns what one has to measure up to; it provides a milieu, a language. But at the same time one can become a plaster cast of somebody else through tradition – using it as a surrogate for the personal self-development of thinking, questioning, etc. Thus there can be a merely external use of tradition in exegesis, or we may have a plaster-cast 'Thomist' in whom authority has taken the place of personal development. Thomas himself distinguishes two ways of teaching theology: one way is satisfied to impart the truth by reference to authorities, and would send the students home empty; the other tries to bring students to understanding.[7] So you need a tradition but you need also the development of self towards the universe of being.

There is, then, an underlying problem and it is personal. Each one of us has his world: it is a solid structure; it is the result of our lives; it has a horizon. And this world is apt to define what I mean by the real. The philosophic point is not to correct our spontaneous attitudes or habits, but to work on the level of what we decide deliberately. We have to grasp that the real is what we know when we make a true judgment.

Now if our view is right – that the underlying problem is a tension between the *Welt* and the pure desire to know – then the solution is dialectical. Dialectic is concerned with three factors.[8] First, it is concerned with the concrete: in the present case, with the concrete subject and his *Sorge*. Secondly, dialectic is concerned with the contradictory: the contradiction is not in propositions but in the subject, for the subject as

7 Thomas Aquinas, *Quodlibeta*, 4, q. 9, a. 3 (= a. 18, if just articles are counted).
8 Where we have 'three factors,' the notes show considerable uncertainty. WAS had written 'meanings' and crossed it out to write 'concerns'; FEC had written 'senses' and crossed it out to write 'factors.'

intelligent and rational consciousness is not identical with the subject of *Sorge*; hence what is real in the *Welt* is not real in the universe of being, and vice versa. Thirdly, dialectic is concerned with change: the contradiction involves a tension, a tension in the concrete, and so heads for change.[9]

2   Positions and Counterpositions

The technical explanation of this dialectic runs as follows. The totality of propositions can be divided into a basic set and a consequent set. The basic set, in the present approach, has to do with knowledge. What is it *to know*? What is *objectivity*? What is *reality*? Propositions on these three topics differ; they are not the same for someone in the universe of being and someone in his own world. In our philosophy the answer to these questions is determined by the subject as intelligently and rationally conscious, but in the opposed notions knowing is looking, objectivity is what can be seen, and reality is what's there. Besides the basic set, there is the consequent set of propositions, consisting of all others. They are consequent, not in the sense of following logically, but in the sense that, as the basic set differs, so all other expressions of reality will differ. That is, the meaning of consequent propositions changes with the meaning of the basic: with every basic meaning of knowing, objectivity, and reality, you give a meaning as well to all other propositions.[b]

Now basic propositions are either positions or counterpositions. They are positions if propositions on knowing, objectivity, and reality are expressions of intelligent and rational consciousness and compatible with its orientation to the universe of being. They are counterpositions if they are expressions which are contradictory to the positions and incompatible with orientation to the universe of being. The counterpositions express *Sorge* and its *Welt* insofar as *Sorge* differs from the pure desire to know and the *Welt* differs from the universe of being.

Further, the fundamental dialectic within the concrete subject heading for change is *manifested*. Insofar as the subject speaks, what he says will purport to be intelligent and rational; but insofar as the subject expresses himself in the counterpositions, there will be a contradiction between what he does practically and what he holds theoretically. No one tries to be stupid and irrational: the claim to be intelligent and rational is implicitly

9 On the notion of dialectic, see *Insight* 217–18, 243–44; in contrast to Hegel's notion of dialectic, ibid. 421–23.

present in whatever a person states; so if his explicit statements do not make intelligence and reasonableness the criteria, he is contradicting himself, there is opposition between the fundamental implicit intention of his utterance and the explicit content of that utterance. Now intelligent and rational consciousness in man is something he cannot forsake or escape; so the dialectic in which he is involved will be manifested: implicitly intelligence and reasonableness are criteria for his utterance; explicitly, if he is in a counterposition, his utterance is opposed to these criteria. He is uttering a counterposition, but his utterance as human claims to be intelligent and rational.

Positions therefore head for development, while counterpositions head for their own overturn. Positions develop. Man asks questions, seeks the right answers, and because positions are not full, definitive, and explicit accounts, they need further development: further questions always arise. On the other hand, counterpositions tend to their own reversal: when the content of the utterance is contrasted with its fundamental implicit claim, there is a manifest contradiction, and the counterposition will collapse.

For that reason, counterpositions tend to be multiple. Authors begin to see the contradiction in which they are involving themselves, and they shift their ground. So too does the man living in the world of his *Sorge*: he also sees contradictions and oppositions in his own operations, and shifts his ground in an effort to maintain his counterposition. There results a series of diverse presentations of the counterpositions. Historically, then, there is not much chance of the disappearance of all counterpositions. But since positions develop, while counterpositions shift their ground, there is change in both of them, and superficially there is no way of distinguishing between the two.

All this is very abstract. What does it mean concretely? Let us offer a concrete ilustration.

Descartes is commonly regarded as a dualist. But a fundamental element in his thought is the *cogito, ergo sum*, which is an appeal to conscious experience (*cogito*) and rational consciousness (*ergo sum*). This fundamental element pertains to the positions: the *sum* is a rational *sum*, a rational affirmation presented with a rational basis, a judgment that claims to reach the real, giving knowledge of reality; and reality here is what is known in true judgment. To that extent, therefore, Descartes is on the side of the positions; further, his position invites development, for Descartes doesn't give a sufficient account of the *cogito*, his account says nothing of what it is to think, nothing of the nature of inference, and so on – there are all sorts of further questions. Still, his statement is a rational position, and therefore open to development.

On the other hand, Descartes has a second thesis – and it too is central for him and a fundamental element in his thought – that material substance is extension, *res extensa*. But how does he know that material substance is extension? If he knows it through the truth of an intelligent and rational judgment, he is still in the positions; but if he knows it by taking a good look at things, 'attending just to what's there,' then extension is a case of the 'already out there now real,' and he is in the counterpositions. Hence there is an element of confusion and ambiguity in the second fundamental element in Descartes. The rationalists – Malebranche, Spinoza, Leibniz, Wolff – develop the first fundamental element; the empiricists take their stand upon the second, but with knowledge regarded as taking a look, and so they bring out the ambiguity of that second element.

Hume was an extremely intelligent and reasonable man, and he gives a persuasive account of knowledge.[10] Now in this account, knowledge is a manifold of sense impressions linked by mere habits and beliefs. But if knowledge is just that, we cannot account for Hume's account of knowledge. So we distinguish between the knowledge he uses to give his account, which is brilliant, and the knowledge of which he gives the account: namely, what he says about knowledge in his account of it. It is this second knowledge that he describes as a manifold of sense impressions linked by habit; in Hume the *author*, however, and in the knowledge he uses to give his account, we have *more* than a manifold of sense impressions linked by habit. Hume is persuasive, not because his knowledge is a manifold of sense impressions, but because it is the product of intelligent and rational consciousness; if it were not, his account would not have been the acceptable and reasonable account it is, even though its content is a counterposition.

Here then we have a manifest tension between the *author* and the

10 It is not clear from the notes whether Lonergan meant this as a second example or as continuing exposition of the single example of Descartes. See *Insight* 388–89, where the two are run together; but see also Bernard Lonergan, *Method in Theology* (London: Darton, Longman & Todd, 1972 [CWL 12]) 21, where Hume is treated alone – as is the case in lecture 2 above, § 1, The Value of Self-appropriation.

author's *statements*. And here too we find the origin of Kant's problems.

3 Metaphysics as Synthesis

We have discussed an underlying problem with regard to method in metaphysics, and it will remain an underlying element in the solution to the problem of method. We will now consider the more explicit side of the notion of metaphysics.

In his *Lectures on the History of Philosophy*, in his account of Kant, Hegel indulges in the gibe that for Kant experience and observation of the world are a matter of a candlestick here and a snuffbox there.[11] Preoccupation with Kant runs the risk of reducing metaphysics to the question whether the candlestick here is a real candlestick, and whether the snuffbox there is a real snuffbox. But we have worked out a notion of being in terms of the completely universal and the completely concrete. Being is completely universal: it includes everything. Being is completely concrete: it includes everything about everything. It is in terms of that notion of being that we developed a notion of metaphysics. Metaphysics is not a concern with the reality of the candlestick or the snuffbox; it is a concern with the universe as opposed to a world determined by a *Sorge*, by a concern. It is concerned with a synthesis.

Besides questions[12] regarding the series of propositions in which one may express one's philosophy, there also arises the more general question, Why do you go about things that way? Why precisely this way of going about things? This is the question of synthesis as such. One can read through a manual in philosophy and say, 'I see nothing wrong with any of these arguments, but what I find totally wrong are the assumptions involved in having arguments, the assumptions involved in trying to settle anything by propositions.' It is possible to pull the rug completely from underneath the series of propositions. If knowing being is a matter of knowing everything about everything, a notion of metaphysics has to be

11 G.W.F. Hegel, *Lectures on the History of Philosophy*, trans. Elizabeth S. Haldane and Frances H. Simson (New York: The Humanities Press, 1955, reprint of 1896 translation), Vol. 3, 444–45.
12 Lonergan prefaced this sentence with, 'As I said last night.' There was evidently a discussion on the evening of August 12, but it was not recorded. There is a similar reference in discussion 4, §5, The Concept of Structure.

of similar dimensions. And so in *Insight* we say that as the notion of being underlies and penetrates and goes beyond all other contents, so also metaphysics is the department of human knowledge that underlies, penetrates, transforms, and unifies all other departments.[13] Metaphysics, then, is conceived in terms of the totality of knowing and the totality of the object of knowing. It is conceived in terms of integration. Earlier we spoke of Thor Heyerdahl, the author of *Kon-Tiki*, who went the rounds among the experts in the field of anthropology and found them all busy picking things out of little holes, and classifying them beside the holes at the top; but no one was going around and seeing what was coming out of all of the holes.[14] The conception of metaphysics is the conception of a discipline that is concerned in some way with what is coming out of all of the holes.

First, metaphysics underlies all other departments, because all other departments are specializations of the total basic inquiry. We have spoken of the pure desire to know, intelligence, intellectual alertness, critical reflection, and we based a notion of being upon that desire to know. What is correlative to the desire is everything about everything. Still, that desire needs at least the occasion, the materials of sense, perception, and imagination, to go from a mere innate capacity to a wonder about something, a wonder about something that is expressed in a question. When it becomes wonder about something, it is wonder about *this* or wonder about *something of this kind*. While that initial wonder is completely universal in its sweep, in its goal, still it leads to something only insofar as there are developed particular departments of knowledge. I see a certain felicity, therefore, in the name, metaphysics, insofar as it means 'after physics.' The other sciences develop, and it is insofar as you are aware of the others as a multiplicity that the further question arises of their integration. Other departments, then, are initiated by wonder as concerned with data of a certain kind. But there is also the total question; as the ground of metaphysics, the total question is something that underlies all other departments.

Secondly, metaphysics penetrates all other departments. The physicist is not concerned with settling what is meant by reality, knowledge, and objectivity; and neither is the chemist, the biologist, the sociologist, the

13 *Insight* 390. The reference was given in the lecture.
14 See lecture 4, § 3, Common Sense and the Role of Philosophy, at note 7; but Lonergan did not at that time refer to Heyerdahl by name.

economist, and so on through an indefinite line of sciences. Each scientist is content to follow the approved methods of his discipline. In fact, one of Husserl's complaints was that the approved methods proper to each discipline become, as it were, a fetish. Further, any attempt to deal with all departments is regarded as just another private discipline, another little department; any attempt to provide a more fundamental ground for the approved methods in each discipline is regarded as an interference of one specialty with another. But metaphysics penetrates all other departments, in a sense, insofar as all other departments have the same principle as metaphysics, namely, intellectual alertness, critical reflection. While the other departments are many, still they seek spontaneously a mutual compatibility and coherence. If the question of compatibility and coherence is to be treated systematically, methodically, there has to be a discipline that is concerned with all.

Thirdly, metaphysics transforms the results of other departments. Metaphysics rests upon a self-appropriation of the subject in which the self-appropriating subject discovers that, besides the man that he is, there is also the man he is committed to being. The subject is fundamentally a tension between what he is and what he ought to be. In the Augustinian phrase, *Homo prout sempiternis rationibus esse debeat.*[15] There is an ideal component in being a man. It is this tension that the existentialists emphasize a great deal. A couple of years ago,[16] Eisenhower sent the Sixth Fleet to the eastern end of the Mediterranean, and at a news conference he was asked, 'Isn't this rather risky?' He replied, 'We have to be men.' In an empirical sense, we all already are men; but there is also the man that we have to be. While this tension, on the moral level, is familiar, it exists equally on the cognitional level. There is development not merely on the

15 This idea can be found readily enough in Augustine, e.g., in *De vera religione* 31, where Augustine says that those who merely apply the law do not judge the law, but the lawmaker consults the eternal law, 'ut secundum ejus incommutabiles regulas, quid sit ... jubendum vetandumque discernat.' J.-P. Migne, *Patrologiae cursus completus ... Series Prima*, Vol. 34, col. 148. But we have not located the exact reference for Lonergan's quotation.

16 The reference here is not to the Lebanon crisis of 1958 (note 5 above), but to the Suez Canal crisis of 1956. In confirmation of this view, we find the same remark in Lonergan's education lectures of 1959 (CWL 10), where, however, he speaks of these events as happening *three* years ago. There is a brief reference also in the existentialism lectures of 1957, where Eisenhower's remark is linked with the phrase, *L'homme se définit ...* See lecture 4 above, note 11.

moral side of man, there is a more fundamental development on the cognitional side, in the transition from a world defined by *Sorge* to a world defined by the pure desire to know, and all the implications in that. Insofar as the metaphysician is a man in whom that development has occurred, he will be able to straighten out the results of the other departments.

Finally, metaphysics unifies other departments.[17] Other departments ask particular questions, but metaphysics asks questions that regard the whole. Insofar as it has answers to the more general questions, it is a principle of unification.

4   Transformation of Scientific Results

The transformation of the results of other departments by metaphysics can be illustrated. Up to the end of the nineteenth century, modern science was involved in a mechanist determinism, and the search for foundations that concerns a certain number of contemporary scientists arises from the fact that the mechanist determinist basis of science has been removed by science itself. In other words, it is not merely the person that is doing philosophy who discovers in himself the opposition between positions and counterpositions. While it may take about four centuries, science eventually develops to the point where it cannot be content with the real world as thought of by Galileo and as more firmly conceived as a result of Newton's work.

The real world of Newtonian science was quite compatible with the results of science until relativity and quantum mechanics were introduced. Relativity[18] removed the space and time in which imaginable entities, even though they could not be seen, were much too small to be seen, at least were imaginable; they were not imaginable with regard to secondary qualities such as color and so on, but with regard to primary qualities that could be handled by the geometer. The imaginable entities

---

17 On the tape this short paragraph follows §4, Transformation of Scientific Results; that order has the effect of interrupting the list of four roles played by metaphysics, so the 1980 edition rightly relocated the paragraph to make it follow immediately on the first three.

18 The structure of the paragraph shows that it was Lonergan's intention to distinguish the separate roles of relativity and quantum mechanics (confirmed by FEC notes), but the transition from one to the other is not sharply defined.

moved in space over time according to determinate laws. Once that is posited, one is involved in a mechanist determinism. It is mechanist because one is dealing with imaginable entities, and only with imaginable entities; anything else is just a complex resultant of that multiplicity. It is determinism because the laws are not on a more abstract level than that of the movement of these imaginable entities; the law is simply that the imaginable moves according to certain determinate principles. That mechanist determinism was not science. As a matter of fact, the development of science eliminated it. First of all, it eliminated the imaginable space and time in which the imaginable entities moved. In the second place, it eliminated the determinate laws. Consequently, physics was left with a problem: What are we dealing with? What are we talking about? What are we trying to know? Prior to relativity and quantum mechanics, scientists were quite content that everything was settled; but afterwards, there arose a problem of their foundations.

Because the problem of foundations exists for contemporary scientists, scholastics of this century have an opportunity they have not had for four centuries. The scientific mind of this century is open; it is inquiring. Of course, this foundational inquiry is more conspicuous in the older men. A man first has to make his name as a scientist, he must get on with his own profession, before he begins to ask these ulterior philosophical questions. Nevertheless, this is taking place in this century. Instead of waiting for the scientists to bring about the elimination of the mistaken philosophic assumption of mechanist determinism, however, metaphysics undertakes the transformation. Insofar as there is operative, existent, a metaphysics as we are attempting to conceive it, one has a principle that will transform the counterpositions in contemporary science. In other words, the scientist expresses what he understands in the data according to the world settled by his *Sorge*, and he may express it in counterpositions as well as in positions. But unless he is a professional philosopher of a certain type, he will not know much about the difference. Insofar as one is a philosopher concerned with positions and counterpositions, one can pick out the element of the counterposition in the scientific expression of the scientific result and eliminate it, reverse it.

There is a principle of transformation in this notion of metaphysics. Not only does it underlie and interconnect, as having the same basis and as concerned with the integration of the other sciences, but it also involves a principle of transformation of their results. The results of the other sciences are the work of scientists, but those scientists are also men. Just as the philosopher has a problem of self-appropriation, of discovery that the self to be appropriated needs to be developed, and that the ideal does not correspond to actual achievement, so too does the scientist. In the measure that actual achievement does not correspond to the ideal, the expression of scientific results will contain the counterpositions. Insofar as the metaphysician is aware of the fundamental issue, he may discern, as it were, how far the scientific element goes, and where the counterposition from the man who happens to be a scientist comes in.

Moreover, metaphysical unification does not involve only a transformation of the results of the sciences insofar as counterpositions are involved in their expression. It also implies a transformation of common sense, and in particular of *my own* common sense. My common sense is the home of my *Sorge*, my world, my horizon. It is its citadel. To insist on common sense, to appeal to common sense, is one of the best ways of avoiding the transition from *Sorge* to the pure desire to know, from my world to the universe of being.

5 Implicit and Problematic Metaphysics

Metaphysics, in the sense in which we are considering it, has three stages: implicit, problematic, and explicit.

Metaphysics is implicit in everyone, because everyone is an instance of empirical, intelligent, rational consciousness, and it is upon the affirmation of a unity-identity-whole which senses, perceives, imagines, inquires, understands, conceives, reflects, grasps the unconditioned, and judges, that our whole structure will be based. Metaphysics works from that affirmation as from a basis. But everyone has a self to be appropriated; that self to be appropriated is the rational, intelligent, experiencing man. The metaphysics with which we are concerned is a metaphysics that is implicit in everyone by the simple fact that he is a conscious subject that experiences, understands, and judges.

Besides the implicit stage in metaphysics, there is a problematic stage. The need for making the implicit explicit is felt, but the explicitation is not achieved. The problematic stage can be general or particular, with regard to particular schools or particular individuals. Insofar as there is a desire for unification of the sciences, there arises a problematic stage.

The problematic stage arises, in particular, insofar as there is a desire for a satisfactory method for the human sciences. In *The Crisis of European Sciences and Transcendental Phenomenology*, Husserl makes the point that, if there is anything wrong with your body or even with your mind, there exist specialists you can consult and from whom you can obtain help. They are specialists in a scientific sense; they are not the old-time doctors of the Greek period or earlier, or the medicine men who know what has worked in certain cases and who conclude that the same thing will help in this case. They are able to diagnose exactly what is wrong; they are able to choose from a long list of tested drugs, and so on, that may help; they are able to draw upon an accumulation of experience in surgery, and so on. If there is anything wrong with your health, there exists a whole array of scientific disciplines at your disposal to help you recover. But, Husserl adds, Europe is sick, the situation in Europe is disastrous, and what do we have to help? Just quacks.[19] While this is just an opinion, still there does arise the question about the human sciences. The human sciences have tended to assimilate themselves as much as possible to physics and chemistry and biology, and in general to the successful sciences. The more that assimilation proceeds, the less able they are to be a help for free men.

For example, nineteenth-century economics has, as it were, two faces. On the one hand, it is ideal. James Mill felt that economics at his time stood in the position of astronomy shortly before Newton. Economics could be just as accurate and just as infallible in its predictions in a few years as Newtonian astronomy became with Newton's publication of his *Principia Mathematica*. This economics was determinist, materialist, and so on. But de facto what nineteenth-century economics did was issue precepts to free men. It told individuals to keep government out of things, *laissez faire*; it told individuals to be thrifty and to be enterprising. Those precepts resulted in an enormous development of parliamentary democracy throughout Europe, and in an enormous economic development. While that economics and its precepts are inadequate, nevertheless they serve to illustrate the difference between a human science as uttering precepts and a human science as predictive, as imitating what the physicist or the chemist does. In the one case, the human sciences issue precepts;

19 Husserl, *The Crisis* ... 269–70 (314–15 in the German). Husserl's language, however, is not so blunt: 'The European nations are sick; Europe itself, it is said, is in crisis. We are by no means lacking something like nature doctors. Indeed, we are practically inundated by a flood of naive and excessive suggestions for reform. But why do the so richly developed humanistic disciplines fail to perform the service here that is so admirably performed by the natural sciences in their sphere?' Ibid. 270.

they tell free people something that free people can do for themselves. But in the other case, insofar as the human sciences aim to predict, insofar as they imitate physics and chemistry, what can they produce? They can produce consultants to central governments; the central governments can only carry out the advice of the consultants by obtaining more power; and there results what is called creeping socialism.

In other words, there exists a fundamental problem with regard to the structure of the human sciences. The human sciences can be conceived as instruments of human liberty and development, or they can be conceived as instruments of the concentration of governmental power,[c] where the individual is incapable of doing anything without government approval of what he is doing and without government financing to enable him to do it. That is just one aspect of this problematic stage of metaphysics.

6 Explicit Metaphysics

Metaphysics becomes explicit insofar as the implications of the pure desire to know and its unfolding are worked out with regard to the structure of reality and the unification of knowledge. So we come to our definition: explicit metaphysics is the conception, affirmation, and implementation of the integral heuristic structure of proportionate being.[20] What does this mean?

We said that being is what can be intelligently grasped and reasonably affirmed. We proposed to do metaphysics in two steps. There is, first of all, metaphysics with regard to this world and, secondly, there is the question of the existence of God.[21] As a first step, we confine metaphysics to proportionate being, that is, to being that is known not only by correct understanding but also by what man can experience and what, by understanding his experiences, he can affirm in true judgments. The experiential element is what differentiates proportionate being from being in general.

What the being is in each particular case – even what proportionate being is – is a question to be answered by a particular science. But, as we

20 Lonergan read the definition from *Insight*, referring his audience to p. 391.
21 On this question, see lecture 10, §2, The Existence of God; also discussion 4, §2, Probability Theory and the Existence of God.

have very briefly indicated in these lectures, and as we have attempted to indicate more fully in *Insight*, the sciences are heuristic. It is not only the algebraist who employs a heuristic structure by writing down 'Let x be the number.' The physicist also employs a heuristic structure by writing down 'Let $f(x,y,z,t) = 0$, where f is any indeterminate function, be the required law.' Where we ordinarily ask, 'What is the nature of ...?' the physicist, with a somewhat more elaborate heuristic structure, asks, 'What is the function that governs these phenomena?' and he attempts to determine that function in two ways. First, he moves up from data through measurements and curve fitting, and the curve will select some determinate function. Secondly, he works down from postulates of invariance and differential equations to the general type of function that will have to satisfy that law. In other words, the physicist moves in from two angles on the law of nature he is seeking, and we called that movement a heuristic structure. This particular type leads to laws and systems, and there is a further development that leads to states and probabilities; but what is being done is fundamentally the same thing that is done by the algebraist when he initially asserts, 'Let x be the number.' The scientist is heading for something, inquiring into something – 'Think about it precisely; give it a symbol.' What is happening? He is anticipating an act of understanding in which he will understand the data in question and all similar data. The scientist not only anticipates the act of understanding, but he also anticipates the expression of the act of understanding in some conception. Where the mathematician says 'x' and the physicist mentions 'some indeterminate function,' in ordinary speech one says 'the nature of ...' What is the nature of light? The nature of light is what we will understand, what we will know, when we understand light. This heuristic procedure anticipates the future act of understanding and its conceptualization, and it uses that anticipation to guide the process towards attaining the act of understanding in question.

Just as there is heuristic structure with regard to acts of understanding, so there is a total heuristic structure; there is the total goal of intelligent and rational consciousness as such. We have named that goal 'being.' When we speak of knowing being, we mean knowing everything about everything. But we do not know everything about everything; we are simply anticipating the totality of acts of understanding and judgment by which we could completely achieve the ideal, the goal, set us by our desire to know. In other words, just as x names the goal of the algebraist, just as 'the indeterminate function' names the goal of a scientific inquiry, so 'being' names the goal of metaphysics. Metaphysics is concerned with the *integral* heuristic structure. It is not content to say that being is what you will know when you know everything about everything. It can become more explicit. It can go on to say that, in any case of knowledge of proportionate being, there will be a component of experience, a component of understanding, a component of grasping the unconditioned and judging; and because the acts are differentiated from one another by different contents, the object known is going to involve a content from experience, a content from understanding, a content from judgment. Consequently, there will be that triple content in the known. The metaphysician not only posits a general x, being, what one will know when one understands correctly everything about everything, but he can also break being up: into being completely, and being that is proportionate being.[22]

Any proportionate being will involve what corresponds to the three contents – this is a fundamental premise in our movement towards a metaphysics of proportionate being – and we can name them potency, form, and act. When science reaches its ideal goal of complete understanding of all phenomena, what will science be? It will be a set of theories verified in any number of particular instances. Insofar as it is a set of theories, it is knowing what is known by understanding; it is concerned with form. Insofar as the set is verified, it is knowing what is, and one is knowing what is insofar as one judges; there is an element of act. Finally, insofar as there are a number of instances for the same theory, in which it is being verified, we have another component that is connected with one's experience, namely, potency.

We have simply attempted to illustrate the idea of metaphysics as working out the integral heuristic structure of proportionate being. That is a fundamental element in the structure. We have not attempted any close definition of exactly what we mean by potency, form, and act; but we have been indicating the type of thing we conceive metaphysics to be. What is explicit metaphysics? It is the subject achieving self-appropriation, knowing himself as a knower, and using that knowledge to deter-

22 The steps in Lonergan's thought are clear enough: being divides first into the totality of being and proportionate being, with the latter subdividing into the (partial) components of being – potency, form, and act. But his oral exposition lacks the careful structure of a written paragraph. See also lecture 9, beginning of §2, Metaphysical Integration.

mine the general structure of his possible object and the relations between the particular departments in knowing that object.

7   Metaphysics and Explanatory Knowledge

Now in *Insight* the various properties of metaphysics are worked out in some detail. I will mention just one which is of fundamental moment for scholastics. If your metaphysics is an implementation of the integral heuristic structure of proportionate being, then you are concerned with anticipating the structure of your knowledge when it is at the stage of completion. You are concerned, therefore, with what is known when insight is full.

For example, we can conceive different stages in knowledge of fire. For Aristotle, fire was one of the four elements; earth, air, fire, and water were four substances. For the immediate predecessors of Lavoisier, fire was perhaps still a substance, but it had a different name; it was not one of the four elements, and it was called phlogiston. Since Lavoisier, fire has been conceived as process, a process of oxidation. We have three accounts of fire. How can those three accounts be of the same thing? Phlogiston is precisely not one of the four elements, and a chemical process is not any substance but just process. Where do we find the common point between the three successive theories, so that we may say that Aristotle's notion of fire was wrong? If he was wrong, he must have been talking about the same fire as the present chemists. What is that fire that is the same? It is the fire that is the object of the heuristic structure. We have sensible data of something burning, and we ask, 'What is the nature of this?' The question receives successive different answers. With the development of knowledge, the particular answers to the question change, but it is the same heuristic structure all along the line: 'What is the nature of these phenomena? What do we know when we understand these phenomena?' That is what is meant by fire, as common to Aristotle and contemporary chemistry.

Now, while this notion of metaphysics is simply heuristic structure, still it is heuristic structure that aims at understanding. If there comes an answer to the question, that answer will be the fruit of understanding. Consequently, while we have to use particular types of information when we are doing metaphysics, those types of information have to be in explanatory form. The metaphysics we are proposing will not appeal to merely descriptive knowledge, but to explanatory knowledge.

For that reason, there is a fundamental difference between the notion of metaphysics we are presenting and what has become fairly common down a number of centuries in scholastic notions of metaphysics. In Aristotle, the predicaments are clearly distinguished; but that is a list of descriptive categories. We arrive at Aristotle's categories most simply by going into the woods, meeting animals, and asking, What kind of an animal is this? How big is it? What is its color? What relations does it have? and so on. They are categories of descriptive knowledge, and descriptive knowledge is science in a preliminary stage.[23] It is something entirely different from science that has reached its explanatory stage. Aristotle himself had a very clear idea of the difference between these descriptive categories, which he sets up in an elementary work,[24] and causes; and he thinks of science as knowledge through causes.[25] However, there has been a tendency to conceive of metaphysics as knowledge, not through causes, but through the predicaments. On the other hand, if you conceive metaphysics as concerned with the total heuristic structure of proportionate being, you must be concerned simply with causes and not at all with predicaments, because a heuristic structure aims at what is known through understanding.

23 But besides commonsense description there is also the scientific description treated in *Insight* 178 and passim.
24 Aristotle, *Categories*; see lecture 1 above, note 5.
25 See lecture 1 above, § 1.2, The Development of the Ideal of Knowledge; lecture 2, § 9, The Expression and Object of Insight in Aristotle.

9

Metaphysical Analysis and Metaphysical Integration[1]

1   Metaphysical Analysis

If intellect is intelligence, it seems a fair question to ask,[2] What does the metaphysician understand? If he does not understand anything, he does not seem to be using his intelligence. If he does understand something, what is it? Traditionally, the definition of metaphysics is that it is the science of being qua being. This suggests that it is not the science of any particular class of beings. It is not understanding what the physicist understands, what the chemist understands, what the biologist understands, what the anthropologist understands, or what the theologian understands. There does not seem to be anything left for the metaphysician to understand.

Again, what he understands does not seem to be being as an abstract residue. One can say that common to all men is intelligence, common to all men and animals is sense, common to men and animals and plants is life, common to those three and the inorganic world is matter, common to all of them and to the angels and to God is substantiality, and common to substances and accidents there is something. What finally is left, after you have taken away what is proper to everything, one may say, is what

---

1 The ninth lecture, Thursday, August 14, 1958.
2 Recording started in midsentence: 'it seems a fair question'; the opening clause is from the WAS notes.

the metaphysician studies. However, that which is finally left is not anything that exists; it seems to be nothing. Whatever you understand, you understand some essence; essence is what you know when you understand. What is finally left after you have removed what is proper to everything does not seem to be any essence.

Again, one could conceive metaphysics as understanding the essence of God, the essence of the *ens per essentiam*. God, understanding his own essence, understands absolutely everything else, everything that is possible and everything that is actual, all in a simple intellectual apprehension that is identical with himself. In that case, if one had God's understanding of himself by which God also understands everything else, one would be a metaphysician who understood something; and indeed, the object of that understanding would be being in its total extension. However, we are not God, and in this life we do not have the beatific vision by which we participate in God's knowledge. Moreover, the beatific vision is something beyond the proportion of our natures; consequently, it does not seem to be what constitutes the metaphysician qua metaphysician.

What, then, does the metaphysician understand, if it is not any particular class of beings, not the abstract residue of all beings, and not the *ens per essentiam*? I do not think that the answer is that the metaphysician understands nothing whatever. What does he understand?

1.1 Analogous Understanding

I think we have to distinguish between two types of understanding. In theology at least, it is necessary to distinguish between proper knowledge of a thing – knowledge of a thing by its essence – and analogical knowledge; and this suggests two types of understanding. When one has proper knowledge of a thing, one is understanding it by its essence; but when one has analogical knowledge, one also has some understanding, an understanding of a proportion, of an analogy.

One may say, then, that the knowledge of the essences of different types of beings pertains to the particular departments of knowledge, and the metaphysician leaves knowledge of those essences to the people working in the particular departments. What will be determined in the various departments are the essences of the different kinds of beings, and that is proper knowledge. But the metaphysician has analogical knowledge. For him, the essences function as a series of x's. When we were discussing the concept of being,[3] we saw that in essence intelligence grasps the possibility of being; because of essence, it raises the question of existence. There is a connection, then, between essence and being, essence and existence; beings are compounded of essences and existences. One might say as a first approximation that the metaphysician is concerned with the proportion between essences and existences, with the analogy of the series x_1/y_1, x_2/y_2, etc., where existences are indicated by the y's and essences by the x's. That analogy is the occupation of the metaphysician. His understanding is analogous. It is an understanding of being and of all being, but it is not a matter of understanding essences proper to each being. Metaphysics is understanding and exploiting the analogy in all being.

This account of metaphysics at least introduces a familiar element.

1.2 The Fundamental Set of Analogies

If, however, we go on to ask, 'Just what are these proportions? How do we obtain these proportions?' I should say that, in the fundamental case, it is by understanding understanding, by insight into insight. The metaphysician's understanding is analogous, and fundamentally the analogies come from an understanding of understanding. In the first instance, they come from an understanding of human understanding, and so we have a metaphysics of proportionate being. In the second instance, one goes beyond the first stage to the absolute being by analogy, and one has some analogous understanding of absolute understanding. That is the root of the analogies employed in metaphysics. It is a matter of understanding understanding, insight into insight.

A standard analogy in metaphysics, that has its origin with Aristotle, is the analogy of form to potency.[a] Aristotle gives an account of it in the ninth book of the *Metaphysics*, in terms of a first type of the analogy of potency to act. What is that analogy in its fundamental case? It is the analogy of insight to data, of what is grasped by insight to what is presented by imagination. Aristotle illustrates this analogy by saying that as sight is to eyes, so hearing is to ears, and taste is to the palate, and

3 See lecture 6, § 2, The Notion of Being.

so on. This illustration is exact. Sight is what we know by insight. We can take a look at eyes, but when we understand the eyes we say that they are organs of sight; sight is the form of the organ that is the eye.

Again, Aristotle elsewhere remarks that the soul is to the whole animal as sight is to seeing.[4] Existence is to essence as judgment is to conception, as affirmation is to what is the affirmed content. As conception results from the combination of insight and data, so essence results from the combination of form and potency. But there we have a second instance of potency and act. Aristotle's illustration for this second instance of potency and act – the relation of form to act – is that as sight is to seeing, so the faculty of hearing is to the act of hearing, *auditus ad audiendum*.[5] We happen to use the same word in English both for the faculty of hearing and for the act, but still, the faculty is the form of the organ, the ear, and the act is distinct from both the organ and the faculty, for there are times when we are not hearing anything.[6]

Our study of knowledge introduces us into the traditional analogies in a fundamental form in which we can control them.[c] We can examine in some detail just precisely what is the relation between what is grasped by insight and what is presented in data. That is a fundamental instance that can be illustrated wherever you can illustrate the relation of form and potency. On the other hand, you will also note that this analogy gives precision to the relation between form and potency. It is not simply that potency is the determinable and form is whatever determines, and you can apply that distinction wherever you please, ad infinitum. We have form and potency when we have the analogy of insight and data. Again, we have the analogy of existence and essence where we have the analogy of judgment and conception. We may have a triple-termed analogy: potency to form to act, as data in the intellectual pattern of experience to insight to judgment.

---

4 Aristotle, *De anima*, II, 1, 412b 10 to 413a 10.
5 The *ad audiendum* may be due to the familiarity of this construction in Lonergan's Latin courses; we would expect *auditus ad audire* in the present context.
6 On the two types of analogy of potency to act, see Aristotle,[b] *Metaphysics*, IX, 6, 1048b 6–9; Thomas Aquinas, *Sententia libri metaphysicae*, IX, lect. 5, 1828–29 (our usage henceforth, *In IX metaph.*).

1.3 Central and Conjugate Forms

Let us return to the relation between what is grasped by insight and what is presented in data, and examine it in further detail. Forms, insights, divide into two fundamental classes that are quite distinct. When data are considered as particular, and a multiplicity of data are referred to a single unity, you have a grasp of form of one type, which we may call central or substantial form. We have insights into data as particular. It is in considering these data that I have insight into the unity of *this* man. Consequently, there is a central form in beings, a central form which corresponds to what is grasped when you say it is one and the same over a spatiotemporal volume of particular data. But when you compare data with one another, build up classifications by similarity, and proceed to work out the relations of things to one another, you arrive at scientific laws. Those laws involve relations, determinate relations of things to one another. A law is an expression of an intelligibility; it involves something corresponding to form. This gives us a second type of form, conjugate or accidental form. There is a determinateness in potency and act that comes from the form. Judgment only says 'Yes.' The form corresponds to data, but it is the ground of the intelligibility grasped in the data. If there are different types of form, there must be different types of potency and different types of act.

Again, we have spoken of higher viewpoints. For a while, intelligence works along with data, under the guidance of certain insights and formulations. When it comes up against difficulties, intelligence starts all over again, reformulating all of its fundamental conceptions. That is the result of further insights that constitute a higher viewpoint with respect to the previous set of insights. In the first instance, higher viewpoints regard the development of human intelligence. But higher viewpoints also have a relevance to the hierarchy in things. (The notion of a hierarchy in things involves a very complex argument that I had best not attempt to summarize.[7]) For the forms on any given level, there is a set of laws. From that set of laws a certain number of schemes of recurrence can be developed. The schemes of recurrence can be brought to light by a physicist, a chemist, and so on. The regular events that occur on that level may be entirely explained by the laws and schemes on that level; but it may also happen that they are not.

7 *Insight* 254–57, 262–67, 437–42.

In the biological unit of the cell, there is taking place a continuous release of chemical actions, and every one of those actions occurs in accordance with the laws of chemistry. But if it is not possible through chemical laws and the schemes of recurrence that can be devised in chemistry to account for the regularity with which those chemical processes take place in the cell, you have to appeal to a higher viewpoint to account for the regularity, and you introduce conjugate forms on the biological level with their laws and schemes. If in the animal you find regularities that cannot be accounted for by the totality of laws and schemes of recurrence on the biological level, you postulate another higher level. You have grounds for another higher viewpoint, in which are introduced the conjugates of the sensitive level. If you find, with regard to men, that all of the laws and schemes of sensitive psychology, which pertain to the psychic level, do not account for the intelligible talk that men carry on, you have to go on to a still higher level and posit intellectual forms that account for human behavior.

The idea of a higher viewpoint, while it was first developed in terms of the development of human intelligence, also provides us with an analogy for the hierarchy of conjugate forms, accidental forms, that are found in single beings. The conjugate acts of a lower level, insofar as they occur regularly and are accounted for by the laws and schemes of recurrence of the lower level, pertain simply to that lower level. If, on the other hand, there is a regularity in the conjugate acts of a lower level that is not accounted for by that level, then there is an information of that lower level by conjugate forms of a higher level. For example, take the flow of images in an animal (insofar as the animal has a flow of images): you do not need to postulate intelligence to account for it. However, the flow of images in a man, with all of the subsequent psychology resulting from the images and ending up in talk, is not accounted for without introducing higher integrations. We can all witness and experience the process of learning, and discover that to be able to talk intelligently, properly, on a matter, one has to have a prior development of understanding. Teaching is principally an encouragement, a help, in that development of understanding. Consequently, Aristotle says[8] that to teach, the fundamental requirement is that you understand. If you do not understand, you are

---

8 Attributing this to Aristotle, Lonergan added, 'I'm not certain, because I haven't been able to find the place again.' The place may have been *Metaphysics*, I, 2, 982a 10–19.

not going to help anyone else to understand. Now it is insofar as there is a higher integration of images and the motor activities involved in speech on the level of intelligence that you have the recurrence of intelligible content in speech, and the domination of speech by an intellectual intention. The relation of insight to data is, in its proper meaning, a case in which a higher conjugate form is controlling an otherwise coincidental multiplicity of conjugate acts on a lower level. When this analogy is pushed to the lowest level, we have, on the side of the accidents, the multiplicity[9] – the empirical residue involved in space-time; and on the substantial, central side, we have prime matter.

1.4 Unity and Distinction

We have put in more familiar terms what I was saying yesterday. Metaphysics is the integral heuristic structure of proportionate being. We are saying the same thing again. What is this heuristic structure? It is the use of a set of analogies, where the analogies have a fundamental determination from cognitional process. The use of cognitional process as the fundamental instance is justified by the relation between knowing and known. Why can we say that all proportionate being will stand within those analogies? It is because proportionate being is what we can know by experience, understanding, and judgment.

We have, then, three types of act, three levels of cognitional activity: the experiential, the intellectual, the rational. As act, these three levels also have content, and the content contained in the act is the content that is known. There is a content corresponding to experience, a content corresponding to understanding, and a content corresponding to judgment. Understanding presupposes and complements experience; judgment presupposes and complements understanding and experience. Consequently, since there are those relations between the acts, there will be relations of a similar sort between the contents. What we experience is what we inquire into; what we inquire into is what we understand; what we understand is what we conceive; what we conceive is what we reflect on; what we reflect on is what we grasp as virtually unconditioned; what

9 Lonergan's words were 'the accidents – the multiplicity – the empirical residue.' Of itself, the sound does not determine whether 'multiplicity' is in apposition with 'accidents' or with 'empirical residue' (and so the object of 'have'). Our option shows in the text; it is confirmed by discussion 2, §2, Inverse Insight and the Empirical Residue.

we grasp as virtually unconditioned is what we affirm. That *what* is the content. There is a unity, then. It is always the same object that is being approached through experience, understanding, and judgment.

While there is a unity, there is also a distinction. The component that you know through experiencing is not the same as the component that you know through understanding. Understanding is not just another experiential element; it is a unification that supervenes upon experiential elements, and it stands in a different order. The affirmation of judgment, the 'is,' is a third component that closes the unity. Consequently, just as one knowing involves three components, so one known will involve three components; and one can establish, by setting up definitions of distinctions,[10] that, of those three components, one really is not the other; they are really distinct. It is a minor real distinction, because it occurs within one and the same being; nonetheless, it is a real distinction.

Form is what in itself is intelligible; it is the component in the known that is known precisely inasmuch as one is understanding. The experienced in itself is not an intelligible, but it is what can be understood; it is related to the intelligible, it is intelligible in the other. Act in itself has a certain intelligibility, but it is an incomplete intelligibility; it corresponds to the virtually unconditioned. Insofar as it is unconditioned, an absolute, it involves some type of intelligibility; but that intelligibility is a dependent intelligibility. It is a virtually unconditioned, an unconditioned that happens to have its conditions fulfilled; it is contingent. It has a reference to the other, and it must have that reference if it is to be fully understood.[d]

Now P and Q are really distinct if P is, Q is, and P is not Q. There is form, there is potency, there is act; but the three are as components in one being, and no one is the other two. Form is neither potency nor act. Form is neither of the other two, because form is intelligible in itself. Neither act nor potency is intelligible in itself, if we are talking about finite act. But one and the same cannot have contradictory predicates; one and the same cannot be both intelligible in itself and not intelligible in itself. If there are contradictory predicates, both of which are to be affirmed, then there have to be different subjects. Therefore, form is not potency, form is not act. That is a distinction that is true; therefore, it is a real distinction, it regards reality.

Again, while both potency and act are intelligible in the other, still it is a different other in which they are intelligible. Potency is intelligible in

10 *Insight* 488–90.

form; act is intelligible ultimately only in a formally unconditioned act, an act that is not simply the virtually unconditioned, but a formally unconditioned that has no conditions at all. What is intelligible only in the formally unconditioned act is not the same as what is intelligible in form.

We may take another angle on this. One can ask, 'Are these three simply posited as real? Are they components of reality, or are they components of reality as known?' We spoke of all three in terms of their intelligibility, and that would suggest that they are components of reality as known. However, if we go back to our definition of being – being is the object of the verb 'to know' – we note that it has an intrinsic relation to knowing. Being has to be intrinsically intelligible; otherwise understanding and understanding correctly could not be knowledge of being.

1.5 An Illustration of Metaphysical Analysis

Enough has been said to indicate that this procedure from a cognitional analysis to metaphysics can be a very expeditious way of arriving with great precision and rapidity at the conclusions that are found in traditional Aristotelian and Thomist metaphysics. Moreover, without a precise cognitional analysis, certain traditional metaphysical questions are very difficult to handle.[11]

Let us consider our human understanding. Suppose it is true that 'so and so' – Socrates, say – understands something.[e] If we have Socrates, we have a human central form, and we have prime matter and existence. If Socrates understands, he has to be able to understand; to be able to understand, he has to have a potency by which he is able to understand. If he actually understands, there have to be acts of understanding; and as these acts of understanding are not merely acts of understanding, but acts of understanding this kind of thing, there is needed a formal limitation, a *species impressa* or an acquired habit, a set of impressed species.

Again, we can say that Socrates, the man in question, not merely has the capacity to understand, but on a certain range of topics he does not have to stop and think before he gives the answers. This is not true of everybody. Every man has the capacity to understand, the *intellectus*

---

11 For the Thomist basis of the issues discussed in this section, see *Verbum*, chapters 1 and 2 (cognitional), chapter 3 (metaphysical).

possibilis. However, this man has the capacity to answer any question in a whole range without stopping to think. As it was defined by Avicenna, *habitus est quo quis utitur quando voluerit*;[12] a habit is what you use whenever you please. One does not have to work up steam to be able to do it. A man who has just the capacity to understand, without any developed intellectual habit, has to learn before he will be able to handle questions in the manner of the man who has learned. That is the element of conjugate form. Thus Aristotle distinguishes between considering and merely having the habit of science. When one considers, one is actually understanding; there is a third element.

Besides the potency to understand, there is also an active principle. We have spoken of wonder, intellectual alertness, and that is the *intellectus agens*;[13] to account for the occurrence of events in the intellect as a potency, you must have an agent intellect that is relevant to the flow of sensations, perceptions, and images. Moreover, when you understand, you are able to define; when you understand, you are able to formulate at least a hypothesis. That is an act that proceeds from the act of understanding by intellectual consciousness.

Further, the *intellectus agens*, when it arrives at a hypothesis or formulation, a *verbum interius*, is not yet satisfied; it has there simply the ground for going from essence to being by raising the question of existence. When the question of existence is raised one has rational reflection, which heads toward another act, the reflective insight in which you grasp the virtually unconditioned. There can be a habit relevant to that grasp. Some people can make judgments more quickly than others; a man familiar with a particular field is able not merely to put forward hypotheses and possible answers, but he is able to say, 'That's what it is.' He has a habit of wisdom; with regard to practical matters, it is a habit of prudence. That reflective grasp of the understanding expresses itself in the *verbum complexum*.

This analysis, in metaphysical terms, is found in the writings of St Thomas. However, you find an entirely different metaphysical setup in Scotus, who explicitly denied insight into phantasm. But in the commentators, as far as I can see, what you find is Scotist psychology forced upon this Thomist metaphysical setup, and it does not make much sense. It

---

12 A definition frequently referred to by Aquinas. A note in the 1950 Marietti edition of the *Summa theologiae* (at 1-2, q. 49, a. 3, Sed contra) attributes the definition to Averroes: *In III De anima*, comm. 18.

13 Lonergan said *intellectus possibilis*, but both the context and his references elsewhere seem to dictate the change to the present *intellectus agens*.[f]

leads to all sorts of disputed questions. The question whether the *verbum interius*, the formulation, is really distinct from the *intelligere*, the insight, is debated rather futilely if there is no clear idea of what an act of understanding is. The tendency of a number of commentators is to conceive the *intelligere* as the activity from the *species impressa* putting forth the formulation. When the formulation is put forth, intellect takes a look at it and knows the universal. There is no act of understanding; only the activity of producing a concept is acknowledged. As far as I can tell, that seems to be the theory of John of St Thomas.

We have given a general sketch of metaphysics and metaphysical analysis on the basis of cognitional analysis. We have a basis, then, from which to deal with metaphysical issues. Three may be considered here.[14]

First, there is the relation between being and essence. Is existence a third component over and above matter and form? Is being all three? Is the *id quod est* the compound of all three, a triple compound? Or is the *id quod est* the form and matter, and does it exercise the act of existence? It's a nice question.

Aristotle does not advert to the act of existence; but in St Thomas, we have a series of relevant texts. In the *Commentary on the Sentences*, the *Summa contra Gentiles*, and the *pars prima* of the *Summa theologiae*, *id quod est* is the compound of form and matter in material things, and simply the form in angels and God. On the other hand, in the *tertia pars*,[15] q. 17, a. 2, ad 4m, there is (fortunately, from my viewpoint) a passage in which St Thomas says that the compound of form and matter is just *id quo est*. If 'form and matter' is just *id quo*, then to have the *id quod* one has to add existence, and we have a third component.

This question is fundamental in the theory of the incarnation, because one and the same is both God and man. If there is a man, we have matter and form; if matter and form give us an *id quod*, in the man Jesus Christ we have one *id quod*, and in the second person of the Blessed Trinity we have another; consequently, we do not have one and the same that is both God and man. That is why, in this passage, matter and form are just *id quo*. Because of this difficulty, in Cajetan the substance, *id quod est*, is matter and form, but subsistence requires the addition of a mode. A mode

14 The 'three' is editorial, as is our use of 'first,' 'second,' and 'third.' But the additions are based on notes taken at the lecture.
15 The notes of was and fec both have the reference to question 17 in Aquinas, though it is not heard on the tapes; presumably, Lonergan wrote it on the board.

must be added for it to be capable of existence, and that mode is missing in the case of the incarnation.

Insofar as you are proceeding from cognitional analysis, you have a means of handling such questions systematically. Your concepts may be of essence – 'humanity' or 'this humanity' – and as such they have only a remote relation to being. If your concept is 'man,' you are seeing the implication of existence in essence; your concept of being involves not only the conception of the essence, the compound of matter and form, but also the intention of existence, the question of existence. Being as *what*, as a concept, an object of thought, is matter, form, and existence, where matter and form give you 'humanity,' and the question of existence, about to be raised, supplies the other component. If you do not have a precise cognitional analysis, this question is very difficult to handle.

Let us take a *second* question. What is the relation of substance and accident? I understand by my intelligence. My intelligence is an *id quo*; it is conjugate or accidental potency. What is it that understands? What is the 'I'? In our analysis of Socrates, we had prime matter, substantial form, substantial act, accidental potencies, accidental forms or habits, and some accidental acts. Is the 'I' that understands the being, the *id quod est*, the whole, or is it just some *id quo*?[16] If you think simply in terms of the predicaments, which occur in the *Corpus Aristotelicum* as an introductory statement and, I believe, as a purely descriptive stage of the science of metaphysics before the question of causes is raised at all, it is almost inevitable that you will answer that the being is just this *id quo*. You have substance, man, and quality, intelligence, and you have potency, form, and act accounting for the man, and potency, form, and act accounting for the intelligence. On this view, the man, the being, is just the substance, and qualities are added on; they come to the substance.

On the other hand, on the analysis of central and conjugate forms that can be worked out from cognitional analysis, what we have is data that we consider in either of two ways: insofar as they are individual, we grasp in these data a central form; insofar as they are of a kind, we reach conjugate forms. It is understanding the same data from different viewpoints that leads to the two types of form. The central form is the comprehensive unity in the whole; consequently, the man is one by his central

16 Lonergan said, 'Is the "I" … the whole, or is it just "this"?' where the meaning of 'this' was fixed by pointing to the blackboard; we have substituted 'some *id quo*' as his probable meaning. See also p. 212, where pointing showed 'this' to mean substance.

form, which is the principle of unity in the whole. On this second view, it is much easier to understand why a change in the accidents is a change in the man.

Thirdly, there are questions of consciousness. Who is conscious? In virtue of sense and imagination we have an empirical consciousness; by understanding we have an intellectual consciousness; by reflection we have a rational consciousness; and when we go on to will, we have rational self-consciousness. But who is conscious? If 'this' is the man, if it is true that the man is conscious, then it has to be this substance that is conscious. How is it conscious? It is conscious by really distinct accidents. If you say that the man is the whole which is one by the substance, then you can say the man is conscious.

That is a general sketch of metaphysical analysis on the basis of cognitional analysis.[17]

1.6 Canons of Metaphysical Analysis[18]

When I presented the manuscript of *Insight* to the publishers, it was first given to a reader who was an English Dominican[19] – just who he was I've not yet learnt – and the question my publisher put to me was, 'How can you teach this?' Apparently, the report was, 'This isn't what you find in the other books.' This question has probably occurred to those engaged in teaching. One may feel that this seems so different from anything that is in the books that it could not possibly be taught. The preceding discussion, however, illustrates the possibility. In other words, you need not work through the general scheme completely every time. I make use of this material continually in my theology classes in dealing with the speculative side of problems that arise, and I do so in terms of the

17 The three questions were not part of the 'sketch,' and concluded with the remark, 'these are just questions I throw out – I'm not too clear about them.' Coffee break followed immediately; on resumption of the lecture, Lonergan made some announcements about the final lecture of next day, remarking that some would miss the second part – 'always the poorer part anyway.'
18 See *Insight* 503–507 on Lonergan's three rules dealing with metaphysical equivalence. He does not use 'canon' there, the word which is used for the rules of empirical method (chapter 3) and the rules of methodical hermeneutics (§3.8 in chapter 17).
19 The reader was Fr Thomas Gilby, O.P., as he himself reported in a lecture given in Australia. We have this information from Fr Thomas Daly, S.J.

fundamental analogies. Aristotle knew about insight; he did not know all forms of all things and from that knowledge conclude to his hylomorphism; he knew about understanding. It was not possible for him to formulate it as we can formulate it today, but he had a marvelous formulation for it, considering the opportunities of language, and so on. If you have a clear idea of what insight is, it is not hard to become convinced that Aristotle knew about it, and that that relation between insight and data is a key to the relation between potency and form, matter and form.[20] Again, it was insofar as St Thomas grasped the significance of the judgment of existence that he complemented the Augustinian emphasis on truth with the metaphysical component of existence, and set up the relation between essence and existence. The analogies, as I have worked them out in terms of cognitional theory from self-appropriation, also played their role, I believe, in the historical development of scholastic thought. By using the analogies concretely, one can give exactly the same doctrine in any particular case.

Moreover, with regard to the method, there is a whole chapter, Metaphysics as Science, that works out a number of rather detailed questions. I draw attention particularly to this point, because it is of fundamental importance: one applies metaphysical analysis, first of all, concretely.[21] Thomist doctrine is not set up in Euclidean fashion. St Thomas proceeds by answering a series of questions, and the marvelous thing about his procedure is not so much the answers as the series of questions. One can set up principles to be able to answer the questions, but the surprising thing is where those questions came from, the build-up they involve, and the mastery of detail. It is a consideration of concrete questions; metaphysical analysis is applied to the concrete. When we have a truth, we know something. If we wish to go on to the metaphysics of that truth, we want, not an abstract truth, but a concrete truth. We want, for example, 'This man understands,' not 'Man understands.' Because what exists is concrete, the first canon is concreteness: deal with the concrete. We may answer general questions in metaphysical analysis, but the way to

20 Lonergan inserted here a reference to the technical terms which, he said, Aristotle had to improvise totally: 'his *to ti ên einai*, and so on; and while they are not the sort of thing that is going to convince someone who is not too sure that any insights exist and not ready to admit that Aristotle had any idea of it, still if you have a clear idea of what insight is ...' (continued as in the text).
21 *Insight* 503–504 (reference from Lonergan).

approach them always is by an analysis of a concrete instance, because it is the concrete instance that exists. It is Socrates who understands; it is not understanding, not cognitional process. Cognitional process is not a being; it is a component; it is something that happens in a being. Deal with the concrete.

The second canon is the explanatory viewpoint. It is more difficult, but it is also very fundamental. I believe that all sorts of difficulties, obscurities, and insoluble problems are caused insofar as metaphysical analysis is attempted from truths that are merely descriptive. Truths cast in the form of Aristotle's predicaments, where you have descriptive knowledge that does not imply any great understanding but only a minimum of understanding, where you have an understanding of things as they are related to us or an understanding of words, are not a sufficient basis for metaphysical analysis. Even if your knowledge on a question is only descriptive, you have to cast it in explanatory form. When your knowledge is descriptive, it merely anticipates the understanding we are talking about, and you have to transpose, as it were, the descriptive knowing into an intention of explanatory knowing in order to enable the analogies to function properly. The analogies are insight into data, and judgment upon formulation. If your formulation is such that it does not involve any real insight into the thing, then you have to introduce the hypothetical insight, the objective of your heuristic structure, to be able to handle it in terms of the analogy. If you seek a metaphysical analysis that will cover absolutely everything, you get confusion and insoluble disputes.

Thirdly, metaphysical analysis is not grammatical analysis; it is not logical analysis. Someone once said to me, remarking on the Thomist synthesis, that it is 'a marvelous synthesis of human psychology, a marvelous synthesis of reality, a marvelous synthesis of *grammar*.' You can get bogged down in words. You may get concerned with the metaphysical significance of a word; but when questions get onto that level, they become hopeless. You must go behind the words to the experiences, the understanding, the rational judgment, to the analysis of the cognitional process at its root. Potency, form, and act are not in any immediate correspondence with words, with grammar. There are elements in grammar that are closely connected; you can emphasize the 'is,' but it is not 'is' as a word that is metaphysically significant: you can have 'is' merely in the expression of an object of thought or in a question. What counts is the rational act of judgment. Again, what counts is not words but the insight. Unless you reduce your truths to the experience, understanding, and judgment on which their expression rests, you are going to encounter difficulties in metaphysical analysis.

There are, then, three points. The first is concreteness, because being is concrete. The second is the explanatory viewpoint. Suppose we have the descriptive expression, 'He is five feet tall.' Now what are the conjugate potencies, forms, and acts in that? I do not think you can handle the question. You have to conceive the measurement, 'five feet tall,' in terms of an understanding of man, and you can see that it shades off into a datum that is not going to be integrated in any explanatory system; it is just going to be a matter of statistical frequency. The third point is that we are concerned with cognitional acts, not talk. The applications of the canons may be complicated, but if you take those directives you can perform metaphysical analysis in terms of central and conjugate potency, form, and act, and explanatory genera and species, and the analysis will be satisfactory; and I think you will also find – although it is a matter of experience – that the root of a large number of disputed questions is simply a violation of those canons.

2   **Metaphysical Integration**

Now we may approach metaphysics from another angle. So far we have been concerned with the general analysis of a being. We have been presenting merely a sketch in terms of a being's metaphysical constituents: central and conjugate potency, form, and act; and the various hierarchies.

However, there is also being as a totality, being as the universe. In particular, there is a special reference to man.[22] It is of special relevance to man insofar as there are the questions of philosophy, and history, and history of philosophy. There are synthetic elements. I speak in terms of emergent probability on lower levels, and they are rather too complex, but the top level within the field of proportionate being is man. If metaphysics is concerned with being qua being, and being is the all-inclusive, then metaphysics has to say something about the all-inclusive. Metaphys-

---

22 Lonergan inserted here, 'For Heidegger, for example, man is the shepherd of being; being comes to light in human living, although that is just *das Seiende*.' This has the appearance of a digression, one which Lonergan perhaps realized, with the mention of human living, was taking him too far afield, into an area where he would have to distinguish *das Sein*, *Dasein*, and *das Seiende*.

ics is not merely analysis of particular beings; it is a view of the whole. The view of the whole in terms of the inorganic, the biological, the animal, comes under the general designation of emergent probability, and I will not attempt to treat that notion here.[23]

2.1 The Significance of Images

Something that has come into great prominence during this century with regard to man is the image. On the one hand, if intellect is not intelligence, if it is just a spiritual reproduction of what you already know by sense with some omissions, then intellect and image are pretty much the same thing, and their difference is accidental. On the other hand, if intellect is intelligence, if intellect is not just a spiritual reproduction of what you already know by sense with some omissions, if intellect is understanding, then there is room in your knowledge of knowledge for a grasp of the function of the image.

Mircea Eliade, in a small book I found very helpful, *Images et symboles*, notes that the rationalist tendency of the eighteenth century led to a devaluation of the image.[24] The emphasis upon reason as the characteristic of man led everyone to want to feel that he was just an embodiment of pure reason, and the image was devalued. That devaluation, however, did not result in any suppression of the image; it did not diminish in any way the power of the image in human living. The effect was simply a depravation of the image. For example, the symbol of Paradise Lost appears in popular modern literature and thinking in the musical *South Pacific* about a never-never land where everything is perfect. The goddesses of Greek mythology appear in modern life as the pinup girl. The image is still there, and it is still performing its functions: but those functions have been depraved, cheapened, lowered.

Eliade makes a second point. The study of images can take place in two ways. There is, first, the clinical manner. Depth psychology has reinstated the importance of the image or symbol. There is the study of symbols in Freudian doctrine and in Jung's doctrine, and the significance attached to them is considerable. But the clinical study of the image considers the

---

23 On emergent probability, see *Insight* 115–28, 259–62, 510.
24 Mircea Eliade, *Images et symboles: Essais sur le symbolisme magico-religieux* (Paris: Gallimard, 1952); trans. Philip Mairet, *Images and Symbols: Studies in Religious Symbolism* (New York: Sheed and Ward, 1961).

image in abnormal cases, in cases where something has gone wrong.[g] According to Eliade, the proper field in which to investigate and grasp the significance of images and symbols is the history of religion, especially primitive religion. In another work, *Le chamanisme*, Eliade investigates the medicine man in the archaic civilization of northern central Asia.[25] He is the prototype of the medicine man as we hear of him in the stories of North American Indians. Eliade's study of the shaman in that civilization on its primitive level is in terms of archaic techniques of mysticism. For Eliade, the image is a transcultural language.[h] One can understand a civilization that is totally removed from one's own, both in time and space and all historical connections, in terms of fundamental images. Those images by themselves constitute a language that is independent of words. Those are a few general notions on the image.

2.2 Mystery and Myth

The connection of the image with the doctrine of self-appropriation that we have been developing is twofold. Our sensitive living is a matter of images that release emotions and affects and result in action. Intellect and reason and will are a higher control. The execution of what we will depends upon our ability to control our psyches and to manipulate them. However, on the side of cognition, insofar as man develops, insofar as he develops first as an animal and then as intelligent and then as rational, the image has a function to fulfil with regard to the whole of human living. The image has to be able to carry the anticipations of intelligence and rationality; it has to carry the dim, imperfect development of the intelligence and rationality that are proper to man. In itself, the image, the symbol, is a sensitive function. But in the integration of man, insofar as the image carries the significance and the ideals proper to intellect and reason and will, we have mystery.

The image has a logic of its own. It is not subject to any law of univocity.

---

25 Eliade, *Le chamanisme et les techniques archaïques de l'exstase* (Paris: Payot, 1951); trans. Willard R. Trask, *Shamanism: Archaic Techniques of Ecstasy* (Princeton: Princeton University Press, 1970). See also Eliade's work, *Traité d'histoire des religions* (Paris: Payot, 1949); trans. Rosemary Sheed, *Patterns in Comparative Religion: A Study of the Element of the Sacred in the History of Religious Phenomena* (New York: Sheed and Ward, 1958).
Lonergan had referred in his lecture to Eliade's 2-volume work on the history of religions. We are presuming he meant the *Traité*, though later Eliade was to produce a multi-volume history of religious ideas.

218 Understanding and Being

Words have to have one meaning or a limited series of meanings; if it is
not sufficiently clear which meaning one is employing, words become
useless. But the image is not tied down to one meaning. It can have a
different meaning today from its meaning yesterday. It can have different
meanings for different people. It can become enriched in meaning as a
person develops. The significance of the religious image, the death and
resurrection of Christ, is a significance that can develop with the whole
religious development of the person; it can be apprehended by the child,
and it can be enriched in meaning with the developed and cultured
adult understanding of human life. The image can carry all levels of
understanding, from the most incomplete to the highest and most complete. Again, because of that multiplicity of interpretations, the image is
not under the law of contradiction. It can mean different things at different times. It is an implement of developing understanding, rationality,
and virtue. On the other hand, the image can also be a block; it can also
function as myth. Living on the level of the image can be a closing
off against the development of intelligence and rationality and virtue.
Considered from this viewpoint, it is significant that Platonism involves
a critique of the gods, a critique of common notions, a critique of Homer.[26]

The notions of mystery and myth are developed at some greater length
in *Insight*.[27] However, the main point is that there is a fundamental
ambiguity in the image. The significance of the image has to be considered
in connection with the polymorphism of the human subject. Man develops as an animal, as intelligent, as rational. He reaches maturity on those
different levels at different times. Yet he can develop as a unity insofar
as the image, the symbol, is capable of carrying higher meaning, of
suggesting and evoking – one does not know just what. It is the means
of carrying the higher; but again, it can run into the aberration of myth
and magic.

The image, then, is a principle of continuity in the developing subject.
Again, it is a principle of efficacy in the developed subject. No development of intelligence and reason can legitimately claim that images were
simply used as a ladder to reach that level of development, and that
images can now be dispensed with. With regard to certain mystical states,

26 Lonergan said, 'a critique of Homer – Hesiod.' Did he mean Hesiod as
   an example of critiques of Homer, or did he mean we must critique
   both Homer and Hesiod? For the former view (adopted here) see *Method
   in Theology* 90–91.
27 *Insight* 531–49, 561–62, 723–24.

that may be true; but apart from exceptions – and mystical states are exceptional – the general rule is that the image is not transcended. Your willing is efficacious in your living insofar as what you will can be connected with images that are efficacious for you. With images and symbols, forces are also necessarily associated; it is not just a matter of producing what you please, in the sense of any image at all. It is an image that in you releases emotion, affection, and action – it is that type of image that is significant.

2.3 The Historical Component in Self-appropriation

That is one aspect of self-appropriation. You can see how that imaginative side enables self-appropriation to project itself not only into the childhood of one's own past but also into the childhood of humanity. It aids an apprehension of man on the grand scale. Again, we have said that the measure of one's self-appropriation is a measure of the meaning or the significance one can put into cognitional analysis; but it is also a measure of the dexterity, the comprehension, of metaphysics, where metaphysics is concerned with being as the all-inclusive or the all-inclusive of proportionate being. We are easily brought to a consideration of the historical component in self-appropriation.

I happen to have remarked frequently that the account I have been giving of cognitional analysis has been facilitated enormously by the development of modern science and the techniques of introspective psychology, which did not exist at the time of Aristotle or Aquinas; they lead to a mode of expression that was not previously possible. That is a general phenomenon. For a man to have self-appropriation, it is not enough for him to *be* empirically, intelligently, and rationally conscious; he has to *know* that he is. Knowing that he is, is conditioned by self-expression, self-manifestation. I think there is something very true in the Hegelian connection between the subjective spirit and its manifestation in objective spirit. One need not underpin Hegel's ideas in this regard with his peculiar metaphysics; but the notion, it seems to me, is both true and extremely significant insofar as one is concerned to understand history. Self-appropriation is conditioned not merely by the fact that one is empirically, intelligently, and rationally conscious; it is conditioned also by that fact as manifested.

The fact is manifested, first of all, in those activities and products that are sensible things, that can be inspected, as it were. They are material creations such as the material creations of modern science. You can go right back to the earliest forms of technology, man using instruments. There is a manifestation of intelligence and reasonableness in the things that man makes, in the way that men behave. That provides a first level of manifestation.

Insofar as the activities and products are linguistic, one has again a fuller and more immediate manifestation. When the level of science is reached, one has again a fuller object upon which one can reflect to attain one's self-appropriation. And when it reaches the level of a succession of philosophies, all claiming different things, one meets the objective manifestation and expression of the polymorphism of the human subject – not merely of his capacity and need to develop but also of the possibility and fact that he develops in quite different ways.

It is possible, I believe and suggest, to classify the differences of philosophies in terms of the measure of self-appropriation. Insofar as the self qua experiencing alone is appropriated – we are quite well aware of ourselves as seeing, hearing, talking, and so forth – on this experiential level, philosophies are materialistic, atomistic, sensistic, positivistic, pragmatist. If internal experience is also included, philosophies are modernist. Modernism[i] makes religious experience the ultimate in religion, while the truths, the dogmas of the church, are only symbols. So long as these symbols serve the experience which is the ultimate criterion, well and good; but when they are out of date, they are simply to be forgotten; the emphasis is on experience. Philosophy that places the emphasis upon experience is one type that keeps recurring in different forms right through the whole history of philosophy.

Besides self-appropriation qua experience, there is self-appropriation qua intelligent. To it we devote the first eight chapters of *Insight*. It yields philosophies of the Aristotelian type, the Kantian type, the idealist type, the relativist type, and the essentialist type. Intelligence is combined with experience, and that is the self that is appropriated. From the different ways in which intelligence is conceived and experience is conceived, there arises another whole type of philosophy.

When self-appropriation qua judging is added, a third type of philosophy is obtained. All three types develop. They develop according to the self-appropriation of the individual, and according to the degree and the mode of self-appropriation that is possible in a given age and a given culture. However, the development of contemporary psychology and the development of the sciences at the present time make possible a much fuller and more exact self-appropriation than was possible before those developments occurred, just as the development of language and writing made possible an earlier self-appropriation of a similar type.

Again, there can be degrees of exclusiveness. Philosophy can be developed on the basis of self-appropriation qua experiencing, deliberately excluding self-appropriation qua intelligent and qua judging. In other words, understanding and judgment may be said to be merely subjective activities that do not count in knowing the real. On the other hand, a philosophy can be open to further self-appropriation, and nuances will arise in that way. You can have self-appropriation qua experiencing and qua intelligent, and be open to self-appropriation qua judgment; but you may still exclude judgment, or implicitly exclude it insofar as it is insufficiently appreciated.

Further, there is not only a division of philosophies. A division of stages in culture may be undertaken along the same general lines. Take the example of Pitirim Sorokin. He performed an enormous analysis according to the best available statistical methods.[28] While he had no great faith in statistical methods and the charts in which statistical results are presented, he believed that this was the only way to speak to the culture in which he was working. Moreover, the work was not carried out all by himself; it was farmed out to different experts in different fields. But my point is that Sorokin worked out a scheme of three types of culture: sensate, idealistic, and ideational. He considered the way sensate culture was manifesting itself in architecture, painting, poetry, and so on, through all of the aspects of human living. Again, he worked out the characteristics of an idealistic culture and an ideational culture in all of the same fields. He was able to set up a cycle. Western civilization, from the Greek period to the present day, has moved through phases of sensate, idealistic, and ideational culture. There is an obvious correlation between sensate, idealistic, and ideational cultures, on the one hand, and the three degrees of self-appropriation, on the other. By using Sorokin's material, one can prolong this analysis of the subject into terms of the development of culture.

28 Pitirim Sorokin, *Social and Cultural Dynamics*, 4 vols. (New York: American Book Company, 1937–41). Lonergan mentioned a discussion of Sorokin 'the other night.' He seems to refer to an unrecorded discussion, possibly Tuesday, August 12.

2.4 Self-appropriation and Historical Study

This raises a further question. Just as from self-appropriation it is possible to set up a technical metaphysical analysis of the single being in its different metaphysical components, so also it is possible to derive categories[j] for characterizing fundamentally different philosophies, differentiated by their level and their period, in terms of the stages of development that become possible in self-appropriation. Similarly, and more generally, this may be done for cultures.[k] The further question is, What does this yield with regard to the understanding of man?

The categories, I should say, provide an upper blade for historical study, the study of the history of philosophy, or the study of the history of cultures, of literatures, and so on. However, it is just an upper blade. In other words, just as in physics, for example, it is not enough to have invariants and differential equations, but you must have measurements going up through curve fitting, so here you do not simply set up categories and deduce the history of philosophy, the course of the history of cultures, and so on. Again, as it is not deducing in the ordinary sense of the word, so it is not deducing in the Hegelian sense of the word, namely, in the precise form of the Hegelian dialectic. However, it has something in common with the use of the differential equations in physics that provide a principle of interpretation for materials that are to be gathered on the lower blade. Thus in history of philosophy, one has to have exact historical knowledge of what the philosopher said, what were the meanings of the words he used at the time and place he spoke, and so on. However, while all this historical work is necessary, by itself it is not sufficient. It is necessary to have the factual side; but if all you have is that factual side, you will also have superficiality. Consequently, the presentation in *Insight* is in terms of a hermeneutics, a theory of interpretation.[29]

The merely positivistic approach to the problem of interpreting a writer, which emphasizes the merely factual side, is typical of history as developed from the nineteenth century up to the present time. It is held that the really scientific part of history is collecting and editing the documents, and making no comment whatever that goes beyond the documents. On this view, then, those who make some brief comment on the documents are a lower type of scientist – if the comments are tightly tied in with the documents, well, they are fairly good scientists, though

29 *Insight* 562–94.

still second-rate. But if you go on to say something more intelligent about the content of the documents, you have begun to speculate; and if you attempt to consider the relations between successive philosophers, that is just wind. That is what I meant in saying that one can be factual and nevertheless superficial.

The first point that I make in working out the theory of interpretation is that all documents and all monuments of the past are simply sensible signs that exhibit a spatial order. All intelligibility that can be given those signs exists formally only in the interpreter and is a function of his capacity to interpret. The 'out there' merely provides a criterion for editing documents or editing pictures of the carvings on sarcophagi, and so on; and the editing simply provides another 'out there.' All interpreting depends upon the ability of the interpreter to move from *his* experiences to imaginative reconstruction of the situation in the past, from *his* understanding to a hypothetical account of the understanding behind those signs, from *his* knowledge of the possibilities of human judgment and the possibilities that arise from the polymorphism of the human subject, to the type of judgments and the type of decisions and motives that lie behind those signs. That is the first point.

Secondly, it is not by understanding as little as possible that you are going to arrive at a correct understanding of the thinkers and actors of the past, but by understanding as much as you possibly can. The correct interpretation of a passage in Kant, Aquinas, Aristotle, or Augustine is not going to be reached by determining what is most obvious to the least intelligent person you can find. The whole problem is to find someone intelligent enough, capable of sufficient intellectual development, to be able to estimate just what point in intellectual development is represented by the author in general or by these particular statements in a given case. In other words, don't be afraid of preconceived ideas. Anyone who has developed beyond infancy has some development of understanding, and the only way to eliminate those ideas is to return to infancy. It cannot be done. The way to deal with the problem of interpretation is to develop one's intelligence as much as possible. It is only in terms of that fullest possible development of intelligence – development to the point where wisdom is not merely a matter of saying what is so with regard to reality, but also what is so with regard to the point of development achieved by man in the past according to the possibilities of different levels of culture – that correct interpretative judgments are possible.

Insofar as your self-appropriation makes you aware of the possibility of settling for a positivist philosophy or an idealist philosophy or a realist philosophy, insofar as you are able to grasp that all of those three are possible ways which may be taken by men living under certain conditions and under certain pressures, and insofar as you are able to grasp the reasons men can have for taking those ways, you are in possession of an upper blade in the study of history of philosophy and history of culture. The fuller your understanding of the polymorphism of your own being, the better understanding you have of yourself and the better possibility you have for understanding others, for projecting from the present into the past and reaching an understanding of philosophers and cultures that constitute the past.

This self-appropriation provides in history of philosophy and in history of cultures an upper blade that combines with the lower blade to close in upon an interpretation. The conditions in which that can possibly be worked out and the type of collaboration required are somewhat complex. All I wish to communicate is the general idea that self-appropriation enables us not only to have an analysis of particular beings in terms of potency, form, act – conjugate and central – explanatory genera and species, and also development (a point I have skipped here), but also to grasp proportionate being as a whole: on the less than human levels, I did it in terms of emergent probability; and on the human level, the categories of a scientific hermeneutics[1] – the last section of chapter 17 – offered some indications.[30]

30 The DJS reel takes us right to the end of the lecture, as is clear from Lonergan's concluding words, 'I think it's time for lunch.' The other reels stopped earlier in the paragraph (LRI at 'upper blade'; WAS at 'less than human levels').

10

Ethics and God[1]

1   The Possibility of Ethics

In *Insight* we noted that we are concerned not to draw up a code of ethics but rather to meet the relevant prior questions. We are concerned with the possibility of ethics. Can ethics be conceived along the same lines as metaphysics?

1.1 Levels of the Good

We distinguish three levels of the good: the good as the object of appetite, the good of order, and value.

The object of appetite is the good on an elementary level. When attained, it is experienced as pleasant, enjoyable, satisfying. But we experience aversions no less than desire, pain no less than pleasure. Consequently, on the elementary level, the good is coupled with its opposite, the bad. However, among our desires there is the detached and disinterested desire to know. While it has its satisfaction in one's own joy in insight, it is not content with satisfaction; the desire to know heads beyond the satisfaction of insight to the further question whether one's insight is correct. Its immanent criterion is the attainment of an unconditioned independent of one's own likes and dislikes, one's own desires and aver-

---

1 The tenth lecture, Friday, August 15, 1958. See discussion 5, where there was reference passim to the first part of this lecture.

sions. Through the knowledge-generating desire there comes to light a second meaning of the good.

The second level of the good is the good of order. Such is the family as an institution, the technology, the economy, and the polity. The good of order is not the object of any single desire, for it stands to single desires as system to systematized. In the family,[2] technology, economy, and polity there is a flow of operations, and a flow of benefits, distributed among the members, resulting from the operations. These operations must be cooperations, and so there are required habits in the individual and some type of habitual structure, in the way of techniques and institutions, that may be implicit in customs, in use and wont, or may be formulated in laws, tribunals, and so on. Finally, there are personal relations. That is the order as realized concretely in human living.

Thirdly, there is value. Value is the good as an object of possible rational choice. Particular objects of appetite are values insofar as they lie within a good of order; it is not sheer appetite but intelligently ordered appetite. A good of order is a value, first of all, because that is the order that happens to exist at any given time; secondly, there is the value in the sense of improving the actual order, value in the sense of avoiding what destroys the actually functioning order.

The three levels of the good correspond to the divisions in our knowing: experience, understanding, and judgment. The object of appetite is a spontaneous object, just as experience is given without any reasons being simultaneously supplied. The good of order is an intelligible unification, something in the way of organization, though it may be much more spontaneous than any deliberately conceived organizing blueprint. Value lies upon the level of judgment; it is the rational choice. Our notion of the possibility of ethics has its grounds in the extension of self-appropriation from the subject as knowing to the subject as both knowing and doing. The object of experience ties in with objects of appetite, the good of order ties in with the grasping of intelligibility, value ties in with the judgment that leads to choice.

1.2 The Existence and Freedom of the Will

The question arises of the precise meaning of choice and of will. Traditionally, will is defined as an appetite that follows reason, an intellectual

2 Recording starts here; the previous material is supplied from chapter

appetite. To have an object of will, there must be a good of order. It is through the good of order, which is an intelligible good, and insofar as objects of appetite are subsumed or placed within some apprehension of a good of order, that the functioning of will can occur.

The existence of will is proved most simply by Aristotle when he remarks that the doctor can kill or cure. If the doctor knows enough medicine to be able to cure you, he also knows several very neat ways of killing you. Knowledge, of itself, does not settle a course of action. The doctor is an example of knowledge, and the knowledge as such regards contraries; knowledge grounds different and even opposed courses of action. Again, if you know how to build a bridge, you also know the most effective place to put the explosive if you wish to destroy it. Knowledge, of itself, grounds different possible courses of action. Because knowledge has that polyvalence, so to speak, that multiplicity of uses, we are led to posit a distinct type of operation, habituation, act. *Will* corresponds to potency, *willingness* to habit or form, and *willing* to the act.

Moreover, the act of will is free. To affirm the freedom of the act of will is not to affirm that it is unguided or indeterminate; there are obviously reasons for our choices. What is affirmed when one speaks of the freedom of the will is that the reasons do not settle the choices. For example, I am going to have lunch at noon, but no one now can demonstrate that I will have lunch at noon. You can establish the matter with a very high probability, but you cannot prove it, you cannot demonstrate it. I might very well fall ill before lunch, and then having lunch would be entirely out of the question. You cannot demonstrate a future course of action. While there are things that can be proved in knowledge, future courses of action are not among them. You can reason and argue about what would be the right thing to choose and what would be the most advantageous thing to choose, and so on, but all of those reasons simply prepare the ground for the choice. You can continue reasoning about the matter indefinitely. Like Hamlet, you can go back to all the preconditions and consider all the possibilities, and then you can consider your considerations, and 'the native hue of resolution[3] / Is sicklied o'er with the pale cast

---

18 of *Insight*, with confirmation from sketchy notes taken by FEC and WAS.

3 *Hamlet*, act 3, scene 1, with a correction of Lonergan's quotation; he had said 'the native hue of action.' *Insight* 611 is almost exact.

of thought.' The cognitional process, of itself, has no immanent term in the field of action. Because cognition has no immanent term in action and does not settle things, the will is said to be free.

As the will is not settled by cognitional antecedents, as you cannot demonstrate from cognitional antecedents the choices that will be taken, still less can you demonstrate choices from lower-level determinants. The lower level does not determine the higher; it provides material conditions.[4] Consider, for example, consciousness. Consciousness has its own orientation, and what one perceives depends upon the orientation of consciousness. Consciousness is not determined simply by the object. We have spoken of *Sorge*, concern, as the root of one's world, and also of a selective inattention that ignores what lies beyond one's horizon. Consciousness itself has a fundamental freedom; it is independent of biological and neural determinants. It is in that sense, it seems to me, that Heidegger speaks mainly of freedom, the freedom of the flow of percepts, the determination of one's world by one's *Sorge* or concern.

1.3 The Ground of Choice

The notion of the freedom of the will brings us to a fourth level of consciousness.[a] We have spoken of empirical, intellectual, and rational consciousness, but we reach a fourth stage, rational self-consciousness, when there arises the question, What am I to do?

We have been speaking of self-appropriation. Now the self that we are attempting to appropriate in the field of knowledge is a self that is guided by absolute or objective norms. It is as though the power of logic were something immanent within me, something quite impersonal. The pure desire to know sets up exigences and tendencies that are opposed to me as a concrete functioning unit with desires and fears. If my cognitional process is guided by my desires and fears, the result is not knowing but simply wishful thinking. There has to be a detachment from self in knowledge. But when the question arises of the free act, of willing, of the practical course of action, I reach rational self-consciousness, and what is at issue is fundamentally myself.[b]

---

4 Lonergan added, 'That's a point that's developed more fully in the book, in terms of the relation between the levels.' See *Insight* 616; more fully, chapter 8, § 3, Genus as Explanatory, and chapter 15, § 3, Explanatory Genera and Species.

When we say that the act of will is free, it is similar to saying that intellect understands. *I* understand by my intellect; *I* choose by my will. The ground of the free act is myself; I am the *id quod operatur*. What underlies an individual's choices? The ultimate reason is himself. We said that choices in their determinacy cannot be reduced to the individual's knowledge; choice comes in precisely because knowledge does not settle the issue. Again, choices cannot be reduced to lower determinants, because the contents of consciousness are largely determined by the orientation of consciousness itself. In free choice, *I* am the ground of the act; *I* am the ultimate reason. Why this act? Because of *me*.

1.4 Choice as a Determinant of Development

Choice is a determinant in personal development and in objective process.

By my free acts I am making myself. The series of my choices gives me the character I have. One can say that all men have the same nature, and that it is in virtue of matter that all men are distinct individuals.[c] But there is also a personal differentiation of one man from another, and that personal differentiation of one man from another is the cumulative product of each man's own free choices. One becomes oneself by one's choices. The ground of choice is myself as rationally self-conscious and making myself. This is the point to Eisenhower's remark, 'We have to be men.' We make ourselves the men we are, and as long as life lasts the process continues. A man can make himself into something, and he can decline again to nothing, he can go to pieces. The free choice, then, is a determinant in my own development, a determinant in my making myself what I am to be. The self that one is, is the self that one becomes. This theme, being oneself, becoming oneself, is of considerable interest in existentialist circles, and it is a very fundamental theme. It is an issue that arises for anyone who is at all reflective, and it provides one of the starting points of existentialist reflection.

This development, like all development, is caught, as it were, between two fires. The central notion is the habit in the will. On the one hand, without development I am characterless, I have not yet become myself, I am not orientated in any specific direction. Just as a person who understands nothing will have to learn before he will habitually be able to answer any question that arises within a given range, so there is needed a development in the will of willingness, a habituation of the will, that comes as a result of making choices. If we are to do those things we do not habitually do, we have to develop in ourselves the willingness. If that willingness has been developed, when the occasion for doing arises we will not have to be persuaded to act. Just as we do not have to learn again those things that we habitually know, so we do not have to be persuaded to do those things we ordinarily do; we have the willingness. On the other hand, though, until one has attained willingness with respect to every right action, one is at a disadvantage in being a good man. When the occasion arises for a right action, we see that it is the right thing to do, and if we have the time, we can go through all the reflections that constitute the persuasion to be willing to act. But usually we do not have the time; we are unwilling; and because we are unwilling, we are unwilling to make the time.

In other words, inasmuch as we have perfect willingness, we are ready to do what is right under all circumstances on every occasion without having to argue ourselves into it. But inasmuch as we do not have perfect willingness, the perfect habitual state of the will, we cannot spontaneously do what is right the way heavy bodies fall. St Thomas remarks that the just man does just actions the way fire rises upwards;[5] he has acquired habitual willingness, the freedom from the need of being persuaded or persuading himself with respect to any just action he may be called upon to perform. That is the idea of the habit in the will. But there is a catch to habit in the will. Insofar as we do not have the willingness, we are not able, on the spot and without reflection, to do the right action; we need to be persuaded, we have to get up the steam to do it. Moreover, insofar as our habitual willingness is for wrong actions, we do them unless we get up the steam not to do them.

We distinguish, then, between the essential freedom of the will and its effective freedom. Essential freedom lies in the very structure of what our knowing is in practical fields, in the fact that that knowing does not result in any practical decision. The decision arises from a further factor, the will, and that further factor is not determined by anything except myself.

---

5 The reference is probably to *Summa theologiae*, 1-2, q. 113, a. 7, ad 4m; that is the reference Lonergan gives in *Grace and Freedom* for the statement, 'Just as the generation of fire results in immediate burning [Latin: '*movetur sursum*'], so the infusion of the virtues results in immediate acts of virtue' (p. 58; see also pp. 56–57).

I am the one. Why this act?[6] *I* choose to do so; the ultimate reason is the *I*. But that *I*, the self, makes itself through its choices, and the choices are free essentially; they are mine. And they could be other; I can always make up my mind to take the time out, to get up the steam to do what is right and to avoid what is wrong. On the other hand, while I may make up my mind, I may also be left behind by life. While one is taking time out, things keep moving on. The world does not give you the time. Again, if one thinks that by sheer effort one is going to achieve ideal willingness, there can result a nervous breakdown of sorts. For example, novices entering the religious life have ideals of perfection put before them before they have acquired ideal willingness, and they think they can reach the ideal by a good strong resolution. By efforts of attention and concentration, they attempt to achieve what should be achieved by acquiring the relevant willingness, the relevant virtue. There results a psychological breakdown, a nervous breakdown of some sort. In other words, there is a physical limit, a real limitation to our freedom. Freedom does not mean that at every tick of the clock we are back again in a state of perfect indifference,[d] ready to do this or that. We have to recognize that our freedom has two aspects, essential freedom and effective freedom.

Because essential and effective freedom may be distinguished, there is a possibility of a meaning when we speak of being able to do right by God's grace. St Paul says: It is God who operates in you, both good will and good performance (Philippians 2.13).[7] St Augustine develops this in his doctrine of grace as operating and as cooperating.[8] He illustrates it from St Peter, who at the last supper told our Lord, Even if all deny thee, betray thee, I will not do so,[9] and yet proceeded to do so. Insofar as Peter said, 'I will not do so,' he had operative grace, the good will. But there are two degrees in having good will: the good will that wants to do it, and the good will that does it. The second degree was had by Peter in his martyrdom when he not merely wanted to do it but actually did it. The

---

6 The question in the lecture was, 'Why do I throw up the chalk?' as Lonergan tossed and caught the chalk he was using.
7 A free quotation, perhaps from memory; the RSV has 'for God is at work in you, both to will and to work for his good pleasure.'
8 See *Grace and Freedom*, especially 2–6.
9 None of the variants in the four gospels expresses it in quite this manner. Thus Matthew 26.33: 'Though they all fall away because of you, I will never fall away' (RSV). See also Mark 14.29; Luke 22.33; John 13.37.

fact that man is free essentially and yet has to win for himself effective freedom constitutes the psychological ground for prayer, for seeking God's help in doing what is right – and not only the psychological ground but also the ontological ground, because psychology is not outside being and so not outside ontology. There are occasions when we all have to get down on our 'benders' and ask God's help.

Besides determining my development, my becoming whatever self I am, the kind of man I am, choice is also a determinant in objective process. A choice results in a course of action, in the occurrence of objects of appetite, in the satisfaction of desires or the realization of the worst that was feared. It results in the actual functioning of the good of order. The actual functioning of the good of order may be excellent or fair or mediocre or poor or disastrous. In a revolution, the good of order of the state vanishes, and violence takes over. Again, worse than a revolution is the total breakdown of the state. Similarly, in an economic depression the good of order continues to function in some way, but there are millions who are unemployed and who are extruded from the order. Choice has its bearing on the improvement of the actually functioning order, or upon its further corruption and distortion. Relevant to this free act, then, is determinative development in the subject, becoming oneself, and determinative development in the objective human process, the social process, the world-historical process.

1.5 The Moral Imperative

One's choice is under an imperative. We said that it was free, essentially free, but that effective freedom was something to be won. While that freedom means that choice is not settled simply by intellect, regularly there can be an exigence from intellect requiring choices of a certain kind and excluding other choices. The rationally self-conscious subject is not only a knower but also a doer, and he is under a rational imperative to act. Just as the subject cannot be rational without making the judgment once the virtually unconditioned has been grasped, so there are practical judgments such that the rationally self-conscious knower and doer cannot be rational[e] without making the choice dictated by practical judgment, judgment upon value.

There is an imperative implicit in the very structure of the rationally self-conscious knower and doer. One can grasp the existing good of order, the actually functioning good of order, as a value that cannot be replaced overnight. One can see that that good of order has certain implications that cannot be violated without a destruction of the good. The good of order is something determinate; if it is something determinate, then there is an opposite to it. We considered the good of order in terms of the family, the technology, the economy, the polity, but there is also an *immanent* good of order in the self-developing subject, in the subject who is making himself by his choices. We have said that self-appropriation leads to a discovery that the self to be appropriated has to develop. Well, that discovery extends right through the rationally self-conscious knower and doer. It is the discovery that willingness is something that has to be developed to increase my effective freedom. The order without and the order within, in concrete practical judgments, can result in the judgment that this is what ought to be concretely, this is what I ought to do, or this is what I ought not to do. In virtue of the coherence of the rationally self-conscious subject, in virtue of the fact that one is a knower and so quite detached and has no difficulty telling someone else what *he* ought to do, and at the same time a doer and consequently also telling oneself what one ought to do, there emerges the moral imperative.

1.6 Positive and Negative Ethics

On this basis, I believe, there can be developed an ethics, that is, a science of the 'what ought to be' and the 'what ought not to be.' I do not attempt to do that here, and I did not attempt it even in *Insight*; we have been concerned with the *possibility* of ethics. We have determinate notions on the good, and we are involved in a necessity of action. Not to choose is not a possible choice; we have to choose. Even if we choose not to choose, at least we make that choice, and in that choice are involved all of its consequences. Shall I go off to the desert? That, to some extent, would be one way of choosing not to choose.

The one point I would like to make is that one may distinguish between the positive and the negative aspects of ethics. It is much easier to develop the negative aspect of ethics, the 'Thou shalt not.' There are many possible objects of choice that are not values, that cannot be conceived as values, and in that case you can demonstrate quite clearly, 'Thou shalt not,' 'There ought not to be this.' Just as there are positions and counterpositions in knowing, for the rational consciousness, so there is the extension of positions and counterpositions in doing, for the rational self-consciousness. That one ought not to do such and such may be demonstrated quite clearly, because the project is involved in an internal contradiction of some sort. The self that is organized on the level of objects of appetite is radically in conflict with guidance by the good of order, any good of order. He wants to rearrange the world about himself; he is an egoist. For the self organized on that level, the good of order is not an objective intelligibility in the way things can be intelligibly arranged and in the way things can function. The good of order, from that standpoint, is the ordering of things around me. Illustrations of egoism are endless.

Just as there is development from a theory of knowledge in terms of intuition to a theory of knowledge in terms of intelligence and judgment, so also there is the moral development of the subject from an aesthetic sphere that is concerned with objects of appetite, with all the refinement of the Cyrenaic, or again with all the crudities attributed to certain types of Epicurean. There is the reversal, the conversion, the transformation, of that type of organization in the subject, to bring him into harmony with the objective good of order. What is good is objectively good; it is the proper functioning of society around one and of the order within one, the justice within the man.

Although it is a complicated enough business, it is relatively easy to demonstrate 'Thou shalt not.' One finds much more written, with much more convincing proofs, on the subject of ethical precepts that are negative. Why? Because positive ethics is the concern of the subject with regard to himself and with regard to the actually functioning good of order in which he finds himself, on all its levels. Positively to do good is to become good oneself, to move from organization on the level of objects of appetite, just as one moves from knowledge organized about intuition, to a self that is in harmony with what objectively is good. The good person says, 'If that's the thing to do, I'll do it.' But that is not easy; one says rather, 'What's in it for me?' So there are two types of organization giving rise to two types of questions: What's in it for me? What ought I do? That is, doing good is not merely development in the subject, not merely asceticism. It is also promoting the good of order in the general case, in the concrete situation in which one lives and in all its ramifications insofar as one can influence them.

1.7 The Course of Human History

To grasp a notion of a positive ethics, especially with regard to the good of order, is to reflect upon history. I will offer a very brief and schematic reflection on history.[10]

There is a series of approximations to the course of human history.[f] As a first approximation we note that man has a history, that human situations change. The whole way in which human life is organized, the benefits that accrue from the cooperation of men – all this changes. That process of change is a matter of situation, insight, policy, counsel, consent, course of action,[g] and a new situation which gives rise to new insights.

There is an objectively functioning good of order, and it functions in virtue of clusters of insights relevant to certain departments, and relevant to all the individuals involved in the order. How is it that the whole situation changes? It changes insofar as situations give rise to insights; one grasps a better way of doing things. The insight, the better way, suggests a policy, a course of action. But a course of action will involve others, and you have to get their consent, you have to spread the idea around. Consent results in action. Because the action comes as a result of a fresh insight, the situation changes. One change in the situation leads on to further insights, and things begin to roll. There is a difference between a paper account of the state and the actual state, a nation, a people that develops. There is a difference between a paper account of the economy and an economy that develops. As the United States entered into the Second World War, Roosevelt spoke of producing 'a bomber an hour,' and something like that was actually done. But the king of Siam might have the same idea, and there would be no question of its being carried out. The difficulty would not be merely a lack of factories and material resources; it would be the lack of people with the discipline to work so many hours a day at a steady job, the lack of technical know-how, the lack of managerial skill, and so on. What can be done in a situation depends upon what was done before. The situation gradually develops.

That first approximation provides, as it were, a first differential equation on development. How does development occur? Situations give rise

10 On cycles of development and decline in history, see *Insight* 222–42, 630–33, 688–93, 742–43. On history, see also discussion 5, §8, Historical Knowledge.

to insights, policies, consent, and courses of action, and consent can be implemented in a variety of ways: people may form a small group, an association for a specific end, or a state, or the United Nations.

Secondly, there can be a break in development at the point where consent is required. From the viewpoint of a positive ethics, the policy may be the right thing to do; it may be for the common good. But instead of consent, there is irrational refusal. Irrational refusal implies irrational action. Irrational action introduces irrationality into the situation. The situation takes on characteristics that it would not have if men were reasonable, and that it should not have because men should be reasonable. The irrationality of the situation gives rise to the 'false fact.'[h]

The notion of a false fact is paradoxical. What is the false fact? It is the actual existence of what should not be. On the international scale, the actual existence of what should not be is the ground of *Realpolitik*:[i] 'We have to defend the nation; everything would be fine if the other people did what they ought to do, but they don't, and so we can't.' Again, it is reflected in the personal field: 'This is the right thing to do, but I have to live.' The false fact leads to a grasp, an insight, that is not so much an inverse insight as a perverse insight. The only way you can survive, the only way you can get things done, is by not being scrupulous, to say the least. There is the mounting irrelevance of intellect and reason, initially in particular cases with regard to particular things, but it gradually builds up. If, for example, a philosopher were to tell the members of the United Nations that what we have to do is achieve self-appropriation and follow reason, they would know he was a fool. Intelligence and reason and the pure desire to know are irrelevant to the world as it is; they are in an ivory tower. They may have an influence upon a small group of individuals, if you can interest them in this sort of thing. But that small group of individuals is not the group that has the destiny of nations in its hands, and even if it did, what could it do about it? We have the sociohistorical surd.

The third level of a consideration of history emerges with the question, What are we going to do about it? At the time of Christ, what was expected was an apocalyptic, eschatological solution: all the wicked people were simply to be wiped out, and the just were to triumph; we were to have the kingdom of God, and God's justice was to prevail. However, that is not the kind of solution that exists. The solution that exists is put symbolically by the death and resurrection of Christ. In other words, philosophical analysis takes you as far as the second approximation, but you must move on to religious and theological thought if you want the solution.

The false fact is to be eliminated. The false fact involves suffering. But suffering can result either in the perpetuation of the false fact by violent reaction, refusal, hatred, and the preaching of the irrelevance of intelligence and reason to the world, or in the acceptance of suffering and, at the same time, the adherence to truth, to the Light. The acceptance of suffering and adherence to truth absorb the false fact. The blood of martyrs is the seed of the church. That is, one may say, a mystical idea, but it works. It is on that level that you understand the New Testament, and that you understand the emergence of a still further good of order that is the mystical body[j] of Christ and his church.

2   The Existence of God

In chapter 19 of *Insight* we deal with the notion and the existence of God.[11]

2.1 Approaches to the Notion of God

The conception of knowing in terms of intuition, confrontation, seeing what is there, resulted, in the Platonists, in positing a first order of ideas, the intelligibles, and a second order of gods that contemplated the ideas. First is the object and then the subject. Because the subject depends upon the object, the gods are in a second order. The same principle is operative in Plotinus. In the first position is the *hen*, the One, and in the second position is *nous*, intelligence. The One is beyond being, beyond knowing, beyond intelligence; being is connected with intelligence, and intelligence involves dependence upon what is known. The same principle results, in Scotus, in the *distinctio formalis a parte rei*, the formal distinction on the side of the thing. Distinctions are not merely real distinctions or notional distinctions; there is an intermediate distinction, and it is worked out in terms of Trinitarian theory. The same thing recurs in Sartre insofar as he maintains that it is a contradiction in terms to think of God as both simple and self-conscious or knowing himself, both simple and personal, because knowing involves duality, and duality excludes simplicity.

11 See also discussion 4, § 2, Probability Theory and the Existence of God.

Now there is another tradition that obviates this difficulty. An Aristotelian first mover is, first, immovable, not dependent upon anything else, and yet an intelligence. How is Aristotle able to hold that a first mover is not dependent, without conceiving a first mover as nonintelligent? On the other hand, how is he able to hold that it is intelligent, without conceiving it as dependent?

Aristotle's position can be understood if you start from the nature of insight. Insight is into presentations, and because it is into presentations it is limited. You understand geometry, physics, chemistry, biology, and so on. Our understanding is always a limited understanding, an understanding restricted to a particular field, because insight is into *these* presentations. But if you posit an immaterial being, you posit a being without senses. That immaterial being, if it is anything, is intelligent, because the intellectual is the only positive meaning that can be given to the immaterial. You want, then, an intelligence that is not an insight into something previously given, because there cannot be anything previously given without the senses.

Aristotle moved from insight to his principle that, in the immaterial order, the understander and the understood are identical: *in his quae sunt sine materia, idem est intelligens et intellectum.* When insight is into data, it is understanding of the other, and it is limited by the other; but when we have an intelligence that does not arise from data, it does not have a limiting object, and it is not confined in that fashion. Consequently, Aristotle conceived a first mover as *noêsis noêseos.* I prefer the medieval translation, *intelligentia intelligentiae,* understanding understanding, to the subsequent translation, thinking thought.[12] If you are a conceptualist, you hold that we can think only about concepts, thought, and you do not attend to the prior act of understanding; so when Aristotle speaks of *noêsis noêseôs,* the only meaning you can give to it is 'conceiving conceptions,' 'thinking thought,' and it does not make much sense. On the other hand, if you are not a conceptualist, it can mean 'understanding understanding,' a transposition[k] of the notion of insight into insight, and we have seen something of what insight into insight yields. (Finally, we may note that in Aristotle there are many first movers; in the *Metaphysics* he considers whether there are forty-nine or fifty-seven first movers. He needs a first

12 For Aristotle's phrase, see *Metaphysics,* xii, 9, 1074b 35. For the medieval translation, see Thomas Aquinas, *In xii metaph.,* lect. 11, textus Aristotelis, § 1096 (Marietti number). See *Verbum* 188.

mover for each one of his spheres, and it is not too clear whether it is all reduced to unity in the end or not.[13])

In St Thomas, the development also proceeds from insight; and, as in Aristotle, brute sensibility is excluded. There is a pure act of understanding. However, there is another aspect to the limitation of insight to which attention is drawn. Not only are our insights limited by sensibility to being of this kind, or limited by experience more generally insofar as they are into this and then that, but also, of themselves, our insights are just bright ideas. We have to ask the further question whether our insights are correct. Insight is limited not only on the side of presentations, but also on the side of judgment, which completes it. The unconditioned that is reached in judgment is a virtually unconditioned; it is an unconditioned only in a sense, in the sense that while it really is a conditioned, still de facto its conditions are fulfilled. Consequently, when we speak of a grasp of a virtually unconditioned, and know that it occurs, we can also consider whether there might be a formally unconditioned, that is, an unconditioned that has no conditions extrinsic to itself, no conditions in any significant sense – it is strictly unconditioned.

Now when we not only consider insight as liberated from the limitations of sensibility, but also raise the question, Is that insight *of itself* unconditioned, or is it just a *virtually* unconditioned, a conditioned that has its conditions fulfilled? there arises the distinction between angels and God as conceptions. As with the many Aristotelian first movers, the angel's fundamental act of understanding is understanding himself. He is an intelligence in act, but the intelligence is a limited intelligence. On the other hand, you can also conceive of an intelligence that is unlimited, that has no conditions. That formally unconditioned gives the meaning of the *ens per essentiam*. We can understand beings; but if I understand a horse, all I grasp is the essence of a horse, not the essence of being. Similarly, understanding man completely is grasping the essence, not of being, but of man. The pure act of intelligence, in contrast, is formally unconditioned; it is coincident with the *ens per essentiam*, that which if understood would be the understanding of everything. Why would the *ens per essentiam*, if understood, be the understanding of everything? Because being is the unrestricted objective of the pure desire to know. It includes everything. If there is, at least in conception as an ideal limit – the way the physicist speaks of absolute zero in temperature – an *ens per*

13 See Aristotle, *Metaphysics*, xii, 8, 1073b 39 to 1074a 15.

essentiam, a being that has the essence of being, then understanding that being would not simply be understanding *it,* but it would be understanding everything, because being includes everything. It is again the notion of the intelligibility of being.

2.2 *The Priority of Knowledge in the Approach*

This approach to the notion of God, to what we mean by God, can be developed much more fully, and it is developed more fully in *Insight.*[14] But a question arises with regard to the priority we have given knowledge in forming our notion. We have not moved from a limited case of act, from act limited by potency, to pure act. We have moved from insight as limited, to an unlimited act of understanding.

First, I think the two processes are equivalent; the same conclusions are reached, although they are reached in different ways. That is apparent from the coincidence of the conclusions to be found in any exposition of the notion or the attributes of God and the conclusions we draw. Why are the two equivalent? It is because being and intelligence are correlative. Being, as we have defined it, is the objective of intelligence, of the pure desire to know. I prefer to begin from intelligence, because in that way all ambiguity of the meaning of being, and the sense in which I am using the term, is eliminated.

One may ask whether in God there is a priority of being over the knowing or of the knowing over the being. Now, if one has a Scotist notion of God, there has to be a priority of being over knowing, because there has to be something to be looked at before one can have the look. There has to be Father and God to be intuited before the Father can intuit himself as both God and Father, at least in thought. There is a priority of the object definitely settled by a theory of knowledge in terms of taking a look, and there follow the difficulties that result in Scotus' proof of the formal distinction.

St Thomas, on the other hand, asks the question, What is the truth of God's knowledge of himself? In general, he says, truth is a matter of the similitude between knowing and known; knowing is true because of a similitude, an equation, an equivalence, with what is known. However, in God's knowledge of himself truth has to be understood as an absence of dissimilitude. In order to have a similitude, you must have a duality;

14 *Insight* 657–69.

but there is no duality in St Thomas' notion of God. *Ipsum esse* is *ipsum intelligere*; they are one and the same; there is no duality. To speak about the truth of God's self-knowledge, it is necessary to shift your notion of truth from terms of equivalence, similarity, or the like, to absence of dissimilarity.[15] Moreover, unless this type of approach is taken, whole sections of Thomas become meaningless. This is true, for example, of his treatment of *idem est intelligens et intellectum*.[16] There can be a diversity between the potency to understand and the potency to be understood; but the understanding in act and the understood in act are one and the same. With regard to God, there is no potency involved; consequently, there is an absolute identity. In order to have a duality, even in your thinking about God, you have to postulate a theory of knowing in terms of the look.

In brief, then, I believe that what I have to say about the idea of being is altogether equivalent to what is said of the *ens per essentiam*. We are not speaking about two different things. When I speak of the *ens per essentiam* in terms of the idea of being, I am speaking about it in a determinate way that excludes misconceptions that, I believe, are well worth avoiding. The *ens per essentiam* is the essence that grounds being intrinsically, and the idea of being is the same thing expressed differently.

2.3 Proofs for God's Existence

So far we have been concerned simply with the notion of God. From the conception of God, we turn to the question of his existence. One can begin by distinguishing truth. Our knowledge of the existence of God is our knowledge of the truth of the conclusion 'God exists.' St Thomas remarks that you know the *esse*, the existence, of God insofar as you know the truth of the proposition 'God is.'[17] Truth is the medium in which we know the real: *verum est medium in quo cognoscitur ens*. This is a fundamental point in all we have been saying about knowing.

How does one arrive at the conclusion 'God exists'? A first way of arriving at conclusions is to deduce effects from their causes, by a priori reasoning. But this way is ruled out for the present question. God is not

---

15 Thomas Aquinas, *Summa theologiae*, 1, q. 16, a. 5, ad 2m. Lonergan gave this reference tentatively; we may refer also to his own *Verbum* 183–91.
16 *Summa theologiae*, 1, q. 14, aa. 2, 4 (reference from Lonergan). The Latin phrase translates Aristotle, *De anima*, III, 4, 430a 4.
17 *Summa theologiae*, 1, q. 3, a. 4, ad 2m.

something that has a cause; he is formally unconditioned. A second way is to argue from the concept itself, and this is the ontological argument. 'The necessary existence necessarily exists' is an analytic proposition, and analytic propositions are knowledge of reality.[18] If your principle of causality is valid objectively because it is an analytic proposition, then 'The necessary being necessarily exists' is also valid objectively. So you know existence through an analytic proposition. However, I do not believe that argument is valid, because I distinguish between analytic propositions and analytic principles. Although I do not subscribe to logical positivism, an analytic proposition, which may be obtained from definitions and rules of syntax, is more or less a tautology. 'The necessary being necessarily exists' can be established to be analytic through definitions and rules of syntax; consequently, it is just an analytic proposition. On the other hand, to have an analytic principle, you must have a true judgment of concrete fact in which there occur the terms in the sense defined in the analytic proposition. In other words, in order to transform this analytic proposition 'The necessary being necessarily exists' from an analytic proposition which depends upon definition and rules of syntax, which is just linguistic convention, into objective knowledge, there is required a true judgment to the effect that there does exist a necessary being. If that judgment is true independently, then you have an analytic principle. In other words, once the existence of God is known, the situation changes; you think of God as the necessary being.

2.4 Extrinsic Causality

The argument for God's existence has therefore to be a posteriori, from the consequences to the antecedent, from the effects to the cause. Because the argument for God's existence has to be a posteriori, there arises the question of the universal validity of extrinsic causality. By extrinsic causality I mean efficient or final causality.

The causality dealt with in pure science is, I believe, internal causality. Pure science is concerned with the intrinsic constituents of being, intrinsic properties of being, just as metaphysics is concerned with potency, form, and act. Questions of efficient and final causality do not arise in pure

---

18 In Lonergan's own position, analytic propositions are not knowledge of reality in the present sense; see lecture 5 above, § 12, Analytic Propositions and Principles.

science, but only in applied science. For example, a town is divided by a harbor, and someone has the idea for a bridge.[19] The architect is called in to design it, and the contractor is hired to gather people to build it, and so forth. What is sought is the utility, the use, of the bridge – final causality. By gathering together people who will build it and providing them with the motivation for doing so, one is seeking efficient causality. When science is applied, even when it is applied to the guidance of experiments, there is the intervention of efficient and final causality – extrinsic causality. But the pure scientist is concerned neither with final causality nor with efficient causality; he is concerned with internal causality.

The question, then, is, Is this type of intelligibility something that can be generalized? Why is there this bridge? There is the end, the utility, the use of the bridge; there are the efficient causes, and the efficient causes produce an effect that per se is permanent. Efficient and final causality are relevant to understanding why the bridge is there. But can that type of intelligibility be generalized? Can we move from the intelligibility of extrinsic causality, in the case of applied science or in any case you please in ordinary human experience or in the concrete effects in nature, to a universal application? Can we say that this type of intelligibility is universally relevant? Or would the use of those principles to go beyond this world be an illegitimate extension?

That is a very fundamental question. The answer depends, first of all, upon what you mean by 'reality.' If you do not mean 'being' by the word 'reality,' I do not know of any way to prove that extrinsic causality expresses principles that are universally valid and relevant.[1] However, if by 'the real' you mean 'being,' then it can be proved that those notions of extrinsic causality that I have illustrated are universally relevant. Because being is intelligible: it is what is to be known by correct understanding; by definition, it is the intelligible. Being has to be the intelligible to be what is to be known by correct understanding, because the intelligible is all that correct understanding knows. That is the first premise.

The second premise is that there are defects of intelligibility in the existing world, and those defects are universal. They cannot be eliminated by any possible development of science in the ordinary sense, that is,

19 The illustration began by referring to a town divided by a river; 'harbor' was an afterthought, probably for local relevance, since a bridge had recently (1954) been built over the Halifax harbor.

science that does not go on to raise metaphysical questions. There is no technique or method of obtaining from physics or chemistry or biology or any other similar science an answer to the question, Why should there be anything at all? A thing is, in fact, because it is a virtually unconditioned; its conditions have been in fact fulfilled. You can explain it provisionally by saying that *this* is because *that* is. But why is *that*? As long as you stay within the limits of the world of your experience, you do not get beyond the virtually unconditioned, beyond that which happens to be because its conditions are fulfilled.

Again, why do these events occur? It may be that these events occur in virtue of some settled scheme of recurrence such as the planetary system. There is the transit of Venus because you can deduce it from the existing scheme of recurrence and previous positions. And similarly with regard to eclipses of the moon or any other event that occurs within the planetary system. But why is there this scheme of recurrence, the planetary system? There are explanations for the emergence of planetary systems, and the explanations lead you into probabilities. But there is no overarching scheme of recurrence, I believe, that accounts for the emergence of schemes of recurrence. The only general explanation for the existence of schemes of recurrence will be in terms of probabilities.

Again, events occur according to laws. But why these laws? Why not other laws? The nature of a free fall is a constant acceleration. But why should it be a constant acceleration with a value g determined by the law of inverse squares? Or why might it not be a changing acceleration? It is not impossible. Similarly, with regard to all other laws, one may ask, Why these laws?

Again, why should there be the precise hierarchy of beings that there is? We concluded to some hierarchy of beings: inorganic, biological, sensitive, rational. But why this hierarchy? Why not another? Some sort of answer may be obtained from probabilities; but the mere fact that you are using probabilities means that a vast array of other alternatives is possible. Why *this* particular alternative?

Finally, the real is being. But you can ask, 'Why should the real be being? Why should the real be intelligible? What are the grounds for that?' For us to have valid knowledge, for us to say anything significant, for us to use our intelligence and reasonableness, it is necessary that being be intelligible; and the only meaning one can give to the word 'real' without falling into a counterposition is 'being.' But why should reality be intelligible? What is the ultimate ground of its being intelligible? Our minds are not that ultimate ground. The structure of our minds provides what is *prius quoad nos* or the *causa cognoscendi*. Just as the moon is not a sphere because it has these phases, but we merely know that it must be a sphere because of the phases, so we know that the real must be being because of the structure of our minds. But there is the ontological question, What is it that makes being intelligible? It is not our minds. The ontological reason for the phases of the moon is the sphericity of the moon, what the moon is; the reason why we know the moon is a sphere is the phases. Similarly, the structure of our minds is the ground of our knowing that the real must be being and intelligible. But there is a further question: What accounts for the fact that the real is intelligible and being?

One can set up a long list of questions. If being is the intelligible, they have to be answered; if being is not the intelligible, there is no possible point to any question or any answer, because by asking and answering questions you would not be knowing anything at all. Since this universe is intelligible only up to a point and then leaves off, giving rise to further questions, we affirm the universal validity of some principle of extrinsic causality. Being has to be intelligible. But the intelligible is not something with respect to which I answer a certain group of questions and, for no reason whatever, refuse to answer further questions. If being is the objective of the pure and unrestricted desire to know, then the questions continue to arise. There is no point where you can arbitrarily say, 'No more questions – supply exhausted!' To answer all of the questions that do arise de facto, you have to go beyond this world, and that means that some principle of extrinsic causality is universally valid.

2.5 The Argument for God's Existence

The third step,[20] then – so far we have been engaged in preliminaries – the third step is the argument that has as its conclusion 'God exists.' The argument can be presented in different ways – in terms of motion, contingence, order, and so on – but there is, I think, one comprehensive way that includes all the rest. In its most general form, the argument is this: If the real is being – I mean, the intelligible – then God exists; but the real is intelligible, the real is being; therefore, God exists.[m]

The minor premise, that the real is being, the real is the intelligible, is established by the fact that the alternative is clearly a counterposition. If

20 This step puts together the two premises stated in the preceding section.

you say that the real is not being, that the real is not intelligible, then you are using your intelligence and your reasonableness to present, as intelligent and reasonable, a judgment; from the very intention and nature of the utterance, you are presuming the validity and the significance of an intelligent and reasonable affirmation. But if it is true that the real is not being, if it is true that the real is not the intelligible, your affirmations can have no significance whatever, and, because they can have no significance, they cannot be intelligent or reasonable. It is only insofar as the real is being that any intelligent and reasonable affirmation can be intelligent and reasonable; if this is not affirmed, you involve yourself in the counterpositions.[21]

The major premise is to the effect that only if God exists can the real be being. Only if there is, at the root of all reality, an unrestricted act of understanding that freely creates everything else that is, and in doing so acts intelligently and reasonably – only if the whole of reality depends upon God, and God is absolute understanding – can it be true that the real is being, that the real is the intelligible. That is the only way in which it is possible that all further questions that arise about this world have an answer. If you place nothing outside the world, there is no answer to those further questions. If you make something finite, some *ens per participationem*, the ground of the world, then it is questionable: the *ens per participationem* gives rise to further questions just as much as this world does. Only insofar as you posit the formally unconditioned, as not only intelligible but also intelligent – and all the other properties that can be deduced from that, which I have not treated here – can it be true that the real is being, that the real is intelligible.[22]

21 The remark was added, 'Note also that this is only one brief way of putting it. It is also relevant to the question of objectivity, or the proof that one knows – it's a proof of that type.' For some other ways of putting the argument, see *Insight*, chapter 19, § 11, Comparisons and Contrasts.
22 Lonergan concluded the lecture with thanks to the participants, with apologies to them for not being able to see them individually more than he did ('The schedule was rather breathless'), and with special thanks to Fr Belair to whom was due the original idea of the seminar, and whose work had brought it about. Fr Belair responded in the name of the President of Saint Mary's University.

EVENING DISCUSSIONS

Introduction

The lectures that formed the first part of this volume were delivered in the mornings in a classroom setting, but in the evenings there were discussion periods in a more informal style.

There are next to no notes of the discussions, but five of them were recorded and are published here: those of Monday, Tuesday, and Thursday of the first week (August 4, 5, and 7), and those of Wednesday and Thursday of the second week (August 13 and 14). It is clear from a morning announcement that there was no discussion period on Wednesday, August 6; there was almost certainly none on Saturday, August 9, and certainly none the last day of the Seminar. There remain the evenings of August 8 and August 12. We have evidence that there was a discussion, that went unrecorded, on August 12, for references the next day to what was said 'last night' make that clear enough.[1] It is possible that there was a discussion also on August 8, which likewise went unrecorded. Nevertheless, for reference purposes, we have numbered 1 to 5 the discussions we possess.

There was a tendency, as is usual in this format, for 'discussion' to become simply questions and answers, and for the questions to wander from the lecture topic. But at the start of the second day Lonergan himself asked for suggestions to improve the evening sessions. For one thing he did not wish them to become another two hours of lectures, and in fact there is substantive input from other participants. Sometimes, indeed,

1 See lecture 8, note 12; also discussion 4, note 11.

two of them would become engaged in exchanges with one another. The majority present, however, discouraged that trend, for naturally their chief interest was in Lonergan's own thought, and the microphone was placed so as best to pick up his voice (some audience contributions being consequently lost).

Of course, questions *did* provide the staple content of the evening sessions, and here the procedure varied. The first evening all the questions came from the floor; later, and in response to suggestions from participants, some questions were submitted in writing. But the floor was always open to interventions, and regularly Lonergan would ask after his responses, 'Does that meet the point?'

Given the novelty and difficulty of his thought, and the great diversity in audience familiarity with *Insight*, it was inevitable that he would spend time repeatedly explaining his position, but the repetition serves a purpose, for the difficulties experienced by his audience have happily resulted in valuable clarifications.

Still, there was at times a sense of frustration, documented in a letter, dated August 6, from Stan Machnik to Fr Eric O'Connor: 'The discussion periods are not only a great strain on Father Bernard but also reveal an unrelenting insistence to impose the misconceptions and the associated terminology he so deliberately and pointedly avoided and argued into its proper purgatory' (Lonergan Archives – used with permission of the author).

In editing the discussions we opted to err, if error it be, on the side of completeness, feeling even less liberty to 'interpret' than we did in the lectures; the latter at least were planned in advance, the train of thought could be discerned more clearly, and it was possible to correct Lonergan's grammar with less danger of betraying his thought. In any case, the very struggle in the discussions to achieve a meeting of minds, though it gives the text a ragged appearance, does reveal the difficulty of getting hold of Lonergan's thought and was not, in our view, to be edited out. Again, when we tried to eliminate the interruptions, we produced a text with unexplained zigzags, or else put words in Lonergan's mouth – a procedure for which readers were not likely to be especially grateful. On the whole the genre of the discussions seemed to justify a lack of finish that would be less acceptable in the lectures.

The remaining details of our editorial policy are simple. We have tried, by using three styles of type, to soften the outlines of the question-and-answer format, and thus provide a more readable sequence. Our editorial paragraphs are in smaller type, and enclosed in square brackets. Questions and input from the floor are in italics. Lonergan's answers and remarks are in standard type. The divisions and titles are ours, and sometimes we have relocated a question to bring it under a more relevant heading, but for better reader control we have recorded in our notes such relocations. It is regrettable that speakers from the floor could not be identified, or transitions from one to another be indicated.

Discussion 1[1]

1   Mathematics and Logic

[Recording was a little late starting. The original question had to do with the cognitional process in syllogisms, especially within mathematics; the discussion then turned to what a computer does. Our text begins with Lonergan speaking to that point.]

The computer operates in terms of zeros and ones, but what it can represent is a symbolic logic, and your symbolic logic can represent whatever propositions you please. A computer will operate from the set of premises provided. To get your premises is another matter: ordinary thinking, even philosophic thinking, usually has not got its premises in a sufficiently accurate form of expression for use in symbolic logic. But insofar as any type of premise is made sufficiently precise you can get what follows.

It seems to me that in a machine like that you can only get what follows when what follows does so mathematically. All men are mortal; Peter is a man; therefore Peter is mortal. This particular individual is included in the all, is included as one unit in the number, and something like that can be handled by a machine; but is that all there is to a syllogism?

1   The evening of Monday, August 4, 1958. The 1980 edition (in questions 1, 2, and 3) included parts of the present § 2, Refusing Insights; of § 7, Self-appropriation and Self-involvement; and of § 9, Appropriation: The Word, the Act.

It is the type of thinking that you get more in mathematics. If you say this, does this follow rigorously or not, under this set of rules and this set of implications? And so on.

You say a conclusion follows in a certain field of implications? Well, how does it follow? As a particular under a universal?

No. As a consequence.[2] If you have 'Whenever there is an *A*, there is a *B*,' and an *A* turns up, as a previous conclusion or in some other way, then you also get the *B* out.

Yes, but when you say, 'If there is an A, then there is a B,' that is the equivalent of a universal.

Yes, but it will be an axiom, or a definition,[3] or something like that. Computers, as far as I know, are not used for that kind of operation; symbolic logic represents the type of thing that they can do. The simplest way to get a concrete idea of it is to take a book such as Prior's *Formal Logic*[4] and see what they are doing when they lay down a set of axioms and the enormous number of conclusions they can get from it. The axioms may be all trivial. Where *P* and *Q* are sentences: if both *P* and *Q*, then *P*. – Fr Wulftange knows more about this.[5]

Is it true that people like Whitehead and Russell practically have reduced all mathematics to mere calculation, so that it can be handled by computer, mechanically?

That ideal is present. Up to the nineteenth century and the discovery of strange geometries, it was taken for granted that Euclidean geometry was the one, unique, necessary, self-evident, absolutely valid geometry. Then they discovered that other geometries were possible; they discovered a whole series of them. And so the question arose, What do we know in mathematics? Do we know anything at all? Can you take any set of premises and call these the axioms, and will what follows from them be mathematics?

---

2 We suggest 'consequence' as a possibility: the tape is not clear.
3 This again is a suggested reading: 'definition' is not clear on the tape.
4 Arthur N. Prior, *Formal Logic* (Oxford: Clarendon, 1955).
5 Joseph Wulftange, s.j., was a participant in the Halifax seminar; he was at this time professor of cosmology, i.e., scholastic philosophy of nature, at West Baden Springs, Indiana, in the philosophate of the Chicago Jesuit Province.

Now the ideal of Russell and Whitehead was to base mathematics on logic. A line is a set of points. And, conceiving a line as a set, you can conceive it as a class: a class of points that is found in this line. You see how you can make your transition from geometry, and from mathematics generally, into purely logical terms. Now the logic they conceived was a purely extensional logic. It is 'all men' and 'all mortals' that they are thinking of: concrete multiplicities, and relations between classes. The logic is developed along those lines; it is the extensional and not the connotational side of logic. And the aim of Whitehead and Russell in the *Principia Mathematica*[6] was to deduce the whole of mathematics from simply logical axioms. Since everyone must admit logic, everyone must admit mathematics: as logic is true, mathematics is true. In other words, the idea was to get away from this condition in which mathematics was placed by the discovery of many geometries.

Well, are there many mathematics as well as many geometries? What is mathematics? The idea of Russell and Whitehead was to base it on the logic. But they were not able to do that. They had to bring in further axioms. They had to bring in an axiom of infinity and another axiom that has to do with the theory of types. Now it is very difficult to formulate the theory of types; it holds that propositions that regard all types are not valid – that is the general idea of it. And, as you can see, that is a proposition that regards all types; so it is not valid. Now how do you get a way of saying that which does not involve this self-referential contradiction?

Since the Russell-Whitehead position was found to be unsatisfactory, Hilbert said: Let's do the mathematics simply as mathematics, from mathematical axioms, not from logical axioms.[7] Then we will do the logic afterwards with regard to our mathematics. So we proceed on two levels: the mathematical, and then the logical which regards the mathematical procedures. Now the mathematical procedures involve infinities of operations; for example, to get 2, you add 1 to 1, to get 3 you add 1 to 2, and so on to infinity: whenever you have a proposition such that, if it holds in the case n, it will hold in the case $n + 1$, you have

6 Alfred North Whitehead and Bertrand Russell, *Principia Mathematica* (Cambridge: Cambridge University Press, 2 vols., 1925–27, 1st ed. 1910–12).
7 David Hilbert, 'The Foundations of Mathematics,' in Jean van Heijenoort, *From Frege to Gödel: A Source Book in Mathematical Logic, 1879–1931* (Cambridge, Mass.: Harvard University Press, 1967) 464–79.

an infinity of operations involved. So they admitted infinities of operations on the mathematical side, but the logic was to be done within finite limits.

The difficulty with Hilbert's approach was the Gödelian Theorem.[8] In the mathematics – simply, in the theory of arithmetic – you get as far as where you can show that any number can be resolved into one set of primes and only one set. Well, if your theory of arithmetic gets that far you can have theorems of limitation; in other words you can prove that something cannot be proved in mathematics. All these theorems of the Gödelian type take some theorem of limitation in the mathematics; then, if it's within the mathematics, it can be transposed into the logic. But when you get a theorem of limitation in the logic, you can prove that something cannot be proved, that something cannot be true, that something cannot be defined, that something cannot be solved by a machine. And that was blocking this attempt to do the mathematics.

A third movement which is fairly dominant at the present time is that of the Bourbaki group.[9] They say, Let's forget about all this logic. Well, that eliminates the Gödelian theorem – the Gödelian theorem too can be transposed all the way up; for example, if you want to do a logic of your logic – and they simply deduce from the axioms.

But the objection against them is, Well, you do a beautiful piece of work on your mathematics, but it is rigid, static. How do you account for the way mathematics has developed up to where it is at present, and how can you go beyond this to the mathematics of the future? There is a static element in a rigid deduction, and there are also other difficulties. So opposed to that static approach you have people like Gonseth who hold that mathematics has to remain in contact with science and with general cultural movements, that that is where the development comes from: the interaction between mathematical thinking, the requirements of science, and the general cultural movement of the age.[10]

8 Ibid. 596–616. Also Kurt Gödel, *On Formally Undecidable Propositions of Principia Mathematica and Related Systems*, trans. B. Beltzer (Edinburgh: Oliver & Boyd, 1962).
9 See lecture 5, note 12.
10 Ferdinand Gonseth, a Swiss mathematician, was one of the three founders of the journal *Dialectica*, and its editor for over twenty years. See *Dialectica* 1 (1947) 5–6; 20 (1966) 3–4; 30 (1976) 3; 31 (1977) 1–202.

2   Refusing Insights

I could offer you this cigar and you could refuse it, because you know very well what cigars are and perhaps you don't like them. But throughout your book you talk about refusing insight. Just how is it possible to refuse insight?

It is not refusal in the same sense. We start in *Insight* with the story of Archimedes. Archimedes wanted to find out whether the crown was of pure gold. He was tending toward the answer not only consciously but also subconsciously, because, at a time when he was not thinking of the problem at all, the solution popped into his mind. A condition of having the insight is having an image in which the insight can click; and insofar as the whole man is orientated, wanting insights, not only consciously but also subconsciously, he is moving towards the insights.

If you want to write a sermon for next Sunday, and you are told about it on Monday, you can jot down thoughts, in any order at all in which they come to mind, put them in a drawer, and pull them out on Thursday. Then you will not only have the thoughts, you will have a plan – or a plan will very quickly come to mind. Likewise, when you are dealing with a problem, if you define it as carefully as you can – all the aspects of it – then put it aside, and take it out six months later, you are more likely to hit upon the solution than if you just stuck with it.

In other words, there is a subconscious and preconscious effort moving towards this insight. Within a person there is a series of levels – physical, chemical, biological, psychic, intellectual – and they have to be working in harmony. It's some form of disease when they are not. And just as there can be an orientation in conscious living that favors the emergence of insight, so too there can be an orientation in conscious living that is opposed to having the insight.

But you don't really refuse insight in a conscious, deliberate fashion?

No, not in the way I refuse a cigar.

The insights are unwanted?

Yes. Here is a story to illustrate that. Harry Stack Sullivan, in a posthu-

---

Among his many books is *La Géométrie et le problème de l'espace* (Neuchatel: Griffon, 1945–55).

mous volume of lectures published by his pupils, treated incidentally the question, What use do you make of dreams? Well, his practice was not to bother too much about dreams; however, he gave an example of the use he made of them. A patient of his, obviously disturbed and suffering, had a dream about a beautiful Dutch windmill, on a knoll with lawns around it; the green was magnificent, the sky was clear, the windmill turned majestically, and so on. Everything was perfect, exteriorly. Then he found himself inside the windmill. And that was a mess, cobwebs and rust – it was impossible to conceive how the machinery could do anything in there. This was the dream he recounted. And Sullivan asked: Who does that remind you of? The man said: My God, my mother![11]

He had been expressing antipathy to his father all through the interview; but just at this point it dawned on him that he had an antipathy to his mother. As a matter of fact, owing to the situation, the mother had so given herself in meeting difficulties from the father that she had become empty interiorly. And this was brought to his attention through his dream, in this symbolic form, and then became explicit through having the question put to him. In a sense this man has not been wanting to understand his mother. Not in any deliberate fashion, the way one refuses a cigar; but still there is a movement away from the insight.[12]

Am I right in saying that you hold – I think you say it somewhere – that ultimately a psychoneurosis, or even just aberrant behavior in general, is based on a refusal of insight which causes an affective disorder, rather than the other way around? Did you say something like that?

A reviewer claimed that I did.[13] No, what I claim is a correlation, and a correlation that says nothing about causality. If there is emotional disturbance, it is going to prevent the images from assuming a certain constellation. You are going to prevent the insight. To what extent it works the other way, I would not venture to say.

Your quotation from Stekel, wasn't that in favor of the suggestion that it worked

---

11 Sullivan, *The Interpersonal Theory of Psychiatry* 338–39.
12 The rest of this section has been relocated here from the end of §4 below, 'Methods' of Gaining Insight.
13 John Wren-Lewis, 'A Bold Venture in Constructive Philosophy,' *The Modern Churchman* 1, 2 (October 1957) 139–43; see p. 141.

from insight to affect, rather than the other way? It seemed to be implied that this is the line that you would take yourself.[14]

That impression arises insofar as Stekel's method is an active method, one. aiming at a *cure*. It is not dealing with the genesis of a psychoneurosis; it is bringing about the cure by a process of reeducation. What you are operating on directly – you are also operating on emotions too in the transference – has to do with insight: you are aiming at insight, you are aiming at a process of reeducation.

But I don't want to say that this grounds a new theory of psychoneurosis. Obviously, any theory will hold that the trouble is more from the emotional side, and more on the sensitive level than the intellectual; but there is a nexus between the intellectual and the emotional simply because there is a connection between the insight and the formed image. Think of correlation rather than causality, and I believe it stands.

Is it possible that neurosis may produce insight?

It is possible. I suppose a man with a persecution mania has a number of insights that other people do not have.

Some people claim that a person in a neurotic state is capable, overstimulated, outdoes himself.

I think that is true. In other words, the mere fact that there is a lack of balance means that there is a greater concentration on some aspects of living, and greater possibilities there.

Would a scrupulous person be an example of that? Nobody is keener on thinking about possibilities, and I suppose that every possibility represents an insight; but what he lacks is judgment.

I think so; it is to the point.

3 Insight as Unexpected

You say that insights are always unexpected. What exactly do you mean by that? I mean, you can sit down with a problem in mathematics, work on it, and see yourself arriving at the insight.

14 *Insight* 200–203.

To say that they are always unexpected is inaccurate: the statement has to be qualified. Insights are of different kinds. There are insights that simply integrate, follow on something that went before – after you have done a lot of problems in geometry, for example, and work habitually. True, you can't solve any problem in geometry without hitting upon its construction; but if you have a lot of practice doing problems, you will hit upon the construction much more quickly. Still, the more fundamental the insight, the less likely you are to be prepared for it, and the more unexpected is apt to be the actual occurrence of the insight. What is true when one says that an insight is unexpected is, it is not a function of any set of rules. It is the starting point for something in the way of new rules.

4   'Methods' of Gaining Insight

There is no pedestrian method of reaching an insight. What comes to mind, as an example of that, is finding the solution of a complicated integral in mathematics, where you have to find some substitution that will throw the data into recognizable form. The people who are really good at this have no notion how they do it. They just see it. There is no method; it is a matter of coming up with suitable substitutions.

No, the integral is a very good example of that. While you can differentiate according to rules provided the function is differentiable, finding the integral is a trick, or very frequently is. It is just reversing the process, but reversing the process is not subject to rules, not to the same extent anyway.

In that case, what do you mean by heuristic method?

Well, that is a further point. What the heuristic structure supplies is a field in which the insight can occur. Insofar as you say that finding the solution to the integral is just a matter of hitting upon a proper substitution, from the fact that you can say that, you already know something about how you are going to arrive at the integral. And saying that much is a heuristic structure towards finding the integral. However, it is not heuristic structure in the general sense; it is heuristic structure with regard to a particular problem.[15]

---

15 The clause after the semicolon is not clear on the tape.

Setting up a heuristic structure, that consists of a number of insights?

Making it explicit does, because it is reflecting upon your previous process and saying that, if you do this, you can eliminate to some extent the element of chance. At least you know what you are aiming at. When Galileo said that science is the mathematization of nature, he did not know what the subsequent mathematical expression of natural laws was going to be, but he knew the kind of thing he wanted.

Is it true that insights are either inherited through traditional education or accidentally stumbled on? You couldn't plan the first insight into a particular field – it would always be unforeseen. You would have to start from something you stumbled on; then through heuristic method go on to the next stage?

That is true, particularly with regard to the latter part. However, there are differences. While it is easier to absorb the insights that are contained in a tradition or a culture, just as it is easier to learn by going to classes, it is not easier for everyone in the class. What a teacher does is provide ordered sensible signs. But there has to be personal intellectual activity for anyone to understand, though he may understand more easily within the culture.

In general, when I say it is not a matter of rules, that statement is to be qualified. My first difficulty was that insight is unexpected; then I went on to shift that to saying it is not a matter of rules. Well, let us shift it again, and say it is not a matter of deduction. It is not setting up rules that infallibly lead to the insight. It is not in the same class as the deductive conclusion. It is more on the side of the premises.

Perhaps deduction is not the word. It is not so much that it is not like a deduction; rather it is not like a cooking recipe, where if you follow the rules perfectly you get the soufflé, or whatever it is.

It's not the *result* of a recipe, it's the *foundation* of a recipe.

5 Self-appropriation and Philosophy

I have always believed that philosophy could be defined in this way, that it is an effort of the human mind to understand the universe of our experience, where understanding means knowing the causes of things, and where knowing the causes means knowing the intrinsic and the extrinsic ultimate causes. What I would like to know is, In what sense is self-appropriation necessary for this purpose? In particular, How much is self-appropriation required for philo-

sophical and metaphysical explanation of that part of the universe that is not rational, for what is not man or rational cognitional process? For example – Fr Wulftange may be able to help us on this, he has been working on cosmology – I was wondering where self-appropriation would fit into cosmology, where you are dealing with inanimate objects. How important is it there?

I think I can answer that by asking another question: What does the philosopher understand?[16]

As far as I can see, he tries to get at what is intelligibly implied in any given data of experience, and what I can see to be clearly implied in any substantial change is what are called prime matter and substantial form, two correlative principles, without either of which you would not have explained the given fact of experience, namely, substantial change. Further, without substance and accident you would not have an explanation of accidental change. But I think that that is intelligible to me without the reference to self-appropriation. Now perhaps it is not as deeply intelligible as it should be, and light can be shed on it by this process of self-appropriation, but that is what I would like to see.

I think that if you build up your philosophy on the basis you are suggesting, what you arrive at after a while is a nest of disputed questions, and you will go round in circles. And besides that, you have a set of specific problems. What is the relation between this and science? What does the scientist understand? Are these atoms substances in my sense, or are they not? You have a set of problems and a set of questions; and you have no method of answering them, solving them. Or have you?

What I have thought the method of science to be is this: to reduce the phenomena of nature to mathematical law, in the sense that scientific explanation is explanation in terms of correlation of particular events with other events, and that correlation is expressed mathematically. And that is all the scientists – as far as I can see, especially with people like Whitehead and Russell – that is all they are interested in. And given that as their outlook and their interest, they do not raise certain questions, for instance about the essential constituents of things.

Supposing someone were to say that this business of investigating

16 Compare lecture 9, § 1, Metaphysical Analysis, where Lonergan asks (and answers) the question, What does the metaphysician understand?

substance and accidents and substantial change is just a survival of a Greek ideal of science, that it is out of date, that we can forget all about it and be just as well off, how would you answer that?

I think I would put it this way, that even when the scientist has given his explanation there are certain things he has not explained. He has not touched the question of the real causes of things; if he limits himself to the expression of mathematical laws, uniting them in theories, he is remaining on the level of explaining correlations between events which he takes for granted to be happening in a real world; but he is not out to explain the real causes of that real world.

Well, suppose he were to ask, What do you mean by the real world and the real causes?

That might be a bit of a problem!

6   Self-appropriation and Truth

Do I understand you to say that self-appropriation at least will have the function of a final criterion for truth?

Part of self-appropriation is uncovering what precisely you mean by 'true' and what precisely your criterion of 'true' is.

I would say that the function of self-appropriation is this. The symbolic logician can set down a series of symbols and say, 'These are my assumptions; my assumptions are $p, q, r, ...$' Well, what are $p, q,$ and r? They stand for propositions, for sentences. What do they mean? It does not make any difference. And he can lay down rules for procedure, and rules of inference, and so on. But it is all in a purely symbolic field – it does not mean anything. What does self-appropriation do to such a set of symbols? If such a set of symbols is your philosophy, it provides you with the means of verification and giving meaning to those symbols: it gives a fundamental definition, a fundamental verification of meaning.

I wonder if this is relevant to what Fr Hoenen[17] has, and what I think Fr

---

17   The reference is probably to Peter Hoenen, s.j., *La théorie du jugement d'après St. Thomas d'Aquin* (Rome: Gregorian University Press, 1946); trans. Henry F. Tiblier, *Reality and Judgment according to St. Thomas* (Chicago: Henry Regnery Company, 1952).

Boyer[18] *has, when they speak of a complete natural reflection as the element relevant to knowing when one has the truth — I wonder whether self-appropriation is the term or result of this complete natural reflection.*

Well, something like this complete reflection is the fruit of self-appropriation. Whether it is exactly the same is another question. And if you have arrived at self-appropriation *you* will be satisfied and you won't worry too much about what they mean, because you will have something in yourself that will be your ultimate court of appeal.

> [Here it was asked to what extent the truth is subjective. Lonergan wished to postpone his answer until he had treated the virtually unconditioned. But a further exchange led to the following immediate response.]

What I am aiming at is a set of ultimate meanings in terms of which everything else can be defined. I was going to say more about this tomorrow morning,[19] taking a cue from a statement in Kant's Transcendental Doctrine of Method. He distinguishes knowledge, '*cognitio ex datis ... cognitio ex principiis*' – it's a division that I don't think is correct – and says that even sciences that are matters of knowledge from principles can, as learnt by someone, really be known merely as a matter of data.[20] He gives an example. Someone learns Wolff's philosophy and knows all the definitions, all the divisions, all the answers to all the objections, all the proofs. But if you disagree with any of his definitions, well, he is lost – it is not in the book. And Kant says such a person becomes just a plaster cast of a man.

Well, what do you do *not* to be just a plaster cast of a man? What do you do *not* to have to depend on somebody's definition, or somebody's say-so, or 'It is the way we always talk'? What do you base your ultimates on? What do you get them from? Is there any method of tackling that problem? And I think that's the use I see in self-appropriation.

There's an element of quiescence in the answers that have been attained. In other words, the tension you describe as preceding insight is resolved in the moment of quiescence following.

18 The reference is probably to Charles Boyer, s.j., 'Le sens d'un texte de Saint Thomas: "De Veritate, q. 1, a. 9",' *Gregorianum* 5 (1924) 424–43; trans. Tiblier (note 17 above) 295–309, 337–39.
19 See lecture 2, § 1, The Value of Self-appropriation.
20 Kant, *Critique of Pure Reason* A836/B864; Norman Kemp Smith: 'all knowledge ... is either historical or rational. Historical knowledge is *cognitio ex datis*; rational knowledge is *cognitio ex principiis*' (655–56).

If self-appropriation is indefinitely perfect, you could say that; but one of the things you arrive at is that it is not perfect, so you do not get complete quiescence.

7   Self-appropriation and Self-involvement

To what extent would you admit a correlation, or would you admit any, between the fact of self-appropriation as described, without categorizing it now particularly, and affectivity, or personal involvement, or commitment?

In chapter 6 of *Insight* I distinguish a series of patterns of experience. Now self-appropriation as relevant to philosophy is in the intellectual pattern of experience, and it is a matter of the maximum detachment. Just as you are not 'involved' in doing mathematics, so you try not to be 'involved' in doing philosophy – although there is a notable school at the present time that insists on the opposite.

It depends, however, on exactly what you mean by affectivity. If you include what I call the pure desire to know along with affectivity, then it is a matter of selecting one affectivity and favoring it against others.

Do you think in such detachment that insights are more right and true?[21]

Insights of themselves are neither true nor false. All that is relevant to insights is that you get them, and whether they are true or false is always a further question. Now the insights relevant to science are of that type, and as long as you are just a scientist, of course you will be missing a lot of insights of other types.

The point in the pursuit of truth is, the more insights the better. In other words, you do not arrive at truth by a *minimum* of understanding. I once conducted a seminar on interpretation,[22] and found that people often have the idea that the less we understand, the less likely we are to have preconceived notions. And that is true. But to arrive at a correct interpretation what you want is *all possible* preconceived notions. And if you are dealing with a first-class author your present preconceived

---

21 The tape is not clear here; possibly the speaker said 'more right than true.'

22 Lonergan had several times given courses, or conducted seminars, on the interpretation of St Thomas – the Thomist use of *verbum*, of *actio*, etc. Possibly the reference is to one of these, for there is no record of his having at this time led a seminar on interpretation as such.

266 Understanding and Being

notions probably won't be enough – you'll need still more. In other words, in interpretation, the closer you approach to understanding everything, rather than the less you understand, the better chance you have of arriving at a correct interpretation. If you are interpreting St Thomas or Aristotle, then the true meaning of the text is not the meaning that is going to be at once obvious to the most stupid person you can find. Your ideal interpreter isn't a newborn baby, who has never understood anything – or very little yet; it's rather the person who has understood as much as possible of everything. Is that to your point?

Do you think there are some insights, at least in some areas, that would be impossible with detachment?

There are insights that arise in ordinary intersubjective living. When you are familiar with people, the slightest sign will let you know what mood they are in today. You meet someone and decide, 'Well, I'll talk to him later!' But if you are in a perfect state of detachment, you lack this kind of rapport with people, you don't understand them that way. – There you have an insight linked with self-involvement, one which is obviously true: it is the way we live.

I am interested in the word 'detachment' from a historical point of view. I was struck very much not long ago on reading a historian who said that only by the widest sympathy and greatest love could any true objectivity be reached in history. It seems to me, in my own experience, that that is true. In other words, it's a case of involvement, as far as history is concerned, rather than detachment.[23]

To become fully involved you have to be extremely detached; there are several angles on that.

8   The Universality of the Pure Desire to Know

I think this morning you were saying that the desire to know is something innate in human nature, that there is a natural desire to know.

I quoted Aristotle to that effect, and also the scholastic distinction

---

23 This question has been relocated from § 10, Self-appropriation and Philosophy.

between natural, acquired, and infused habits.[24] However, such expressions presuppose a metaphysics.

But if this is something necessary and universal in human nature, is it not peculiar that it remained for the Greeks to 'bring home the bacon' after fifty million years?

The answer to that, of course, is a theory of history, in which you account for what happened in the previous fifty million years. Karl Jaspers, in *The Origin and Goal of History*,[25] disagrees with Hegel's view that the axis of history is at the incarnation. He places the axis of human history in the period from about 800 to 200 B.C. And he contrasts civilizations that existed at that time in Greece, Judea, Egypt, Persia, India, and China, with antecedent civilizations. It was in the breakdown of these massive civilizations, he argues, that one has the burst of philosophic reflection and of individualism: it occurred precisely because those civilizations were not working, because they had come to a breakdown.

Take people in Canada or the United States: prior to the recession, the breakdown of 1930, the depression, and still more so prior to the First World War, there was not the disquiet, the concern, about economics and international affairs that became widespread later. The experience of the society, because of those catastrophes, favored a certain type of reflection upon social affairs. And still more does the present situation favor such reflection, where you have a rather universal anxiety about big questions. – I'm just giving you Jaspers' account of history; it is one way of answering a question about what happened in the previous fifty million years.

Now, if you compare the results of that reflection in these different areas, the Greeks bring home the bacon because they were interested in reflection on technique.[26] It was concomitant with the development

24 See lecture 1, § 1.1, The Pursuit of the Unknown.
25 Karl Jaspers, *Vom Ursprung und Ziel der Geschichte* (Zürich: Artemis, 1949); trans. Michael Bullock, *The Origin and Goal of History* (London: Routledge & Kegan Paul, 1953).
26 The tape records Lonergan saying that the Greeks succeeded because 'they were interested in technique'; we edited this as 'interested in reflection on technique,' basing our interpretation on the way Lonergan later in this response distinguishes the Greek way from that of other civilizations which also were interested in technique. See also *A Second Collection*, ed. William F.J. Ryan and Bernard J. Tyrrell (London: Dar-

of mathematics. The Egyptians knew all about surveying, and they knew how to make a right-angled triangle, because otherwise you could not mark off the land properly. They knew about 3, 4, 5 – if you get those three lengths for the three sides, then you will have a right angle. And the Babylonians did a lot of calculating. The Mayans, I believe, had the most accurate of all calendars – more accurate even than ours. But it was on the level of technique, of getting results. What the Greeks asked was, Why must it be so? They seized on that question. It happened there.

You get the further steps of catching on to just what it is to catch on, in the idea of insight. But to express that is extremely difficult. Whenever you express, you are in concepts and judgments. All through the book *Insight* you have always words, concepts, judgments – they are there in the book. But the insight is something behind. By a sort of psychological method you can suggest this self-appropriation to people and urge them to take it up. But it is a technique of reflective psychology.

I am quite certain that Aristotle knew about insight. I am also quite certain that Aristotle did not talk about insight the way I do. And the same is true of St Thomas. My arguments that there is insight in St Thomas are indirect: he would not have said what he did, had he not known about insight. But at that time there did not exist a technique – not in St Thomas' time, much less in Aristotle's time – there did not exist a technique of reflective psychology such that people would know what you meant if you started talking about insight. Does that meet your question?

I'm still not convinced that the pure desire to know is something universal in human nature. Everything depends on coming in contact with people who stimulate you to develop your intelligence – it's nothing human nature comes equipped with.

That question is not material to my position: we can arrive at discussions about human nature later on. It will be quite sufficient, until we get into metaphysics where that type of question arises, if now we find that we ourselves want to understand something, if we have the experience of asking the question, Why?

---

ton, Longman & Todd, 1974) 23–24, where there is mention of a technique that is 'characteristically Hellenic ... of reflecting on propositions' at a second level.

But with regard to the fact that there is a desire to know, I think if you examine children you will find evidence for it. They keep on asking questions, and stop only because they begin to find that the answers aren't forthcoming or cannot be given, or because they are discouraged more than helped. It is often impossible to give them answers, but there is a terrific flow of questions. And what does it come from? You don't teach them to ask questions.

But is that true in all cultures?

Well, that is a further point. I haven't investigated that. But there has to be something there to start with, for it to occur in any culture. However, as I said, that is not material to the argument.

How can you make a general theory of this appropriation of your own rational self-consciousness, and claim it is valid for everybody, except by making an exhaustive tour of inspection of everybody? How can you be sure that everybody's mind is going to work that way?[27]

Well, to be certain of that would presuppose a metaphysics, and until we get to the metaphysics we don't bother about being certain. You write the book and they read it, and if they find themselves intelligent and rational, I think that they will agree.

But why do you think that they will agree?

I have metaphysical reasons for that.

In other words, I think that philosophy is a matter of the engagement of personal responsibility, and I am concerned with the individual coming to find intelligence and rationality in himself, so that he won't be a plaster cast of a man, but will be able to think these things out for himself, and make up his mind about them.

But in order to say that everybody does that in the same way ...

Well, I don't have to do that, do I? And I don't attempt to do that. But I suspect that it will happen, and if you want more than a suspicion, then you move to metaphysics.

---

27 This question and the rest of this section have been relocated: the first three exchanges from § 11, Further Use of One's Insights, and the next two from § 13, Objectivity.

What might be insight for one person might not be insight for someone else, in this process of self-appropriation; for example an insight might be had already.

Yes. In other words, there is no one determinate route of arriving at a goal. Several people can arrive at the same goal by different routes. Secondly, people can arrive at different goals by different routes. Insights that occur to one won't have occurred to another, and insights that occur merely incidentally and have no importance in one man's life will be of great importance in another's life.

Even objectively, then, what might be an insight for one person might not be an insight for another person.

Well, not a significant insight, or not an insight that occurs. But I don't want to use the word 'insight' in a way that would strip it of all meaning; if you say it is an insight for one person and not an insight for another, does the meaning of 'insight' depend upon the person? I don't want to accept that logical implication.

9 Appropriation: The Word, the Act

Would you mind explaining just why you chose the word 'appropriation' to describe this function?

I did not want to talk of phenomenology, because that would involve me in difficulties with a whole series of people. It is a word that occurs in English without too definite a meaning, without tying you down too much. But if you use a more technical term, you get involved with explaining the difference between your position and what you mean, and the positions of a whole series of other people. In other words, you are just creating for yourself unnecessary difficulties and unnecessary blocks. I have no particular love for the word 'appropriation'; I just want to communicate something with it.

'Appropriation' often has the connotation of 'taking away from' – at least to an American, who thinks of the congressman reaching into the national pocketbook to take funds for this or that. And somehow that has resulted in creating a kind of a block in my own mind.

I can see that; and in that case, forget it. But if you think of the word in a religious context – appropriating one's religion, appropriating the truths of one's religion – or think of Newman's use of the word 'realize,' anything like that will do. You have self-appropriation insofar as you don't merely understand but advert to the fact that something happened in consciousness.

You said you did not want to become involved in arguments with the phenomenologists. Do they have terms that might be confused with 'self-appropriation'?[28]

Suppose I said that the first part of *Insight* was concerned with the *phenomenology* of knowledge, that as yet I am not saying whether knowledge is this or that or anything else, but I am giving you a grasp of the essence, I'm giving you an essential description of what goes on in your mind when you inquire and understand and judge. That would be a way of describing the first part of the book, to say that it is phenomenological. As a matter of fact Fr Dhanis[a] asked me, 'Your book is more or less the same sort of thing as Hegel's *Phenomenology of Spirit*, isn't it?' Well, I do not want to be involved in Hegel's idea of phenomenology, or the series of meanings that occur in Husserl, or in Heidegger's use of it, Buytendijk's use of it, and so on. That would be an endlessly long technical discussion: an endlessly complicated investigation too, and then all sorts of arguments with all the specialists in these fields – whether I was using 'phenomenology' in the correct sense. In other words, it would be creating an enormously complex situation.

I have less of a problem with the word than with the act. It seems that human knowledge is a complex of judgment and concept and image, as you said this morning. We think of insight ordinarily as something which is included in that judgment and image and concept, whereas you speak of it as something behind this. Now this seems to make it some kind of mystical thing, a transcendental self that we grasp behind judgment. Many people are very unhappy with this. They say that you cannot get behind the self judging to the pure self.

There is a sense in which you can't, and there is a sense in which you can. To define them, to pick them out, is rather complicated. You need an accurate expression of your own philosophy; also an accurate account of theirs, and start showing in which sense the statement you refer to is true and in which sense it is not.

But the answer to the question, insofar as I have it, will be in chapter

28 This question has been relocated from § 10, Self-appropriation and Philosophy.

11, where we arrive at our notion of what it is to know – experience, understand, and judge – and we ask, Am I a knower? Do I experience? Do I hear sounds? Can I prevent myself from hearing sounds?[29] And so on. Am I intelligent? Well, even if I wanted to play the fool, the stupid fellow, I would want to do it well, I would want to do it intelligently. Now when I answer, I say something that I claim to be true about me, so we have more questions. Am I reasonable? Am I concerned with truth? Is alchemy just as good for me as chemistry? Astrology just the same as astronomy? Myth just as good as history? Or do I want one and reject the other – in a very, very fundamental sense?

Well, those are just indications. But you discover yourself as intelligent, as rational. You discover yourself as intelligent and rational, not in the sense that you look into yourself and find something with the label 'rationality' on it, the way you look at a map and see a point marked Calcutta. It is like verification: I will use that as an example. You want to verify the formula that pressure by volume is equal to a certain constant. You take the pressure at a certain time, and you find what the volume is; then you write both down and multiply it out for your constant. You repeat the process, trying for a series of values of P and a resulting series of values of V, and a constant verified all along the line. What does the verifying mean? Well, there is a factual element to it, a given element.[30] All you see is a gauge for the pressure, a dial on which the pointer stands at certain positions. And that seeing could be done by anyone: you need not be a scientist to do it: it is just there. You do not even have to understand the numbers, insofar as this purely given element is concerned.

Now self-appropriation is a matter of adverting to what is given; it is merely that 'adverting' to what is given; it is adverting to what is given insofar as you have to be present to yourself for others to be present to you. It is bringing to light data, constructing the sort of telescope or microscope or experimental situation in which such advertences can occur. But it isn't the understanding, and it isn't the affirmation that follows on the understanding. It is merely this given part, as it is in verifying that pressure by volume is some constant: that is, in verifying

29 Lonergan answered his own question: 'Well, not here tonight.' He is surely referring to the noise that so often disturbed the discussions; see also lecture 6, note 5.

30 On this use of 'factual,' see lecture 1, §2.2, Insight in Euclid; also note m to that lecture.

an abstract proposition, a formula. You don't verify what you see. And it is not one act of seeing or one set of measurements that suffices for the verifying; it is a whole series, and the longer the series the better. Moreover, if one really good set of measurements were to contradict it, your result would throw the whole formula out. The verifying is never coming across a real instance that provides you with an exception. But verifying isn't just taking a look. That is a condition for verifying. And self-appropriation is providing the conditions for verifying, when we come to questions such as, Am I a knower? What is truth? What is judgment? What is understanding? And so on.

10   Self-appropriation and Philosophy

Once we discover the self that is present behind these acts of knowing, how can we incorporate this into a systematic philosophy? It seems that, as soon as we do, we must be making judgments about it, and does not the experience, the awareness, of subjectivity escape when you try to systematize it?

The first step: understand what it is to know. If you discover invariants in your knowing, if you find that your knowing always conforms to certain general rules, then the relations you find between the acts of knowing imply relations between the contents in the activities of knowing. And if this is true for all knowing, you know something about the possible object of human knowledge; and if you know something about the possible object of human knowledge, you know some metaphysics.

Moreover, you know something about metaphysics that is not a matter of self-evident principles from which you deduce according to the norms of essentialism or pure reason. Your metaphysics has a verifiable element. When someone wants to introduce a fourth element besides potency, form, and act – such as the Scotist or Suarezian mode – you can say to him, 'If there really were some fourth element, there would have to be some fourth level in your knowing. Please provide the evidence through self-appropriation that that fourth element exists.' Or, again, if he wants his fundamental analysis to be Aristotelian, not in terms of potency, form, and act, but simply matter and form – hylomorphism – you can allege against him the fact that we judge, that we are interested in truth, not merely in experience and understanding. Is that OK?

Yes; in fact, it's a marvelous review of the book. But there is a question which I don't ask you to answer now, though I hope it will come up later – on your statement that the structure of your acts of knowing implies the contents of your knowing, what you call the isomorphism of knowing and being. It's a crucial issue. Do you take that up when you discuss objectivity?

Not precisely there. Objectivity is connected with it, is a presupposition of it. But I don't think there is any real difficulty there, any serious difficulty. It may seem very tricky and smart though.

11   Further Use of One's Insights

To arrive at this knowledge of the invariants of human knowing, you must have insight into some situations, and you must know that you have these insights. What do you do with them then?

The first step is adverting to insight as an occurrence. But if you become familiar with a series of instances of insight you begin to catch on to what it is tied in with. It is related to inquiry: it is what inquiry heads for. It is related to sensible and imaginative presentations: they are what you have insight into. It is related to conceptions, definitions, hypotheses, suppositions: insofar as you have insight you can have all of these. Then, insofar as you arrive at such formulations, there arises a further question, Is it true? – You get moved on to a third level. And when you arrive at truth, well, you may be at a dead end for that question, but further questions arise and you start over again. Now you discover in this process an invariant pattern, and there you have the invariant pattern in the knowing. But whenever you know, there is a known – you have contents of different kinds – and this gives you your invariant pattern also in your object.

If I have a bunch of insights, not knowing whether they are true or false, where do I start to try to verify them?

Try the concrete judgment of fact in chapter 10. The point is that you can so qualify things as to make a verifiable judgment. For example you can say, 'Well, at least I had an insight, though it may not be right.' And you are right in that judgment: you have had an insight.

In commonsense insights – to take perhaps the easiest type of example – when you move into a new situation, and you do not know the people, do not know how they do things, well, you are pretty cagey for a couple of weeks or a couple of months, until you get to know what the attitude of the people is, what they think about this and that, the way they do things. And the same in dealing with people. You get to know people, you know what to expect from them, what they will do under certain circumstances. You have a series of insights that you gradually accumulate into a sort of cluster, insights into the way this fellow reacts. And you size him up, whether this is the day to ask him to do something. You may be wrong, but then you correct your cluster. In other words, the insights accumulate, and single elements in them lead to qualifications and corrections, they complement previous ones. The process does not run off to infinity. It closes into a circle, and you get to the point where you say: Well, I am familiar with that situation, I know what to do there.

But you can never be sure?

Well, in common sense, are you ever absolutely certain about things like this? You head towards certainty. Questions of absolute certainty go on to a more technical type of philosophy. But you can always qualify, break it down. You won't be certain that he will say yes or no, but you can be certain he will say something.

12   Philosophical Presuppositions of the Theory

Does the description of the different instances of insights presuppose a certain conception of what understanding is or how it can be exercised?

From the side of presuppositions you can always say that, when you make any statement, you are presupposing a theory of knowledge and of metaphysics. But my answer to this is that, even though there are presuppositions, we will handle questions in theory of knowledge, and a complete theory of knowledge and metaphysics, better later on than now.

Do you see the point when we draw circles and see that in some cases they intersect, and in this case they will have to intersect – does that click or does it not? Do you get it or do you not? And if you don't get it in this case, well, there are other cases in which you do get it. And if there is a significant increase in knowledge in such cases, well, let us call that insight. In other words, one can say that in the first ten chapters of the book I'm presupposing that insight is best described as an event.

Compare German philosophy. For example, Karl Jaspers' book on truth[31] gives a magnificent description of a whole series of terms in the German language connected with knowledge, *Geist* and *Bewusstsein, Bewusstsein überhaupt, Vernunft* and *Verstand*, and so on. It is a description that is easier for me to understand because of my views on insight, but it nowhere speaks about insight explicitly. Now he is approaching cognitional process there through the terms used in the German language, but I think that you could justify speaking of insight as an event by appealing to the psychology of insight.

Of course, you can also ask whether I am not supposing an Aristotelian and Thomist type of metaphysics in talking about an event. Well, de facto probably I am. But lots of people talk about events without Aristotelian and Thomist presuppositions. And in general my approach is not from what is logically prior to what is logically posterior. Neither is it an approach from what is metaphysically prior to what is metaphysically posterior. It is an approach from what is pedagogically prior, and I believe that the first thing to do is to pin down this event, insight.

13 Objectivity

Whatever be the phenomenology that we use – whether that of Husserl or that of Sartre or the one that you yourself prefer – necessarily, in connection with phenomenology, the question of objectivity arises. Now they say that Husserl's position on phenomenology has logically led to a new sort of idealism. This may be precisely why you didn't want to use phenomenology: you didn't want to side with Husserl. But where does the question of objectivity come in in your position? And by objectivity I mean what is really real. Where would that come in?

That comes in with the question of truth and true judgments. The fundamental opposition, I think, is very well put by Maréchal.[32] You can have an analysis of knowledge in which the critical element is the experience, the confrontation, the given, the sense perception; if you make that the decisive element, you are on Kant's side. Or you can

---

31 Karl Jaspers, *Von der Wahrheit: Philosophische Logik, Erste Band* (Munich: R. Piper, 1947). Only short selections have been translated into English.
32 The discussion here, on the role of Maréchal, sheds light on our reconstruction of the end of lecture 7 (not recorded); see note 23 to that lecture, also discussion 4, §6, Maréchal, Kant, and Lonergan.

make your decisive element the judgment, what is true, and then you are on St Thomas', the realist side. And there are a lot of scholastics who do not agree with Maréchal.

Besides, you see, that position of Maréchal, placing idealism as a halfway house between realism and materialism, or positivism, implies that the Kantian Copernican revolution was not revolutionary enough. On another view of realism, you can have realism as the halfway house between materialism and idealism.[33] And that is the fundamental existential question, the personal question; it is one of the big difficulties raised by *Insight*, and it is raised by pushing systematically the assertion that intellect is intelligence.

Now to discover the objectivity of things, should we start with analyzing judgment, and judgment without connection with sense experience, or should we start simply with the data of sense experience admitted as an independent reality?

I don't think that the question of the validity of sense is philosophically of great significance. In other words, sense experience is an integral part in our knowledge of reality, our direct knowledge of reality; to have knowledge at all you have to have sense knowledge. But if sense experience is the decisive point, then it will play the same role in your philosophy as intuition does in Kant.

What is the implication of what you call judgment, when you say that, if you give importance to judgment in your philosophy, then you are a Thomist. Now what is the implication of this judgment, what does it contain, what are its elements?

'It is' or 'This is' – affirmation, rational affirmation. Take the position of Kant, who starts with the assertion that intuition is of appearances: we have no intuition of things themselves. Now if intuition is the decisive part in knowledge, that statement of Kant's is valid only insofar as there is an intuition of 'intuitions of only appearances.' But, for everyone, if it is true that intuition is only of appearances, well, you are finished: you have settled the matter on the level of truth. If Kant's statement is true, then intuitions are only of appearances. In other words, implicitly Kant is acknowledging that truth is the decisive factor when he makes that statement.

I don't know if I am being clear, getting the point across. There is

33 See also the passage quoted below in § 14, Two Realisms.

an implicit appeal to the ultimacy of truth, that is contained in the statement, 'Intuition is only of appearances.' It is by truth, therefore, that we get to know reality. And the whole question is whether Kant's proposition is or is not true. But Kant's philosophy is not built in a way that is compatible with the fact that the decisive element is truth. Because, for possible knowledge, the criterion in Kant always is the possibility of connecting it with an intuition. And that is why you get into these logical difficulties in Kant. But they are only symptomatic.

In the structure of the judgment you put sense experience, of course?

Some judgments presuppose sense experience in their content. But if you say, for example, that you had an insight, the judgment of the fact that you had an insight doesn't necessitate sense experience. You are not asserting sense experience or the content of sense experience when you affirm the fact of an insight.

But what is the most existential judgment?

Well, that judgment is existential if you really had an insight.

What is the first insight then?

Chronologically?

Ontologically. I mean the one that would give an existential basis for all the other judgments. There must be one which has a maximum of existentiality, I should say.

We are not yet on the level of judgments when we have insights; and *the* act that is both insight and judgment and has a maximum of existence to it is God's self-knowledge of the beatific vision.

14 Two Realisms

Could I ask for an explanation of a few lines in the Introduction to Insight? *Their meaning didn't quite get across to me. You speak of 'the discovery ... that there are two quite different realisms ... an incoherent realism ... that poses as a half-way house between materialism and idealism and ... an intelligent and reasonable realism between which and materialism the half-way house is ideal-ism.'[34] I have difficulty getting hold of that, and my difficulty is increased now,*

34 *Insight* xxviii.

because you just mentioned two sorts of idealism, where also you use the image of a halfway house.

I don't think I spoke of two idealisms. I meant to say exactly the same thing as in the passage you quote about two realisms.

Could you go through it again?

It is not an easy point. As a matter of fact, it is a fundamental point. But it will become clearer in the course of the two weeks, and if it does we are achieving an awful lot. Roughly, however, is it truth that is decisive, and is it simply truth that is decisive? That is the position that is relatively easy, for a Catholic and for a theologian, because a Catholic says, 'I believe ...' and there follows a list of propositions; they are truths, and they determine his religious life. Likewise for a theologian: fundamental in his science are the truths of faith. On the other hand, if you want to be a modernist, you will say that what counts is religious experience. Truth, well, it has a certain symbolic value, and the propositions – such as the two natures in one person in Christ – no doubt helped the Greeks of the fifth and sixth centuries in their religious experience, but they aren't very helpful today, and so we can forget about them. Truth is not the decisive thing in the modernist,[b] it is religious experience – intense religious life – and you adapt these propositional symbols to the exigencies of the age.

You can see how the position that truth is the decisive factor is all-important in theology, and how it is easier for a theologian to take that step. Philosophically religious truth is a very extrinsic consideration; philosophy has to stand on its own feet. When you define the real as *id quod est*, that which is, you define the real as what corresponds to truth. You set up a correspondence between truth and reality. If you think, however, that your judgment is true because you already know reality, and you look into yourself for a prior act that decides what this judgment really means, this act can be merely a rubber stamp placed on judgment, a rubber stamp placed on some prior act.[35]

---

35 The end of the discussion was not recorded; the DJS tape brings us to this point, the LRI tape stopped a line earlier, and the WAS tape in the first sentence of the final paragraph.

Discussion 2[1]

1   Insight and Its Conceptual Expression

[Recording started late, and the first question has been lost.]

We distinguished between insight and conception this morning. The insight names the act, the event; and different insights have different contents: understanding why circles will intersect is different from understanding why the external angle must be greater than the internal opposite angle. There are different ideas involved, and the idea is the content of the insight. I have probably been speaking of insight generally, and using the word indifferently to refer both to the act and to the content. But later, when we become more precise, we will use 'idea' to refer to the content and 'insight' to refer to the act.

Is the relation between concept and conception that of content and act?

There is possibly room for some sort of distinction there. The question about conception gives rise to difficulties, at least historically. In Aquinas, for example, the concept does not seem to be conceived as an act, but simply as a content. However, I don't think that way myself. Certainly judgment is an act, and judgment for Thomas was an expression in the way the concept is an expression; I would therefore be

1 The evening of Tuesday, August 5, 1958. The 1980 edition included (in questions 4 and 5) parts of the present §7, Self-appropriation, Hegel, and Kierkegaard; and of §9, Western Culture and the Scientific Ideal.

inclined to say that there is an act for conception too. So again you have the distinction between act and content.

In this morning's talk you seemed to make the concept or conception something over and above insight, an enrichment, or something added.[2] From what you had written previously,[3] I always understood you to mean by concept or verbum *the same as you mean by definition, in which you have the expression of insight, of what you have understood – when you have understood something, then you can define – as if there were really no difference between the content of your insight and the content of your concept except that one is the expression of the other. But now you seem to bring in this idea of a further generalization, a general formula.*

Well, there has to be some difference in the content, otherwise you have no proof that they are two acts.

That helps account for a question I had never been able to figure out: Why do we ever have to have contents, and why all the talk about contents? But there is a further problem: How much is just added by the mind, and how much is taken from reality?

I think that there are differences between the content of the act of conception and the content of the act of insight. I thought that we gave a fairly clear illustration of it, when we caught on to the fact that Euclid did not have an adequate proof for his construction of the equilateral triangle, that he had been using an insight surreptitiously. I tried to formulate that yesterday morning and did not succeed; we did it again explicitly this morning and found that it is quite an elaborate process.[4] And also the effort at general conception involves the introduction of a scientific ideal, as illustrated by Socrates. Socrates *did* something when he introduced universal definitions.

There is not a change in position at all, then, with regard to your own work: concept is still definition.

Yes. Definition is one illustration of it.

What is the difference between that and insight? Insight is knowledge of what

2 See lecture 2, §§2–5.
3 The reference is probably to *Verbum*, passim – for example, 23, 24–25, 82–83.
4 See lecture 2, §2, The Nest of Related Terms.

is relevant, and only of what is relevant, to some given sensible presentation of data. That seems to me to be knowledge of the essence or nature of something; but then, you say, over and above that we go on to a further act whereby we express to ourselves what we have understood. That just seems to be adding further complications to an already complicated problem.

I think that there are clear distinctions between the content of the concept and the content of the insight. The insight is the enriching moment – the grasp of the actual intelligibility, in Thomist terms – that is potentially in the phantasm ...

A particular phantasm?

All phantasms are particular ... that grasp enables you to select from the phantasm the parts of the form as distinct from the parts of the matter. And that selection is a process of abstraction.

In the *verbum* articles I distinguished between apprehensive and formative abstraction, and you have the same viewpoint there again.[5] I worked out the articles in function of Trinitarian theory where, if you are going to use the psychological analogy at all, you obviously have to have a distinction between the understanding and the concept.

Further, if you presuppose a metaphysics, then your systematic proof of the distinction between insight and concept, between *intelligere* and *dicere*, is from objects. Acts are specified by their objects: unless you have different objects you have not got different acts. Thus you have different objects for concept, insight, and sensible presentation. In your concept you include common matter, in Thomist terms. Your insight adds form to the sensible presentation; it grasps the intelligible that is in the sensible.

Is what the insight grasps merely particular or does it achieve a certain generality?

It has at least *virtual* generality, because similars are similarly understood.

The point bothering me was: it seemed to have a little more than that virtual generality, because it grasps necessity, and necessity does seem to introduce immediately the notion of universality. Even on the level of insight, you say these two circles must intersect. We don't yet know why, in the sense that we can

5 *Verbum* 151–68.

write out a formula showing under what conditions the circles will intersect, but we see that they must intersect. And this seems to introduce universality. Or is this just hindsight on our part, when we are analyzing further what it is we have actually got insight into?

Well, at least there is this difficulty of hindsight. In other words, as I stressed this morning,[6] when we express the content of the insight, we are already using concepts. When I say that in the insight we grasp the necessity of this curve being round and these circles intersecting, I am already using words, and behind my words are judgments and concepts. So I am using this further part in knowledge to give an account of some prior part in which there are not yet concepts, judgments, or words. I described that earlier part by using the word 'necessity.' But it isn't necessity in general; at least it isn't any general concept of necessity yet. It is the basis for a general concept of necessity.

This morning I thought I understood that point, but on reflection I'm not quite sure I do. It seems to me that yesterday when, in your parable, as it were, we had grasped the fact of necessity in that particular case, but had not yet formulated it, we were still at the stage of insight. But we had already spoken of necessity in words; therefore, we had already conceptualized the necessity.

In other words, we hadn't perhaps formulated this insight but we had already used words, and therefore concepts, at what you might call a lower level of organization, in order to express this insight while it was still at the stage of insight, before it was actually formulated.

So I am wondering how far there is always a necessary connection between the use of some concepts and the expression of an insight, even when the insight is still at the level of insight with regard to the total complex you happen to be interested in at the moment.

I think that is a very complex and difficult question. It seems to me that the artist expresses his insights in his work of art, certainly without using any generalized conception such as we attempted today for the intersection of the circles. Is there conception in some other form? If you want to argue from the texts of St Thomas you would say so, yes. Does it occur that one catches on to something, or does one have the feeling that one had caught on to something, and can't recall just what

---

6 See lecture 2, §4, The Content of the Insight – where Lonergan deals with the psychological fallacy.

it was? Would that be the case of an insight occurring without conception? I think that there are all sorts of odds and ends that come in on that issue.

Some people would say, 'If you haven't got the exact words you haven't got the insight.' They wouldn't use those words but they would say, 'You're not quite sure until you've labeled exactly what it is that you are thinking.'

I think that there is an element of truth in that: our thinking includes expression in language. But that there is not some incipient stage when the words fail us, or that failing to find words is always a proof that we have nothing in our heads, nothing at all – I am not quite so sure of that.

With regard to the difficulty you raised, comparing yesterday and today on this case of the equilateral triangle, and then the general statement on the conditions for the intersection of circles, one might say that there are two distinct insights: an insight into this particular case, and then an insight into the general question of when the circles intersect. And really this morning we were formulating that further insight.

But I don't think those questions can be settled until we get on into systematic metaphysics, questions such as: What is? Is it the same or different? What are the criteria of identity and difference? And so on. There we are really asking metaphysical questions about insight and conception, but at this stage of the game they are not important.

I am only trying to get clear exactly what you were using as an example of insight in this particular case – how far what was happening yesterday was an example of insight and how far it was something else. I take it, then, that as far as the primary insight is concerned in that particular example, it stops at the stage where we simply made our construction, and recognized – by the very fact of using those two circles, without raising any problem about it – recognized that they are going to intersect. Perhaps even before saying, even to ourselves, 'They are going to intersect.' So that when we say 'They must intersect,' we have actually formulated this insight. Is this true of what you said so far?

Yes, approximately, yes.

If you have the distinction between the insight and the conception, it seems to me that there is going to have to be some process between the two, whereby you finally end up with the conception itself. And I was wondering whether that means that you have an insight into the intersection of the circles, and then a second insight relative to the formulation?

Yes, I think so. In that case the process is reflective, as when you ask yourself the further question, When will the circles intersect, when will they not? On a more delicate level there is process between insight and conception, and between grasp of the sufficiency of the evidence and judgment.[a] That process is illustrative of what is meant by intelligent consciousness and rational consciousness.

How would you qualify the sort of evidence that you have on the level of insight? You say that there is evidence on the level of insight, that the object of insight is something evident. Then you have evidence also on the level of conception, because you discover in conception a sort of 'whyness': 'why this is so,' 'when it is so,' and 'why it should be so.' You have two instances then of evidence: what is the difference between the two exactly? One seems to be more imbedded in sensibility, and the other more detached from sensibility and more on the intellectual level.

The word 'evidence,' I presume, does not mean anything more than the psychological fact of the insight? The psychological fact of the insight enables you to select – and this is the process of conception – to select from the data in a transformed way, the necessary and sufficient conditions for having the insight. When you have the insight as to why this curve must be perfectly round, namely, because all the radii are equal – well, we have already expressed it there, and gone beyond the insight. But it is because, in just having the insight, we see a necessary connection between the equality of radii and the appearance of the perfectly round curve, that we are able to go on and define a circle as the locus of coplanar points equidistant from a center.

Is definition the only element added to insight?

Yes.

In insight do you see that it must be so, whereas in conception you would have the 'why it is so'?

No, we are not yet strictly at the level of judgment. I think that there is a danger of the psychological fallacy cropping up continuously in any discussion of this matter, and by the psychological fallacy is meant the fact that, while the psychologist uses words and judgments and concepts, still what he is talking about need not be yet in words, or yet at the level of judgment, or yet at the level of conception. Consequently, though I describe what is grasped by the insight as a grasp of necessity, of a necessary link, still we have not arrived yet at the concept of necessary link, and much less the judgment.

I do not understand. If we see the necessity we see it through our intellect, necessarily we conceive it. But I don't yet see the necessity of having a conception if it is already in the grasp that you have in insight.

In the insight what you do is add intelligibility to the sensible data. The sensible data or the imagined data are potentially intelligible. At the moment of insight you have actual intelligibility,[b] you click.

At this moment do you not also have conception?

Well, maybe temporally. But you can formulate your insight incorrectly. I have frequently tried it with a class, giving them the insight into why the circle is round, and then defined the circle as the locus of points equidistant from a center and applied that definition to the outline of the map of Africa, where all points on the outline are equidistant from the center of the earth.

It may be that your insight was not complete, then?

That may also be true. In other words, they did not advert to the absence of the condition, coplanar. As a matter of fact, the possibility of the development of the sciences – of the fact that the sciences move from one system to a higher viewpoint, which is another system – the possibility of that movement is that the insights expressed by the lower system are expressed inadequately. You do a certain amount of arithmetic, and then you discover difficulties about your fundamental concepts – what you mean by 'equals' and what you mean by 'one'--and then you need to redefine your whole set of fundamental concepts. You do that in algebra.

The fact that you express it more adequately, is that not a sign that you have another insight?

Yes. You have a higher viewpoint – at least in the example I gave, you have a higher viewpoint. Do you express it more adequately? In a sense, yes, because in this conception, at least the type of conception that we are talking about, we are trying to express the insight universally, to give a formula that covers every case. We are trying to do what Socrates was trying to do with the Athenians, to give an account of bravery that would hold for every instance of bravery. But this brings up differences in patterns of experience, and we have not treated that yet: it comes up at the beginning of chapter 6 in *Insight*. What Socrates is also trying to do, fundamentally, is introduce the intellectual pattern of experience into Athenian life. But the Athenians for their practical purposes knew well enough what it was to be brave and what it was to be cowardly, and so on for the rest of the virtues, even though they could not satisfy Socrates with their definitions. That movement towards a universally accurate definition is a movement towards the realization of an ideal that we call science, an ideal that is developed in the history of culture.

2 Inverse Insight and the Empirical Residue

What is the connection between experience and inverse insight and the empirical residue?

Experience is what is presupposed by inquiry, insight, and conception. If your mind is perfectly blank you cannot ask any questions. Experience is what eliminates the blank, supplies materials to ask about.

The way I define inverse insight is this: you anticipate an intelligibility, and then you demonstrate that there can't be intelligibility of the type that was anticipated. For example, the irrational, the law of inertia, special relativity, and so on – they are inverse insights. You have them also in probability, and later, in the dialectic – human affairs.

The empirical residue differs from the inverse insight insofar as there is lacking this element of anticipating an intelligibility. No one expects the physicist to have different explanations for different instances of colors of exactly the same shade. De facto you cannot give different explanations for colors of exactly the same shade, but no one expects you to do so. That is why I call empirical residue these cases of inverse insight where people don't anticipate any intelligibility at all.

What you are getting at there by inverse insight looks suspiciously like experience on the level of intelligence. Would that be true? For instance, when this morning[7] you said that 'This point is not that,' it was basic that there was no understanding: it is experience on the level of intellect.

7 See lecture 2, § 13, Inverse Insight.

Insofar as I state, 'This one is not that one,' obviously I am making a judgment.

Yes, but I am talking about the prior stage of the given.

And that mere multiplicity in the given prior to any understanding and conception is the empirical residue, insofar as you must not expect any explanation for this given.

Well, could you therefore say that you are getting at that by some sort of intellectual experience, using 'experience' for that aspect of the intellectual act by which you are getting at this empirical residue?

It can be called intellectual experience in the sense that there is experience, and intellectual advertence to the absence of intelligibility relevant to this experience. In other words, it is not simply experience when you say it is empirical residue. You have also noticed that there is nothing to be understood with regard to it.

Why do we sometimes anticipate an intelligibility and sometimes not, when in both cases there is no intelligibility to be grasped? Why are we surprised sometimes that there is no intelligibility and other times not? You say for the 'here and now' that no one expects that it should be intelligible, and so we're not surprised when we are told it isn't; but for constant velocity we do expect that there should be some reason, and we are surprised when we find that it is a part of the empirical residue.

I never asked myself what the reason would be. De facto people are always surprised at the law of inertia, and there have been lots of efforts to try and account for it, in terms of inequalities and properties and so on. On the other hand, people spontaneously generalize. They would be surprised if exactly the same experiment, performed under exactly the same conditions, yielded different results because the places were different and the times were different. I suppose it is that attitude that we formulate in such statements as 'Similars are similarly understood.' Well, perhaps the answer to your question is that we made the discovery at such an early period that we don't worry about it at any later period. I wouldn't offer an opinion on that.

> [At this point various suggestions were made to explain our attitude to constant velocity, for example, the influence of prior insights. Discussion continued with the following suggestion.]

*How much of this difficulty about constant velocity is due to our own nature,
our own physiological and psychological frame? If you shut your eyes you are
quite indifferent to whether you are in constant velocity or at rest. The human
frame only feels acceleration.*

I think there is a very good point there. It reminds me of Merleau-
Ponty's work on the phenomenology of behavior,[8] and he has another
book, in which a large number of our sense perceptions are explained
in terms of our own bodies.[9] – That is as far as I can take the question
but he works it out in beautiful detail. In a sense, I believe his work is
an attack on behaviorism.[10] But an awful lot of our perceiving would
not be possible without our bodies, not merely that we need our senses,
but that we need the whole body.

3   Induction

*You mentioned the principle 'Similars are similarly understood,' and you say
that using that principle solves the problem of induction. Could you amplify
that a little for me, please?*

'Similars are similarly understood' is a truth based simply on the analysis of insight or advertence to insight. You can't understand differently, and you don't try to understand differently, if the data are exactly
the same, similar in all respects, in two different cases. With regard to
the problem of induction, you have to distinguish it from the problem
of accurately formulating just what you get in a given insight; that
problem is not solved at all by 'Similars are similarly understood.'

8 Maurice Merleau-Ponty, *La structure du comportement* (Paris: Presses Universitaires de France, 1942); trans. Alden L. Fisher, *The Structure of
   Behavior* (Boston: Beacon Press, 1963).
9 Maurice Merleau-Ponty, *Phénoménologie de la perception* (Paris: Gallimard,
   1945); trans. Colin Smith, *Phenomenology of Perception* (London:
   Routledge and Kegan Paul, 1962).
10 Lonergan added some incidental information on Merleau-Ponty: 'He is
   a professor at the Collège de France – I think he has recently moved
   up from the Sorbonne. There is a book on him, an account of his philosophy, by Alphonse De Waelhens, the man who wrote on Heidegger.' – See
   Une philosophie de l'ambiguité: l'existentialisme de Maurice Merleau-Ponty (Louvain: Publications Universitaires de Louvain, 1951). De Waelhens' book
   on Heidegger: *La philosophie de Martin Heidegger* (Louvain: Editions de
   l'Institut Supérieur de Philosophie, 1st ed., 1942).

Again, the certainty of the truth of the generalization is not solved by 'Similars are similarly understood.'

Once that is grasped there is no problem as to why people generalize. The whole problem is to prevent them from expressing their generalization inaccurately, or making generalizations that they cannot establish. But the generalization itself ceases to be a problem.

4   Insight in Art

You said something about the artist's insight and something also about the phenomenological approach. In both cases there is a selection of data. In both cases there is an insight: I presume that the description of the selection of what is relevant in the phenomenological approach supposes an insight, otherwise you couldn't select it; but an artist also selects. Is there something common there?

I think so. I think the tendencies of the later Heidegger illustrate that, because what he is really giving in his later works is a philosophy of art.

But an artist does not give you a philosophy of art.

No. But phenomenology has led Heidegger to a philosophy of art.

So the difference would be in the material object. For the artist, say, the story of a human life; for the phenomenologist, selecting materials which will lead to a scientific formulation, if they are pushed. There must be a difference; they are not just the same, are they?

No, they are not the same. They have quite different claims and aims. But again you can say that Aristotle's philosophy is the same sort of thing insofar as it is a philosophy of matter and form without going on to the act of existence. In other words, what is common to phenomenology, to the artist, and to Aristotle, is data and insight.

Yes, but Aristotle formulated his insights.

Yes. Aristotle formulated his insights as a system. The phenomenologist formulates his by drawing your attention to the data in the intelligible constellation that he wishes to communicate, and he goes about the matter more systematically, more in the scientific manner. The artist simply produces the work, with no commentary – he leaves that to the critics, the interpreters.

Is there a point at which the scientist becomes an artist? I remember hearing an historian talking about his investigations into the House of Commons in the nineteenth century. He used punch cards and an IBM machine to work out as many correlations as he could between different factors that he thought would be illuminating. Well, he found after a while that the mystery was deepening rather than anything else.

The only connection between the scientist and the artist that occurs to me at the moment comes from Lindsay and Margenau; it is in the last chapter of their book *Foundations of Physics*, when they move to the fundamental presuppositions of the physicist, and express them in the artistic terms of simplicity and elegance: they say that in the last resort a physicist is an artist, or something like that.[11]

Not quite in the same sense, though, is it?

No. But when they come to fundamentals, what the physicists appeal to are artistic criteria of simplicity and elegance. The comparison is not exact – de facto simplicity and elegance have different criteria for them and mean different things to them from what they do to the artist.

In one case they come as the end of the work: the artist consciously aims at elegance and simplicity; in the other they come as a presupposition: one of the tests of the validity of the theory in physics will be its elegance.

I think that, when Lindsay and Margenau give this formulation of the basis of physics, they don't mean to go into it philosophically, but simply to give brief indications.

Regarding the parallel between artist and phenomenologist, I don't see how the insight the artist has or the form the artist grasps could possibly be expressed conceptually.

I think that you are perfectly correct on insisting on the differences between them. What is common is the absence of attention to the reflective level of truth, reality, being; that does not come up explicitly. They both remain on the level of experience and insight.

Yes, but the difference seems to be that in one case you can proceed further, in the other case it does not make sense to ask the further question. You can say,

11 Lindsay and Margenau, *Foundations of Physics* 528.

I suppose, of a work of art that pretends to be representative, a picture of London in 1688 or some such thing, 'Is this really what London looked like?' But in general, if you take something which just pretends to be an abstract work of art, it does not lend itself to the procedure that moves into those further stages. It does not seem to make sense to apply the conceptual level of thought, or the judgmental level of thought, to a symphony. And if this is so, does it not mean that the fundamental insight is different, or that the form is different altogether, that it is not an intellectual form? I am a little disturbed by this because one so often reads or hears of intelligible form in art, but it would seem not to be intelligible at all, because it does not permit of conceptualization at all, and the question of judgment does not arise.

I think that you are correct in drawing attention to differences, and I would not want to dispute them. On the other hand, there are, I think, similarities that are significant.

You say that the artistic insight does not admit conceptualization. When we get onto probability, I think we will find the insight there involves an element, a closeness to the sensible data, that cannot be got into the conceptualized system. And the absence or the presence of the possibility of such more concrete insight makes the difference between the classical and the statistical structures of investigation. So that you have there a point of community.

Again, while the phenomenologist may be said to provide data for more systematic conceptualization, still, he would not go on to that as a phenomenologist: his work is finished. That work is quite definitely not artistic in the strictest sense. On the other hand, it fulfils a function that has certain similarities to the function of art. The function of art – one way of conceiving it, I simply want to suggest, not to define – regards the harmony that is involved in the artistic work and is communicated to the percipient, and it is beside the point to try to conceptualize that. And the phenomenologist too, in his attention to data and his presentation of them, fills in a mode of communication that is quite distinct from the more systematic conceptualized mode of communication.

So I think that there are certain similarities; but I certainly would not want to argue for any sort of identity. Is artistic insight insight in the same sense as in phenomenology? Is it insight in the same sense as in geometry, or science? Those questions remain.

[Here there was an exchange between two participants on the question whether we apply judgment to a work of art, one holding that we do – the judgment whether it is good, beautiful, etc. – the other wishing to confine discussion to the point reached in the lectures so far, where there are no presuppositions about metaphysics. The discussion continued with the following remarks from the floor.]

The statement that conceptualization is beside the point is ambiguous. You might mean that it is beside the point for the artist – it isn't what he wants to do, and with that I agree – but I don't mean it's beside the point in that sense; I mean that it is logically improper.

I wonder if one is misled by certain forms of art, where there is an apprehension of an intelligible form, where the mind delights in the work – for example, when you call a mathematical proof beautiful. There is aesthetic appreciation of the pattern of the argument. But is that something accidental? It may not apply, for example, to certain paintings or pieces of music. Does it depend on the particular art? A poem, a novel, or a play may be intellectually pleasing. Can you try to conceptualize in these cases, but by reason, not of art, but of what is incidental to art? That may explain what I meant by saying 'logically improper' instead of 'beside the point.'

Is there a distinction between the two?

There would be if by 'beside the point' you meant that the artist as such isn't interested in forming a concept – in the same way as the phenomenologist as such is not interested in that.

Another example: the carpenter, teaching someone his work, is not interested in producing theories, but simply in teaching modes of procedure which can be imitated. You might say it's beside the point there. Again, a golfer can play golf without understanding the mathematical theory of the flight of the golf ball. You might say it's beside the point to go to the mathematical theory, when you are teaching someone to play golf, not do mathematics. If that's what you mean by beside the point, I should agree; but that's not all I would want to say.

I think it would be difficult to work out at the present stage the differences between 'logically improper,' and so-and-so not being interested, and so on. Probably when I said that it was beside the point, I meant logically improper inasmuch as it is no part of the idea of art.

5 Intellect as Intelligence

Yesterday you said that intellect was intelligence. Could you explain that, please?

In the history of scholasticism, you find the theory of grace worked out

in St Thomas with a very definite psychological content. By the time
you get to the sixteenth-century theologians, that psychological content
has disappeared. There is a purely metaphysical content. Shortly
prior to St Thomas only the psychological content existed: the metaphysics had not been attempted.

Or take Trinitarian theory. It has a definite psychological content in
St Thomas, and the psychological content very shortly was removed
from it and vanished.

The same sort of thing can happen in psychology. You can use the
word 'intellect' or *intellectus*, and have a series of metaphysical definitions of types of intellect, and the operations of intellect, and the conditions of the operations of intellect, and do the whole theory of intellect
without any psychological contents being involved – or only minimal
psychological contents, such as the universal concept, and the truth
of a judgment. And when I said intellect is intelligence, I meant to
express a disagreement with that viewpoint. In other words, I don't
believe that there is any intellect that is not intelligence ... in the sense
that what is not intelligent cannot be labeled intellectual.[c] And I think
that, if you apply that, you will find it is quite a broom.

Intelligence, then, is just the ability to grasp the intelligible?

Yes, to grasp it correctly.

6   Understanding and Perception

[Here there was an intervention by Bernard Lonergan's brother, Gregory, who was a cartoonist of considerable talent, and also a humorist.
His aim was to set forth his understanding of his brother's cognitional
theory, and ask whether that understanding was correct; it is impossible,
however, to transcribe his talk, partly because it depended on cartoon
illustrations at the blackboard, partly because laughter at his humorous
remarks drowned out much of the exchange. At the end, Bernard
responded, using Gregory's example of seeing a tree.]

There are some omissions; for example, the psychological. The eye and
the optic nerve are the organ of sight, and the brain too. Besides the
organ of sight there is sight. Sight stands to its organ as the soul stands
to the whole body. The movement, the change, in the organ involves a
change in the faculty of sight, the form; it is the *motus coniuncti*. You

have a sense impression of a tree; you see the tree from a particular angle. And that is not yet a perception of a tree. In what you have represented in your diagram – brain, eye, optic nerve, and so on – you are talking on a physiological level.

But it is a good place to jump off into the other.

All right, make the jump. Corresponding to the organs there are forms, such as the senses. The modification of a sense gives rise to a sensation. Any particular sensation is just an element in a horizon of possible sensations. You never saw Saint Mary's University: you saw it from this angle, from that angle, from in front, from behind, and so on. You can have an infinity of different sense impressions of Saint Mary's University by walking along the front. But when you talk about Saint Mary's University you mean the integral, the horizon that contains all the different sense impressions of Saint Mary's University that you could have, if you walked the whole way around and came inside and went through all the corridors and rooms and so on.

I am not talking of the intellect yet, but of the difference between sense impressions and perception. You don't get to intellect until you start asking why. You can have all sorts of sensations and sense perceptions without asking why. It is from the moment of intellectual alertness, intellectual curiosity, wonder – it is when these commence, that you have what is called the illumination of the phantasm. When the class wakes up! They are not just hearing. They are wondering why. And the insight is what answers that wondering, that why.

That wondering why, centered in the intellect, is it independent of the senses?

Well, you have to have sense perceptions, sensations, to have something to wonder about.

Then where is the connection between wonder and sense perception?

Well, it starts things going on the intellectual level. You have the movement of consciousness as long as you are having sensations and sense perceptions, and a flow of images and desires and affects and so on, and a certain emotional tone. That is empirical consciousness. When wonder intervenes, you have the start of intellectual consciousness: you want to understand something. And that wanting to understand deals with these images, and in the images grasps forms, has insights into the images, and expresses them in conceptions. If there is no intellectual wonder, there is no intellectual operation. It hasn't started yet.

Would you describe the role of intellectual operation as related to perception?

Let us sketch it more diagrammatically.[12]

There is a flow of sensations. They are integrated into a flow of perceptions insofar as the sensations take their place within horizons; that is Husserl's terminology – he has done a lot of reflecting on this sort of thing. The perceptions give a profile, an *Abschattung*. The perception is a horizon that will contain a whole series of these possible sense perceptions. The perception can have a flow filled out with images, whatever their source is – memory and so on – and this is governed by various psychological laws. All this occurs within empirical consciousness.

Then there is intellectual consciousness. You have your intellect, agent intellect, the source of wonder. Wonder starts, there is something that excites your curiosity, you wonder why about something. We have a flow of images, but we have gone past the stage where we wonder about trees, so they are not good examples for anything intellectual; what we have been dealing with mostly these last two days have been geometrical images because they are easier than any others to pin down. When wonder arises with respect to an image or a presentation, you have what the scholastics named the illumination of the phantasm. The sensible presentation is now a problem for you. The phantasm, the image, is said to be the instrument through which the possible intellect receives a *species impressa*, an impressed form. Why is it a form? It grounds an intellectual habit. If you once catch on to something it sticks with you. It is a different type of memory from sensible memory. If you do your geometry correctly, if you really learn it, you do not forget it. There is quite a difference, then, between intellectual memory and sensitive memory, and what that means is again form in the sense of habit. Once you catch on to something, once you have the idea, you are able to operate on your own, you do not need the teacher. Really what you need is a whole set of such forms to have a habit.

12 Lonergan's point here: we need a more schematic diagram[d] than his brother Greg's artistry provided.

The insight is act limited by that form, and the concept is the expression of the insight; when you have understood something, you can express it in a concept. In your example, you have understood how to use the word 'tree'; you may not have understood anything about the tree, but you can say, 'This is a tree' – 'tree' is the appropriate word to use when I am seeing this. However, there are all sorts of further questions involving that 'is,' which we may get on to next week.[13]

7   Self-appropriation, Hegel, and Kierkegaard

Would you indicate again how self-appropriation solves the difficulty in Hegelian interpretation?

I have not yet said how self-appropriation answers it. The difficulty is this: The pursuit of knowledge, the pursuit of a science, the pursuit of a philosophy, is the pursuit of something that you don't know yet – otherwise you would not be pursuing it – and to account for that you have to appeal to some sort of ideal. While there are tendencies in us, such as wonder, wanting to understand, wanting to understand things correctly, still, historically, it is clear that the expression, the conceptual formulation, of this ideal has been inadequate, that we move towards a more adequate conceptual formulation of the ideal. You have the Aristotelian idea of science, Galileo's idea of science, the idea of science that became possible with Newton, with Einstein, with the states and probabilities of quantum mechanics. The ideal of science in its development shifts; it becomes more precise. We stop looking for things that we were very much concerned about in previous periods.

Now using a Hegelian terminology, one can say that any explicit formulation of the ideal is abstract. It does not fully represent what is being expressed in this abstract fashion. That abstraction, the fact that it is abstract, reveals and will bring to light an alienation. The ideal, because it is different from the subject that it expresses, because it does not adequately express the subject, will be alien to the subject; there will be a tension between them. Nonetheless, letting that ideal work out its full consequences will bring to light ever more clearly this element of

13 See lecture 6, §2, The Notion of Being.

alienation. Consequently, it will be a means, a mediation, towards attaining a more adequate expression of the ideal. For the Hegelian this process runs right along with his philosophy. The objection can be put: no matter how we attempt to formulate the ideal we are seeking in philosophy or in science, it is always going to be making explicit what is implicit; it will always suffer from its abstractness; it will always give rise to alienation and mediation and a higher reconciliation. You can take it either in a relativist sense, where the process goes on indefinitely; or in the Hegelian sense, where we get into the Hegelian system.

A complete answer to that difficulty I did not attempt, and I cannot attempt it until we get a good deal further on. We would have to cover a lot of things that we hope to explain during the lectures. But the idea of self-appropriation, the ideal as conceptually formulated, is going to be abstract; there is no eliminating an element of abstraction there. In other words, even if you filled the world with encyclopedias, you would still not be giving everything.

But insofar as there is self-appropriation, insofar as one moves towards what has to be present for other things to be present to it, one is dealing with what conceptually is implicit still, but is de facto my empirical, intelligent, rational consciousness. It is functionally operative in my knowing. There is an escape from the abstraction insofar as I turn to the sources that are functionally operative in my inquiries, my investigations, my attempts to formulate. And insofar as the subject himself is a concrete being, in the measure that he has self-appropriation, in the measure that he has moved in on the basis as it operates, whence the ideals get expressed, he perhaps has a starting point towards meeting it.

To remain with your Hegelian analysis, you proceeded with the argument to show that the notion of being becomes the notion of nothing, and then you said that the Hegelian process leads to a toppling towards either the Marxian or the Kierkegaardian approach or attitude.[14] *I don't understand very well this toppling towards the Kierkegaardian.*

A few things about Kierkegaard in general: One of his fundamental questions was, Am *I* a Christian? That question is transposed in modern existentialism, Am *I* a man? What is it to be a man? Is it enough to have a birth certificate? The idea is that man is defined not by a static

14 See *Insight* 373-74.

essence but by an exigence. Being a man is something you become. So also in Kierkegaard's question, Am I a Christian? Is it enough that I was born in Denmark and am automatically a member of the State Church of Denmark? Am I Christian because of that? Or is being a Christian something more? He was concerned with what he was and that type of question. Kierkegaard is very much concerned with the states of the individual in his development.

Not being able to judge that he is?

No, it isn't a problem of knowledge, it's a problem of what he is. Whether he knows it or not is another concern. But he is concerned with the fact that he is the realization, or he *should be* the realization, of some 'what ought to be'; that is one way of putting it. It is a concern with existing, not in the scholastic sense of what de facto is, but in the deontological, normative sense. It is the type of question raised by Kierkegaard that is extremely difficult to answer within the Hegelian system: Kierkegaard considered that it could not be answered within the system.

That concern with moral and religious values that you have in Kierkegaard is one type of difficulty that arises against the Hegelian system. The other type arises with Marx, who said he turned the dialectic upside down – whether he did that or not is another question. Here you pick out certain elements in Hegel, for example, the succession of the feudal state of society, the bourgeoisie, the fourth estate and everything of this kind. There is a concern here with external human affairs as they concretely happened, and it sets up another kind of opposition. However, that is just a matter of the symmetries.

8   The Quest of the Ideal

You said that when you start seeking knowledge you are seeking an unknown, and therefore you set up an ideal; where does the ideal come from if the whole thing is unknown?

The fact that you are seeking enables you to objectify the ideal you are putting before you as a goal. The unknown goal, as an ideal, is an interpretation of the fact that you are seeking, that you are 'heading for' something.

Regarding inquiry: intellectual activity arises with the question for understand-

ing. Now this question expresses the ignorance of the intellect, but it also expresses knowledge, because you would not be able to posit questions if you did not know something about what you question. I wonder whether we have to go to a certain habitual knowledge that the intellect has, so that we can formulate a first question?

Psychologically, what is first is the question in the sense of wonder. It is not the formulated question, the question you put in words, nor the precisely conceived question that you have in your mind, but the intellectual dis-ease and desire; and it is not those words – they are just ways of expressing the matter. You can ask which comes first, food or the hunger? But in the order of potency and act, it is the hunger that desires, it is for the food, and you get the food because of the hunger. Similarly there is a hunger of the mind that manifests itself in this wonder, in this trying to understand, and that effort to understand is something that is first psychologically.

In the metaphysical analysis of intellect what is first is the *intellectus agens*. When Aristotle divides intellect, he says that in intellect as in everything else there is an agent and a patient, and therefore, there is an agent intellect.[15] And that is the source of intellectual motion, and of the illuminated image – that is, the image that is intellectually a problem, a question.

Whether you can go further back may be a question, but at least psychologically you do not have to go further back than that, and there is no use appealing to something to account for that primary psychological fact.

> [An airplane passing overhead drowned out an intervention that evidently had to do with questions. Lonergan continued.]

Oh yes, questions. But I am talking about something that is prior to questions, when I am talking about this wonder; or I am talking about the root question, the fundamental question. Certainly as soon as questions are put in words, or even in concepts, you have gone beyond the mere agent intellect. You have to have, at the starting point, psychologically, what Aristotle referred to in the phrase: Wonder is the beginning of all science and philosophy.[16]

15 Aristotle, *De anima*, III, 5, 430a 10–14.
16 See lecture 2, § 2, The Nest of Related Terms.

9 Western Culture and the Scientific Ideal

Is this ideal, that is involved in the search for the unknown, comparable to Whitehead's explanation of why science arose in western Europe and in Christian lands, and not in the Orient – because the Christian faith provided a climate of opinion that God and the universe are orderly?

The two are not equivalent. This is from *Science and the Modern World*[17] by Whitehead, is it? Even in the pre-Christian period you have a difference between the Western world and the Orient. I remember having a theological student, a Hungarian, who had been some years in Japan;[e] he had a story about a missionary working in a small village, who spent six years convincing the bonze in the village of the principle of contradiction. When he got him to admit that – in other words, that the difference between religions was not the same as the different routes up Mount Fujiyama: they all went towards the top and it didn't make any difference which way you took – when he got the bonze to think in terms of what is true and what is not true, when that point was made and he got him convinced of the relevance of the principle of contradiction in the field of religion, then the bonze and all the village became Christians. That principle was the fundamental point.

In general, in the Orient, you have not got what exists in the West as a result of Greek science and Greek philosophy. Those traditions are not in the mentality, within the culture; they are not taken for granted. I believe it was UNESCO that found that, while Catholics and Protestants and Jews and agnostics from the West can all discuss education, questions of culture, and so on, and at least understand one another, it is an entirely different question when you start talking with the Indians and the Chinese and the Japanese, and so on – unless you are dealing with specifically Western sciences.

There came to the Western world through the Greeks a cultural development, not merely a development within certain intellectual sciences that were apart from the culture, but an influence upon the whole culture, that is not to be found in the same way in these other countries. Just as the fact that Russia never had a medieval period, such as the West had, results in fundamental differences between

17 Alfred North Whitehead, *Science and the Modern World* (Cambridge: Cambridge University Press, 1953; 1st ed., 1926).

Russian thinking, I believe, and Western thinking, and these are cultural differences.

Now undoubtedly – I am inclined to agree with Whitehead here – the Middle Ages, with their concern to answer questions, had an influence on the rise of science. Take the twelfth century: what are they doing? Well, they collect all the documents, and devise series of questions. For example, in Abelard's *Sic et non* you have a list of reasons for one side of the question, and you have a list of reasons, equally authoritative, for the other side – right through a series of questions. You have the same thing in Gratian's fundamental collection of canons and laws – it's the basis of all canon law, this work done by Gratian – where canons are cited for and against various possibilities.

Then it was up to the canon lawyers and the theologians to try to make some harmony out of this situation, to try to make the authorities say the same thing. So the work done by these collectors in the twelfth century formed the basis of the speculative effort of which the achievement, for example, of St Thomas Aquinas is just a particular instance. The work was going on all the time from all different viewpoints, and as a result there was created a climate of opinion that was definitely favorable to science. As a matter of fact, the beginnings of modern science go right back to that time – science does not simply begin with Galileo, with nothing before him. There were all sorts of discussions going on even in a much earlier period: Roger Bacon is not an isolated example. Although their production was not anything like that of later centuries, still the study that has been done on the history of medieval science reveals an enormous background behind the work that came to fruition in the sixteenth century.

I wonder if you would make a comparison, in this process of wonder and then insight and concepts and judgments, between the scientist and the pragmatist. Dewey's problem solving, for instance, is in steps that in some way seem similar. Is there attention first, in your concept of insight, attention that is expressed before you get the wonder?

Wonder is a species of attention. I am not too familiar with Dewey, but we have not yet reached the plane where philosophic differences arise. Any philosopher can have experiences, understanding, and judgment. But the way he will emphasize one or the other, his orientation in regard to those activities – you can get all the different philosophies out of differences there.

10   The Concept of Being

You said in one of your lectures that insight precedes judgment. Can this be reconciled – of course, it's not necessary to reconcile it – with Gilson's affirmation that the very first concept, the concept of being, is obtained through a judgment, and that therefore the very first insight we have will consist in a judgment? In his position the first concept we have, the concept of being, is in fact a conflation, made up of two elements – an affirmation of that which is, and your apprehension of that, an apprehension limited to essences. There you have an affirmation of something that exists, and therefore necessarily the intervention of judgment. Therefore you would not get the first intelligible aspect of reality through an insight but rather through a judgment which would, in that case, be the first insight.

We will be batting this around more fully later on. But briefly, at the moment: This wonder is heading towards being, and the fact that you head towards being through insights in the sense in which we have spoken of them gives you your component of form or essence in being. This applies to any being you can know, since it is going to be through understanding that you know it. But since your understanding is always just a 'what might be,' without settling the question of whether or not it is, your concepts give rise to a further question – *An sit?* – that is going to be answered by a yes or a no, It is or It isn't. So that your notion of being is something much more fundamental than any particular insights ...[18]

18 The LRI reel runs out here, in midsentence; the WAS reel had run out toward the end of §9, Western Culture and the Scientific Ideal, and the DJS reel early in the first question of §10, The Concept of Being.

Discussion 3[1]

[All reels lack the opening words. As the sound begins Lonergan is listing questions given him in writing, '... and the third page is on patterns of experience.'[2]]

1   Common Sense

On common sense, two questions. First: *Do the processes of experience, understanding, and judgment apply to common sense?*

I would say, yes.

A second question: *Is the reason why you prefer to base a phenomenology of knowledge on the exact sciences rather than on common sense because of the difficulty of distinguishing experience, understanding, and judgment in common sense?*

It's not so much the difficulty of distinguishing them as the difficulty of giving any exact account of them.

If one wants to speak of a commonsense insight, one starts from where so-and-so is; but to give an adequate description of how much he already understands, and how much and what is to be added to

---

1 The evening of Thursday, August 7, 1958. The 1980 edition included (in questions 6, 7, 8, and 9) parts of §8, Patterns of Experience; of §9, Common Sense and History; and of §14, Applied Science.
2 See §8 below, Patterns of Experience.

that, is to give a biography. Either you have to begin from the infant, explaining the first insights it has – and that's a matter of considerable difficulty, especially when it comes to testing it – or you begin with a person whose intelligence has developed to some degree. And to what degree has it developed? That will depend upon subjective factors and objective situations, and where you are is very difficult to determine. Again, what's added to that by an insight is very difficult to pin down. You can't easily say, 'He has got hold of this much but something needs to be added here.'

Again, from the viewpoint of judgment, it's extremely difficult to give a satisfactory account of a commonsense judgment. I attempt one in chapter 10 of *Insight*. It's a very simple one, a matter of presupposing a person being familiar with a certain routine and understanding it perfectly. Some change occurs in the routine: he comes home from work and finds the windows smashed, water on the floor, smoke in the air, and the smell of fire. And he makes a judgment. He doesn't say, 'There's been a fire.' He says, 'Something happened.' If you can pin down a commonsense judgment in that fashion, in terms of a familiar situation, when some change occurs in it, well, it's possible to give some account of that type of judgment. But as you can see, it's a very limited account of common sense and judgment. So now you have not only all the problems of the prior development of intelligence, but also all the problems, repeated in a different fashion, of the prior development in the person's judgment.

Further, judgment matures. It has a different period of maturation from intelligence. Children start understanding from a very early age, but you say they reach the age of reason at seven, and are minors until they are twenty-one. Aristotle holds that youth is not capable of a proper study of ethics.[3] So there is the factor of development and background – so much of judgment depends upon a person's background, on the context of judgments he has already made; and that also makes it very difficult to speak about commonsense judgments.

In the sciences, on the other hand – because they aim at universality, at a technical vocabulary, at enucleation of every step in the processes by which they arrive at determinate answers – it is much easier to pin things down.

That's the reason why I prefer to begin from the more exact sciences,

3 Aristotle, *Ethics*, 1, 3, 1095a 2–13.

from the field in which the activities of intelligence and reason go on under controlled conditions. Just as the physicist or the chemist doesn't want to base his conclusions upon ordinary situations – he wants a laboratory in which he can have purified materials and very delicate instruments, and completely control his experimentation – so the processes of intelligence and understanding, that occur under the controlled circumstances of mathematics and scientific research, provide a much more satisfactory field in which to obtain fundamental, clear, and exact notions of what precisely is meant by insight or conception or reflection or judgment.

2   Common Sense and the Patterns of Experience

The first set of questions was on common sense in general. Then come questions on *the relation between common sense and the patterns of experience*.

In general, I conceive common sense as a mode in which insights accumulate. They do not accumulate towards the realization of an ideal of universal, orderly, valid knowledge. That ideal is not functioning in common sense, which is a much more spontaneous process.

The question then: *Is common sense a pattern of experience distinct from the four patterns of experience mentioned in the text?* – In the text there are considered the biological, aesthetic, intellectual, dramatic, and practical patterns of experience; so, first, is common sense a pattern of experience distinct from these?[4] – *Or is it identified with any one of them? Or is it identified with the sum total of all the patterns? Or is it a partial aspect of all the patterns?*

Common sense occurs, ordinarily, it develops, in the dramatic and practical patterns of experience. The aesthetic pattern of experience also has its common sense. Scientific knowledge begins from common-sense knowledge, but starts moving away from it because of its own aims; it has its specific end. Common sense, as a mode in which insight develops, is something common, I prefer to say, to some of the patterns. Is that enough?

[The remaining questions in § 2 came from the floor.]

---

4 The lines in roman seem to be Lonergan's own, interpolated into the question as he read it.

It would be the same aspect of some of the patterns of experience, but not necessarily of all?

Not the intellectual pattern, which begins from common sense, but moves off towards the realization of other ideals.

About the aesthetic, for example, and presumably all the other patterns of experience: Would it be true to say that they occur, generally speaking, in a mixed form, in which you might say that the aesthetic – or the dramatic, as the case may be – dominates? So that perhaps, at least in a human being, there is no pattern of experience which excludes common sense?

I would not say that any of them excludes common sense. The intellectual pattern begins from it and also has to use it. The scientist has to have a certain amount of common sense; otherwise he wouldn't be able to find his way into his lab.

I wasn't thinking of the intellectual pattern so much as of the lower levels. What of the aesthetic pattern, for example? I forget how you define it, but it hasn't got the same practical aim as common sense.

I use the aesthetic pattern to indicate the possibility of a transition from the biological to other patterns of experience. Also to provide an underpinning of the dramatic. The dramatic is, as it were, a specialization, or an extension, of the aesthetic. – But on my aim in drawing up those patterns of experience, I want to say something presently, because in the fourth section tonight I have a set of questions on that.[5] Is that enough for the present?

3   Common Sense and the Conjugates

Thirdly, then, I have a question on *the relation between common sense and the experiential and pure conjugates.*

Experiential conjugates are terms defined by the relations to us. The definitions ultimately come down to some content of experience. What do I mean by 'red'? Well, I mean what I see under such circumstances as the present where I'm looking at the flag. I see the red cross in the center. You explain what you mean by 'red' by saying,

5 See §8 below, Patterns of Experience.

'Something like this.' And the same for sounds, tastes, and so on. What you ultimately appeal to is some element in experience.

On the other hand, the pure conjugate is a term that is defined from verified correlations. It's contained in laws. For example, understanding exactly the electric and magnetic field vectors in Clerk Maxwell's equations:[6] what are they? They are the terms that satisfy these equations. Mass is another example. Temperature also: temperature, as we illustrated the other day, is not an experience, not the same as feeling hotter, or feeling cooler. The iron rung here feels cooler than the seat of the chair, but they're at the same temperature. Temperature, then, is a pure conjugate. It's a notion that's defined by being contained implicitly within certain correlations. – At least, that's one way of going about it, and it seems to be the most satisfactory.

Now the question: *Is common sense sufficiently distinguished from the exact sciences by saying that the former understands experiential conjugates while the latter understands pure conjugates?*

Well, that's part of the differentiation, but I think the fundamental differentiation is the difference in the ideal you're pursuing. Common sense is a spontaneous questioning, a spontaneous clustering of insights, and the use of spontaneous multiple modes of communication in which the community, as it were, hands on[a] the development of understanding that has been acquired. And also, to some extent, develops it and adapts it to changing circumstances.

4 The Ideal of Common Sense

[The questions in the next three sections, §§ 4–6, coming from the floor, interrupt the series of questions on common sense and the conjugates, but we leave them where they occurred in the discussion.]

But you never seem to state that ideal. There seems to be an ideal you can state for science, but what is the ideal for common sense? The practical fact?

The question is, What is the ideal in common sense? Let's go back to our self-appropriation. I think we'll get to the root of these patterns of experience that way.

We started off speaking of self-appropriation as though there were

6 See *Insight* 80.

something quite determinate within us that we were going to find, and we were going to use that as a basis. And we reached a point this morning where we look in ourselves, and what do we find? Not something achieved, but rather, perhaps, something to be achieved. In other words, we develop. Our intellects at the start of life are like a board on which nothing is written, and intellect is gradually actuated. The process of actuating intellect involves a new component in the man. And as that intellectual component develops, the total balance changes, and you get a change of orientation in living. Now the more the intellect is developed, and the more the balance is changed, the more the orientation also is changed; and the patterns of experience that we describe in *Insight* are just rough indications of the possibilities of diversity and differences in combinations in modes of living.

But to ask what the ideal of common sense is, is like asking, What's the meaning of life? Well, it's something we're trying to find out. You live without knowing why, until you do find out. And you live according to the best ideas you can get hold of, and look for better ones. Or, you don't worry about it.

Perhaps the most relevant thing with regard to those patterns of experience is this: The ones I give are simply indications of the fact that people differ from one another, that they live in different ways, that this or that is a possibility, and so on. What I'm trying to indicate is the possibility of different components that can enter into human living. I'm not trying to offer a set of formulae and say, 'Now you have people of this type, with so much of the dramatic pattern and so much of the practical, and a little dose of the aesthetic now and then,' and find a chemical formula under which you'll be able to classify types of human beings. But I wish to indicate the potentialities of man in a general way.

I was wondering if you could express this notion of an ideal in terms of the quest for happiness, with the intellectual side as one facet of it.

You could, but if you did you'd be raising questions. The 'quest for happiness' can be very ambiguous. Aristotle asks whether a good friend should love himself, and he answers: Well, he shouldn't love himself in the ordinary meaning of the word. However, it's different if what he wants for himself is wisdom and virtue – he has to will for himself wisdom and virtue, which are the best things in the world;

otherwise he can't be a friend either to himself or to anybody else.[7]

In other words, the quest for happiness is not too clear a notion, and to start off by explaining just what you mean by happiness is to presuppose the results we're aiming at in *Insight* rather than to prepare the way for them. At least, that's the way I felt about it.

Well, I think it would have to be a vague notion of happiness in the beginning, with a sharper delineation of it as one goes through life itself. One person would seek at least partial fulfilment of happiness in the speculative order, another would seek it in the practical order – in the order of common sense – a third would seek it in the arts. Then of course there's a different balance of them all.

Yes, but I see these difficulties. If you start off from happiness as your fundamental goal, are you not prejudicing your account of knowledge as a means towards obtaining happiness? Is your knowledge, that is a means for obtaining happiness, going to be objective knowledge, or is it going to be wishful thinking? You create for yourself the set of problems that are inherent in the ambiguities of the notion of happiness.

Moreover, eudemonism isn't altogether satisfactory, even theoretically. The intelligible good is the good of order, and man can want the good of order, not merely for himself, but for other people. If one is a good Communist, one wants to give the good of communism not only to the Russians, the Chinese, who have its benefits already, but to the rest of the world. – It seems to us a very perverse notion.

But on that desire of the good: If you mean by the good simply that which everything desires, *id quod omnia appetunt*,[8] it is true, but it doesn't do justice, at least not without an awful lot of explaining, to the precise nature of intellectual appetite. Intellectual appetite is for the good of order, and for my good as part of the order. And if I set my good ahead of the good of order, I'm being immoral. Just what the good of order is, is a further question.

In other words, I think that if you want to make the good your basis, well, you can go to Marcel, who approaches being through the good[b] – I think that's putting Marcel's approach to philosophy in a satisfactory

7 Aristotle, *Ethics*, VIII, 4, 1157a 16–19; IX, 4, 1166b 2–29; IX, 8, 1169a 12–15.
8 Ibid. I, 1, 1094a 3.

way. My concern is not a philosophy; my concern is the technical end: on the structure, the method of science, prior to the method of theology. You'll see from that why I didn't go about things that way, with a basis in the good. And I simply indicate my reasons for not caring particularly for that approach, because I think that an adequate account of the good presupposes an adequate account of intellect.

Would, then, the ideal for common sense, in the sense in which you're using the term, really be a process of problem solving? Is that the nearest you can get to it for common sense?

It's more than problem solving, though that's a large part of it. But to say what it is, to answer that question really – for that we would need a metaphysics in terms of which we would know exactly what we mean when we say that something is, and 'This is not that,' and 'This is in potency,' and 'This is in act,' and so on. In those terms it's fairly simple to state the ideal. Namely, the ideal is the goal of potentialities, and as a matter of fact man's potentialities are infinite. But it's by trying this and that and the other thing that we gradually come, through our development, to discover what we're really for.

The means and the end are the same at this point?

Well, they can be confused. Common sense is a limited type of development of intellect, and it's guided largely by practical ends. Descriptively, what does a man of common sense do when you start raising theoretical problems? He'll either excuse himself, or he'll ask you, 'What's the good of it?'

There's a limit to questioning, that arises in common sense, but is set aside when you move into theoretical science. And to move into theoretical science, or the pursuit of knowledge for its own sake – that is possible at any stage of human development. A child can ask astounding metaphysical questions. But development is required for this effort to be sustained, and it is required not only in the individual, but also in the social milieu. At least, it seems to be so in the history of philosophy. Does that meet the question?

5   Common Sense and Prudence

Could you remark on the relation between what is traditionally called prudence and what you call common sense?

Traditionally prudence is *recta ratio agibilium*.[9] And it's a judicial habit. It regards judgment, and judgment with regard to what act is to be done. It's judgment as to *whether* it's to be done, as opposed to art, namely, understanding *how* to do it.

In common sense, insofar as it's practical, it's knowing how to do things, and it's art. Insofar as it's judicial – I'll try to say something on commonsense judgments tomorrow[10] – it may be a question of what is so, and it may be a question of 'Should I?' or 'Should I not?' In that case it's prudence.

There's a little more to prudence than deciding whether you should or should not act.[11]

Well, if you take the 'should' and 'should not' in their full sense ... What more is there? What are you thinking of?

It's a matter of choosing apt means to achieve your end – that's also a part of the virtuous man, there is prudent judgment in that sense; also of establishing worthy ends for yourself. All that is included in the idea of prudence, isn't it?

Insofar as it's a matter of hitting on the right means to achieve an end, the successful ones, it seems to suggest art more than prudence – the fellow that knows how to do it. Insofar as it's a matter of choosing ends, it comes under 'should' and 'should not.'

It seemed to me, when I was reading your section on common sense, that most of what you say about common sense can be said about prudence. I was wondering, as I read that chapter, if prudence couldn't be defined as the acquired habit of acts of common sense?

In chapters 6 and 7, where common sense is considered simply from the viewpoint of understanding – at least that's what I'm trying to communicate there – I'd say we are on the level of art. De facto, judicial elements keep coming in. I don't think it's worth while to try to exclude them, because what I mean by judgment I only explain in chapters 9 and 10. So probably there is a good deal that might be

---

9 Thomas Aquinas, *Summa theologiae*, 2–2, q. 47, a. 2, Sed contra, quoting Aristotle (see *Ethics*, VI, 5, 1140a 25 to 1140b 4).

10 See lecture 5, §9, Concrete Judgments of Fact, and §10, Judgments on the Correctness of Insight.

11 This question, and the remaining exchanges in this section, have been relocated from §6, 'Insight' in Apes.

connected with prudence in those chapters. But I think that prudence, taken as *recta ratio agibilium*, correct human behavior – I suppose that's the translation of it – needn't be purely judicial, though ultimately perhaps it is.

Your description looks a lot like what St Thomas called the potential parts of prudence[12] – habits of foresight, being able to profit from experience, and so forth – things that surround the actual prudential judgment rather than prudence itself.

Good. That satisfies; I've no difficulty about that.

What you have in Aristotle, and then in St Thomas, is the discussion of intellectual activity in terms of intellectual habits. You have five intellectual habits: two practical, art and prudence; and three theoretical, intelligence, science, and wisdom.[13] And anything you say about intellect is bound to be in terms of the actuation, the development, of some of those habits; and insofar as common sense is concerned with the practical, it will come under either prudence or art.

The virtue of prudence actually joins the intellect and the practical. It's an intellectual virtue in a sense, but it's also directed toward action. In that sense, it has a lot in common with what you are describing in common sense.

Yes. There's a difference in viewpoint, insofar as when I'm talking about common sense, I'm talking about the type of knowledge that is not developed under the ideal of building up a rigorously valid body of knowledge. And my question is, What is the nature of that development of intelligence?

But it can be put in many other ways.

6   'Insight' in Apes

How would you differentiate the insight that you describe as proper to common sense in man, from the insight that psychologists speak of in certain higher types of apes, and what not, in problem solving?

The differences seem to be recognized.

12   The reference is surely to Thomas Aquinas, *Summa theologiae*, 2–2, where q. 51 is on the potential parts of prudence (but foresight is treated in q. 49, a. 6).
13   Thomas Aquinas, *Summa theologiae*, 1–2, q. 57; there is reference there to various loci in Aristotle's *Ethics*, VI.

First of all, what is the limitation to insight, so-called, in apes? The experiments were done by Köhler,[14] and his favorite chimpanzee was known as Sultan. What Sultan could do was use means to an end, and he could do so when the means and the end were within his range of vision. If you put a banana outside the cage, he could put out his arm and get it – he had no difficulty about that. Put a banana a little farther outside his cage, so that he couldn't reach it with his arm, but with the aid of a stick he could reach it, then if the stick and the banana were simultaneously within his range of vision, he'd seize the stick and pull the banana in. But if the stick were outside his range of vision, he wouldn't do it.

The limitation in the apes, as far as experimental knowledge goes, simply put, is that they're not capable of free images. Man forms free images.[15] He's able to imagine circles, squares, etc. In other words, he's able to use his imagination in a way in which a beast doesn't.

And the ordinary exercise of common sense, in concrete particular situations, would involve in man free images like that??

All men are capable, more or less, of free images, unless they are extremely retarded.

Now, where does the difference lie between insight and this use you have in apes – the use of means towards an end, as long as the means lie within the range of vision? In other words, when the ape picks up the stick and reaches out for the banana, or, if the banana is still further out, takes two or even three pieces of a rod and joins them together – he can do that too, if they are within his range of vision, join the pieces together, reach out and get the banana – in that case there is an exercise of imagination. He sees the three pieces of the rod, he picks them up and puts them together, and reaches out to the banana. But if you scatter the three pieces about the cage, with the banana outside, he isn't able to make the free image, the freely constructed image, of having one part here, and another part there, bringing it all together, going over to the banana, and getting it. – That is, as I remember, the result of those experiments; there may have been something subsequent to them.

14 Wolfgang Köhler, *The Mentality of Apes*, trans. (from 2nd rev. ed.) Ella Winter (Harmondsworth, Middlesex: Penguin Books, 1925; Pelican Books, 1957).
15 See *Insight* 274.

Now what is the difference between insight and that type of imaginative construction? Well, if all we knew about men was that they do
that sort of thing, we'd have no grounds for drawing a distinction. But
there are all sorts of manifestations of human intelligence that don't
come under that category – there's never been any success in teaching
language to an animal.ᶜ Insight, insofar as it bases the capacity to give
universal definitions, and so on, moves into an entirely different category from any type of imaginative construction.

You say you would not yourself use the word 'insight' for what the apes do in
relating means to end, since it doesn't go beyond imagination, but would you
agree that the word could be so used?

I wouldn't presume to legislate for the usage of the Queen's English.

7   Common Sense and the Conjugates *(continued)*[16]

The next question is on the relation between common sense and the
experiential and pure conjugates: *Does common sense fall under the exact*
sciences insofar as experiential conjugates are a particular class of pure conju-
gates? Or, are experiential conjugates basically irreducible to pure conjugates?

I should say that they are a particular class. In other words, experiential
conjugates arise in the relations of things to us. But we are among
the things. So they are a particular category, that of the relation of
things to us, and therefore of things to one another.

Wouldn't there still be some difference between the appearance of 'red' and the
verified, scientific explanation of 'red,' and therefore in that sense you could
not subsume it as a particular class?

If you limit the verified, scientific explanation of 'red' to what the
physicists do, yes. However, if you include the biologists and the
psychologists, and so on, you include all the 'things' related to one
another. On the other hand, the knowledge of the experiential through
the relations of things to one another, through the scientific formulation, is general and mediated – and I think I have a few more adjec-
tives somewhere, where I treated that topic.[17]

16 The series of written questions is resumed here, after the 'digressions' of
   §§ 4–6 from the floor.
17 The reference seems to be to *Insight* 394: 'the inclusion of descriptive
   relations in metaphysics is implicit, general, mediated, and intellectual.'

The next question is: *In verification must the exact sciences always terminate in experiential conjugates?*

In verification what one has is a set of requirements and their fulfilment, and the fulfilment, I think, will always contain an element of experiential conjugates – I don't see how you can get away from that – in other words, epistemic relations.

May I ask a question connected with the last two? The word 'pure' seems to suggest that in some way one escapes from what one must almost call the contamination of personal experience. One becomes objective in the sense that one gets outside the realm of personal experience.

Now against that it would almost seem that one could reduce the pure conjugates to experiential conjugates, rather than make the latter a subclass of the former – on the grounds that, as you said just now, in verification you are bound to come back to experiential conjugates. In other words, ultimately everything has to be described, presumably even at the level of explanation, in terms of what we have experienced. So that, even in terms at several removes from what we've experienced, even in dealing with a higher order and a much more abstract concept, there is still something that is ultimately tied down to what we've experienced. In the sense that we don't experience, for example, electrons, obviously in that pure conjugate we have something which is independent of experience to a certain extent. But I'm still not quite sure even then of the meaning of the word 'pure' because even in that case we don't get right away from experiential conjugates.

I think I started off using 'pure' and shifted to 'explanatory' in the course of the book.[d] And what I mean by it is: There are basic terms that are defined by referring them to your senses, and there are other basic terms that are defined because they're contained implicitly in verified correlations. And that is, simply, the meaning of 'explanatory' or 'pure' conjugates – such as the notion of mass.

When you put in 'verified' correlation, this does in a sense relate it again to experience.

Oh, yes.

When I first read this section, I had the impression that there would be only one pure conjugate for each of the experiential conjugates. But, as I thought it over, it seemed to me there might possibly be a dozen pure conjugates to explain the experiential.

For instance, in the case of 'red' there would be one experiential conjugate, but I might explain 'red' in terms of wavelength, I might explain it in terms of chemical combinations, I might explain it – as an artist might – in the sense of a composite of three or four different colors. So would I have there three pure conjugates?

I wouldn't attempt to predict how many pure conjugates people are going to find, and I don't hold for any correlation between the two types of conjugate: there are as many pure conjugates as are necessary in the science, when it reaches the stage where it has the complete explanation of all phenomena.

But you speak of science as though it were a unique thing, whereas at least today there are a multitude of sciences.

I mean all the sciences, the complete explanation of all phenomena – whatever number of sciences are needed for that.

Do you think the conjugates can ultimately be reduced to one pure conjugate?

I don't think so. For example, I am convinced that I have both intelligence and will.[e]

But let's say the experiential conjugate is of 'red.' Will that ultimately be reduced in all the sciences to one pure conjugate?

Insofar as 'red' is something that's transmitted by radiation, you have a connection with physics. Insofar as the thing that is red is chemical, you will have a chemical account of it. Insofar as seeing red doesn't occur without organs, you'll have a physiological and psychological account of it.

So we're going to end up here with distinct sciences.

We're going to end up, as far as I can see, with the bifurcation of nature.
    And I think the reason for it can be put perhaps in a very simple way. If you start measuring, you can measure the length of that wall by the length of this table, the length of this wall by the breadth of the chair, and use different units in every measurement; then you can compare all these things with one another, and never settle upon some unit of measurement that you can use for measuring everything. It's much simpler to use one unit, the centimeter or the inch, in all measurements – then you can translate, compare any two things with one

another by comparing their measurements in terms of this unit – than to measure Tom's height by Dick's, and Dick's by Harry's, and Harry's by Joe's, and so on. In the latter you have all the same information, but it's written down in a much more complex form. I think the tendency towards the pure conjugates can be perhaps put on as simple a level as that. Now the question, In verification, must the exact sciences always terminate in an experiential conjugate? is followed up: *If so, is the distinction between common sense (for example, the sun goes round the earth) and verified science (the earth goes round the sun) the intervention of an insight and pure conjugates which are verified by the help of experiential conjugates?*

The two statements as they're put – the sun goes round the earth, and the earth goes round the sun – are presented without the qualifications that are needed to bring out the difference in meaning that lies behind them.

In ordinary speech we say the sun goes round the earth, because that was held to be the truth up to about the sixteenth century – by most people, not everyone – and since then we haven't changed our language; we've kept on speaking according to the appearances.

From the viewpoint of mere relative motion, it's probably a matter of indifference whether you say the sun goes round the earth, or the earth round the sun. From the viewpoint of explaining mass velocities and accelerations, it's much simpler to account for the spinning of the earth, an inertial spin on the earth, than to account for a terrific velocity in the sun in its enormous orbit around the earth every day.[f] And, consequently, scientifically it's probably more satisfactory to say that the earth goes round the sun.

Now that difference is much more than a matter of pure and experiential conjugates. In other words, to put that question in terms of pure and experiential conjugates seems to me to put a question in a very complex fashion. Could you break it down?

What I was trying to get at was the concept of scientific laws. On the experiential level, it appears obvious that the sun is going round the earth. In the next step, your scientific laws, the pure conjugates are indifferent whether the sun goes round the earth or the earth goes round the sun – that is, referring to Newton's laws of gravitation and his laws of motion, and so on. Then, when you come to verify them, there seems to be some difference of opinion in scientific circles: you'll find some scientists who seem to say it's a matter of indifference and the only criterion you have is a criterion of simplicity: it's simpler to say that the earth goes round the sun than the other way round. Is that true? Or is it a matter of fact that the earth goes round the sun?

It's a matter of fact if it's true.

But what I'm trying to find out is, How do I tell whether it's true or not?

I think that's a scientific question. In other words, does a physicist devise criteria by which he can judge in some cases whether there exists an absolute motion? Is that your question?

> [The response from the floor is not clear; it seems to reject the search for absolute motion, and to restrict consideration to these two particular bodies. Lonergan continues:]

Take, for example, Newton's bucket experiment. He filled the bucket with water; he twisted a rope, hung the bucket from the rope, and let it spin. The bucket was spinning for some time before the surface of the water became a paraboloid. The rope finally stopped untwisting, the bucket stopped, and the water retained its paraboloidal surface. I think you have a proof there that it's the water that's accelerating.[18]

And it wouldn't be just a matter of simplicity?

I think you can say it's a matter of simplicity too. The alternative is so complicated that I don't think anyone would want to think it out.

> [There were short exchanges here in general agreement with what had been said. Then, a request that the original question be read again (with the remark, 'I'm not sure I understood it,' to which Lonergan replied: 'Well, I'm not either'). The question is read again, *Is the distinction between common sense and verified science the intervention of an insight and pure conjugates which are verified by the help of experiential conjugates?*]

If the question means that science differs from common sense insofar as it arrives at insights that have a general statement and involve pure conjugates, yes.

---

18 See *Insight* 153–54, on the bucket experiment. There is an abbreviated reference there to Edwin Arthur Burtt, *The Metaphysical Foundations of Modern Physical Science: A Historical and Critical Essay* (London: Kegan Paul, Trench, Trubner & Co., 1925); see pp. 249–50, where Burtt gives a long quotation from Newton's own account of the experiment.

[The questioner interjects: 'Yes, that's what I was trying to express in my book.'[19] The written question continues, and Lonergan reads on.]

If so, is it true to say that experiential conjugates are not affirmed in the exact sciences but are rather the conditions for affirmation?

First of all, the experiential conjugates. There is their description from a commonsense viewpoint – 'It's a bug' – and from a scientific viewpoint, where you get a very precise classification. In both cases our knowledge is simply descriptive: relations of things to us. Now that scientific description, although it's science on a preliminary level – it hasn't reached explanation yet – still it's scientific, dealing with terms that ultimately are defined by their relations to us, to the contents of our experience. So, insofar as science is descriptive, on the preliminary level of description, it's involved in experiential conjugates.

Again, even when it's on the explanatory level, all verifying, and all setting up of experiments, and so on, is in terms of the experiential conjugates. You don't get away from your epistemic relations. And I think you hold that the epistemic relations are affirmed scientifically?[20]

Yes, I do; but I didn't know how far you would carry that.

8   Patterns of Experience[21]

On patterns of experience: The question begins, *Are there patterns of experience besides those listed in the text?*

Quite possibly. I'm not attempting an exhaustive account of possible patterns of experience. I'm trying to break down the notion that a man is some fixed entity. Psychologically we develop. And for every stage of development, in every stage of human culture, and history, and society, and so on, you have different developments. Everyone has something ... Human lives are not all the same. What is the possibility of that? What are the types of factor that enter in?

19 We are unable to identify the speaker or the book referred to.
20 The 'you' refers to the same unidentified participant.
21 The following five questions seem to be the ones announced as the tape began recording: 'and the third page is on patterns of experience.'

Is the pattern of experience distinguished by its end? Speculative for truth, and so on?

Insofar as you're able to tie down a pattern of experience ... you arrive at something that's abstract.

The question continues, *If so, what are the ends of the four patterns of experience?*

Well, we didn't agree on the first part, so we may drop the 'If so ...'

How would you go about indicating the superiority of the speculative pattern of experience to the others, if that is the case?

It is the case with regard to general knowledge. In other words, if what you're seeking is universally valid knowledge, then you have to be in the intellectual pattern of experience to get proper results.[22]

What is the superiority? I don't hold that the intellectuals are a superior race. But I think that, with regard to all human conduct, there is a dependence upon knowledge. And insofar as human life enters into the complexities that develop in cultures, and develop in civilizations, and so on, general knowledge becomes a necessity. And the way to arrive at it is through the intellectual pattern of experience.

Again, the question can be put from the viewpoint of an antiintellectualist philosophy. But when anyone attempts to hold such a philosophy, he's usually, I think, involved in some sort of a contradiction. In other words, he's claiming that the intelligent and reasonable thing to do is not to bother too much about intelligence and reason. I think, in other words, that there is a primacy of the intellect in the human makeup, and it leads anyone who tries to get away from it to contradict himself, or betray himself.

Is it true to say that, in the speculative pattern of experience, insight terminates primarily in verified concepts – in knowledge of being, which is concrete, and our knowledge of it is also general, and so on[23] – *but in common sense insight terminates primarily in practical living?*

If the meaning there is that common sense short-circuits the problem of generalized conception, if that's the meaning, yes, that's what I say.

22 Lonergan added a remark that sounded like, 'That's more or less tautological, I think.'
23 The lines in roman seem to be Lonergan's own, interpolated into the question as he read it.

[Further questions this evening were from the floor.]

What exactly is the purpose of identifying the patterns of experience?

The point in the book is to draw attention to the fact that the account we've been giving of insight in mathematics and science isn't the whole man, that man is intelligent in quite other ways, that ordinary living is intelligent, that that exercise of intelligence occurs within the context or the orientation of a mode of living.

It also opens the way to a questioning of the complete satisfactoriness of one's own mode of living. It undermines the appeal to common sense as the ultimate tribunal that settles all philosophic questions: 'After all, philosophers are a little weak in the head, or they wouldn't be doing that; the real ultimate answers come from the man of common sense.' – You'll find in chapters 6 and 7 a good deal of doubt suggested in one way or another about the omnicompetence of common sense.

Now that questioning of the omnicompetence of common sense seems to me a very good propaideutic to philosophy. It does something towards persuading people that after all there may be some relevance, even for them, of a bit of philosophy. It has a philosophic moment also, insofar as in the later stages of the argument everything will turn upon positions and counterpositions, and positions are defined in terms of the intellectual pattern of experience. And while the counterpositions can do a lot of appealing to common sense, we've already disqualified that witness a little bit.

It seems to me that the patterns of experience that affect common sense are also going to, at least indirectly, affect scientific knowledge. And since each person's pattern of experience is definitely different, to some extent that is going to color the insights and the scientific judgments that each person makes. Now my question comes up: How does one ever hope to reach a community of science, with all these various patterns of experience?

Well, the scientists do it. Is your problem scientific or philosophic?

... or just psychological!

As far as the scientists go, first of all, the scientific method has implications such that errors and oversights are systematically worked against.

By other scientists?

Yes, in the whole group. And it's also true, of course, that science itself can be misdirected owing to mistaken commonsense assumptions. I think that's pretty well established from the recent revolution in science that we've had. Galileo and Newton – their scientific thinking philosophically is either a mechanist determinism or is very closely allied to it. And the basis of that mechanist determinism is direct realism[g] – elementary notions of what knowledge must be, and reality must be, and so on – that can be laid perhaps at the door of common sense, although not strictly commonsense judgment (it's more complicated than that). But I think there are mistaken notions that have been existing in science in the past and have gone unperceived; it's only with more recent developments that further advance in science involved jettisoning such notions.

It seems to have worked itself out fairly well in the experimental sciences, but when you come down to philosophical matters, it would appear that these patterns of living have infiltrated more penetratingly into philosophical thought, and I'm wondering what hope there is, or how it would be possible to, shall we say, straitjacket, these patterns of experience.

Well, the possibility – the first step – lies in advertence to them. As for further consequences, I think we had better leave them till later – the business of positions and counterpositions is definitely an attempt to deal systematically with that problem.

9   Common Sense and History[h]

This may be what you want to deal with later. But I would like you to say more about common sense and the questions that arise around the concept of history – how you keep a concept like common sense with a concept such as history.

Is the suggestion that a review of history suggests that there's nothing common?

No, but if you go into modern views of history, such as arise in the nineteenth century, you get in some of the more sophisticated varieties, the notion of the Age of Reason, the idea that common sense will be overcome, where people won't have to live any more at the level of common sense. This raises a question.

Ah, yes. Well, I don't believe that common sense is going to be superseded. Because common sense is specialization in the concrete and practical, and we always need that. But the ideas on the dawn of the Age of Reason and so on, where common sense is looked on as a form of error, where everyone will become scientific – is that the point of the question?

Yes.

I think that those ideas are associated with a particular philosophy, and a reasoned disagreement with them could only come with a precise discussion of that philosophy.

My own position with regard to that matter would be that common sense is the one competent judge within its own field. There can be all sorts of aberrations introduced into human living and so on, but it's a distinct type of thing that's behind the aberrations from the common sense we've been describing. This common sense is a certain type of accumulation of insights according to a certain mode – for example, the fact that among primitives it's recognized that in certain aspects of their living they're perfectly intelligent and reasonable. That there exist these other aspects, the aberrations – the fact can be explained in various ways. Mythic consciousness[i] is quite a question, just what it is, and what are all the factors that enter into it, and so on.

But I think that common sense is a valid and necessary part of human knowledge. If your logician lacks common sense he won't know how to connect his logical laws with things that people are actually saying and meaning. And if a scientist lacks common sense, his own living will be a mess, and probably a lot of the practical side of his scientific work will be a mess, and so on. In other words, insofar as one has the common sense appropriate to one's work and position and conditions of life, one is successful in dealing with the concrete and practical. Does that do something to meet the question?

Is common sense part of the human condition? Inevitable to being a man?

I'd say that, yes. At least, as I have understood it and attempted to pin it down. I'm dealing with something I defined, not with something that you pick out ... I think I have enough of a definition of common sense, as a determinate type of accumulation of insights, to be able to say, when difficulties come up – such as, 'How stupid these people are! What ridiculous things they did!' – to be able to say, 'Well, that's not what I mean by common sense.'

10 Varia: Teaching, Grace, Starting Point

I have a very practical question about teaching. If people are trained in science, even if they don't become scientists at a high level, do you feel that this kind of thinking will influence their commonsense experience to such an extent that it would help them?

Well, I think if they have common sense, it will.

Is it because science is so poorly taught as a rule that you can find people who have had a great deal of science but, as far as developing insights are concerned, are not very competent?

In ordinary living?

Yes.

It may be due to an unbalanced training. It may be that their interest in science is compensating for social deficiencies, and so on. I think there are all sorts of factors that enter into that problem.

The way you speak, it seems to me that self-appropriation would be expected, but I don't think that as a matter of fact it happens without divine appropriation, or something like that. There seems to be a surd there. I wonder if self-appropriation is basic enough.

No, in other words God's grace is prevenient.

Is your beginning with self-appropriation a subterfuge?

As I said the first day, I don't believe in discussing the possibility, or the method, and so on, of a philosophy. I think the method is identical with the philosophy itself. But I started off from this stuff on self-appropriation to provide the series of lectures with a sort of framework; then it has a certain utility, but it isn't the be-all and end-all of everything. In other words, there is room for further steps. What we start from is not the measure of where we hope to end.

I just wonder if we will ever end there, if we don't start there.

If the method is deductivist, you don't. But deductivism, I think, is just a mistaken ideal. The last thing some people want to accept would be either the abstract deductivism that you find in Scotus or Ockham, or the concrete deductivism you find in Spinoza and Leibniz. And yet the norms that they expect *you* to meet in *your* thinking are precisely the norms that can be taken from such a deductivism.

I understand that, but I think it is just as hard to get them to accept self-appropriation as it is to accept divine appropriation.

But then I'd be giving a course in theology.

When you're dealing with a man of common sense, and just common sense, to whom nothing makes any difference unless it has practical consequences, how can you get him intrigued with the ideal and to begin thinking about the universal and necessary?

It's a different problem in every case. But he has potentialities. Scientists, when they achieve fame in their department, have a tendency to turn to philosophy, and that potentiality is within everyone.

However, a philosophy is a very technical – highly sophisticated, if you please – sort of thing. It's not the necessary means of salvation, or anything like that.

It's not irrelevant to living.

Oh no, I wouldn't say that either.

11   Certitude in Common Sense

In regard to your distinction of common sense as concerned with concrete situations, and what to do, and so forth: in your book you lay a lot of stress on the fact that the set of insights in function of which common sense operates is incomplete, all the time. I was wondering if that has anything to do with, or does it depend upon, or is it the reason for, Aristotle and St Thomas repeating so often that there is no absolute certitude when we get down to particular human actions.[24]

What do you mean by absolute certitude?

Aquinas says that in the speculative sciences, we do have that certitude: with the metaphysics, and so forth. As far as the common principles of ethics go, we have absolute certitude; but when it comes down to particular applications – I'm thinking of questions of positive obligation – it's very hard to nail it down

24 Thomas Aquinas, *Summa theologiae*, 1–2, q. 94, a. 4. See also q. 96, a. 1, ad 3m, where Aquinas refers, on the question of certitude, to Aristotle (see *Ethics*, 1, 3, 1094b 13–22).

and say positively, A person must do this or do that. I think the terms in other articles that you have written are: You can make up a dialectical syllogism in these matters, but you can never make a demonstrative syllogism with regard to it.[25] *Are those two things bound together?*

Well, you have ethics coming in, and freedom, and common sense. A number of factors are involved in your question, I think.

With regard to certitude, the type of certitude arrived at in common sense is: Manifestly, de facto, that's what's right. That's the most you ever get – right, or correct, or true. It's true that this lighter is on this table. Not necessarily so.

Can it be true without being necessarily so?

The 'necessarily so' is simply using the principle of identity: If it's there, it's there. That's the only necessity involved – in the fact. And it's only a set of facts that enables me to make the judgments: that I have these insights, and know these words, and know that's the correct way to employ them – they're all facts too. That contingent element, namely, is found in all these instances.

Again, 'It's necessarily so' – in the sense that, if it's there, it's there – is also eternally true. It never could be true, it never will be true, that at this particular moment it's not there.

That's true with regard to speculative propositions. Here we're dealing with common sense.

Is it a speculative statement to say the lighter is on the table?

It's not practical, not something to do in the realm of common sense, of practical action, to which common sense seems to be directed.

Oh, I see – with regard to positive courses of action. Well, they're not demonstrable. The cliché: that's the proof of freedom. You can't prove that I'm going up to have coffee in three-quarters of an hour.

---

25 See *Insight* 611–20 on contingency in practical matters; on the dialectical syllogism appropriate to such contingency, see Aristotle, *Prior Analytics*, I, 1, 24a 22 to b 12; *Topics*, I, 1, 100a 29 and I, 10–12, 104a 3 to 105a 19. Lonergan refers to Aristotle's notion of dialectic, *Insight* 217, and surely had these passages in mind; but he may have referred more specifically to the dialectical syllogism in his classroom lectures, which George Topp, the questioner, attended at Regis College, 1948–52.

12   Science and Common Sense

A few days ago you quoted Merleau-Ponty.[26] *I don't know if you would agree with him. He doesn't use the word 'common sense' but speaks of consciousness-in-the-world-with-others. He seems to give a sort of superiority to this situation of man in the world over science. Because, he says, science comes after; science would have no meaning unless it recurred to this existential reality. And he says there is the same difference between, say, common sense and science, as there is between seeing a map and traveling. In one case you have more reality, because you do experience them. So science would be always something abstract. Therefore, you always leave something out of your real experience, your real knowledge of the whole world.*

We fortunately don't have to choose either one or the other. You can have both – in some limited extent: one can't travel over the whole world, have a thorough tour of every town in Canada, such as I believe you had yesterday in Halifax.

But can we absolutely affirm that science as such is a sort of ideal that we must reach? That we must try to move off, as soon as we can, from common sense?

Oh no, I wouldn't assert that.

There seems to be a greater richness ...

In the concrete.
   There is in Europe, especially since the war, a terrific antipositivist and antiidealist movement. And that takes at times an antiscientific turn precisely because of the intimate association there had been in the past, in their culture, between idealism or positivism and science.

13   The Dramatic Pattern of Experience

In identifying the patterns of experience, do you assume that we're moving in an intellectual pattern of experience while we identify the other patterns?

If we want to do it with complete objectivity, yes.

And supposing we weren't in the intellectual pattern of experience?

To say, 'supposing we weren't,' is perhaps supposing something that's

26 See discussion 2 above, § 2, Inverse Insight and the Empirical Residue.

a bit incoherent. If I'm in the dramatic pattern of experience, thinking of you, and the impression I'm making on you – not too explicitly, because the dramatic pattern of experience has these overtones, but they're not explicit – then I'm not engaged in thinking about my pattern of experience. To be in the dramatic pattern of experience is to be *not* thinking about it. If I spoke as though I were an actor, I'd be consciously in the dramatic pattern of experience. And being consciously within it is already acting it, or not being in it, in a sense. Insofar as the actor *acts* as though he weren't acting, he's a good actor.

On the other hand, to attempt an analysis, or a study, or an account of what you mean – well, your interests are in the object merely as an object, and you're out to say just what it is in all its respects. And if you're doing that properly, you're in an intellectual pattern of experience.

You're never sure of a thing like that, whether you are in the intellectual pattern?

There are doubts that can arise. If you want to settle the question by introspection, there are doubts: you're not sure. But read your stuff over a year later; get other people's opinions on it. You're making checks that say, 'Well, this is good enough for the purpose I had in mind.'

14   Applied Science

I wonder what your criterion of science is – whether it is universally valid knowledge, or the idea of pure conjugates. I'm not sure what your definition of science is, and how it affects practical relationships.

The sciences aim at a complete explanation of all phenomena. You can ask what a phenomenon is, what an explanation is, what a complete explanation is, and then we step into approximations to a certain extent.

Up to 1900 there was an ideal of scientific explanation that is not operative at the present time. In other words, the ideal itself develops in the pursuit: a full account of what explanation is going to amount to will develop. But we attempt self-appropriation: What occurs in us when we understand? And, in that way, from the properties of that act of understanding, we're able to block out an account of explanation that's independent of the different stages of the development.

I was wondering what you would say about medicine, for instance.

Medicine is an applied science.

Yes, and the way the personal relationship comes into medicine seems to raise difficulties about the idea of pure conjugates.

Yes, very definitely. Medicine is an applied science: the medical doctor has to go to university and learn an awful lot of biology and pharmacology and a large number of other things, but he also has to have a good bedside manner, and all that's connected with or evoked by that expression. And his work is the pursuit of certain effects in the individuals who will be his clients. And it's certainly entirely a practical task, and it's a task that's governed by common sense in the concrete situation. His theoretical knowledge provides a sort of background that guides him in diagnosis, that guides him in prescription, that guides him in surgery, and so on. But it's not enough to be a surgeon or a diagnostician, if you're going to have patients and get along with them.

And probably there are also psychological problems connected with the patient and the doctor – a good general practitioner will know not a little about them.

This goes back to the point made before, that common sense in the proper meaning of the term, as I attempted to define it, is a permanent and necessary component in human knowledge.

15   The Cognitional and the Ontological

The ideal that moves the intelligence and becomes explicit through acts of understanding, is it an act of knowing or the known?

It's a desire.

What attracts, moves, the intelligence?

Desire. The desire to know.

What moves as an end?

As an end? The final cause. According to St Thomas we have a natural desire to know God by his essence,[27] and that includes knowing every-

---

27 Thomas Aquinas, *Summa theologiae*, 1–2, q. 3, a. 8.

thing else. And that Thomist theorem, I think, is the ultimate answer to that becoming more and more explicit.

You say the ideal of knowledge, of the intelligence, becomes more and more explicit through acts of understanding. It would seem the intelligence would be led to a more perfect act of understanding.

That's one way of putting it – the way Aristotle puts it.[28]

Would it not be the formal or immanent finality of intelligence, rather than what we could call the transcending finality, that would move every being according to its own measure? It is not, I think, the thought of the intelligible.

I don't quite follow the argument.

The intelligence is not led to the most perfect act of understanding, but to be satisfied by what is the most intelligible object, which is identified with pure thought, as a matter of fact.

Oh. Well, the precise formulation of the finality of intellect will presuppose an account of reality and being, potentiality, act, finality, and so on. You have a distinction between *finis quo* and *finis cuius*, *finis qui*, and so on.[29] You can speak of finality as the object – your objective beatitude – or the act by which you attain the object, and so on. I think those distinctions can be made, but they don't involve a material difference, at least in the present stage, do they?

Only the fact that, if the ideal of knowledge is going to integrate all parts of knowledge – which is to me very attractive – it seems that what will be integrating all parts of knowledge in one person will be the most perfect act of understanding, and that all the intellectual activity of man will be finalized, we could say, or would be moved – understood as moved by an end – by this perfect act of understanding. When I reflect on that I don't think it's quite correct.

Why not?

Because it will seem to privilege the immanent finality of the being, apart from what is the true finality.

28 Lonergan may have in mind what he said about Aristotle in lecture 1 above, §1.1, The Pursuit of the Unknown. See also his references to Aristotle on human ignorance and human progress, *Verbum* 38–39.
29 For Lonergan's own use of such distinctions, see *Collection* (CWL 4) 19–20, and ibid. 260, note *d* to chapter 2. Possibly *cuius* stands for *cuius gratia* here.

How do you determine what is the true finality?

I wouldn't mean that it would involve formulating it explicitly, but certainly the first act of understanding is an act which is produced by the object, the connatural object that is attained at present, and the perfect act of understanding, it seems, would be to insist on the object[30] *rather than the end.*

What difference does it make materially?

Materially it means that the act cannot be separated from its conditions. Two things are to be distinguished ...[31] *Not the act measuring the end, but intelligence measuring the end.*

I have no difficulty with what you say.

For me personally there is a big question here, because it seems that we could easily be led to introduce the act of understanding as being the measure of everything else, the measure of being.

Don't you think that's true? Doesn't it measure everything? For example, how does St Thomas prove that intellect is a passive potency? Because an intellect fully in act would be infinite, the infinite being. And if that proof is true, then intellect is the measure of being. And if it's the measure of being, then it's the measure of everything – *pars prima*, 79, 2.[32]

I would consider that a conclusion from the analysis of being.

Does St Thomas conclude it from an analysis of being?

I wouldn't argue on that.

Is there a text in which he concludes this from an analysis of being or is there not? He explicitly uses the argument I gave.

I know that when he wants to make an analysis of understanding, certainly his starting point is understanding as a form of being, understanding as a modality of being. Because he says, in the De veritate, *that whenever we want to analyze*

---

30 The word is inaudible on the tape; 'object' is a conjecture.
31 We cannot make out from the tape what these two things are; one of them may refer to the intelligibility of the object.
32 See Lonergan's use of this article of Aquinas passim in *Verbum* – for example, p. 85; the whole of chapter 2 of *Verbum* is relevant to this topic; in particular, on intellect as measure, see p. 60.

any reality we must start from that which is common to any being.[33] *So I would deduce that this is true even of the finality of understanding.*

De facto St Thomas presents his psychology in metaphysical terms. That's his regular mode of presenting it. And he does it because it's the most economical way of doing it, because he's engaged in theology.

He also holds that the *priora quoad se* are, at the other end, the *priora quoad nos.*[34] When he wants to establish the essence of the soul, he says: You begin from the object, you consider the act, you go from the act to the potency, and from the potency to the essence of the soul. And the object is something psychological: it's what is known in the act, and the act is something psychological. In that case it's from the essence of the soul that you establish, deduce, the order *quoad se*: the potencies, and the acts, and the objects. In the other order things are cognitional.

Now the two are equivalent: just starting at one end or the other. There's no absolute, necessary way of beginning. It's according to the sort of question that you're treating that you begin one way or the other. Don't you think so?

I have something on that in the paper before the American Catholic Philosophical last Easter. You can find it in the Proceedings.[35] I have the proofs, but haven't seen the finished form.

16   Philosophy and Theology

I wondered about the distinction between philosophy and theology. It seems to me you can do away with it now because the ideal, as it becomes more explicit, could become more explicit by incorporating theological data.

The distinction is not so simple as it was – that's perfectly true. As soon as you get to existential philosophy, concerned with man as he is, in his actual human situation, you don't give full answers to his questions until you step into theology.

The answer to the problem of evil in this world is not a philosophic answer, it's a theological answer. And if your philosopher is concerned

33   The locus referred to in the *De veritate* of Thomas Aquinas seems to be q. 1, a. 1.
34   Lonergan discusses this regularly in the context of his Trinitarian theology: see *Collection* (CWL 4) 117–27.
35   *Proceedings of the American Catholic Philosophical Association* 32 (1958) 71–81; the paper is reprinted in *Collection* (CWL 4) 142–52.

mightily, not with the set of questions that it's useful to give students preparing them for a course in theology, and that aren't strictly theological, but conceives his philosophy as dealing with the problems of man in this world, he will be including in what he calls philosophy questions that traditionally are theological.

Now the distinction between philosophy and theology is one thing, and the separation of them is another. You have the distinction between philosophy and theology in the Middle Ages. You get the separation in Descartes, very clearly worked out. We're working out the philosophic side of things, and we want a set of criteria entirely independent of theology. The distinction has moved into separation. And you get it much more so in the rationalist, where it becomes systematic, where they don't want to have any theology at all.

There is a problem of distinguishing philosophy and theology,ʲ but I'm not prepared to give an account of the distinction off the bat. I think there is a distinction, though, because there are such things as revelation, and so on.³⁶

36 The LRI reel brings us to this point; discussion, it seems, continued; the DJS and WAS reels both stopped during the question of this last section.

Discussion 4[1]

[The recording started with Lonergan in midsentence, but it is clear he was just beginning the evening discussion.]

1 Immanent and Projected Intelligibility

... the first pair[2] of questions sent to me tonight regard a review in *The Modern Schoolman* of *Insight*, by James Albertson, a Jesuit, who I believe is also a doctor in physics from Harvard University.[3] I've no objection at all to the kind remarks in the review, but further questions are raised that call for an answer.

The first is: what have I got to say about this – *the characteristic feature of the entire study, the absence of a distinction between the intelligibilities immanent in objects and patterns of experience, and those intelligibilities projected by the knower into objects and patterns of experience?*[4] That distinction is illustrated by the reviewer by distinguishing between regularity, separateness, and sequence – intelligibilities said to be immanent in the object (separateness: *A* is not *B*; sequence ... [these are not his

---

1 The evening of Wednesday, August 13, 1958. The 1980 edition (in questions 10 and 11) included part of the present §7, Intellect as Intelligence, and the whole of §15, Social Science.
2 The second question is taken up in §2, Probability Theory and the Existence of God.
3 James Albertson, S.J., *The Modern Schoolman* 35 (1957–58) 236–44.
4 Albertson 238. The quotation is not quite verbatim.

further explanations; they're mine]; sequence: *A* follows *B*; regularity: whenever you have *A*, you get *B*) – and on the other hand, intelligibilities that are projected, namely, necessity, unity, relation. And, as he says, a mathematical theory of the event will bring you from regularity, separateness, and sequence to necessity, unity, and relation.

Now in what sense is the first set immanent in the object and the other projected? The only sense in which I can see that that could be asserted is that it's easier to suppose that the first set is a matter of pure experience, while the second set is not. But as a matter of fact, both sets involve operations of intellect. Whenever there's anything precise, concepts are being employed. Sense data lack precision. You get precision in your sense data insofar as they are subsumed under concepts. At least, I think so.

However, the point to the distinction between immanent and projected intelligibilities is of course that it is a distinction which is necessarily made by an empiricist or a naive realist. The immanent intelligibility is the one you know by taking a look at what really is there, and the projected one is the one that you think out in your mind and don't see in the object. And since I disclaim both empiricism and naive realism, I consequently have no use for that distinction. For me, the significant distinction is between intelligibilities that are affirmed in true judgment and intelligibilities that are not affirmable in true judgment, because we don't know intelligibility by taking a look. (If your criterion of reality is a look, you *have* to distinguish between the immanent and the projected, or perhaps reject all intelligibility entirely, and say, That's *all* subjective.) All insight is a content. What you get or grasp by insight is not yet known to be true. There's a further requirement, a reflective act, in which you affirm what you grasped by insight. And there are conditions for the affirmation, and the conditions have to be fulfilled before the affirmation can be rational.

So the logical position is to say: *No* intelligibility is objective – if you're going by the look.

However, if you hold that the criterion of reality is truth, then you divide intelligibilities differently. There are those that enter into true judgment, and they are knowledge of reality because they are truly affirmed. On the other hand, if you grasp intelligibilities but do not see your way to place them in certainly true judgments – you may place them in probably true judgments, or possibly true judgments – then you don't know yet whether they are parts of reality, whether they pertain to the real or not. And if you judge that the thing is not so, does not conform to this intelligible law, or whatever way you conceive the intelligibility, then it does not pertain to the real.

In other words, from one viewpoint on knowledge a distinction between immanent and projected intelligibilities is plausible; but if your criterion of knowledge of the real is truth, then the only relevant division of intelligibilities is between those truly affirmed and those not truly affirmed.

2   Probability Theory and the Existence of God

The second question was, *If probability is necessary, then the universe itself* – this is a quotation – *as a whole is not intelligible, so that the real is not completely intelligible, and he cannot for example conclude that God exists.*[5]

In that statement there are a number of elements involved. First of all: 'If probability is necessary.' To say that anything is necessary is not for me an ultimate mode of speech. The one necessary being is God. If this universe is knowable through laws of probability, not simply classical laws, if a statistical element is not merely a cloak for ignorance but knowledge of this universe, well, it's knowledge that's true as a matter of fact; it's not a matter of necessity. Statistical laws, as far as we can make out – I give reasons in *Insight* – are part of our knowledge of reality in fact.

'If probability is necessary, then the universe itself as a whole is not intelligible.' And to that effect he had cited a work by David Bohm. 'David Bohm has recently arrived at such a position,' namely, that the universe as a whole is in the last analysis by nature unintelligible, if statistical laws are relevant to knowing it.[6]

Now there are two issues, it seems to me, involved. First of all, is probability so conceived that it implies that, if the universe were a matter of probability, then the universe is not intelligible, or by nature unintel-

---

5 Albertson 244. Again, the quotation is not exactly verbatim. The numbering in this section is confusing. Lonergan's first 'First of all' seems to deal with a preliminary point on necessity. When he comes to the real question, he sees it as involving 'two issues,' and his next 'First of all' takes up the first issue, probability. The second issue will be intelligibility. See also note 7 below.

6 Ibid. The reference there is to David Bohm, *Causality and Chance in Modern Physics* (London: Routledge and Kegan Paul, 1957) 167–68. On this point see also lecture 3 above, §5, Probability Theory.

ligible? I think that that possibly is true in certain senses of probability. If what you mean by probability is determined by two elements, first of all a definition of a probability aggregate, understood simply as an exclusion of regular law in your data, then that first element is an exclusion of intelligibility. If your notion of probability itself is conceived as a limit to actual relative frequency, when the frequency increases beyond all bounds, then you're placing any intelligibility that may be involved in probability at infinity. So your two statements combined can and possibly do imply that an object to which this concept of probability was applied would be unintelligible by nature. So we can grant that there may be a concept of mathematical probability that if applied as such to the universe would be tantamount to saying that the universe is unintelligible.

However, if that concept of probability is applied to the universe, as the same reviewer says, it has no implications about actuality. In other words, it seems to me that such a concept of probability has no relevance to any empirical science. The statistics, or probability theory, as used in the sciences, is something that is verified or not verified. Quantum mechanics doesn't stand on the basis that, while these equations bear no relation to the position of the spectral lines and their intensities, still at infinity they might; it's because these equations give us exactly the results we want.

In other words, to have a probability theory that fits, that is useful to an empirical scientist, you have to have implications with regard to actuality. If there are no implications with regard to actuality, then I don't see how there can be any relevance to an empirical science.

And in the third place,[7] such a notion of probability bears no relation whatever to the notion of probability evolved in *Insight*. The reviewer seems to presuppose that what I'm trying to do is express in popular form the mathematical theory of probability. What I'm concerned to do is to work out, from the limitations of classical laws as such, a basis that leads to a theory of probability which is relevant to empirical science. The mathematical theory of probability, even from a mathe-

---

7 Here 'third' seems to make a third point on the first of the two issues, probability. Then Lonergan proceeds to the second issue, intelligibility, and comes to 'a third point'; this could be considered a third point on intelligibility, but is probably to be taken more generally, as a third point in series with the two issues of probability and intelligibility.

matical point of view, is in difficulties. You can find those difficulties in Lindsay and Margenau, for example – their exposition of the theory of probability when they go into the business.

So much for the probability side.

Now with regard to the intelligibility: What is the intelligibility of probability as I affirm it? Well, probability as I affirm it is the intelligibility in what Aristotle would call the per accidens – that's St Thomas – the *kata symbebêkos*. Aristotle's conception of the terrestrial process is that it is a coincidental process.[8] Any event presupposes a cause acting *now*. Why does this cause act *now*? Well, you have to invoke some other cause to account for the 'now.' And why does *that* cause act now? You have to invoke some further one. And the cause that accounts for this other agent acting now is a cause per accidens. There is no nature that is such that it will cause other things to act now. Its nature is some universal property.

This is the Aristotelian theory.[a] Consequently Aristotle deduces the eternity of the world, and the fact that this terrestrial process is a coincidental process. To account for the regularity and continuity of terrestrial process he goes on to his theory of the influence of the heavens. That's where the theory of the influence of the heavens comes in, in Aristotelian theory.

Where does probability make a difference between Aristotle's account and the coincidental process? It's insofar as probability is the assertion of an intelligibility in the coincidental itself. Probability as conceived in *Insight* is an affirmation of an intelligibility within a field that classical law is not capable of handling.

So probability is not simply unintelligible as we conceive it. It presupposes the inverse insight that classical law cannot handle certain types of event, cannot provide a systematic general explanation of certain types of event. But through probability theory, you get the next best: you get something that's general, regards all cases, and so on.

Now there is a third point there. Is this unintelligibility that is involved in Aristotle's per accidens, and that is presupposed by probability – since probability finds some limited intelligibility in the coincidental process – is that such as to invalidate the proof we offer of the existence of God?

Here one has to distinguish between the intelligible and the nonintel-

8 See *Insight* 129, 664; also *Grace and Freedom* 77.

ligible, and subdivide the intelligible into the intelligible in itself and the intelligible in the other.[b]

Form is intelligible in itself. It's what you know by insight, by understanding. It's as much of the thing as you know insofar as you're understanding it. And that is a pure intelligibility. But potency, the empirical residue, is not intelligible in itself. It's intelligible in form. The empirical residue as such is a limit to the intelligibility we find in data. But insofar as one fully grasps the nature of form, I believe one finds a certain intelligibility in the empirical residue, in potency. Potency has an intelligibility, not in itself, but from its form.

Again, act – existence, or event – is not intelligible in itself. It's contingent. You know existence or event through judgment, through the proper content of judgment. That proper content results from a grasp of the virtually unconditioned. The virtually unconditioned is a conditioned whose conditions happen to be fulfilled. Because the conditions *merely* happen to be fulfilled, the act is contingent. There is a defect of intelligibility in act. Act is not intelligible in itself. The existents in this world of our experience have not an intelligibility in themselves – we postulate a cause for them. If the universe were completely intelligible in itself, it would be impossible to argue from the universe to the existence of God, because you'd have no reason to go beyond the universe to attain complete intelligibility.

So the universe, if there's a valid argument for the existence of God, no matter how you formulate it – in terms of causality, or finality, or anything you please – in every case you're appealing to some type of intelligibility, some specific or generic type of intelligibility.

If the universe were in itself completely intelligible, then intelligence would have no lever, no fulcrum, by which it could go beyond the universe. There has to be a defect in the intelligibility of this universe to have arguments that will take us beyond the universe, to complete the intelligibility.

And that's quite clear from any of the arguments that are employed. In any of the arguments from causality you argue from the contingency. Or, you argue from the order of the universe not being accountable for by the universe; in other words, it's there as a fact, but if you have an intelligible order, the existence of that intelligible order is not accounted for without an intelligence. And so on. You are always arguing from some defect in the intelligibility of this universe.

So insofar as it's an objection against the possibility of proving the existence of God by the procedures employed in chapter 19 of *Insight*, then there's a failure to distinguish between intelligible in itself, such as form is, and intelligible in the other, such as you have in act and potency.

Does that meet the question?

Very much, yes.

3   The Content of Heuristic Structure

A second question: *If one defines metaphysics as a heuristic structure, does one imply that it is exclusively so? In other words, which of the following propositions is true? (1) The intelligible content of the heuristic structures is exclusively supplied by the particular sciences, or (2) the intelligible content of the heuristic structures is partly, concerning the general determinations of being, provided by metaphysics, and partly, namely, as concerning the particular determinations of being, provided by the sciences.*

First of all, I note that defining metaphysics as a heuristic structure is a definition that primarily regards the metaphysics of proportionate being. We first deal with the metaphysics of proportionate being, and then we go on to metaphysics of being as such, or in general, or in the general case.

And that division means that certain theorems that you have at present – where you haven't got that division of metaphysics – are found in the second part. For example, theorems regarding participation, and limitation of act, and so on, theorems that regard the intelligibility of being in the general case, do not arise in the metaphysics of proportionate being, but only when you go on to being in the general case.

Now, with regard to the content of heuristic structure, the expression is ambiguous. The heuristic structure in itself is a content. When one is talking about the heuristic structure, one means something very definite. And to find out exactly what it means may require considerable effort. But there's something to be grasped and affirmed when you're talking about a heuristic structure: the heuristic structure itself is contentual. But further by the content of the heuristic structure you also mean what fills in this structure.

The content of the heuristic structure as such is the content of the metaphysics. The content that fills in the heuristic structure will be the content of the sciences, or of common sense, according to the nature of the question.

Now one mustn't think of the content that the heuristic structure itself is as a sort of scheme that's rather dead, passive. It is a content that not merely embraces all the different departments of science; it also is a content that transforms them insofar as the expression of scientific conclusions at any given time involves counterpositions: that is, it's also critical of the science. And similarly it's critical of common sense insofar as common sense is involved in the counterpositions.

Moreover, this content that pertains to the heuristic structure that is metaphysics is isomorphic with the content of cognitional theory. It is through[9] the structure of our cognitional activities that we're able to say how it will account for the procedures of the sciences, and at the same time transform their results, and further discuss and come to conclusions with regard to the relations between the sciences – the way they fit together.

Again, the content of the integral heuristic structure that is metaphysics is a content that develops. The sciences develop. The development of the sciences enables us to have a much more accurate account of our cognitional processes. It was impossible for Aristotle to know the way in which insight works out de facto in the sciences, some three hundred years before Christ. What the sciences have achieved in our time is something that just passes imagination, and still more would you be expecting the impossible if you expected a theorist of knowledge in Aristotle's time to anticipate just the way in which the empirical sciences have developed.

In other words, a development of the sciences enriches our knowledge of our knowing. Now what the scientist is really confident about is not scientific conclusions, but scientific method. His conclusions are always probable and capable of revision, and he knows that. But he knows that he's contributing to a process that's on the right track.

And it's this methodical element, development especially in method, that is significant to cognitional theory. It makes cognitional theory much more precise. Because your metaphysics is isomorphic with your cognitional theory, development in cognitional theory involves the possibility of development in the metaphysics. That development in the metaphysics, once certain fundamental positions are attained, is

9 The word 'through' is sheer conjecture; a cough drowned out Lonergan's words.

not revolutionary, but evolutionary. In other words, think of the experience of science in its first stages: what science has achieved up to now has been the emergence of something that was totally alien and unintelligible to common sense. It revealed a new world. It's exhibited in Whitehead's contrast of his two tables.[10] But that is not the sort of thing that keeps happening over and over again. We get on to the nature of scientific theories, you see *why* that happens, and just what leads to it, and so on.

When we worked out the affirmation of the subject we showed that that self-affirmation was not subject to possible revision, that any hypothesis of a possible revision involves a reaffirmation of that structure of the subject which we had already established. In other words, just as cognitional theory can show that its attainments are definitive, that you have a special case in consciousness that you haven't got in the sciences, so there's a coincidence of the descriptive and the explanatory in an account of knowledge that can't be had in the empirical sciences. Because of that coincidence, it's possible to arrive at results that you can show are not open to revision.

In other words, the very nature of revision presupposes this structure you've reached. Similarly, at further stages in the development of the metaphysics, there are ways of showing that this result is permanent. You can get theorems of that type, I believe, in cognitional theory.

But that doesn't mean that you have nothing more to learn about knowledge. You have *something* permanent, something fixed, something in the way of a structure. But you can find out more details about the elements in that structure. And some of them – you can determine that they too are not open to revision, that they're invariant. And insofar as you can build up an invariant account of cognitional structure, you can build up an invariant account of the structure of the thing; or the integral heuristic structure as a metaphysics of the object.

Again, to put the matter from a different angle, we've spoken in the sciences of a scissors-like action. The scientist works from data through measurements to graphs to curve fitting to laws. And that's the lower blade of the scissors. At the same time, he's working down: from postulates and invariants of his differential equations. And the two close in upon the function that's the law he's looking for. And that's a

10 Earlier in the seminar Lonergan had spoken of *Eddington*'s two tables. We give the reference in lecture 1, note 8.

description of classical physics. But you can show that the same sort of thing is operative in any science.

Now, just as there is a scissors-like action proper to any given science that has reached the explanatory stage, that has got beyond the merely descriptive stage represented by the classifications of botany, and reached an explanatory stage where it's dealing with laws – just as there's a scissors-like action within any science in its explanatory stage, so if you think of the totality of the sciences, each with its own pair of scissors, you can conceive all the sciences as a lower blade in a single bigger pair of scissors, where you have determinations coming up from the sciences, especially from the methods of the sciences, and determinations coming down from the self-appropriation of the empirically, intelligently, and rationally conscious subject. Now this second big pair of scissors is concerned with the radical structure of the entities that are being investigated in each of the particular sciences; it's also concerned with the relations between the different levels of reality investigated – for example, by chemistry, biology, sensitive psychology, rational psychology – so what it is trying to close in on is, first of all, the internal structure of each being, and, secondly, the relations between different levels of being. And, consequently, insofar as it's closing in on the relations between different levels of being it's also closing in upon the relations between the different sciences.

The concept then of metaphysics is dynamical. It's something that develops. Insofar as the sciences develop you know about knowledge, and consequently you know more about the integral heuristic structure in the whole of knowledge.

It's something concrete. By being we mean everything in all the aspects that things have: the totality of the aspects of everything. It's concrete.

Potency, form, and act – terms we'll introduce tomorrow, in a more satisfactory way, I hope – are defined by their relations to one another. On the one hand, therefore, their contents aren't determined, but on the other hand, you can use those terms to refer, not simply to whatever has this relation to this other, but to *all* of what has this relation to the other. And you save the concreteness of being, and the developing character of human knowledge, by that type of approach to metaphysics.

Is that OK?

4 The Parallel of Cognitional and Ontological

May I ask a question on the general problem of how we know that the structure of being is in accord with the structure of cognition. It would seem that there are three possibilities. Either, Kantian-wise, that we can't know that the thing itself corresponds to the structure of our knowledge, but all we can say is, roughly speaking, that this is the only way in which we can interpret it, so this is the way our mind works.

Or, secondly, that we can know in some way that our mind is such that it is proportionate to the being which it knows.

Or, thirdly, there's of course the unsatisfactory possibility of some rather more arbitrary preestablished harmony.

And it seems, fairly obviously, that you're distinguished from Kant by relying on the second alternative, and I wondered exactly how you establish that. The objection suggests itself that what might be happening, is what Eddington, I think it was, described in terms of the net – it's a very common simile, lots of people have used it – the net which catches fishes which are proportionate to the size of the holes in the net. Our knowledge having mesh of a certain size, as it were, catches parts of reality and you can't say that there's no other part of reality in the sea, because our net can't catch it.

Now I may have missed the explanation of this somewhere along the line, but I would be glad if you could run over it.

The way I approach the thing is this. First of all, I say what I mean by being; and, secondly, I ask whether being in that sense is the real world.

Being is what we know by correct understanding, by the totality of true judgments. That's what we mean by being. *Ens est id quod est.*

Now supposing a man goes to work on a question, and has a large number of acts of understanding, which as far as human cognitional process goes, lead him to make judgments that are correct, that are pronounced correct, according to the immanent criteria of human knowledge ...

Immanent – that's the problem.

Yes, according to those immanent criteria. Experiential objectivity – it's given, it's not merely produced by my imagination. Normative objectivity – it's according to the exigences of the pure desire to know, of intellectual curiosity and critical reflection; there has not been significant interference from desires and fears, it's not been anything that can legitimately be characterized as wishful thinking. At the term of that process, with regard to each judgment, I arrive at the virtually unconditioned.

By my understanding I have conceived; by my experience I particularize my conceptions; by my judgments I make affirmations: *A*, *B*, *C* – each of which is properly defined – exist. I know a universe of being, where being is defined as what you know in that way.

Now, is that the real world? Might not the real world be something totally different from that? That's the question?

Well, it's just a matter of the parallelism between the three levels of cognition and potency, form, and act. I'm not so much worried about the part which I think you've just been dealing with, it's just that ...

The parallelism?

Yes.

Well, first of all, the answer to that question is of course to ask the man what he means by the real world. And if he means by the real world what he knows intelligently and rationally, then he means being by the real world. And if he doesn't mean something that's the fruit of his intelligence and rationality, well, we needn't bother about him.

The further question: Why is this structure in knowledge a structure in reality? Why is it not simply a structure that arises insofar as I am knowing it? That's your question?

I think that's probably it.

That ties in with different types of intelligibility. Well, more fundamentally ...

First of all: being. Insofar as being is what is known by correct understanding, by true understanding, then by definition being is intelligible. It's what you know by understanding, and the intelligibility is what is known by understanding in this cognitional process.

Now you can either say that intelligibility is identical with being, so that if there are differences in intelligibility there'll be a structure in being; or, you can say the intelligibility is only in the subject, it's not in the object. If you take the first, it's a matter of comparing the different senses of intelligibility – intelligibility in itself, intelligibility in the other, and different types of intelligibility in the other – to see that there'll be that structure in the being. If you say the intelligibility is just in the knower and not in the being, then you're making the being an unknowable. Because what you know by understanding correctly is intelligible.

I think the whole question arises from bad habits of thought somehow. I think when it shakes down in my mind, I shall see why the question really in a sense doesn't arise.

Well, there is the conflict of the developing subject involved in it, I think. I think in other words that that problem in its traditional form is the problem of the real distinction between essence and existence. And historically we've had all sorts of people holding there is a distinction, but it's just a distinction in our minds. And for me the point to the controversy is: The problem doesn't lie in the word 'distinction,' it lies in what you mean by reality.

Insofar as people conceive the real as what is known by intuition, confrontation, looking, and so forth, there's no possibility of proving the real distinction. It's only insofar as the real is what is known by true judgment, and real distinction by comparative negative judgment, *A* is not *B*, that you have a possibility of proving the real distinction.

In other words, a proof of the real distinction – which is the same sort of thing as there is in our structures: what I call the structure of the mind is the same as the structure of the object – resides in a transition, in the conscious, explicit rejection of one type of cognitional theory and the acceptance of the other.

5   The Concept of Structure

[A question here was almost inaudible, but had to do with the meaning of structure – in being, in knowing.]

Well, what is meant by structure in either case is a set of entities having relations of a certain type to one another, and the relations that you have in the structure of knowing are relations of empirical, intelligent, and rational consciousness; and as such, unless the object you're talking about has the structure of another intelligent, rational consciousness, you won't have structure in exactly the same sense.

What is the difference? The question was put last night on the passage about the obverse and reverse of a coin:[11] the distinction between the intelligible and the intelligent, the reasonable and the grounded. A technician makes a machine. The machine is not intelli*gent* but the man who makes it, who designs it, has to be intelligent; he has to know how to adapt means to an end, and he needs intelligence to invent a machine of such and such a type, or adapt someone else's invention, to make of it a better type of machine, and so on. The man is intelligent, the machine is intelli*gible*. Your relations in cognitional structure are of the type 'intelligent'; your relations in the material thing, for example, are of the type 'intelligible.' The concept is intelligible, it isn't intelligent, but the insight is the act of a man qua intelligent, and the concept is intelligible because it's a product of the insight, or of the man with the insight.

OK?

It seems that in being the structure has to be complete, whereas in knowing the structure can stop at understanding ...

[Some of this question was inaudible, which may explain why Lonergan answers only what seems to be the first part.]

Part of the structure of being has to be complete, and another part doesn't. You haven't got accidents, or what I call conjugates, floating around on the loose. They always presuppose a substance, with the exception of the Eucharist. You have to have the substance: if it doesn't exist, you haven't got one; and if it does exist, it's complete qua substance. But the accidents needn't be complete. We have a capacity to understand, but it isn't necessary that we actually understand all about everything, just because we have a capacity to understand. That isn't complete.

6   Maréchal, Kant, and Lonergan

There's a point about the relationship of your thought to Maréchal's that I can't get straightened out. It came up in discussion, and a student of Maréchal asserted that Maréchal makes the finalistic concept of intellect a premise for a certain objectivity – and I thought then, if so, that indicated a radical difference

11 The question surely refers to *Insight* 323, but there is no tape of the previous evening's discussion by which we can verify this; see also lecture 8 above, note 12.

from your thought, where there's no premise, as far as I know, for knowing; that is, there's no super-knowing by which you can validate knowing simpliciter. *Now, more recently, that opinion on Maréchal has been challenged, and I'd like to know what you think of Maréchal's position, first of all with regard to that point, and how it compares with yours.*

Well, first of all, I'd best explain that my knowledge of Maréchal's position was acquired largely by osmosis. When I was a student of theology, there was a man of the same year, an Athenian who entered the Sicilian Province, and studied his philosophy at the scholasticate in Louvain.[12] At that time Maréchal was teaching psychology, according to his ideas, and the professors of all the other subjects were also teaching their subjects in accord with Maréchal's ideas. So he picked up Maréchal, not by studying Maréchal's book, but by being in the milieu, that is, the philosophy in his course. And I did a fair amount of my studying with him – we prepared our final exams together, and so on. And I picked up a good deal of Maréchal that way. Familiarity with the ideas. I learned a lot from him.

But you can see that there is no direct connection. It was part of my own development, my living and talking with him, discussing with him, and he happened to have a knowledge of Maréchal that hadn't been within my ken before that.

'Maréchal makes finality of intellect a premise.' Yes, Maréchal will argue that the order of *ens* is noumenal. He is arguing more or less in direct relation to Kant. He is a recognized commentator of Kant, first of all, and his fifth volume, I think it is, *Le thomisme devant le criticisme Kantien* ...[13]

12 Lonergan will presently identify his fellow student as Stephanos Stephanou. For nearly fifty years Fr Stephanou has been professor (now emeritus) at the Pontifical Oriental Institute in Rome; he belongs to the French Province of Jesuits.

13 Maréchal's fifth volume is entitled *Le Thomisme devant la Philosophie critique*; his third volume, *La Critique de Kant*. Possibly Lonergan has conflated his memories of the two volumes. On Maréchal, see also lecture 7 above, §2.5, The Problem of Objectivity, and discussion 1, §13, Objectivity.

   Since only half of lecture 8 was recorded, the rest of side 1 of that reel was used for the beginning of this evening's discussion. This meant that midway in the discussion, recording was interrupted while the reel was turned. Both was and djs bring us to the point reached in the text; the lri reel had stopped a dozen lines earlier. All three begin the next part in the same way: there was a sentence ending with the word 'Maréchal,' and Lonergan goes on to say, 'What I do in *Insight* ...,' as in the continuation of our text.

... What I do in *Insight*, what I've been interested in, is, What precisely do we do when we understand? And the problem dealt with in *Insight* is a double problem:[c] What happens when we understand? And why is it that so little is said about it? The reason why so little is said about it is that, if you acknowledge that intellect is intelligence, you can't have any satisfactory theory of knowledge without putting your whole weight on the true judgment.

Now you can see from that that my thinking has not been a function of Kant's thinking, in any sense at all. It has been concerned with the question, What do we do when we understand? My philosophic development was from Newman to Augustine, from Augustine to Plato, and then I was introduced to Thomism through a Greek, Stephanos Stephanou, who had his philosophic formation under Maréchal. It was in talking with him that I came first to understand St Thomas,[d] and see that there was something there. After all, St Thomas had insights, too! If he didn't have insights, he didn't mean anything.

7 Intellect as Intelligence

You emphasize that intellect is intelligence. Could you expand that again for a moment, say what it is you're getting at there?

Well, I think if you look up the type of Latin scholastic manual that was still current between 1926 and 1929, when I was studying philosophy, you'll find an account of intellect that doesn't at any stage have anything to say about understanding anything. You form concepts, and they're little nuggets. And they're functions of the thing; they're not dependent upon any intelligently conscious process; they're first; the first element of intellectual knowledge is the concept. Then you compare concepts, and they're either contradictory, or necessarily related, or neither the one nor the other. Then you make judgments, and you make judgments in virtue of the sufficiency of the evidence. And what's the evidence? Well, it's your concept ... At any rate, the simple things to be grasped about knowledge are, on the one hand, sense data and, on the other hand, words. From your sense data you can build up your theory of sensation in terms of knowing the sense data. From the words you can say we have to have knowledge of universals. You have principles, because these universals are necessarily linked together. And they're analytic: the predicate says just what's in the subject. There aren't any synthetic ones; if you say there are, you're a Kantian. There's no relevance of inquiry, understanding, the development of understanding, the way understanding develops, and no clear, explicit account of what exactly critical reflection is. We ask the question, *An sit?* But what goes on? What precisely is that moment in your knowing? Where does it come from, and what does it lead to?

Again, we speak of weighing the evidence. I believe that my account of reflective understanding is, in different terms, but roughly equivalent to, what Newman calls the illative sense.[14] Newman was concerned with that same problem, What's the ground of the assent? The ground of the assent is grasping the sufficiency of the evidence. I worked it into a formula for an insight, the virtually unconditioned, that eliminates the metaphors.

Now that's one aspect to it, the factual side, what happens when we know. There's another side to it. When you propound such a theory of knowledge, people say, So that's what our knowing is – Ah, but it isn't knowledge of reality! Your insights, they're not infallible, they're what might be true! And how do you know? How do you get to certainty?

Again, the insight isn't taking a look at the essence of the thing. It's a development of intelligence that occurs gradually, and that may eventually arrive at knowing the essence of the thing. And if that type of knowledge is true, not merely of the sciences, which they're quite gaily ready to admit – that is, that the sciences only know what's probable – but even of common sense, if common sense is a matter of understanding and making true judgments too, and not a matter of looking at things, well, where's your real world? Why aren't you an idealist?

An exact account of knowledge raises the epistemological problems in a real fashion, not merely in the sense of refuting adversaries, but also in the sense of solving personal problems – and not how I am going to help other people that are in difficulties, but how I'm going to help myself! The intrusion of epistemological problems in a real, significant way is a disturbing event. That is what I mean when I say, Intellect is intelligence.

Now I believe that when Aquinas is talking about intellect, he's talking about understanding. Not always: the Latin verb *intelligere* doesn't have

14 On Newman see lecture 5 above, note 3.

the same set of connotations as 'insight' and 'understanding' in English. But there are clear occasions when it does. The simplest is Thomas' argument against the Averroists, who held that each man had an imagination, but that each man didn't have his own possible intellect. The possible intellect was another one of the separated substances. Avicenna held that the agent intellect was a separate substance, but that each man had a possible intellect; Averroes said that the possible intellect also is separate.[15] And Thomas' argument was an *argumentum ad hominem*: If this man, my adversary, hasn't got a possible intellect, it can be shown that *hic homo non intelligit* – this man doesn't understand; and *si non intelligit, non est audiendus* – if he doesn't understand, there's no reason why we should listen to him.[16] Unless you give *intelligit* the meaning of understanding in that sentence, the argument doesn't have much point; but it's obvious to everyone that, if a man doesn't understand, there's no reason why we should listen to him. There are other indications, too, that Aquinas meant 'understanding' by *intelligere*. But in the medieval period of philosophic development, when introspective psychology was not a technically developed procedure, it was only by loose indications that a thinker who really did know a great deal about intelligence could express himself. That's why it is possible to think my interpretation of Aquinas wrong. My first *verbum* article in 1946 was met with an explosion[17] – this isn't what scholastics mean by intellect at all!

8   Probability and Determinism

I wonder if you would care to say more fully what are the grounds for your position regarding the big discussion of determinism at present. Are you holding that we could, on philosophical grounds, by an analysis of knowing, have predicted that the scientific determinism of the last century would prove invalid? In other words, are there philosophical grounds for some sort of indeterminism? And in what sense would that indeterminism be related to the probability that you are speaking of in the book?

15 On Avicenna see lecture 7 above, note 12; on Averroes see *Verbum* 78–79, 173.
16 On Thomas Aquinas see *Verbum* 78, where a number of references are given; see also ibid. 218.
17 Matthew J. O'Connell, 'St. Thomas and the *Verbum*: An Interpretation,' *The Modern Schoolman* 24 (1946–47) 224–34.

I think that the view of determinism overlooks a step between a scientific system and the solution of a concrete scientific problem. That step is the occurrence of an insight that selects which laws are relevant to this concrete situation, which elements in this concrete situation have to be measured, and with what degree of accuracy the laws are to be applied to these elements when we work out a solution, and so on. There's that mediating insight; there's a level of intelligibility that's closer to sense, that mediates between sense and scientific system.[18]

Now insights of that mediating type can occur, and do occur, not merely in the solution of particular problems, when the scientist is confronted with a particular problem and wants to apply his laws to it, but also when a man who knows the laws uses insights of that type to set up ideal cases.[19] Insofar as concrete reality conforms to such ideal cases you have determinism – insofar as the planetary system is periodic, you can have accurate predictions indefinitely, provided the planetary system isn't upset. Because the periodicity of this concrete system involves insights on that lower level, it isn't simply the general solution to the n-body problem that you're dealing with.

Now what are the concrete conditions of the real being a sufficiently close approximation to some such ideal case? Determinism presupposes that that must be so in every case; in other words, that every concrete case corresponds to some construction that insights can use to mediate from your general system. But if that is not so, then probabilities start becoming relevant.

Could that have been predicted last century? Well, it would involve a very exact theory of knowledge, and so on.

That's not precisely what I meant. What I meant really was this: It would seem you're asserting here that from a philosophical analysis of the act of knowing it's possible to exclude determinism.

No. There are structural features of our universe that favor probability – long periods of time and large numbers are relevant to understanding it, and so on. All that the abstract argument does is exhibit another possibility besides determinism in that sense.[20]

18 *Insight* 46–53.
19 See lecture 3 above, §4, The Limitation of Classical Procedure. In *Insight* 46–47, the terms 'anticipatory concrete inferences' and 'imaginative model' are used, as well as 'ideal or typical cases.'
20 Some lack of clarity in the response required heavy editing here.

But it exhibits it as a possibility. In other words, would you say that the question is still open for decision in science, whether or not the ultimate status of theory ideally would be deterministic or indeterministic? Is that still an open question?

I'd say that the probabilities are very slight for the deterministic.

But there is a possibility?

Possibility is compatibility with fact in this case, and I work out a number of criteria of what would follow on the indeterministic and what would follow on the deterministic. In other words, I'd say the question is this, that theoretically both are possible, and you choose between them by hypothesis and verification. And I think that there is an awful lot of evidence of a very general type favoring the indeterministic types of probability theory.

Well, suppose you take the concrete instance from David Bohm mentioned by Albertson.[21] Here we begin from the consideration of the explosion of a radioactive atom, and if we take the Niels Bohr theory, then you would suppose that this is in principle something indeterminate and indeterminable. In other words, it's unpredictable in principle. Over aggregates, over large numbers, it is possible to predict the frequencies, but for single instances it is impossible in principle to know the reality well enough to be able to predict that. Now would you suppose first of all that that position philosophically is more probable?

No, I don't think that's philosophic at all. I think it involves a large number of concepts that I would define differently, or want to examine a lot more carefully. The notion of probability itself implies the notion of prediction. As I work out probability there's no incompatibility between probability and accurate prediction in each single case. For example, in casting dice, there's no suspension of any of the laws of mechanics. In the probability in death rates, there's no suspension of any law of medicine or biology. And these are cases that come under probability as I conceive it. In other words, probability is concerned with general knowledge on a level where you don't have the type of insight that yields the scheme of recurrence. It's a limitation on *general* knowledge.

In other words, could you put this from the Aristotelian point of view, by saying that it arises because it's the passive potency of the object to be influenced by other objects outside of the system, of which we cannot now take cognizance?

21 See note 6 above.

It's concerned with the occurrence of system.

Of a closed system?

You can be enclosing processes that needn't have this scheme of recurrence within. If you're enclosing a system with a scheme of recurrence, you have accurate prediction in the general case. And if you're enclosing a system without a scheme of recurrence, then your only general predictions will be probabilities.

Just one last point. The sources of probability here in your view would be in a sense the assumption of a closed system, whereas an open system is always possible, so to speak. In other words, there's a scientific assumption here of a closed system, which is necessary for scientific prediction, but is in fact always only an approximation. Would that be ultimately the source of probability?

Well I don't think my remarks on closure[22] bear on the issue. I think there's an obscurity in the notion of closure. I think what closure really means is this: You have a scheme of recurrence that is not interrupted, or not upset; and when you're speaking of a case of probability, you don't have a scheme of recurrence, and you don't properly have a closure.

9 Form and Act

[There was an almost inaudible question here, having to do with form and act.]

Form is intelligible in itself. Contingent act, finite act, is not intelligible in itself. It is intelligible in the other. Existence and events are contingent; they're what corresponds to the proper content of judgment. The proper content of judgment depends upon a virtually unconditioned. A virtually unconditioned is what in fact is unconditioned – in fact has its conditions fulfilled. There's a limitation on the intelligibility there, and for that reason you are led to postulate efficient causes to account for contingent existence and contingent events.

[The next question was also inaudible; from the context it seems to have been something like, Did you say that contingent existence is not intelligible?]

22 On closure, see *Insight* 47, 52.

No, I said it was not intelligible *in itself*. When you have your efficient cause you do account for this contingent existence, this contingent event. But its intelligibility involves a relation to the other, a dependence on the other. Its intelligibility is not enclosed within itself. Form is the nucleus. It's what we know insofar as we understand. But only an object that is exclusively form is totally intelligible in itself – an object, a reality, in which its form is also its act, by identity. Then you have total intelligibility in itself.[e]

Form, where it's just a component of the real, is the nucleus of intelligibility intrinsic to that reality. Essence is intelligible in itself; material essence is intelligible in itself because, while essence includes both form and potency, or form and matter, and the matter or potency is not intelligible in itself, still it is intelligible in the form, and you've included the form in the essence.

> [Another inaudible question had to do with the relation of existence to essence.]

Yes, well, the act of existence stands to the form as judgment to concept. The other day[23] we saw that the intention of being takes the concept of essence and sees in it the possibility of existence. Now just as the judgment of existence[24] is related to the concept of essence, so existence is related to essence – there is an isomorphism.

10 Intelligence in Contemporary Thomism

I'd like to return to a question asked a few minutes ago, the question of intelligence. With regard to the traditional interpretation of Aquinas' cognitional theory, I know some who maintain that actually the preliminary or earlier moments in the knowing process have been taken into account, and have been discussed on the manual level, even by people like Siwek[25] and Raeymaeker[26]

---

23 'The other day' may refer to lecture 7, § 1.5, Understanding and Experience, and § 1.6, Judgment and Experience; see also lecture 6, § 2, The Notion of Being.
24 Lonergan actually said, 'the concept of existence' – surely a slip of the tongue for 'the judgment of existence,' though he does admit there is a concept of existence also.
25 Paul Siwek published a manual with the title *Psychologia metaphysica* (Rome: Gregorian University Press, 1948).
26 Louis de Raeymaeker published a manual in two languages, *Metaphysica generalis* (Louvain: E. Warny, 1931), and *Philosophie de l'être; essai de*

and most certainly by André Marc.[27] *Would you agree with this observation? I think it's sort of a banal question, but for my peace of soul ... Do you think it might be that the traditional interpreters, even since the turn of the century, have actually taken into consideration the earlier moments in the process, but have done so in very mechanical terms, as though this were a nonconscious and a-conscious, automatic process which goes along its merry way from insight into the phantasm, as they would interpret it, with intelligence coming out in full dress and all at once in the concept? Whereas in your own position the process from the word go is strictly conscious and can only be interpreted, as far as the text of Aquinas is concerned, and can only be analyzed, if someone wants to do it afresh, in terms of consciousness and introspective psychology.*

Well now, that way of putting it is essentially what I mean. The people who say that intelligence comes to light in the concept are using their intelligence; I'm not implying that they're not intelligent and not using their intelligence; they're doing both: they are intelligent, and they're using their intelligence ... But to see intelligence as a distinct moment governing the formation of concepts – that's another matter.

I haven't read all the manuals. I spoke of manuals available to me at a certain period in a certain place. Hoenen in an article in *Gregorianum* in 1933,[28] dealing with the first principles of science, with axiomatic systems, and so on, wanted to show that it's not only the term that's abstracted from phantasm, according to Aquinas and Aristotle, but also the nexus between terms. That was his thesis. He convinced himself that that was the case in Aristotelian and Thomist doctrine; that's the burden of the article. But that terminology – that from phantasm are abstracted not only terms, concepts, but also the nexus between concepts – you won't find either in Aristotle or in Aquinas. That language is purely Scotist – terms, with a nexus between them. You'll find that in Scotus,[29] but you won't find it in Thomas. I've never run across Thomist texts of that type, as far as I can remember; that isn't his way of speaking. What he says is that what you abstract from phantasm is *species* – *species* is translating Aristotle's *eidos*; that is what Aristotle says

---

synthèse métaphysique (Louvain: Editions de l'Institut Supérieur de Philosophie, 1946); trans. Edmund H. Ziegelmeyer, *The Philosophy of Being: A Synthesis of Metaphysics* (St. Louis: B. Herder, 1954).

27 The reference may be to André Marc, *Dialectique de l'affirmation: Essai de métaphysique réflexive* (Paris: Desclée de Brouwer, 1952).

28 See lecture 1, note 13.

29 The references are in *Verbum* 25, note 122.

about abstraction; he doesn't talk about abstraction in the same way as Scotus; but he too talks about *eidos*.

Moreover, Hoenen says that in the roughly seven hundred years that had elapsed from Thomas to the writing of his article, there were seven scholastic writers that he'd been able to find who had adverted to this possibility. And very few of the seven agreed with the thesis that Hoenen was proposing.

The terminology employed by Hoenen, and the negative results he had when he compared Aristotle and Aquinas with the succession of scholastic writers, suggest that there has been an eclipse of the act of understanding. If you want to say what's grasped by insight, you have Aristotle's expression: form, *to ti ên einai*. It's not a matter simply of a nexus between terms; it's also that, but to describe it as a nexus between terms is a special case relevant to mathematics. Unity is another case – substantial unity. And if what is grasped by insight is form, what is expressed is related concepts. The presentation, the attention, has been so concentrated on the universal and the concept that the notion of the concept has permanence. But conscious intelligence is missing.

And it's missing in a most conspicuous fashion, because in Thomist Trinitarian theory, the procession of the Son from the Father is a matter of conscious intelligent process. That's the point to the psychological analogy – the difference between conscious intelligent process and mere causality.[30] Mere causality involves a real duality. The cause cannot be identical with the effect. You can get around that identity – not completely, because you don't completely understand mystery, but to some extent – insofar as the generation of the Son is an intellectual generation – conscious intellectual process, such as concept from insight.

Now theologians have been doing Trinitarian theory extensively, every one of them, but that has completely disappeared in Trinitarian doctrine. Even the most brilliant of them, like Billot, say that imagination is just as good an analogy.[31] In that sense I say that there hasn't been the recognition. And also in the sense that epistemological problems take on a reality that they didn't have before.

30 See lecture 5, §3, The Act of Reflective Understanding.
31 Ludovicus Billot, *De Deo uno et trino* (Rome: Gregorian University Press, 7th ed., 1935) 358. Introducing the *verbum* articles Lonergan referred to the 1910 ed., p. 335 (*Theological Studies* 7 [1946] 349); these paragraphs were omitted from the book *Verbum*.

But it's impossible to generalize about manuals.

And again, when I talk about intelligence, I'm not meaning that men aren't intelligent. That's the possibility of the counterposition. The man *is* intelligent, and he's highly reasonable, but the account he's giving of knowledge doesn't do justice to his own intelligence and reasonableness. That conflict is the basis of the counterposition and the reason why the counterposition heads for a reversal.

11   Insight and the Beatific Vision

Would you care to go into the relationship between your notion of being and the beatific vision as an act of insight?

Well, the beatific vision is another mystery. But, first of all, we can understand the essence of a man, we can have an understanding of human nature, of animal nature, of plant life, of the inorganic world. We're understanding a particular type of being. But what's behind my concept of the *notion* of being is this: once you set down, posit, that intellect is intelligence, that abstraction is an intelligent operation in which you omit the irrelevant and grasp the essential – such a notion of abstraction means that you cannot have an abstraction of a concept, being, because to have abstraction in that sense, you have to grasp the essence of being; and to grasp the essence of being you have to have the *ens per essentiam* as the object of your knowledge, and know that object by its essence. And knowing the *ens per essentiam* is the beatific vision in Thomist theory.

Is the word 'insight' very apt here?

Well, insight, insofar as it presupposes a previous knowledge, is not apt. But I say it's an act of understanding. And it's an act of understanding that doesn't lead to a further reflective act, because it's the totality of intelligibility.

There would be judgment ...

Just as in God essence and existence are identical, so in the beatific vision grasp of essence is also knowledge of existence.

Do you think it would be expressed in an eternity of judgments ... inexhaustible?

Yes, I suppose so. But it's just hypothesis; we really don't know. It's a plausible account of the thing.

The theory of the beatific vision is involved in another glorious complex point, the vital act – a bit of metaphysics that blocked most of theology. It blocked the theory of grace, blocked anything pretty well that involved knowledge or will. However, that's a very complex question.[f]

12   Judgment and Cajetan's Analogy of Proportion

Would you care to explain the differences between the theory of judgment as grasping existence and Cajetan's position of grasping the relation between essence and existence in the judgment?

Well, insofar as I know Cajetan, his theory of being is in terms of a functional relation between essence and existence.[32] What's the unity of the notion of being? The unity of the notion of being is that the essence of *A* is to the existence of *A* as the essence of *B* is to the existence of *B* – the analogy of proportion. And that's an adequate account of the notion of being, as long as you're thinking of this being, that being, and the other being. But that involves precision. I distinguish between precision (prescinding) and abstraction. You abstract what is essential and omit what is incidental, irrelevant. But prescinding is a matter of considering one question at a time. You may consider the issues concretely or abstractly; but you're considering just this question. And to think of being solely in those terms is to omit the notion of being as the universe, as everything. And when you omit that, you omit the integrating aspect of metaphysics. Is that sufficient?

Still, in an individual judgment in regard to the particular being, you would be grasping the relation of the intelligibility to actuality?

Yes, just as we did in working out the concept of being yesterday, or the day before:[33] the procedures of intelligence, the intention of being, the grasp in the essence of a relation to existence, the consequent question, Is it? and the affirmation. In other words, you can add onto Cajetan's analogy the relation between conception and judgment. And that gives me my isomorphism.

---

32 For Cajetan on this question, see *Insight* 368–71.
33 See above, note 23.

13 Common Sense

A slight problem, which I know you will take in stride. It deals with common sense. The knowing procedure – your three levels, with the object being – is the knowing procedure in common sense the same as the procedure in science?

It involves the three levels, yes.

The object of knowing is being, the everything about everything. Is that the object of common sense?

No, common sense is a specialization.

Something of the everything, then?

Yes.

In common sense don't you revert back to the real out there now? When you've gone up through the process ... you have to get back to it.

You never leave it, you need never leave it. Do you leave it in common sense?

Leave what in common sense?

In other words, you say, You go up to judgment, and how do you get back?

Right, back to the outside world, to the real out there.

The question of the difference between knowing as taking a look and knowing as having its significant moment in true judgment is not a question for common sense; it's a philosophic question.

Well, you have to think in order to use your common sense.

Yes, but you don't have to have a theory of common sense to have common sense. And a theory of common sense is not a thing that common sense can work out.

But if you're going to use common sense you have to affirm judgments. You have to ...

Yes, you have to do all that. But do you have to have a theory of judgment?

You don't need the theory necessarily, no.

And common sense is a specialization of knowledge. Just as there are certain types of knowing that are no business of the chemist, but belong to the physicist, and so on all along the line, so common sense is another specialization of human understanding. It's for dealing with the concrete in practical living. And the man of common sense de facto is guided by his judgment. If you stop him and ask him whether the real is what's already out there now, or what you know in a true judgment, he'll say, 'It's what's already out there now.' But then he's talking outside his specialty; you're asking him a philosophic question. If you ask him, 'If it were true that there weren't a machine down here,[34] would there really be one?' he'll say, 'No, it would have to be merely an appearance if there really weren't one there, if it weren't true that there is one there; that would be a hallucination.' If you ask him why, well, he'd be in difficulties, because he hasn't contrasted the different components of his knowledge and separated them and worked out a theory of them. But if you get commonsense people to do some commonsense action, you'll see that they use their judgment – when they're not sure, they hem and haw and avoid the issue, put it off, and so on.

They use the same knowing procedure.

You have the structure.

But it's directed towards different objects?

Yes, and it's developed in a different way.

14 Common Sense and Science

Would some people object to your making such a clear distinction between commonsense thinking and scientific thinking? Unless you put it all in the object. In other words, people in the realm of common sense do do what we would consider sometimes scientific thinking; they have to abstract, and they have to make at least for themselves some sort of propositions, analyses, and theories. And yet all the way through you have made almost an iron curtain between a commonsense thinker and a scientific thinker. I'm not sure I feel there's that much difference. I can understand that science is more universal; but the process that you might go through in thinking about politics or economics or

34 The 'machine down here' – presumably pointing to the tape recorder.

human relations or anything else has the same elements as the scientific process has. So is the distinction really in what they deal with?

Well, the root of the distinction, as I drew it, was that by common sense I meant insights that accumulated, headed towards a basic nucleus, such that by adding further relevant insights on each occasion, different ones, one would be able to deal successfully with the situation.

And this is what is done by most people in everything except the highest mathematicians and scientists?

No, I don't believe that the man of common sense is concerned to arrive at what universally is true. Insofar as he does, he's an incipient scientist. In other words, if you draw a distinction by defining what you mean in one case and in the other – and that's the only way you can set up an intelligible difference between them – then there arises the problem of application, and you'll get borderline cases, and so on.

15 Social Science

Would you say something about the social sciences generally. Is there a problem there?

I think so. The problem is that where your object is an empirically, intelligently, rationally conscious subject that develops in his intelligence and reasonableness, you're dealing with an entity that, even from the viewpoint of your scientific method, has to be approached in a manner essentially different from the study of atoms or plants or animals. And it's only insofar as the human sciences will be willing to expect some philosophic commitments or, on the other hand, be masters of all possible philosophic commitments that they'll be able to think on a level that is truly human in their human sciences.

If the economist, in his analysis of the economy, is concerned to make plain to people as individuals that certain procedures are just as intelligent as stepping on the accelerator and the brake at the same time, he's talking to them as men. And they by their use of their intelligence and reasonableness will individually or cooperatively be able to carry out his precepts and avoid grand-scale blunders. But if he thinks of economic activity as predictable events in the same manner as the nineteenth-century physicists did, or as statistically probable events, he's dealing with an objective manifold, and his only way of dealing with it will be through government, or through propaganda, or through psychological conditioning, or through the police state, or what you please. The link between the human science and its application will not be human; it will be subhuman. It's a problem of considerable dimensions – a number of dimensions that are all pretty enormous.

16 Heuristic Structure and Metaphysics

There's another point that leaves me restless, in connection with this business of heuristic structure. This morning[35] you gave an example of heuristic structure: what is the nature of fire? – the definition or the description that has been given in history a propos of this. Now 'What is the nature?' would be the heuristic structure, and 'nature' – would that be the concept?

Yes.

Suppose we take the reality of change or becoming. Suppose as a metaphysician I answer, describing change in terms of potency and act. Are potency and act other heuristic concepts? Or are they fulfilling to a certain extent my heuristic structure 'nature'? Or should I simply rely on sciences to answer the question?

Well, I think a number of different elements are involved in the question. First of all, with regard to the notion of being – I don't think you can get a metaphysical argument from the fact of substantial change to hylomorphic composition in terms of matter and form, because, if you could, then the total conversion of the substance, the bread, into the body of Christ, as defined by the Council of Trent, would be metaphysically impossible. Therefore that argument is only physics.

Another angle: once the scientist arrives at his laws, either he meets a layman who asks him what the real really looks like, or he asks himself, because he's also a layman when he's off duty. And he tends to give an imaginative picture.

Similarly, once you arrive at your metaphysics, you'll be tempted to answer questions by saying, 'Well now, let's start it going and see how it works.' And I think those questions of that type are of the same category, the same kind.

It's a question of where you draw the line, where metaphysical questioning ends, and it's a fundamental methodological question. But I think that a line can be drawn, and has to be drawn. You set up the

35 'This morning' likely refers to lecture 8, §7, Metaphysics and Explanatory Knowledge.

structure, but the function of the structure, the utility of the structure, is not to replace your scientific inquiry; it's to provide a fundamental semantics. For example, what do you mean when you say this? Would you mean anything different if you said that? Insofar as you can distinguish a certain number of metaphysical elements, and say, There are these and none but these, then you're able to say that this range of propositions are all saying the same thing. They're true if there's this metaphysical entity, and they're not true if there isn't. On the other hand, you can say there are other propositions involved, distinct metaphysical entities; there are distinct conditions of their truth. You would have an operative semantics. It's the sort of thing that's very useful in theology. You eliminate an awful lot of disputed questions with that technique.[g]

In other words, one isn't to think of the explanatory value of a metaphysics in terms of concrete problems.[h] Leave those to the scientist. There are problems on a much more fundamental or complex level, which you develop your metaphysics to handle.

What the metaphysician would provide, then, to the physicist are conditions?

Well, he separates positions and counterpositions in the physicist's utterances.

Do I understand from that that I have to abandon the whole Aristotelian explanation of change, or what I thought was the Aristotelian explanation? I don't mind abandoning it ...

I don't agree with it. I don't think the argument is a metaphysical argument.[36] And of course the fundamental problem from the viewpoint of the Aristotelian position is to say where Aristotle's physics ends and where his metaphysics begins. And the theory developed in *Insight* offers a systematic solution to that problem.

I think that Aristotle in his *Physics* violated his own principles. He, or at least the Aristotelian corpus – it's very difficult to say what is from Aristotle – but in that body of writings he distinguished his predicaments from causes, and science is conceived in terms of causes.[37] But

---

36 Lonergan took this position twice in answering the questions in this section, but modified it in the course of the exchange ('perhaps I should qualify what I said before').

37 See lecture 1, § 1.2, The Development of the Ideal of Knowledge, and the references to Aristotle there in note 5.

Aristotle's *Physics* is fundamentally a theory of motion, and motion is defined as the incomplete realization of three of the predicaments. Local motion is an incomplete realization of being there, being in a place. You're not in any place when you're moving; you're on your way to some place. Where is it? You get involved in the continuum, if you want to say where a moving body is, and Aristotle didn't have the differential calculus to get the idea of that type of analysis of a local movement.

Again, quality, or change of quality – what's called alteration, *alloiôsis* – is change in the *sensibilia propria*, in color, hot and cold, wet and dry, smooth and rough, and so on. What is 'becoming white'? Well, it's an incomplete realization of 'being white.' What is 'heating'? It's an incomplete realization of 'being hot, at a certain intensity of heat,' and so on.

Similarly, for quantity.

The categories, the predicaments, form the basis, then, on which he develops his theory of motion. Science becomes not a reduction of reality to its causes – certain knowledge of things through their causes – but knowledge of things through the predicaments, so that science, instead of advancing from description to explanation in causes, starts circling around within the descriptive field.[i]

The definitions I worked out, of potency, form, and act, are exactly what Aristotle uses in his psychology. Eye, sight, seeing, are potency, form, act. The capacity to will, habits of will, and acts of will are potency, form, act. The possible intellect, habits of intellect (the acquisition of a science), and acts of understanding are potency, form, act, again – all analogous to prime matter, substantial form, and existence. And that in Aristotle, I believe, survives, when systematically collected. But Aristotelian physics has doubled back on the descriptive element, and that's why it was a block to the development of science. And that's what sets the problem of just what kind of a department of philosophy cosmology is.

> [There follows a question, barely audible, that seems to move from the previous observations to the problem of the argument for the existence of God based on change, and asks whether something along the lines of Aristotelian hylomorphism is not required for the Thomist notion of the immutability of God.]

Well, not exactly. Insofar as the negation of change is based upon that argument, it would be. But there are other types of argument for that exclusion of change from God. If you have change, you have some sort of finality. You have some sort of potentiality, imperfection, some perfection to be acquired. And if you posit unlimited act, well, you're excluding the possibility of change in quite a different way from the argument from the supposition of matter. In other words, matter isn't the only type of potency. It's by the negation of potency, capacity for development, that you get the immutability of God.

> [There follows a further question, again only partly audible, that asks whether, while Aristotle lists his changes according to the set of the predicaments, he does not also analyze them in terms of causes. The question ends as follows.]

I still don't quite see why he has to be condemned for mixing up change with the predicaments, even if he did so, because he also appears to have thought of change concurrently in the metaphysical sense.

There are two distinct questions there.

With regard to involving the predicaments in the *Physics*, I think that seems to be quite clear. And the theory of motion involved in the *Physics*, and the presupposition that change of quantity presupposes change of quality, and change of quality presupposes local motion, that buildup gives you his world order.

Now as to the other question, regarding change in terms of potentiality, insofar as you have a being that changes, you have a case of potentiality. But perhaps I should qualify what I said before. If you conceive metaphysics in terms of necessity and impossibility, you haven't got from change a metaphysical argument. But if you conceive metaphysics, as I do, as what is true as a matter of fact in our knowledge – there are factual conditions for it – then metaphysics differs from physics, not in terms of necessity and impossibility, but on the *level* at which it considers the same reality. Metaphysics considers the same reality with the same degree and type of factual knowledge as you have in physics, but it does so as a total integrating function. So in that sense of metaphysics you can have metaphysical arguments from change. And they are metaphysical in the sense that they don't exclude the possibility of the contradictory. You've given a further clarification there. There's a qualification to be put on what I said before – in terms of the different senses of metaphysics I hadn't connected the transposition from the way I thought out metaphysics to the way metaphysics is involved in these single metaphysical arguments.

I take it that these facts which you feed into your structure to produce a metaphysics are not the phenomenological facts.

No, fact here is not on the level of the phenomenon.

17 The Upper Blade

I found your picture of the creation of knowledge very interesting – that facts are produced from phenomena, either in science, or human behavior, or economics, or any field. And man's human tendency to generalize and theorize – he wanders around gathering wool until suddenly theory and facts are observed to fit. But this appears to take place in all subjects. Wherefore, do you have a super-theory? In what field does this operate? What is the upper blade?

Well, insofar as you grasp this theory of knowledge you see that it has implications. And those implications are such that they don't fit in with what is often or spontaneously thought to be so. And that spontaneously thinking things to be so, and taking things for granted, occurs not only in common sense but also in the sciences. In terms of that opposition and conflict, which works out on a rather general level of the polymorphism of the subject – it's developed in terms of that – you can divide basic propositions, propositions about knowledge, into two sets: a set called positions that is compatible with this structure of knowledge, and another set that is incompatible with it. And insofar as any thinker is de facto intelligent and reasonable, but what he's saying is in the second set, the counterpositions, he's in a conflict. It's a conflict between himself as intelligent and rational, and what he's holding, advancing.

I don't understand. Why is there a conflict between intelligence and what he says when these positions are contradictory to fact?

I'm not saying that he sees that. I'm saying that what he says is in conflict with what he is.

I don't know in what field of knowledge ...

Well, take your nineteenth-century physicists and their idea of physical reality, and compare it with the present-day one. If you trace back the origin of their view of reality, you'll find, I believe, that its ground has nothing to do with science, but is philosophic.

And this higher blade is concerned with, is derived from, cognitional theory, and one of its functions, just one of its functions, is the elimination of counterpositions.

I was asking a more specific question: What is the origin of the theory, or whatever you want to call it, which acts as the top blade of the upper set? The lower blade is the structure of knowledge which you have created out of ...

No, no, no. The upper blade is this structure of knowledge, and your lower blade is your scientific elaboration of data.

Yes, in your picture, this is in the lower set of shears. But you have another upper shear ...

In any science there is an upper and lower blade operative. Insofar as you consider the sciences as a whole you can work out a theory of knowledge, and one case of the theory is the relation between this structure of knowledge and the sciences.[38]

And the sort of ideas which operate as this upper blade — where does this come from?

Well, it comes from self-knowledge. And consequently, it's controllable. If you involve in your upper blade things that can't be established from cognitional theory, you have an empirical control to eliminate them. But that empirical control is not empirical in the sense of sense data. It's empirical in the sense of the data of consciousness, the analysis of cognitional activity.[39] It's a fact, in the sense that it's a fact that I think I'm intelligent, I think I'm reasonable, and so on — the sort of thoughts that are hard to avoid.[40]

---

38 The tape is obscure at this point; our editing gives only a probable reading, but the relation between the structure of knowledge and the sciences corresponds to the upper and lower contexts of *Insight* xxv–xxvi.
39 On generalized empirical method as including data of consciousness, see *Insight* xi, 72, 243, 333, 382, 423.
40 Recording went right to the end of this discussion, as is clear from Lonergan's 'I think it's time,' found in the LRI and DJS reels. (The WAS reel – no. 6, side 2 – starts the way the other two do, but soon shifts to the end of lecture 8, and then to the first part of discussion 4; the second part of the discussion is largely missing.)

Discussion 5[1]

[Only the first two questions, it seems, had been given to Lonergan in advance. After he dealt with them, discussion was freewheeling.]

1   The Pure Desire to Know and Charity

I have two excellent questions. I don't know if I will be able to answer either of them. The first is, *Would you speak about the relation between the pure desire to know and charity as described by the apostle?*

I think it would be easier to say something on that in the lecture tomorrow morning when we treat of the idea of the good as it works out concretely in society.[2] In that we will show how the pure desire to know works out into a social situation with its implications, and it will be simpler then to add the differences involved in charity. The theme is one that has become somewhat celebrated, especially since Nygren's work on *Eros and Agape*[3] – Nygren is a Norwegian theologian, I believe.

---

1 The evening of Thursday, August 14, 1958. The 1980 edition (in questions 12, 16, and 14, respectively) included all of §2 (Kant on the Primacy of Practical Reason), §5 (Suffering), and §7 (Self-appropriation and the Christian); also in questions 13 and 15, parts of §3 (Archetypes), and §9 (Isomorphism and Objectivity).

2 Lonergan does touch on this question next morning in lecture 10, §1.7, The Course of Human History; but the course of discussion led him to treat it more fully this same evening: see §5 below, Suffering, and §6, Love and Ethics.

3 Anders Nygren, *Agape and Eros*, 2 vols. (London: SPCK, 1932, 1939).

2 Kant on the Primacy of Practical Reason

The second question is, *Would you also speak of Kant's doctrine of the primacy of the practical reason?*

I can't say anything as a Kantian specialist. But I may be able to offer some heuristic structures with regard to that question.

It is interesting to note that the stoics had a very elevated moral doctrine, while in their epistemology and their views of reality they were materialists. It illustrates the point that one can have self-appropriation and grasp its implications in the moral field and not do so in the more complicated field of cognitional theory and metaphysics. Morality is something closer, more intimate, to the development of the person. And, of course, that remark is using my own heuristic structure to a great extent and the stoics very slightly – just using a historical fact, a general characteristic of this doctrine.

In Kant, one has something similar: a theory of knowledge that excludes, to a great extent, knowledge of reality and, at the same time, an ethical doctrine of remarkable elevation. And the fact that the ethical doctrine seems, at least to me, superior to the doctrine on knowledge and on metaphysics is parallel to the instance of the stoics. In Kant it works out in somewhat greater detail. I think there are indications of just how much this could be worked out in an actual study of Kant precisely on that point.

In the *Critique of Pure Reason* the conditions for a possible experience are not the same as the conditions for a possible course of action. A possible course of action regards something in the future, something you are going to do, not something you know. The conditions are not exactly the same, and so Kant can attribute validity to the ideas of reason or the ideals of reason from the viewpoint of action that he cannot from the viewpoint of knowledge. If, as Maréchal does, one introduces finality into one's notion of knowledge, one is giving the same validity to pure reason or to some correction of pure reason that Kant acknowledges in practical intellect. I say 'some correction,' because Kant's *Critique of Pure Reason* is really an attack upon types of philosophy that are deductivist in the Spinozistic fashion.

Maréchal's work is largely a function of the study of Kant, and this

---

Lonergan's memory was faulty on the title, and on Nygren's nationality – Swedish.

idea of introducing finality into the account of knowledge seems to have been one of his fundamental notions. I'm speaking through a knowledge I have more through osmosis than through direct study of Maréchal's texts; he is a rather formidably voluminous writer; his *Le point de départ de la métaphysique*[4] is five volumes. But at least part of Maréchal's idea seems to have been that to introduce finality in the intellect would be to confer on speculative intellect the same type of validity that Kant acknowledges in practical intellect. But because of the role that Kant ascribes to intuition in knowledge, he cannot at the same time give primacy to judgment, and he cannot at the same time give primacy to a finalistic view of knowledge, namely, that knowledge is something we move towards, not something we build upon intuitions. The cognitional element, for Kant, is very closely related to this intuitional element, that is, through the intuition knowledge has direct relation to reality or to its object.

That is something on the question, and it is very far from being any venture upon an account of Kant's actual thinking or a study of his works or anything like that. It is an idea that may perhaps be of some use to someone studying Kant on that question. It is a very good question.

3   Archetypes

[From this point on, questions were put from the floor.]

On images; I think Jung has a doctrine of archetypes. I think it is a matter of primitive images that recur everywhere, and he tries to give them some kind of psychological validity. How would your doctrine of development be related to that type of thing? Could you suggest whether those images arise by virtue of probability from neural states, or whether you think they would be evoked from a higher level, related to the pattern of thought?

I would suggest that they regard typical situations, concrete human situations. For example, the *puer aeternus*, the son who is always a boy to his mother, even when he is fifty years old: the mother always sees him as a boy. That is something that was suggested to me: just how much that fits in I don't know. I haven't done any study of these archetypes that Jung claims exist, but it seems that these images are

4 Joseph Maréchal, *Le point* ... (see lecture 7, note 23). In response to a question, Lonergan gave an approximation to the specific title of the 5th volume.

recurrent in quite different civilizations. You find the same thing in Eliade. Jung claims that his patients or clients would come up with things that you find in Chinese myth, when this particular patient certainly knew nothing about Chinese literature or mythology and so on. I think they would have to be explained by the nature of man and the concrete human situation. Intersubjectivity has an awful lot to do with it, the relations between persons, mother and child, husband and wife, father and son, and so on – and recurrent human situations. But on a detailed discussion of them I would not venture.

There was a very interesting study from the viewpoint of Heidegger's existentialism by a person who I believe was in this field. It was a very short book, *Dreams*, and was translated into French with a preface of about 125 pages. The man contrasts dreams of the evening or the night, which are more or less a consequence of the previous day, and the dreams of the morning, when the existential subject, the *Dasein*, is preparing to exist. The projects of the day and so on are beginning to take shape and they do so in the dream state.[5]

Father White, the English Dominican,[6] seems to put a great deal of faith in some of Jung's ideas. Some others consider Freudian ideas as much more compatible.

There is the fact that Jung speaks a good deal about religion and the importance of religion. He makes such statements as that, in the majority of the people that come to him, the reason ultimately is a religious one. But then the question arises, What does Jung mean by religion? and one can say that, even if he has an inadequate idea of what religion is, still there is something there. I was told by a man who has a certain amount to do with psychiatrists generally in Montreal that they take a very empirical or an eclectic attitude; when cases arise before the age of 25 they apply Freudian technique; 25 to 35, they apply the individual psychology of Adler – the man is making his way

5 Binswanger, 'Dream and Existence,' in *Being-in-the-World* 222–48. Lonergan was still not able to recall Binswanger's name; see lecture 2 above: §6, The Difference between Empirical Data and the Concept, and note 18. He noted, however, the influence of Heidegger (on Binswanger), and added that the name could be found in his bibliography of the previous year (for the Boston College lectures on existentialism [CWL 18]).
6 The reference is to Victor White, *God and the Unconscious* (London: The Harvill Press, 1952); there is a Foreword by C.G. Jung.

in the world; and if he has difficulties after 45, he wants peace of soul, and they use Jung.

4 Insight and Ethics

[Another question asks about the relation of insight to the field of ethics.]

I hope to speak of that tomorrow morning, but briefly now regarding ethics. Just as there is the structure of knowing that is isomorphic with the structure of being and the structure of philosophies – the diversities of philosophies express the polymorphism of the subject, and the diversities of cultures express the polymorphism of the subject – so self-appropriation contains a deontological element, what ought to be, on a cognitional level, as in Eisenhower's remark, 'We have to be men.' So there is a structure of doing that is a prolongation of the structure of knowing, and from that structure moral ideas can be derived. We will have some greater detail tomorrow morning.

5 Suffering

I don't know whether you are going to get around to this tomorrow, but if God is good and is all-powerful how does it come about that he tolerates the suffering of innocent people and children? Either he is not all good or he is not all-powerful.

The premise is that suffering is unmitigated evil and that, in this life, justice is on a purely individual basis, and I think both of the premises can be questioned.

First of all, with regard to God's justice in this world: God's justice in this world is simply his will following his wisdom. Insofar as God's will is conceived as executing a conception of his wisdom, and that conception of his wisdom is an order of the universe, a total order of the universe, God is just insofar as his will follows his wisdom, his intellect, just as we are moral persons insofar as our choices follow our right reason.

Now God's plan, the reason why God chooses such a world as this, can best be conceived as a self-manifestation – or that is one way of conceiving it. The end of creation is the glory of God, the manifestation of God. The degree of manifestation that occurs in a universe will vary with the type of perfection that is desired in that universe. As St Augustine says, divine wisdom thought it better to permit evil rather than to create a world in which no evil would exist.[7] In evil in its fundamental form, which is sin, there is the irrational, the 'what has no reason.' God doesn't cause that, he permits it. Dealing with that question, so that it has a meaning, is a rather technical point, but I believe it can be established. And he permits it, perhaps one might say, because insofar as it is permitted, you can have in a finite universe something of the tension that represents and expresses the infinite good.

The matter, in abstract terms, is apt to be highly unconvincing, but Christians know from the incarnation, from the life that the Son of God chose to lead on earth, that he chose suffering and death, and his suffering and death were the results of sin. They were the results of sin, the sin of Judas, the sin of the leaders of the people, the sin of the Roman governor who did a shabby job of justice. According to the New Testament, they're the sins of the world: it wouldn't have been part of the divine plan to allow sin so to rise against the God-Man were it not for the sins of all the world. And in the Gospel of St John, there is the constant contrast between light and darkness, between those who come to the light because they aren't afraid of their works being manifested and those that reject the light because they do not want their works to be known. There are the rather violent denunciations of the Pharisees, such as in chapter 8: your father is the devil, who was a homicide from the beginning.[8] Sin is the source of evil in this world insofar as this world is a human creation and a human product. It involves an objective surd, and that surd is stopped, it is absorbed, only insofar as there is suffering. Suffering is, as it were, the absorption of the surd of sin.[a]

I am using metaphors. Let's put it more concretely. Poland is invaded, and so many million people are killed off. If you appeal to any conceivable scheme of human justice, how could you set that right, without causing an equal amount of further suffering? Sin leads to suffering, and it is only insofar as suffering is accepted in the spirit in which Christ accepted it that the surd of sin is, as it were, wiped out.

7 Augustine, *Enchiridion, sive De fide, spe et caritate* 11 (PL 40, 236); used by Thomas Aquinas, *Summa theologiae*, 1, q. 2, a. 3, ad 1m.
8 RSV: 'You are of your father the devil, and your will is to do your father's desires. He was a murderer from the beginning, and has nothing to do with the truth, because there is no truth in him' (John 8.44).

Otherwise, it keeps perpetuating itself in social evil, and not merely in physical suffering but in the further darkening of the mind, further weakening of the will, or indifference of the will. And it is insofar as there is this acceptance of suffering that a halt is called.

On the other hand, there is the resurrection of Christ, and the resurrection of Christ is presented in the New Testament as the work of God the Father. It is the Father who raised the Son from the dead. On the one hand, you have the work of man, as sinning; on the other hand, you have the work of God, raising his Son from the dead. This is a religious viewpoint, the way the sufferings in the world are conceived by the Christian, which I offer as more convincing than a purely abstract treatment of the matter such as can be done to some extent from a philosophic viewpoint, in terms of the dialectic and the turning point. And that work of the Father is an illustration of those words of St Paul in the eighth chapter to the Romans: To those who love God all things work for the good.[9]

In the death and resurrection of Christ we have the tremendous symbol of Christianity that interprets for us the meaning of life. The Christian knows that if the master has suffered, there is nothing incongruous in his own suffering; and he knows that as the master rose again, so the Father is able to transform, to make all things work unto the good. That understanding of the meaning of human life that is mediated to us through the death and resurrection of Christ, as through a symbol, an image, is something on which our intellectual and moral and spiritual lives can develop, and in their development see more and more of its profundity. And that is God's expression of himself to us.

So why did God not choose a different world as a manifestation of his wisdom? We can have some glimmer – a glimmer of understanding – that perhaps in this world God is manifesting himself.

What God is – the answer to the question, *Quid sit Deus?* What is God? – is something we do not know. We don't know God by his essence in this life. We have only analogical knowledge of him. But that has been God's revelation of himself to us, and insofar as in humility and simplicity we accept things as they are, we can advance to a knowledge of God and an intimacy with God that will leave us convinced that what, as philosophers, we may call his wisdom and his goodness

---

9 RSV: 'We know that in everything God works for good with those who love him, who are called according to his purpose' (Romans 8.28).

are in truth wisdom and goodness – surpassing wisdom and surpassing goodness.

As you see, the question of suffering, like all concrete existential
questions, heads on to the religious, to the supernatural. Just as there is
a self-appropriation that involves a development in us and implies a
development in us – to be men – so the situation that is the human
condition leads us on further to what we name the supernatural life,
to a life in which God loves us in the full sense of love. Love involves
a quasi identification. When two people are in love their thoughts are
about *us* – what are *we* going to do, what do *we* need? It is all spontaneously so. There is a quasi identification involved. And in the fact that
God became man as our savior, there is that same manifestation of
love, and it is that aspect of love, of God's love for mankind in the full
sense of loving – a self-giving, to which we respond with a self-giving –
that there is in charity something away beyond any ethical structure
that can be based upon the pure desire to know. It presupposes an
advance made by God as a lover, in the full sense of loving, and it
means our response, and it means our response in which we love one
another because we love God – and if we don't love one another we
don't know God, in the words of St John's epistle.[10]

6   Love and Ethics

*I wonder if I could ask whether, in view of the last few remarks, it is possible
to structure love on the same three levels, the corresponding levels of intellectual
operations?*

Yes, it is not so easy to structure love that way. The three levels are
relevant to ethics. Let us start there.[11]

There is the *good as the object of desire*. There is a scholastic phrase,
Bonum est id quod omnia appetunt;[12] the object of our desire is the good,
the objects of our fears are evil. That is the experiential level.

---

10   RSV: 'Beloved, let us love one another; for love is of God, and he who
   loves is born of God and knows God. He who does not love does not know
   God; for God is love' (1 John 4.7–8).
11   Lonergan again referred to next morning's lecture, remarking that questions were heading into it all the time; in fact, this discussion replaced
   much of what he presumably had planned to say in the lecture.
12   Aristotle, *Ethics*, 1, 1, 1094 a 3; Thomas Aquinas, *Summa theologiae*, 1, q.
   5, a. 1, and passim.

There's the *good of order*. The good of order is very well represented negatively by an economic depression. In an economic depression there is no lack of material, there is no lack of capital, there is no lack of people willing to work, and there is no lack of people willing to buy, but things don't run, they don't work. You can prime the pump, and you get a single burst of water going round, but it doesn't keep going round as when the economic system is functioning properly. You can keep priming and repriming and build up an enormous national debt, and still things aren't clicking. It was the World War that started the real economic upturn after the depression of 1929, to some extent anyway, or so some economists insinuate. What is lacking in such a situation is the good of order.

And what is this good of order? It is the dovetailing of one thing with another that you have when the economic system is functioning properly. *A* makes shoes, *B* wants shoes and makes something else, and the whole thing clicks together, and it works. The difficulties, of course, why the thing periodically does not work, the reasons for that, are more complex. But there is a good of order. That good of order is, as it were, a system that links together, that conditions the satisfaction of desires, of one's own desires, by one's contribution to the satisfaction of the desires of others. That is the way it works out in an economic system.

Again, you have the good of order in a family, a family as an institution. It is a mode of living. Just as an economy involves modes of living, performing certain actions at certain times, and so on, similarly in the family; and the thing so works out that everyone is ever so much better off than if they weren't together.

There is the good of order of the polity, the state. These objective schemes of recurrence – you have a good breakfast this morning, you have a good breakfast the next morning, and you keep on having a breakfast every morning; you have a job to do that interests you today, and you'll have it tomorrow, and so on. The thing keeps recurring, and the schemes of recurrence, the recurrences in each individual life, depend upon occurrences in other lives. And the good of order is when the whole thing clicks together. It is *good in the intelligible sense*. It is the object of an insight.

There are people who are ardently devoted to communism, and there are people who are ardently devoted to individualism, but what either of them wants is not a house and a Rolls Royce or a Lincoln and so on. It is not food or drink, it is not clothing or housing: it is a system, an intelligible order, a way of doing things. That good of order is also an object of human appetition, and it's something quite distinct from the object of desire in a much simpler sense. The object of desire is an object for the satisfaction of *my* desire, but a person can very sincerely desire that the Russian people have the advantage of an individualistic or a free economy. We think they would be much better off if they had that, and possibly a Russian may think that we would really be better off if we had the advantages of their system. In other words, the object of desire is a good for yourself, but the good of order regards the right way of doing things.

That good of order is known by an accumulation, a cluster, of insights. And generally, those clusters of insights are parceled out among the members of the community. In the family the father knows what it is to be a good father; he doesn't know so much about the wife's job. And the wife knows what it is to be a good wife and mother and so on. Each one is an expert in his own function, his own contribution to the whole. He knows what he has to do as a minimum and what he can do as a maximum. Anyway, that is the good of order.

A good of order involves a flow of benefits, of fruits, from the good of order, in all the different ways in which the order may be realized. The flow, the series, of classes for the students of a university is a series of benefits. In any good of order it gives rise to a flow of benefits of different kinds. The flow of benefits involves a flow of operations, and the operations have to be cooperations, each one doing his part. The cooperation involves the development of habits internal to the individual, and at the same time the development of a common ethos, an understanding of what the other fellow will do in the community. If you don't know what the other fellow is going to do, you don't know what to do yourself. You have to understand one another. As the community develops into ever larger scale you get the emergence of customs and laws and so on – regulations, arbitration, an external mechanism for community of decision. And that is on the habitual level: the internal habit and the habit of the community as a whole. The habits also involve personal relations – the personal relations of master and slave, of father and son, of husband and wife, of friends or companions.

The good of order so conceived is a flow of benefits, a flow of operations, suitable habits of knowing and willing and choosing and doing in individuals, suitable institutions, where institutions are understood as, as it were, the form uniting the individuals involved in this way of life. That good of order is an intelligible good, an object of a cluster of insights, and the cluster may be parceled out among several individuals. That is the good of order as it is in human living.

There is a third level, the level of choice. People write a *Utopia*. They desire things to be ordered in an entirely different way. And if you try to implement a utopia at once, well, you would be destroying the whole good of order that exists, and it would be a long time before you would have another. But there is always the question, Is the order we have disrupting? And it is always disrupting to some extent. Can it be improved? It always can be improved to some extent. And there, there arises the question of value. The whole order as it exists is a value, that is, something that can meet with rational approbation, something on the level of judgment. And the effective approbation is the act of will. Just as on the side of knowing you have experience, understanding, and judging, so with regard to the good you have the multiple good through objects of desire, you have the good of order in which these emerge, and you have *good in the sense of value*, which is the object of the practical judgment 'This is worthwhile' and the subsequent choice.

Now, having done so much we can say something about the question with which we started out. The pure desire to know can set up the good of order, and it can understand it, it can even understand suffering to a certain extent, but that *eros* of the mind, that pure desire to know, sets up exigences that are beyond our capacity for fulfilment in our present state. We understand that in terms of the doctrine of original sin. But the grace of God is both a remedy for the moral impotence we suffer as a result of original sin and also much more than that. It is a correction of the disintegrating and disruptive tendencies of human society and of individual living, but it also introduces that gratuitous self-donation of God, his initiative in loving us in the full sense, where love means something like quasi identification – the love of God in that sense of self-donation, like entering into the married state, living together, sharing one's life with another, and the quasi identification that that involves.

The incarnation is a first expression of God's self-donation to us. In the incarnation God gives himself to humanity. And the gift of the Holy Spirit at baptism, the instant of justification – the Holy Spirit being the love of God, the subsistent love of God – the gift of the Holy Ghost in sanctifying grace, in the state of sanctifying grace, is the personal self-donation of God to the individual soul, and that is charity on God's side, and at the same time it is the infusion of charity: the love of God is poured forth into your hearts by the Holy Spirit who is given to you (Romans 5.5).[13]

That gift, that pouring forth of charity, the love of God, into our hearts by the Holy Spirit who is given to us, is the gift of charity, the supernatural virtue of charity. It sets up a further good of order in this world, which is the mystical body of Christ and his church. So, just as this self-giving of God is something that lies beyond any possible exigence or conclusion, any possible exigence of human nature or conclusion of man's thinking about the world – loving in the full and intimate sense of the word involves a free initiative – so this mystical body of Christ is a further, higher integration of human living. It is the transition from the *civitas terrena* that can be constituted by a pure desire to know, to the *civitas Dei* that is founded on the love of God and the self-revelation of God.

7   Self-appropriation and the Christian

You leave much of this to the Epilogue in Insight, *and you move into these ideas without much intimation of where you are going till you get there. It seems to me that, in a philosophy that's based securely on self-appropriation, when a Christian appropriates himself, he is going to find at the very deepest level the mystery of faith, and that if he does this his philosophy will almost inevitably move along lines like Marcel, for example, a philosophy which issues positively from his Christian commitment and is a-metaphysical. Yet you seem to do without that. You work along lines that are not based on Christian commit-ment. Does the act of faith in any way make it difficult for a philosopher to do this?*

As I said the other day,[14] religion can be an enormous help, and it can

---

13   RSV: 'and hope does not disappoint us, because God's love has been poured into our hearts through the Holy Spirit which has been given to us' (Romans 5.5).
14   Wednesday, August 13. See lecture 8, § 1, The Underlying Problem.

be a hindrance, in self-appropriation. It can be a hindrance if there is not a religious development concomitant with the cultural development of the individual. If the individual develops as a child in a religious atmosphere, and then his religion remains at what was excellent in a child and is childish in a man, well, there is an obvious lack of balance in the total product, if as a man he is a very highly cultured individual. Now it could occur that such a person would not want to touch anything in his religion, would not want to develop on the intellectual side of his religion, because he would be afraid of upsetting everything, he might think it's essentially childish. – I'm afraid that is just feeling around. But, thinking the thing out, the question can be put in so many different ways. One might ask, 'Is there properly a distinction between philosophy and theology, once philosophy becomes concrete?'

That's really what I'm trying to ask.

Well, once philosophy becomes concrete, as it does in existentialism, you can't have ultimate answers without going into theology. The notion that philosophy is something that can be done by reason, by one's native endowments of intelligence and reasonableness, presupposes that your philosophic questions are restricted to the per se of human nature. As long as you keep your philosophic question bottled up within those limits, the enterprise is quite possible. As soon as your philosophic question, put upon the philosophic level, really admits no answer except beyond it, well, you are raising the type of question that moves one from one level to another, from one department to another. And such questions necessarily arise because all fields are related: while there may be many fields, still each of us has only one mind, and the other fields exist insofar as no particular field is going to answer all the questions that will arise in that mind.

How can one go about philosophic questions in the traditional sense without restricting philosophy to the per se? How can one conceive one's philosophy? Insofar as philosophy was restricted to the per se there was a considerable amount of essentialist influence. And that essentialist influence made it quite easy to restrict philosophy to the per se. Insofar as metaphysicians say, 'Well, your study of being is not a study of essences, it is the study of concrete existence,' you've pulled one of the pegs from underneath that other conception of philosophy. Insofar as that conception is concerned with man, it is concerned with human nature per se, as man would be in any state in which God might create him; then there are further details that regard man as existing in this world which we leave to the theologian.

How can that difficulty be handled? Well, I think one way of handling it is the method employed in *Insight*, namely, the moving viewpoint. You raise questions of a certain kind and carry them so far and broaden the issue. You do it again and again, and by the time you get to chapter 20 you jump over. And if you use the business of the moving viewpoint you can be dealing with the concrete and restricting yourself for a considerable period of time to issues that are purely philosophic. That use of the moving viewpoint has implications that become explicit only when I start talking about the method of metaphysics: it can't be a matter of a systematic deduction where you have the whole system at once, where you lay down your axioms and implicitly you immediately have the whole system. A moving viewpoint means that you have several starting points. Does that say something?

Yes, because it is a much less artificial distinction.

Yes, the approach in *Insight* is that idea of the moving viewpoint, and it evades the difficulty of saying, 'Well, in philosophy we are concerned, insofar as we speak of man, with man as he might be in any possible world,' which immediately creates enormous difficulties on any concrete approach to metaphysics or anything else. It is the type of conception that is associated with the method of Scotus; Thomas does not ask about possible worlds. With Scotus, unless you are asking about possible worlds, you are not doing science, because Scotus was concerned with necessary propositions that would be true in any possible world, and consequently, his discussions become scientific insofar as he is talking about any possible world. But you have an entirely different slant in Thomas. What Thomas is doing is seeking the intelligibility of *this world*, trying to see the wisdom of the divine plan and counsel in *this world* – just as the empirical scientist is not concerned with what the law of gravity *might* be, but with what de facto that intelligible law is in this world. Knowledge is a matter of asking *quid sit?* and *an sit?* and getting the answers, and repeating the questions on slightly different topics, gradually developing.

8   Historical Knowledge[b]

I was just thinking about historical knowledge. It is seldom in history that you can say, 'It is so.' You are almost continually saying, 'It seems' – although sometimes you can say, in a negative way, 'It is not so.' But in historical knowledge if you say, 'It seems,' then is that just a cluster of insights?

The problem of history as a science is an extremely complex problem. Collingwood in, I think, his *Idea of History*[15] – incidentally, he did some rather remarkable historical work, I believe, on the Roman wall in the north of Britain or something like that, so he *was* a historian – illustrates his concept of history as science, at least one aspect of it, by a detective story in which all the clues were planted and all the witnesses were lying. The detective's problem was to find out what really happened by seeing why the clues would be planted and why the people were lying. In other words, it was an idea of history that was independent of human testimony as something you can trust. And that is, as it were, one approach to the notion of history as a science.

You can have history that attempts to evaluate testimony: this fellow is trustworthy, and this fellow, we know from these other reasons, is quite unsound – and you can grade them in between.

There can be false ideals in historical inquiry. German exegetes during the nineteenth century spent a great deal of time trying to reach the historical Jesus, to get behind the gospel to what really happened and what really was said, and they came to the conclusion that it couldn't be done. You can't reach the historical Jesus. And, for example, in Brunner's *Mediator, Der Mittler*,[16] you have the contention – and there is something the same in *Insight*[17] too – that that type of historical aim is mistaken. It is not seeking to arrive at truth, it is seeking to reconstitute the image of the past, the cinema of the past, and the soundtrack of the past, where you haven't got the evidence for doing so. The astronomer with a great deal of very exact observation and measurement and very precise laws can occasionally discover the existence of a planet he can't see, by deduction. But you can't reconstitute the course of a lifetime from a set of documents which you don't believe in, and even when you do accept the documents as valid, well, you find all sorts of problems. That is the problem of history, a misconception of history, that can arise in terms of an empiricist attitude,

15 R.G. Collingwood, *The Idea of History* (Oxford: Clarendon, 1946) 266–74. For his historical work on the Roman wall, see Collingwood, *An Autobiography* (Oxford: Clarendon, 1939), chapter 11, Roman Britain.
16 H. Emil Brunner, *The Mediator: A Study of the Central Doctrine of the Christian Faith*, trans. Olive Wyon (London: Lutterworth Press, 1949).
17 *Insight* 582.

wanting to know, 'Well, what really happened?' In other words, 'Let us describe' is what he wants.

You can have history under a relativist influence – there is a celebrated Dutch historian, Huizinga, who in a volume dedicated to Ernst Cassirer entitled *Philosophy and History* had an essay, 'On the Nature of History,'[18] and it was to the effect that history is a culture interpreting its past to itself, and the interpretation varies with the present, so that you have German history of, say, 1810, 1840, 1870, 1900 – I'm picking the dates at random – because the German culture was in a different mood at these successive dates, and you have different interpretations of the past. They are *all* interpretations of the past, and they are all history, and there is no way of settling the matter. So you can also have the history of the French written by the French, you can get the history of the French written by the Germans, and so on. There are all sorts of interpretations of the past by the present. History is purely relativist.

Can there be an approach to history in terms of truth, the third level, judgment? I think that there can be. Just how much it can achieve, and so on, is a very complex question. It depends an awful lot on the type of thing you are investigating. But it's that question that to some extent I'm dealing with in the section of chapter 17 on canons of hermeneutics.[19] The fundamental problem is the problem of interpretation, and how you arrive at a correct interpretation. Insofar as there are counterpositions active and successful within the field of those writing history, insofar as most historians certainly would not be interested in any methodical discussion, this more or less puts the historians, the people who did the work, in the same class as the physicists who are very good at performing experiments but not so hot at the mathematics. A situation is created by quantum mechanics and relativity: the people who could do the experiments, for a while anyway, were complaining, 'I don't know what on earth I'm doing or what I'm doing it for, but these mathematicians know, and I know they can't perform these experiments. I'm doing the experiments and they are doing the thinking.' Well, if you could get an elaborate theory of the

18 Johan Huizinga, 'A Definition of the Concept of History,' in Raymond Klibansky and H.J. Paton, eds., *Philosophy of History: Essays Presented to Ernst Cassirer* (Oxford: Clarendon Press, 1936) 1–10.
19 *Insight*, chapter 17, §3.8, Some Canons for a Methodical Hermeneutics, pp. 586–94.

method of history, you could create something of a similar situation in history. But I wouldn't try to carry the question any further than that.

This problem of historical knowledge seems to be peculiarly pertinent to apologists.

It is. What occupies people a great deal is what is called fundamental theology: the history of the canon; the historical value of the gospels, and of the epistles of St Paul; the dates at which they were written, how you can establish it. There is what is called the lower and the higher criticism, the history of the texts, the families of the texts, and so on – their relative value, their distribution, how much you can infer was known of this particular writing of the New Testament by Ignatius of Antioch, who certainly lived at the end of the first century – indications from him – and so on. There are all sorts of criteria, and it is an extremely complicated business.

9   Isomorphism and Objectivity

I would like to get back to something you were talking about this morning.[20] I have seen some eyebrows raised about the isomorphism between the structure of knowing and the structure of being as being, not as known. Some think you are putting the cart before the horse.

I'm putting the cart before the horse[c] for people who know by taking a look!

There is a fundamental decision; you can't have it both ways. With regard to the precise issue: Is or is not being intelligible? If it is not, there is no reason for supposing that you could know it by understanding or by judgment, and, if it is something you can't know at all, then it is outside the field of possible questions or suspicions. It is nothing. Insofar as being is what is to be known by intelligent grasp and reasonable affirmation, then being is intelligible, because the intelligible is just *what* is grasped.

Now you can say that that being is really nothing, it is not the 'really real.' I can understand your difficulty. You want to say that that being is just a subjective activity: *I* understand, *I* make my judgment, *I* do all the understanding and judging as correctly as you please, and I arrive at judgments, and I say, 'This is, and that isn't,' 'This is, and that is,'

20 Lecture 9, § 1.4, Unity and Distinction.

and 'This is not that, and I am this.' And I get, by some quite incredible mystery, something that corresponds to what people think is the 'really real.' But still it is not the really real; I don't know the really real that way; when you really know it, you have an entirely different access to it.

That is a perfectly intelligible difficulty, and I think that is a very normal difficulty. But I spent a considerable part of my life dealing with it, and I have an account of it, I'm able to explain it. The 'real world' for people with that difficulty is what corresponds to one's *Sorge*, one's concern, and one's concern is not exclusively a matter of the pure desire to know. One's concern includes all of one's sensitivity, all of one's intersubjectivity, all of one's affectivity, and so on and so forth. It involves the whole man, not this tiny little thread of the pure desire to know that is found in us at times – when you do an awful lot of arguing and proving, then it's there. And that is what the real world corresponds to, and that real world is had by us in a more elevated fashion. It's also had by the animals – that familiarity with the real world by use and wont. And by intellect when necessary – when absolutely necessary you'll get down and think out a problem – but that is just an interruption of normal living!

I too am bothered by this. I feel that the question of isomorphism is not quite the same as the difficulty of objectivity. I'm not bothered about the objectivity now at all. Now I have a very simple and naive little analogy here that came into my head.

Well, just a moment.[21] Are you satisfied with this business on objectivity?

Yes.

Then who else wants more?

I have a pure desire to eat. I go to the butcher's and buy some meat which I cook and eat. Now in order to eat the meat I have to do three things: I have to obtain it, I have to cook it, I have to eat it; and that which I obtain is what I cook, and that which I cook is what I eat – there is a complete unity. Now one might argue that since I have had to perform three operations on the meat, there

21 The written word does not show what is happening here. Lonergan has been answering a difficulty on objectivity, when a third participant begins a question on isomorphism. Lonergan asks him to wait, till he is assured the question on objectivity has been dealt with to everyone's satisfaction. Then he turns to the discussion of isomorphism.

are three elements in the meat, one which I obtain, one which I cook, one which I eat [a passage omitted here] Now this is my puzzle. I am convinced in a sense by this isomorphism, because I happen to believe in potency, form, and act, and I happen to believe in your analysis of cognition, as far as I understand it, and there is a perfect, aesthetically delightful, dovetailing between the two, but what I don't quite see is the logical cogency of the leap from one to the other: I'm not denying at all that the fact that I understand it shows that it is intelligible. If someone says, 'Well, are you really sure that this meat is obtainable?' I say, 'Yes, I've got it,' and if they say, 'Well, are you really sure that this meat is able to be cooked?' I say, 'I cooked it,' and the same with eating: obviously it's eatable, because I've eaten it. Well, now, there is no question about the reality of the meat or the reality of the operations that I've carried out. The fact that I can be sure of the validity of my judgment is precisely granted me, as I see it, by the fact that, in the first place, the object of them is given, in the second place, that I understand them, and in the third place, that I have judged about them. There is no criterion outside this process by which I need satisfy myself about the objectivity. All I am worried about is this three-decker.

This business of the three components, the three decks, is grounded in the cognitional process. It is found in three acts. The three acts have not the same content: it is not meat, meat, meat. It is experiencing, and that content is an intelligible, but it is not an intelligible in itself, it is an intelligible in what will be grasped in the next step ...

Now that sounds to me, if I may barge in, as rather like saying that the meat insofar as I have bought it is not cooked, and I agree cooking it is something additional to buying it; but nonetheless it is all the meat that I have bought and all the meat that I have cooked. And supposing one wanted to offer an analysis of being, for example, simply as form and existence. We have to admit that perhaps not the whole of the being is intelligible; let us say, some being has form and some is formless – any absurd metaphysical supposition you like. Maybe it is there on other grounds, but how can I guarantee that the elements in the being correspond precisely to these three elements in knowing without getting Kantian?

Well, what do you mean by getting Kantian?

I mean without regarding what I say about being as justified simply on the grounds that this is the only way that my framework of knowledge allows me to understand it. In other words, without saying, 'Well, the noumenal may not be as I take it to be; I can't really say anything about the ultimate structure of being as it really is; all I can say is that the being which I experience as I experience it has this structure.' I can see that. But we are claiming not to be Kantian, and I haven't been under the impression that you have been Kantian, but I am not quite certain how one can escape being Kantian at this particular point.

Well, I'm not certain that you wouldn't be more correct if you thought I was Kantian, in your sense. Insofar as the objection to Kant is that Kant introduces categories which the mind imposes or adds to the intuitions of sense, and if he didn't have this imposition of categories from the mind, if his knowing was purely intuition, then his doctrine would be all right – that is one objection to Kant, and I think it is mistaken. I think what is wrong with Kant is not that he doesn't make enough of intuition but that he makes too much of it, that he makes so much of it that he doesn't grasp the full significance of judgment. The argument about the structure of being is from the structure of the mind. If you want to say that this being with this structure is merely a product of the mind, and not a knowledge of what really is, then the difficulty about the objectivity of my notion of being recurs – and that is the difficulty I was dealing with. Insofar as that difficulty about objectivity is answered, then there is no possibility of any *argument*, that is, any appeal to intelligence and reason, that can produce a real that's distinct from what has already been named being. Does that meet the issue?

It certainly throws a certain amount of light on my difficulty. I find it too complex at the moment to be sure whether I have followed you right through.

It is a crucial point in the business. These things become clearer by taking a step further and going into the metaphysics. Why is it that our minds are capable, by understanding and judgment, of knowing what really is? It is because they are created participations of the uncreated light. St Augustine held that we knew truth not by looking outside us, but within, and not properly looking within but in a changeless light, an incommutable light, contemplating the eternal reasons.[22] And St Thomas takes up this doctrine, which was current among Augustinians in the Middle Ages, and he says, 'Do we look at the eternal reasons? Do we judge things by the eternal reasons?' When Eisenhower said, 'We have to be men,' he wasn't appealing to what we

22 Augustine, *Confessions*, 7, 10 (PL 32, 742).

are, he was appealing to what we *have to be*. And that is a simple type of example of what Augustine meant by knowing things in the eternal reasons – it is Platonist, somewhat, in its inspiration. And, St Thomas says, we judge things by the eternal reasons not in the sense that we take a look at the eternal reasons, but in the sense that the very light of our intelligence is a created participation of the uncreated light that is God himself.[23] Just as the uncreated light that is God himself is the ground of all possibility and actuality – it is a real omnipotence – so this created participation of the eternal light, that *is* our intelligence, that comes to light in intelligent and rational consciousness, is an *intentional* omnipotence, a capacity to ask questions about everything and, by understanding and forming concepts and making judgments, to know them.

I think, actually, what I had failed to see is that the answer to this question of the isomorphism is precisely the same as the answer you gave a while ago about objectivity.

True, but the question of isomorphism is a further question, and it has several angles, and they are not all the same. One of the angles is the question of objectivity, but it is not the only one.

  Let us try, therefore, to distinguish the different stages in this iso-morphism.[24] We have three levels in our cognitional process, an experiential, an intellectual, and a rational. And to take the simplest type of example, we will suppose that there does exist a perfect circle, and on the experiential level we see it, and we see radii drawn, and we see measurements made, and they are not accurate just to so many decimal places – we will suppose that they are accurate to *infinite* decimal places. The conclusion is that every one we measure – and we will suppose that we measure an infinity of them: put the thing in the concrete, measurements made an infinite number of times, all coming out equal. That is on the level of experience; it is a matter of seeing: seeing the figure, seeing the ruler, the measuring instruments set beside it, the tests made, and so on. Then there is an intellectual level, in which we grasp the necessity of roundness, which is an appearance, as following from the equality of the radii. Here what we know is

23 See, for example, *Summa theologiae*, 1, q. 84, a. 5 c., from which Lonergan had quoted a relevant phrase, *Verbum* 74; other references, *Verbum* 84, note 175.
24 Lonergan explained his point with the help of a blackboard diagram.

necessity. The intellectual level adds necessity, an intelligible necessity, linking different data. We ask whether in this instance that necessity really is found, and we reach the virtually unconditioned. There
is a necessity if on inspection this is perfectly round, if there are no
bumps or dents – we make the tests on the curve, and the radii are
really equal; we suppose that those tests can be made – they can't, but
we are just doing an illustration. We reach fact, the virtually
unconditioned.

There is the element, then, of data, intelligible necessity, and fact;
you can have intelligible possibility just as well, if you are considering
the empirical unity, and fact, as with the law of gravitation.

Now we have three acts, or three levels of activity, and they presuppose one another – just as cooking the meat presupposes buying it, and
eating it presupposes cooking it. These three levels are mutually
related, and complementary – the second presupposes and complements the first, the third presupposes and complements the second, as
cognitional activities. As contents they yield the judgment 'This is a
circle,' or whatever you please. 'This in fact is a circle; it satisfies the
definition of a circle.' The circle is the reality affirmed. Insofar as
these three coalesce as components – not merely in one process of
knowing, three acts, but as contents – we have the three components
relevant to what we mean by this existing circle.

Now those three components are distinct as notions, they are notion-
ally distinct. With regard to the three components as contents in my
mind, you can say that P is not Q and P is not R and Q is not R, where
P, Q, and R are these three, and you consider them as notions – there
is a notional distinction, as contents in the mind. And the proof is that
what is grasped here, what is grasped by insight, is intelligible in itself;
the data are not intelligible in themselves, they are merely given, they
are intelligible in the other. One and the same cannot have contradictory predicates. A cannot be both B and not-B. You cannot say the
content 'data' and the content 'intelligible necessity' are really just
one content with two predicates, two aspects, because the aspects are
contradictory: one is intelligible in itself, the other is not, and intelligibility is a relevant predicate to these contents.

Similarly fact, again, is a content that is not intelligible in itself. It is
intelligible in the other, but it is not intelligible in the other in the
same way as data are intelligible in the other. The data become intelligible within the form, but the fact leads you to further questions for its

intelligibility – Who produced this perfect circle? and so on. That is a further type of question: you have to account for the fact. So we have three distinct contents.

Now, when one considers the being posited by the judgment, one includes the three contents in what one knows about the being. One can ask, Are those contents intrinsically constitutive of the being or are they not? If they are intrinsically constitutive of the being then we have three mutually exclusive components that are intrinsically constitutive of the being. If they are not intrinsically constitutive of the being, then the being lies outside the field of possible knowledge, because all you know about the being is what you know through data, understanding, and judgment.

You had something?[25]

It's not about the isomorphism, it's about the objectivity – the argument concerning objectivity. Is it the same sort of argument you use with the sceptic when you get him to talk, and he involves himself in contradictions?

Fundamentally it is.

In one case there is a dialogue, and in the other there need not be.

Yes.

Well, is it not confusing? Here you are in an analytic type of thinking – you are not concerned so much with the fact of knowledge –

I am concerned not with the fact of knowledge in general; I am concerned with whether this particular theory of knowledge is a fact.

Yes, but I think the questions generally regard the factualness of this bit of knowledge or that bit of knowledge of anybody who happens to know something, and in your theory you have an analytic component, that is to say, there must be a proportion between the known and the knower, and that does not regard the factualness of any bit of knowledge, it regards the analysis of knowing or the relationship between the known and the knower.

Well, yes, but it is the sort of thing that is established by an argument of that type, is it not?

Yes, but my point is this, that when you answer these questions by having recourse

---

25 Lonergan invites another participant to bring up a question he had tried earlier to raise.

to an analysis of knowing, I think it is confusing a little to those who are
concerned with the fact of knowing. The only answer to the fact of knowing is
the question as to involving yourself in contradiction.

Well, as I understand the question, it is this. I'm concerned with working out an analysis of exactly what knowledge is and I'm presupposing
the fact. I'm not concerned to refute the sceptics. This argument about
the objectivity is the same type of argument as is employed in refuting
the sceptic, therefore – is that the difficulty?

Well, it's the point on which I'm talking.

Well, the answer to it is this, that insofar as I am analyzing knowledge
I analyze the act of insight and its relevance in chapters 1 to 8, and
judgment in chapters 9 and 10, and I come to the fact that understanding is as described to some extent, and judgment is as described, in the
affirmation of the knower – each one satisfies himself that he has a
certain amount of intelligence and reasonableness that he can not get
rid of. And the fact comes up there.

Then the question of objectivity arises naturally. It is a real problem.
It's a problem created by the polymorphism of the human subject – the
fact that he's a subject that develops, and has equilibria of different
kinds according to his development, and there are conversions in the
process.

And there, there arises the point of positions and counterpositions.
Really, the argument about the objectivity of knowledge is showing it's
a counterposition, and counterposition is part of the technique of doing
metaphysics – the distinction between position and counterposition.
This business of counterposition ultimately does reduce itself to the
same type of thing as Aristotle's argument with the sceptic: Get him to
talk.[26]

When you say there's a real problem of objectivity, then you mean there is a real
problem of defining it.

There's a problem of defining objectivity, first; and, secondly, there's
a problem of accepting it.

Of accepting that definition.

---

26 *Metaphysics*, IV, 4, 1005b 35 to 1006a 28. See also lecture 6 above, § 1.3,
   Self-affirmation.

Yes.

Yes, but that's a question of knowledge in general. But it's not a problem for any particular item of knowledge. People know spontaneously, and there's no question ...

Oh, yes. Yes. You mean the question of immediate realism?

Yes.

In other words, we know being ...[27]

---

27 The was reel brings us to this point, but runs out in midsentence. The DJS reel had run out several lines earlier (at 'intelligence and reasonableness he cannot get rid of'), and the LRI reel some lines before that (at 'as I understand the question, it is this').

Lexicon of Latin and Greek
Words and Phrases

Translations were sometimes given by Lonergan in a free style, and we use these (indicated by 'L'), even though they have not a dictionary correctness. Words and phrases commonly found in English dictionaries are not included.

Latin Words and Phrases

a simultaneo: by simultaneous (meaning), by definition (L: from the concept itself)

actio: action, activity

actio dicitur dupliciter: 'action' is used in two senses

actio dicitur tripliciter: 'action' is used in three senses

an sit? quid sit? is it? what is it?

auditus ad audiendum: hearing for hearing (L: the relation of the faculty of hearing to the act of hearing)

bene esse: to be in a good state (L: not just existence, but fruitful existence - applied to philosophy)

bonum est id quod omnia appetunt: the good is that which everything desires

causa, causae: cause, causes

causa/ratio cognoscendi, essendi: the cause/reason of knowing, of being

civitas Dei: the heavenly city (city of God)

civitas terrena: the earthly city (realm)

cogito, ergo sum: I think, therefore I am

cognitio ex datis ... cognitio ex principiis: knowledge from data ... knowledge from principles

cognoscere: to know, knowing
compositio ex causis: assembly (synthesis) out of causes (elements)
conditiones materiae: the conditions (of being) of anything material (space and time)
cuius gratia: (that) for the sake of which

dicere: to speak, to utter a word (interiorly: to formulate a concept)
distinctio formalis a parte rei: a formal distinction from the side of the thing

ens: being (i.e., a being)
ens est id quod est: a being is that which is
ens per essentiam: being whose essence is being
ens per participationem: a being that participates in being
esse: to be, being
essentia: essence
est: it is

finis cuius (gratia): the end for the sake of which
finis qui: the end which (attracts)
finis quo: the mode in which the end (attracts)

habitus est quo quis utitur quando voluerit: habit is that which one can exercise at will
habitus principiorum: habitual knowledge of principles
hic homo non intelligit: this man doesn't understand
homo prout sempternis rationibus esse debeat: man as, according to the eternal standards, he ought to be

id a quo: that from which
id quo: that by which
id quo est: that by which (a thing) is
id quod: that which
id quod est: that which is
id quod omnia appetunt: that which everything desires (L)
id quod operatur: that which acts
idem est intelligens et intellectum: see in his quae . . .
in his quae sunt sine materia, idem est intelligens et intellectum: in the immaterial order, the understander and the understood are identical (L)
intellectus agens: agent intellect (for Lonergan: spirit of inquiry)
intellectus possibilis: intellect as receiving
intelligentia intelligentiae: understanding of understanding
intelligere: to understand, understanding

intelligibile in sensibilibus: the intelligible in the sensible (L)
intelligit: he understands
intentio entis: intention of being
ipsum esse: being itself
ipsum intelligere: understanding itself **(ipsum esse, ipsum intelligere** may be used of God, but may also be used in a finite sense when the meaning is simply intensive)

materia individualis: individual matter
motus: motion, change, activity
motus coniuncti: change in (or activity of) the composite (i.e., of the ensouled organ)
motus in imaginem est idem ac motus in imaginatum: motion (tendency) toward the image is identical with motion toward what is imaged

non asserendo sed recitando: not affirming but reporting

omnia: all things

per accidens, per se: (occurring) by chance, (occurring) as a rule
percipi: to be perceived
potens omnia facere et fieri: able to create all things and to become all things
priora quoad nos: the things that are first in regard to us
priora quoad se: the things that are first in themselves
prius quoad nos: the first for us (see **priora quoad nos**)
propter quid: that on account of which (i.e., the explanatory cause)
puer aeternus: eternal boy

qualis quisque est, talis finis videtur ei: 'the end appears to each man in a form answering to his character' (Ross translation of Greek)
qualis unusquisque est, talis et finis videtur ei: (variant of **qualis quisque . . .**)
qui, quo: see **finis qui, finis quo**
quid: what
quid est? what is it?
quid sit? what is it? what might it be?
quid sit Deus? what is God
quidditas: the essence, quiddity (whatness)
quo: by which
quoad nos, quoad se: in regard to us, in regard to themselves
quod: which
quod quid erat esse: what a thing was to be (the Ross translation of Aristotle has simply 'the essence')

recitando, non asserendo: reporting, not affirming
recta ratio agibilium: correct judgment on human behavior (L: correct human behavior)
res extensa: a thing with extension (in space)
resolutio in causas: breakdown (analysis) into causes (elements)

sensibilia propria: the objects proper to particular senses (as color is proper to sight, in contrast to size which is perceived by both sight and touch)
si non intelligit, non est audiendus: if he doesn't understand, there's no reason why we should listen to him (L)
simpliciter: simply (not from some particular viewpoint)
species: species, form
species impressa: a species imprinted (on the mind)

verbum complexum: a composite word (i.e., a judgment)
verbum interius: inner word (for Lonergan: concept or judgment)
verbum: word
verum est medium in quo cognoscitur ens: truth is the medium in which we know the real (L)

Greek Words and Phrases

aition tou einai: the cause of being
alloiôsis: alteration
dioti: that on account of which (see **propter quid**)
epistêmê: understanding (L)
hen: the One
heurisko: I find
kata symbebêkos: per accidens, coincidentally, the 'as it happens'
logos: word, idea, reason
morphê: form
noêsis noêseôs: understanding of understanding
nous: intelligence (L)
ousia: essence
sophia: wisdom
syllogismos epistêmonikos: explanatory syllogism (L)
synesis: (moral) judgment
to on: the being, the real
to ti estin: what something is (L: definition)

Editorial Notes

The purpose of these notes is indicated in the preface to the volume (p. xviii). The number in square brackets at the beginning of each note gives the page to which the note refers. References to Lonergan's works are abbreviated, but full data follow below in Works of Lonergan Referred to in Editorial Notes.

As in volume 4 of the Collected Works, the notes are seen as having a transitional value. Further, the value varies with the reader's need – one can only try to conceive the needs of a general reader, and provide notes that are a happy mean between too much and too little.

Lecture 1

a [4] **method ... achievement:** this early reference to method as subsequent to achievement is later expanded: 'There is ... a paradox ... in the very notion of a scientific method ... normally scientific development is a jump ahead of scientific method. Performance comes first. Once performance occurs ... there follows reflection. Only as a series of diverse reflections are pieced together, do there begin to emerge ... the prescriptions of a scientific method' (1985b: 13, in 'Method: Trend and Variations').

b [5] **a natural desire to know:** this desire, traced back to Aristotle here, is a key idea in Lonergan's Thomist studies (see, for example, 1967a: 53, 81, 86–87), notably in the context of the natural desire to see God (whence the paper with that title, 1988: 81–91). *Verbum* (1967a: 35, note 160) links Aristotle and Aquinas on this point.

c [7] **theorems:** a word with a long history in Lonergan. His 1940 dissertation defined it as the scientific elaboration of a common notion (1985a: 19) and illustrated it by the theorem of the supernatural, so fundamental in his theology of grace and in theology in general. Its subsequent history can be followed in *Insight* (1957a: 742), *De intellectu et methodo* (1959a: 64, where it is distinguished from single hypotheses as an overarching view), etc. The term does not occur in his student writings in the *Blandyke Papers*, but its use in the present volume suggests a link with the interest in Euclid characteristic of that early period.

d [8] **science ... knowledge ... through ... causes:** A preoccupation of Lonergan at this time was the evolution of the very notion of science, as distinct from the evolution of the sciences themselves. As early as the *verbum* articles he had seen that conceptualists stressed Aristotelian certitude, while neglecting the Aristotelian knowledge through causes that requires understanding (1967a: 211). But he came to see the need of a radical critique of Aristotle. A month earlier he had lectured at Marquette University on The Nature of Knowledge in the Natural Sciences (1958); his course the following year (Gregorian University, 1958–59) lined up a series of stages in the evolving notion, from pre-Aristotelian ideas through Aristotle and Newton to modern times (1959a: 26–30; see also 70–71); the sixth in the education lectures of the following summer (1959b) was on The Notion of Science, with a long section on The Transformation of the Notion of Science. There is a particular question on the scientific status of philosophy and theology; see note *c* to lecture 4 below. On the general question see also note *h* to lecture 4, note *i* to discussion 4 below, and note *e* to chapter 2 of *Collection* (1988: 260–61).

e [9] **order of discovery ... order of doctrine:** Lonergan's own Trinitarian theology (1964a) is structured throughout by this pair of notions; the order of discovery, *via analytica*, structures the first volume, and the order of doctrine, *via synthetica*, structures the second (see the whole first chapter of that second volume, pp. 7–64). A succinct guide to the pair and their application to the Trinity is the 1954 essay 'Theology and Understanding' (1988: 114–32, esp. 117–27), but the idea goes back to the early work *De ente supernaturali* (1946), which is structured in the order of doctrine, and to the 1946–49 Thomist studies (1967a: 61–65, 206–14).

f [11] **essentialism:** briefly refuted already in a *verbum* article (1947b: 412–13; 1967a: 105–106), this ism became a special target in the 1949 paper 'The Natural Desire to See God' (1988: 81–91; ibid. 270–71: notes *h*, *i*, and *j* to that paper; also ibid. 106, in 'A Note on Geometrical Possibility'). Very interesting is the remark of 1958, 'You will find that in *Insight* this radical rejection of essentialism is worked out in detail' (1988: 149) – interesting because the word 'essentialism' does not occur in *Insight*! 'Essentialist' occurs in the lectures Intelligence and Reality (1951a: 16), but only as one in a list of philosophies.

Relevant to the whole question is Lonergan's repeated reference to Scotus as studying possible worlds, in contrast to Thomas Aquinas who studied the actual world: Scotus and 'the deduction of the abstract metaphysics of all possible worlds' (1957a: 406), and 'we are committed to the sobriety of Aquinas ... and ... reject as methodologically unsound the Scotist view that a question becomes scientific when it is raised with respect to all possible worlds' (ibid. 679; see also 1964b: 554–55, 563). This in turn is relevant to the question of the absolute power of God, or what God could do in the series of possible universes: 'Distinctio inter potentiam absolutam et potentiam ordinatam non invenitur apud S. Thomam' (1959a: 30); but 'fourteenth-century theologians ... were forever distinguishing between what God could do absolutely and what he may be expected to do in this ordered universe ... since God absolutely could do anything that did not involve a strict contradiction, there rapidly followed first scepticism and then decadence' (1973b: 6; see also 30–31). On possibility see notes *l* and *r* to chapter 6 of *Collection* (1988: 273–74, 274–75).

g [15] **presence to oneself:** see note *n* to chapter 11 of *Collection* (1988: 293), on the history of this idea in Lonergan; add to that note a reference to *De constitutione Christi* on consciousness as that 'per quam subiectum ... sibi praesens efficitur' (1956: 131); also ' ... eo ipso quod subiectum ... operatur, semper sibi praesens efficitur ex parte subiecti ... ' (ibid.) In the lecture at Marquette University, presence to self is equated with consciousness (1958: §§ 20–23). Lonergan's first stab at this problem was perhaps in the notes *De conscientia Christi*; here he speaks of the presence of operations – 'ipsae operationes ... quodammodo adsunt. Quae operationum praesentia est duplex' (1952a: 4, § 10) – and goes on to a distinction (later dropped) between experience (passive aspect of operation) and consciousness (active aspect).

The related question of the presence of person to person is studied in *Divinarum personarum conceptio analogica* (1957b: 230–32), in the context of the indwelling of the divine persons. The same work refers to consciousness as presence to oneself (166).

h [16] **rational self-consciousness:** this is Lonergan's usual term in his *Insight* period for what he will later call responsible (fourth-level) consciousness, though the term is sometimes used for the total range of consciousness: 'What on earth is meant by rational self-consciousness ... by inviting it to take possession of itself?' (1957a: xix). Some readers have found the usage strange, and Thomas Daly suggests the possibility that it was an import from Hegel (*The Phenomenology of Mind*, v, B: The Realization of Rational Self-Consciousness through Its Own Activity); see *Insight* [1957a: 611], where, after listing the ways one becomes empirically, intellectually, and rationally conscious, Lonergan goes on: 'But I become rationally self-conscious inasmuch as I am concerned with reasons for my own acts.' It is worth noting that in chapter 18 Lonergan oscillates between 'rationally' and 'morally' self-conscious: 'So it is that the empirically, intelligently, rationally conscious subject ... becomes a morally self-conscious subject' (ibid. 599); this is very close to 'responsibly' conscious, and of course responsibility is a topic: 'freedom possesses not only the negative aspect of excluding necessity but also the positive aspect of responsibility' (619).

There is a history to be written on consciousness of 'self' and its evolution in Lonergan's thought. The idea appears in the *De conscientia Christi* (1952a: 5), 'Quarto, de conscientia sui ... ,' and (ibid. 6), 'Qui enim est et sui conscius est ... '; but the interest there is in Christ's consciousness of the beatific vision rather than in his consciousness of self. It appears also, though not in so many words, in chapter 11 of *Insight*: an 'obscure yet familiar awareness' of what I mean by 'I'; '"I" has a rudimentary meaning from consciousness' (1957a: 328); I judge this chapter to be written after *De conscientia Christi*, but before August 1953. The idea comes finally into sharp focus in *De constitutione Christi*: 'conscientia est sui suorumque actuum experientia stricte dicta et interna' (1956: 83); and this clarity is carried into the present work (lecture 6, § 1.2, The Unity of the Subject as Given), where the consciousness of self is concomitant in all conscious activities. Usage, however, remains fluid: Lonergan can say in the Halifax lectures that we become conscious of self on the level of decision (lecture 1, § 1.6, Summary: 21), where he means that the self is responsibly involved in a new way on the level of decision.

See also notes *b* and *e* to lecture 10 below (self-involvement, moral consciousness, etc.), note *a* to lecture 10 below (levels of consciousness, self-consciousness and self-knowledge).

i [16] **looking:** numerous references are found in the Index of *Insight* (1957a: under Knowing and looking); a succinct account is given in *Collection* (1988: 214–19), in the chapter 'Cognitional Structure'; see also note *c* to discussion 5 below.

j [18] **talk ... get the thing cleared up:** see *Insight* (1957a: 290), 'Talking is a basic human art; by it each reveals what he knows and provokes from others the further questions that direct his attention to what he had overlooked.'

k [23] **the diagram:** an echo of what Lonergan wrote as a student thirty years earlier, 'The Form of Mathematical Inference' (1928a: 126–37); there, after several references to visualizing the figure in order to understand the proof, he drew the modest conclusion, 'the diagram is more important than ... is ordinarily believed' (134–35). Thus, in his very first 'publication' he is already on the track of insight into phantasm. Possibly Fr Charles O'Hara alerted him to the significance of the diagram; see *Caring* (1982: 2).

l [25] **take all possible positions:** this 'imaginative experiment,' as he called it a few lines earlier, is another echo of his first writing; there, dealing with the very same problem in geometry, he invites us, in what he called 'a kinetic generic image,' to 'imagine the line CB [the side of the triangle] swinging round as on a pivot ... Every instant we see a different triangle and in the infinity of triangles seen' we find our proof (1928a: 134). It is still 'insight into phantasm,' but the phantasm now is moving. See also note *b* to lecture 2 below.

m [25] **You just see facts or the factual:** 'fact' is used loosely here (see also discussion 1, § 9, Appropriation: The Word, the Act, 272), perhaps in the sense of 'mere matters of fact' (1957a: 652); quite different is the sense of 'that clear, precise, definitive, irrevocable, dominant something that we name fact' (ibid. 331), where 'fact' is the virtually unconditioned following on what is intelligently grasped. See *Insight* on 'the lucid, fully rational factualness that contrasts so violently with the brute factualness' of the empirical residue (ibid. 517). Note also that in *Insight* 'fact' covers both existence and occurrence (1988: 152).

Lecture 2

a [36] **self-affirmation:** Lonergan's ways of dividing his book, or sections of it, vary with his purpose; here he would show the movement through the stages of cognitional process: the nest of terms in the first two levels (chapters 1–8), the terms of the third level (9–10), actual third-level exercise of judgment (11). A few years later he saw the book as dealing with three questions: cognitional theory (the three levels of this become one question), epistemology, and metaphysics (1974: 37, in a 1967 paper). There is still some variation, however, in his divisions: in a paper at the University of Guelph (1973c), he saw cognitional theory as handled in chapters 1–8, epistemology in chapters 9–13, and metaphysics in chapters 14–17, with chapters 18–20 a separate division said to be improved and revised in *Method in Theology*; but a letter of September 14, 1977, to Timothy Lynch (used here with the latter's permission) gives the divisions as 1–10 (cognitional theory), 11–13 (epistemology), and 14–17 (metaphysics).

Michael Vertin recalls a lecture to the Canadian Philosophical Association, May 31, 1974, with a division similar to that of the Guelph paper, but suggests that we not 'read too much into a remark intended simply to supply an intelligible, if only approximate, characterization of a very complex book to an audience ... largely unfamiliar with the historical and systematic context of Lonergan's approach' (personal communication). – Advice we may adapt and apply to any attempt to divide the book too exactly according to the hindsight provided by later questions. (As we go to press, we learn that there exists a tape recording of the 1974 lecture.)

In any case, at the time of writing *Insight* the two main divisions (Insight as Activity, Insight as Knowledge) were said to answer the two questions 'What is happening when we are knowing? ... What is known when that is happening?' (1957a: xxii). For detailed divisions, there are summaries passim throughout the book; see also '*Insight* Revisited' (1974: 267–76), and 'An Interview with Fr. Bernard Lonergan, s.j.' (ibid. 221–22).

b [37] **move the circles towards one another:** another example of Lonergan's 'kinetic image' (see note *l* to lecture 1), but with a difference; in the previous example the image moved through an 'infinite' number of possibilities in one range, to show what 'must' be in all of them; here the image moves through an infinite number of possibilities in various ranges, but only in one range have we the complexity of conditions required for the intersection of the circles.

c [40] **would not deal with that answer at this time:** Lonergan's notes for his lectures on existentialism at Boston College the previous year have three pages setting forth Husserl's position, followed by a page, Critique of Husserl's 'Krisis' (1957d: 7–9, 10).

d [44] **understanding what phenomenologists are doing:** the same Boston College lectures put it succinctly, 'Phenomenology is an account, description, presentation of the data structured by insight' (11).

e [49] **syllogism ... not simply a matter of valid conclusions:** this was a long-time concern of Lonergan, going back to his student paper 'The Syllogism' (1928b), where already there was a search for the intelligent factor that distinguished the operation of syllogizing from the operation of a slot-machine (35), and a concern 'to take the reason as acting only because of a reason' (36). It was this paper (not 'The Form of Mathematical Inference') that was thoroughly reworked and published fifteen years later as 'The Form of Inference'; though it dealt with logic, Lonergan regarded it as 'a first step in working out an empirical theory of human understanding and knowledge' (1988: 16); see also the 1954 paper 'Theology and Understanding' (ibid. 114–32), where he labels it 'a grave mistake to suggest that there is some opposition between understanding and Aristotle's syllogism' (117).

f [51] **the cause of a thing's being something:** 'On being something' is the title of a sheaf of seven pages in the Lonergan Archives (Batch 1-A, Folder 6); they predate the summer of 1953 when Lonergan moved from

Toronto to Rome; topics are 'being something' as limited, as specified, the being of something as contingent, as empirical, etc.

Lecture 3

a [77] **indeterminacy is not presupposed:** *Insight* (1957a: 93) speaks of 'the indeterminacy of abstract classical laws and the nature of the consequent statistical residues' – where statistical theory clearly presupposes indeterminacy. But that refers to the order of knowledge; see also: 'the concrete cannot be deduced in its full determinacy from any set of systematic premises' (99); 'classical laws can be applied to concrete situations only by adding further determinations derived from the situations,' which determinations have a 'non-systematic character' (100). Indeterminacy does not, then, regard the ontological order: it 'does not mean that the further determinations are not related to one another by law' (100–101). It is the ontological order that is in view in the present text, for Lonergan goes on at once to say, 'The mechanics of tossing a coin or of casting dice is an entirely determinate process.'

b [81] **other canons ... the same chapter:** five of these six canons pertain to the classical phase of empirical method; the lectures, Intelligence and Reality, given while *Insight* was in preparation, have two 'basic principles' instead of the six canons (1951a: 7). The principle of 'exclusion' corresponds closely to the canon of selection, admitting 'only systems that involve precisely defined sensible difference.' But the principle of 'relevance' is not as clearly thought out (ibid.); it seems to combine elements of the canon of relevance (seeking what he will call immanent intelligibility), of the canon of operations (ongoing: additional data, higher viewpoints), and of the canon of parsimony (empirical terms must 'admit experimental proof'). In fact, one can easily combine or differentiate at will aspects represented by different canons. In this very paragraph of his Halifax lecture Lonergan introduces into the canon of selection an element from the canon of parsimony: his 'second elimination' rejects theories 'that ... are not verified.' Indeed, he can also forget his own usage: Quentin Quesnell has noted (personal communication) that in chapter 17 of *Insight* he uses canon of relevance when he means canon of parsimony (1957a: 582, line 8) – possibly a carry-over from his 1951 usage.

c [82] **sensible consequences:** speaking here of empirical science in the stricter sense, Lonergan limits the relevant data to those of sense, but his generalized empirical method, so basic to his views on science, includes the data of consciousness as well (1957a: xi, 72, 243, 333, 382, 423; see note *c* to lecture 4 below).

In the Regis College lectures he gave while writing the book, Lonergan apparently explained why the canon of selection limits science to the field of the 'testable': 'Why only sensible data? – traditional – data of consciousness have same structure but are personal' (1952b: 25; from lecture §5 – undated, but §4 is dated December 9, 1952, and §6, January 13, 1953).

Lecture 4

a [93] **a problem:** the problem is handled in a complex set of divisions and subdivisions. Our analysis, and the basis of our editing, is as follows. The immediate dilemma regards the inclusion of mathematics and science in the operations studied for self-appropriation. Objections to including them are handled briefly, but when Lonergan argues in favor of their inclusion he presents an objective aspect (94–98) and a subjective (98–103). The objective subdivides into abstract and concrete considerations, but it is 'minor' compared to the 'fundamental' question of the subjective side (98, 99).

b [94] **enough ... common to everyone:** the 'enough' sounds like a content of common sense, but *Method in Theology* makes a precise distinction here. 'As a style ... common sense is common to mankind. But as a content ... common sense is common not to mankind but to the members of each village' (1972: 272–73). 'So there are as many brands of common sense as there are differing places and times. What is common to common sense is, not its content, but its procedures' (303). – There is a parallel distinction to be made in the 'specialization' of common sense. Both now and later, common sense as a type of knowing is called a specialization in the concrete and practical; see *Insight* (1957a: 175, 180 [with specialized departments], 226, and passim); also discussion 3 below, §9, Common Sense and History: 'common sense is a specialization in the concrete and practical' (323–24); discussion 4, §13, Common Sense: 'common sense is another specialization of human understanding. It's for dealing with the concrete in practical living' (361). Likewise in later work: 'the *commonsense* development of intelligence that specializes in the concrete and immediate' (1985b: 37, in 'Aquinas Today ... '). But besides the specialization of common sense as a single type, there are also the many specializations of the brands within common sense: 'Because common sense is so specialized, there are diversities of common sense,' and 'The notion of specializations of common sense' shows how incomprehension results when classes are stratified (lecture 4 of this volume, §2, Common Sense as Intellectual: 91). But Lonergan is moving to a usage in which specialization applies par excellence to science: 'Science is the clear-cut paradigm of specialization' (1985b: 40, in 'Aquinas

Today ... '); common sense as a type is called undifferentiated consciousness (1972: 272), whereas in *Insight* (1957a: 180) it was a differentiation, and the varieties are the 'brands' referred to above (1972: 276).
A thematic treatment of specialization is found in *A Third Collection*
(1985b: 36–40, in 'Aquinas Today ... ').

c [94] **a scientific pursuit:** the intention here, it seems, is to apply this label
to philosophy; in any case, Lonergan rejected the claim of the natural
sciences to the exclusive use of this label. A first point, 'as there are
sciences of nature, so also there is a science of man. As the sciences of
nature are empirical, so also the science of man is empirical'; but if its
practitioners 'rule out of court a major portion of the data' (those of
consciousness), they 'deny the empirical principle' (1957a: 235; but
see note c to lecture 3 above). Further, chapter 16 of *Insight* has the
title Metaphysics as Science, and theology is considered 'queen of the
sciences' (743).
   Frequently, however, science is used in distinction from philosophy;
further, along with Lonergan's evolving notion of science (see note d to
lecture 1 above), there is developed the notion of scholarship (1972:
233–34), so that he will list '*scientific ... scholarly ... philosophic*' as three distinct developments (1985b: 37, in 'Aquinas Today ... '). As for theology,
when the question came up in the Dublin lectures on *Method* in 1971,
Lonergan remarked 'that there are eight functional specialties in theology, and that you do very different things in each one of the eight. I think
we had better go through the eight before we decide what parts of
theology can be called scientific and what parts can be called scholarly,
and what can be more safely referred to as "academic disciplines"' (1971b:
question 1 of session 2, August 3).

d [94] **quasi speculative ... really ... practical fashion of common sense:**
this is an edited version; Lonergan's phrase was 'the speculativo-practi-
cal fashion of common sense.' He may be referring to the 'omnicompetence' of common sense, in which case the relevant locus is the section
on commonsense eclecticism as a philosophy (1957a: 416–21); see also
his remarks on linguistic analysis as a philosophy (1972: 254–56).

e [96] **the fundamental theological problem ... is a problem of integration:**
Lonergan gave various expressions to the fundamental problem, and saw
the problem of integration in various ways, according to the context of
the moment; thus, the early context was his work on the theology of grace,
when the theological problem of moral impotence pointed to the inadequacy of empirical human science; later the context was the transition
from scriptural categories to dogmatic, and later still the transition to a
pluralist expression of faith.
   But the many contexts and the various expressions converge; thus, he

asks what kind of systematic categories we should use today to express a prescientific faith, and remarks, 'Hoc est fortasse maximum problema scientiae theologicae nostri temporis' (1959a: 65); again, 'the task of doing genuine history and on that basis proceeding to theology confronts contemporary Catholic theologians with the most basic and far-reaching of problems, the problem of method' (1974: 96, in the paper 'Belief: Today's Issue'); yet again, 'The whole problem in modern theology, Protestant and Catholic, is the introduction of historical scholarship' (1977: 103; see also *Collection* [1988] 278, note *n* to chapter 7, and 282, note *r* to chapter 8); and still again, 'in the nineteenth century there was a very superficial notion of the problems of theology. They were afraid of skepticism and relativism, merely philosophic problems. But the theological problems were the notion of history, the notion of critical history, interpretation, exegesis' (1982: 104–105). The convergence of these expressions is seen from a remark of Lonergan on 'what Method is about: surmounting differences in historicity' (letter to F. Crowe dated March 3, 1980).

The problem of integration is another way of putting most of the same questions; it is a topic passim in *Insight* (1957a: see the Index), with the theological aspect coming into focus in chapter 20; the Epilogue even states that 'this problem [the integration of theology, philosophy, and the empirical human sciences] ... in a large measure has dictated the structure of the present work' (743–44); see also note *h* below, on wisdom as integrating. If integration is later seen as a problem of history, as in the quotations of the preceding paragraph, it is because there has to be real integration of past and present in the history that happens (1972: 175), and cognitive integration in the history that is written, of what we and our predecessors hold, giving account too of our differences. See also note *f* to lecture 10 below, note *h* to discussion 3, and note *b* to discussion 5.

f [100] **the classical *Gymnasium***: Robert Doran reports a conversation he had with Lonergan on Eric Voegelin; to a remark on the latter's classical erudition, Lonergan replied, 'He learned it all as a child; it was a wonderful preparation for his future work, and something quite lacking in our educational system.'

g [101] **knowledge of this ... specific character**: the Introduction to *Insight* begins by saying 'the question is not whether knowledge exists but what precisely is its nature' (1957a: xvii); it is hardly a mere coincidence that the same point is made early in these lectures; see lecture 1, § 1.2, The Development of the Ideal of Knowledge (12), 'just knowing that knowledge exists is knowing something very abstract. What kind of knowledge exists?'

h [101] **you have ... certitude ... But ... the problem of integration is ignored:** certitude as the conceptualist ideal of science was sharply criticized in the *verbum* articles (1967a: 211–13); in its place Lonergan would substitute understanding, and would give wisdom, which is the 'highest, architectonic science, a science of sciences' (68), an integrating function. This function still pertains to wisdom a decade later in *De intellectu et methodo* (1959a: 17–22), but eventually Lonergan transposed Thomist wisdom in the sublations of intentionality analysis (1985b: 52, in the paper 'Aquinas Today ... '); then wisdom as a virtue in the single person would be complemented by the wider function of the scientific community (ibid. 14, 19, in the paper 'Method: Trend and Variations'). See also 'Questionnaire' (1984: 4), 'Aristotelian science ... could be a habit tucked into the mind of an individual. But no individual knows the whole of any modern science,' and so wisdom would involve interdisciplinary studies (1972: 22–23, 132, 366–67).

i [102] **the level of our times:** a phrase from Ortega y Gasset that evidently impressed Lonergan; see the original Preface to *Insight* (1985c: 4). Further evidence of Ortega's influence is found in the lectures on education (1959b), where the first lecture lists three 'new factors in contemporary education ... the masses ... the new learning ... specialization' – it is in *The Revolt of the Masses* (London: Unwin Books, 1961) and *Mission of the University* (Princeton: Princeton University Press, 1944) that Ortega y Gasset develops his notion of 'the height of the times.' The idea remained with Lonergan in *Method* passim, 'the understanding to be reached is to be on the level of one's times' (1972: 350); 'To operate on the level of our day is to apply the best available knowledge and the most efficient techniques to coordinated group action' (367).

j [106] **in the very early months of life:** surely a humorous remark, not a position on the question so much debated today, on when human life begins.

Lecture 5

a [113] **'because' ... within a spiritual being:** the point made so briefly here is amplified in the Trinitarian theology of the *verbum* articles. 'There are two aspects to the procession of an inner word in us. There is the productive aspect ... There is also the intelligible aspect: inner words do not proceed with mere natural spontaneity as any effect does from any cause; they proceed with reflective rationality; they proceed not merely from a sufficient cause but from sufficient grounds known to be sufficient and because they are known to be sufficient ... The inner word of defining not only is *caused by* but also is *because of* the act of understanding' (1967a: 199). And Lonergan goes on to explain that only the second aspect, because of, is applicable to the procession of the Word in God.

b [113] **between *quo* and *quod*:** in the lecture Lonergan added the fuller Latin, 'id quod intelligit' and 'id quo intelligit' – the neuter usage probably because 'id' refers implicitly to 'principium,' a term regularly used in the theology of the hypostatic union; see 1956: 117–18, and 1988: 154–62 (in 'Christ as Subject: A Reply').

c [114] **'Yes, yes,' and 'Nay, nay':** Lonergan liked to refer, in the context of truth, to these phrases from Matthew (5.37); see 1988: 126, in 'Theology and Understanding'; also 1976: 10, 127.

d [118] **general form of the grasp of the virtually unconditioned:** Lonergan's main point here, of course, is to 'exhibit' the virtually unconditioned (see note *e* below), not to ground judgments generally in premises which are themselves judgments. But there is a historical interest in the general form of his syllogism, that of the hypothetical argument, If ... then ... ; but ... ; therefore ... In 1943 (1943a) he had argued that 'the form of inference is the simple hypothetical argument' (1988: 5, in 'The Form of Inference'). In his student paper 'The Syllogism' (1928b) he was already moving toward that position (34, 48, 50–51, and especially 51–57), but had reservations on third-figure arguments: 'Neither the syllogistic nor the hypothetical form of Fig. 3 seems satisfactory' (64). On the concern of the young Lonergan for the role of intelligence, even in logic, see our editorial note *e* to lecture 2.

e [119] **the syllogism exhibits ... the prospective judgment ... as a virtually unconditioned:** Lonergan put this principle into practice in his own theology, with resulting clarity in his theological arguments; see the 'proofs' of his 'theses' in his theology manuals. The later emphasis on conversion does not invalidate this rigor: conclusions still follow, but within a horizon, and it is through conversion that we establish a new horizon, select 'the frame-work, in which doctrines have their meaning, in which systematics reconciles, in which communications are effective' (1972: 268). 'Conversion transforms the concrete individual to make him capable of grasping not merely conclusions but principles as well' (ibid. 338). Again, 'Proof always presupposes premises, and it presupposes premises accurately formulated within a horizon. You can never prove a horizon' (1973b: 1; also ibid. 12).

f [121] **Something happened:** Lonergan's procedure here combines two cognitional operations that are separated in *Insight* – the realization of change (explained in chapter 10), and the expression of it in the words 'Something happened' (which supposes some of the notions of chapter 17).

That is, chapter 10 of *Insight* does not take up the expression 'Something happened' *as expression*, but simply explains the realization, be it wordless or expressed. Thus 'the fulfilling conditions are found on the level of presentations ... of the occurrence of acts of seeing and smelling' (1957a: 281–82). Again, 'the weary worker not only experiences present data and recalls different data but by direct insights he refers both sets of data to the same set of things ... a second level of cognitional process is added to a first. The two together contain a specific structure of that process, which we name the notion of knowing change' (ibid.). Now, as Lonergan goes on to say, one can make a statement about that change and affirm it in a judgment. The judgment will be expressed in words, and the meaning of the words will involve a different insight, but Lonergan does not, in these pages on Insights into Concrete Situations (283–87), analyze what happens in the expression as expression; the key loci for that are found in chapter 17; see, for example, §2.4, Truth and Expression (553–58), and §3.3, Levels and Sequences of Expression (568–73).

Here, in the Halifax lectures, his procedure is different; the two operations are combined in rapid sequence. The worker returning home 'has in his presentations and memories the fulfilment of the conditions for saying that something has happened, and in the meaning of these words, Something happened, he has the link between those conditions and the judgment, Something did happen.'

The point becomes especially relevant in the present lectures when Lonergan comes to analytic propositions and says, 'The link between the conditions and the conditioned is given by rules of syntax, the way in which words combine to make complete sense' (127). This case is partly the same, and partly different; see our note *i* below.

g [123] **the dream is disconnected, and lower factors have control:** this is very much the position and partly the language of the *verbum* articles (1967a: 63–64), but in 1976 Lonergan could speak more positively of 'dreams of the morning' in which 'the subject is anticipating his waking state ... anticipating his world and taking his own stance within it' (1985b: 131, in 'Lectures on Religious Studies and Theology, Second Lecture: Religious Knowledge'). – The change may be due to his further reading of Binswanger; there are rather extensive references to him in lectures of the next year (1959b: 154, 283); the still unexplored card files (Lonergan Archives) have an entry with notes on Binswanger's *Traum und Existenz*, the French translation.

h [124] **judgment ... of invulnerability:** judgments on the invulnerability and correctness of our insights, judgments that there are no further relevant questions – i.e., judgments as a means of validating judgments – are involved in a vicious circle unless we have recourse to the self-correcting process of learning. 'So it is the process of learning that breaks the vicious circle' (1957a: 286; see also note *e* to lecture 6 below). – The self-correcting process is an enduring factor in Lonergan's cognitional theory; see, for example, 1985b: 103, 105 (in the paper 'Healing and Creating in History'), and 174 (in the paper 'Natural Right and Historical Mindedness'). But a computer search showed that 'self-correcting' does not occur in our text for *Understanding and Being*; it is a reminder of how much of *Insight* the lectures had to omit.

i [127] **the meaning of this collocation of words:** see Lonergan's distinction between nominal and essential definitions (*scientia nominis* and *scientia rei*). 'Nominal definitions express one's understanding of a linguistic system ... Essential definitions express one's understanding of a real system' (1988: 94). See also note *c* to discussion 3 below.

Now a linguistic system has its own reality, and analytic propositions could, if someone wishes to construct a new language and find people to use it, be brought under that heading. But, as Lonergan will presently say (127), 'we can have as many [analytic propositions] as we please.' Do they give us any significant knowledge? 'Not yet. This indefinitely large group of possible analytic propositions is just a set of possible ways of talking ... it is not a significant part within the field of knowledge.' See 1957a: Analytic propositions 'suppose nothing but the definitions of their terms and ... rules of syntax' (403); 'they rest on rules of syntax and on definitions of terms, and all such rules and definitions are regarded as mere suppositions' (409).

Insofar, however, as it pertains to knowledge, there is truth, the truth rests on a virtually unconditioned, the link between conditions and conditioned is empirical in the remembered experience of hearing the sounds or seeing the inkmarks on paper, but the truth is insignificant except for the esoteric few who bother with that language.

j [128] **the ontological argument is valid if God exists:** since God exists, the force of Lonergan's argument, taken literally, is to declare that the ontological argument is valid. – But Lonergan has telescoped his point; see *Insight* (1957a: 670), where we read that we have a relevant analytic principle only if we can affirm in a concrete judgment of fact that God does exist.

k [130] **those in Paris:** the interesting question is the source of Lonergan's acquaintance with the Bourbaki school, and with the series of logicians and mathematicians who are mentioned in discussion 1 below, § 1, Mathematics and Logic. But Lonergan's sources in general need much more study than they have received; on the present question, we can only refer to his notes for the lectures on mathematical logic (1957c), with their numerous bibliographical references; it is my personal recollection that an important source that year was Jean Ladrière, *Les limitations internes des formalismes* (Louvain: Nauwelaerts, and Paris: Gauthier-Villars, 1957), a book that had come into his hands just before the Boston lectures. His card index (Lonergan Archives) has several entries on relevant questions, with Ladrière named as source.

Lecture 6

a [141] **the subject:** the term occurs passim in *Insight*, but it was Lonergan's work on the consciousness of Christ that brought the question into focus; see his *De constitutione Christi* (1956: part 5, *De Conscientia Humana*, and part 6, *De Conscientia Christi*); also 'Christ as Subject: A Reply' (1988: 153–84; note the remark, 162: 'The notion of the subject is difficult, recent, and primitive'). The topic was treated in its own right in a 1968 lecture 'The Subject' (1974: 69–86).

b [142] **One and the same ... 'person':** 'One and the same' echoes the language of the Council of Chalcedon, *hena kai ton auton ... unum eundemque* (Denzinger-Schönmetzer, *Enchiridion symbolorum* ... §301) – it is one and the same who is consubstantial with the Father, and consubstantial with us. The controversial word 'person' is omitted from this lecture, but elsewhere we find: 'what does everyone understand by a person? We mean *somebody*, someone, not something ... not just a known object, not just a force ... not just a law ... not just a Platonic idea ... not a Platonist One ... ' (1963: 2). Late in life Lonergan returned to these questions: 'Christology Today: Methodological Considerations' (1985b: 74–99; see §6, The Meaning of Chalcedon, 89–90, and §7, Person Today, 90–94).

c [146] **That is the present question:** these paragraphs on the four senses of 'object,' and the related one of lecture 7, at the beginning of §2, The Notion of Objectivity (170–71), were the occasion of long and fruitful exchanges among the editors, too extensive to be repeated here; but it is clear that Lonergan's thought has advanced significantly since he wrote *Insight* five years earlier, and that these passages must be part of the basis for investigating that advance.

d [152] **you utter a concept:** the regular usage in *Insight* is 'formulating' a concept; 'utter' is perhaps an unconscious carry-over from Lonergan's Trinitarian theology, where he speaks of the Father 'uttering' the Word – he would hardly speak of the Father 'formulating' the Word.

e [155] **the right notion of being to acquire wisdom ... wisdom to settle what the right notion of being is:** Lonergan regularly breaks the vicious circles logic cannot escape, by invoking the dynamism of human spirit and the self-correcting process of learning (see note *h* to lecture 5 above).

An image he sometimes uses in this context is that of the spiral, as in *Insight*: 'one's understanding gradually works round and up a spiral of viewpoints' (1957a: 186); and in *Method*: 'Such is the hermeneutic circle. Logically it is a circle. But coming to understand is not a logical deduction. It is a self-correcting process of learning that spirals into the meaning of the whole ... ' (1972: 159); 'One advances in knowledge along a spiral' (208). In the present application, growing wisdom leads to a more accurate notion of being, the more accurate notion of being leads to deeper wisdom, and the process continues in a spiraling motion (see note *k* to lecture 7 below, also 1959a: 19–22).

Lecture 7

a [156] **an objective fact ... just a kaleidoscope:** Lonergan, of course, presents this view simply as a possible position. But in the rigorous sequence of *Insight*, this 'possible position' is not excluded till chapter 14: neither chapter 12 nor chapter 13 takes a position for realism against idealism. 'Thirdly, our notion of objectivity begs no questions. Just as our notion of being does not decide between empiricism and rationalism, positivism and idealism, existentialism and realism [see the paragraph on pp. 349–50] ... so also our notion of objectivity is equally open' (1957a: 384).

b [157] **questions ... bothering some of you:** the pedagogical difficulty of the lectures, surfacing here, was enormous, partly from the side of a traditional Thomism critical of Lonergan's work on Thomas, partly from the side of a secular philosophy unfamiliar with scholastic problems – and from every side the sheer difficulty of Lonergan's thought.

c [161] **Nature gives us nothing in act:** this echoes the *tabula rasa* of the scholastics, denying innate determinate items of knowledge, and referred to a little later as the 'blackboard on which nothing is written' (162). But to be set against it is the dynamism of spirit, which *is* in act and by nature brings determinate items to act. In § 1.3, The Notion of Being as Natural, see these remarks: 'You do not have to teach people the principle of contradiction; they know that by nature ... ' (162). 'Knowing being is natural insofar as we have natural potencies and some natural habits. The whole of our knowing is not by acquisition ... part of it is had from nature' (163). The two sides of the question have to be taken in a context of mutual conditioning.

There is a parallel in the Thomist statement that our knowledge is 'partim ab intrinseco ... partim ab extrinseco' (*De veritate*, q. 10, a. 6 c.); the intrinsic factor of intellectual light already contains in some way all knowledge: 'in lumine intellectus agentis nobis est quodammodo omnis scientia originaliter indita' (ibid.); but it is not enough for determinate knowledge: 'est ipsum lumen non determinatam cognitionem alicuius faciens, quousque apponatur aliqua de quibus est iudicandum' (ibid. q. 12, a. 12, ad 6m) – hence the need of an element 'ab extrinseco': 'praeter lumen intellectuale in nobis, exiguntur species intelligibiles a rebus acceptae' (*Summa theologiae* 1, q. 84, a. 5 c.); 'principium nostrae cognitionis est a sensu' (ibid. a. 6, Sed contra).

d [165] **potentially in the image:** Lonergan's full account, here and elsewhere abbreviated, assigns four steps to the process from potential to actual in the area of understanding. 'The imagined object as merely imagined and as present to a merely sensitive consciousness (subject) is not, properly speaking, intelligible in potency; but the same object present to a subject that is intelligent as well as sensitive may fairly be described as intelligible in potency. Thus, pure reverie ... illustrates the intelligible in potency. But let active intelligence intervene ... there is wonder and inquiry ... the imagined object no longer is merely given but also a something-to-be-understood. It is the imagined object as present to intelligent consciousness as something-to-be-understood that constitutes the intelligible in act ... Finally, inquiry and wonder give place to actual understanding ... ' (1967a: 174–75).

The full sequence, then, is the following: (1) Not intelligible in the context (scil., of animal consciousness). (2) Potentially intelligible, as in the mere reverie of a human imagination. (3) Actually intelligible, as in the scientist asking why. (4) Actually understood, as in the scientist reaching insight. (It is then a further and quite distinct sequence from insight to judgment – see our next note.)

In the telescoped presentation of the present lecture, and quite often in Lonergan, the first and third steps are omitted, and it is the second and fourth steps that are in question: 'potentially intelligible' and 'actually understood.' Further, 'actually intelligible' is sometimes used for 'actually understood'; see note *b* to discussion 2 below, on its use for the fourth step, though strictly it belongs to the third.

e [167] **particularized:** just a few months earlier Lonergan had detailed the process from data through insight, concept, particularized concept, to existence. 'Still, you will ask, just where did existence come in? Was it some one of the data, or was it their totality? No, any and all the data are quite compatible with phenomenalism, pragmatism, existentialism; but none of these philosophies include Aquinas' *actus essendi*. Did, then, existence come in with the insight, or with the concept, or with the particularized concept? No, idealists and relativists know all about insights, concepts, and their particularization; and to suppose that these activites yield more than an object of thought is simply essentialism in its radical form. But, then, what can be the origin of the notion of existence, if neither sense nor understanding suffices? I think that, if you will go back over the process just described, you will see that the notion of existence emerged with the question whether the particularized concept, this thing, was anything more than a mere object of thought. In other words, just as existence is the act of being, so the notion of existence is the crowning component in the notion of being' (1988: 151, in 'Insight: Preface to a Discussion'). More succinctly in his study of the Thomist verbum: 'The essential necessity of inner words ... is the necessity of effecting the transition from the pre-conceptual quidditas rei materialis, first, to the res, secondly, to the res particularis, thirdly, to the res particularis existens. The transition from quidditas rei to res, say, from humanitas to homo, occurs in conception ... ' (1967a: 193).

f [168] **the whole is greater than the part ... that is fundamental in all cognitional theory:** Lonergan never understood in a simply quantita-tive way the principle of whole and part; rather, he conceived it in terms of a metaphysical whole and metaphysical parts, ens quod and entia quibus. When his interpretation was questioned, as it was at the time of the verbum articles, he did not yield on the main point, but he did take the opportunity, when the articles came out in book form, to rewrite the relevant paragraph. Compare 1947a: 45 with 1967a: 57–58.

Here in 1958, at this intermediate point, he is quite cautious about his interpretation: 'What might be the relevance of the whole being greater than the part, as something fundamental in all cognitional process, is the transition from the id quo to the id quod.'

g [174] **infallible:** Lonergan had found the infallibility of intellect (insight) in both Aristotle and Aquinas (1967a: 175–76, see also 63, 178; 1957a: 406–407). For other relevant passages, see Collection (1988), Index under Infallibility.

h [175] **illusions and hallucinations:** this is a brief treatment of a question, that of the 'illusory or hallucinatory,' that Lonergan had brought up earlier this year (1988: 151, in 'Insight: Preface to a Discussion'; see also note n, ibid. 288); at that time he referred his audience to Insight (1957a: 280–83), but the Halifax lectures give more attention to the question than does that locus. – Possibly the question had some personal interest, for in his existentialism lectures he had referred to the problem of 'inte-grated conscious living,' and his own childhood experience that 'illness, fever, easily moves to delirium' (1957d: 23; see also 1982: 136).

i [177] **years ... about eight hundred:** Lonergan probably has in mind here such authors as Abelard (1079–1142) and Gilbert de la Porrée (1076–1154); regularly he refers to them as marking significant steps in scholastic cognitional theory (see the indices of A Second Collection [1974] and A Third Collection [1985b]).

j [178] **where one chooses to start:** it may make no difference 'per se, strictly in principle' (Lonergan's actual words) where we start, but that seems to regard the objective field in which cognitional and ontological are isomorphic; if our 'principles' include the more subjective field of pedagogy, development, and method, then it is clear that for Lonergan it makes a great deal of difference where we start.

k [178] **smaller circles ... bigger circles:** described elsewhere as the 'spiral' of learning (see note *e* to lecture 6), a figure which shows how the transition is made from smaller circle to bigger; a diagram in the WAS notes (29) illustrates this with a row of bigger and bigger circles, and an arrow running through them all, pointing from smaller to larger.

Lecture 8

a [183] **not ... static coincidence, but ... a process of becoming:** the 1957 lectures on existentialism (1957d) have a number of relevant headings, such as The Dilemma of the Subject, Subject and Horizon (*my* universe, defined by my horizon, contrasted with *the* universe; the existential gap between one's horizon on oneself and what one really is), Horizon and Dread, Horizon and History.

b [185] **with every basic meaning ... you give a meaning ... to all other propositions:** see, for comparison: 'the meaning of every other term changes with changes in the meaning of the terms, knowledge, reality, objectivity' (1957a: 426); also, 'every statement made by a realist denotes an object in a realist's world; every statement made by an idealist denotes an object in an idealist world' (1988: 199); also, 'An idealist never means what an empiricist means, and a realist never means what either of them means' (1972: 239).

c [195] **human liberty ... governmental power:** bureaucracy was a lifelong target for Lonergan's criticism, as various notes and drafts in his unpublished papers show (Batch 1-A, folder 9, 6; folder 10, 11). Some of his thinking got into print: 'governmental functions ... have been multiplying and accumulating for a century under the evil influence of a mistaken economic system' (1943b: 5); 'The principle of progress is liberty, for the ideas occur to the man on the spot ... on the other hand, one might as well declare openly that all new ideas are taboo, as require that they be examined, evaluated, and approved by some hierarchy of officials and bureaucrats' (1957a: 234); more fully in the 1975 paper 'Prolegomena to the Study of the Emerging Religious Consciousness of Our Time': 'the large establishment and its bureaucratic organization is a fourfold source of that conjunction of dissatisfaction and hopelessness that is named alienation and foments revolutions' (1985b: 61). The topic still occupies

Lonergan at the end of his life, in the unpublished economics typescript which he was reworking in his last years, *An Essay in Circulation Analysis* (CWL 15).

Lecture 9

a [202] **the analogy of form to potency:** a shorthand expression for the fuller account given a few lines below – as form is to potency, so insight is to presentations; it is the recurring analogy of proportion. It is another usage when Lonergan speaks of the analogy of matter, the analogy of intellect, the analogy of meaning, etc.; in these cases various analogates are referred to one main concept (see 1988: 283, note *a* to chapter 9; also 274, note *q* to chapter 6).

b [203] **Aristotle:** fragments in Lonergan's papers contain little indices of Aristotelian usage, including the term 'potency' (Batch 1-A, folder 9, 1), and his card files show extensive indexing of Aristotle.

c [203] **we can control them:** the notion of control, pervasive in Lonergan, gives a clue here to the organization of the following paragraphs. The effort is for what, a few years later, he will call the control of meaning (1988: 235, and note *d* to chapter 16: 309), and the present question is, How can one control the meaning of the metaphysical elements and their analogies? The theory runs through § 1.3, Central and Conjugate Forms, and § 1.4, Unity and Distinction, to be exemplified in § 1.5, An Illustration of Metaphysical Analysis. – This emphasis on control needs to be kept in perspective through attention to an equal emphasis on openness; see the indices of *Insight* (1957a), *A Second Collection* (1974); also *Method*: 'Such a structure is essentially open' (1972: 141), and *A Third Collection*: 'man's ... unrestricted openness to the intelligible, the true, the good' (1985b: 32). On the importance of control in theology, once one has abandoned deductivism, see *Method*: 'Then, what is paramount is control of the process' (1972: 270).

d [207] **reference to the other ... to be fully understood:** the next two paragraphs tell us something of what it means to be intelligible and under- stood in 'the other.' In a philosophy which stressed the act of understand- ing, this was a crucial question, and Lonergan had his theory well worked out at an early stage: 'positiva intelligentia est vel *tou* intelligibilis in se vel *tou* intelligibilis in alio; in se intelliguntur forma et essentia; sed materia intelligitur non in se sed ex consideratione formae; et exsis- tere contingens non intelligitur in se sed ex dependentia ab exsistere necessario et in se intelligibili' (1973a: 64). Again, 'individual matter is not intelligible in itself but only in its relation to the *per se* universality of forms ... contingent existence is not intelligible in itself but only in its relation to the necessarily Existent' (1967a: 193). More fully: 'Strictly and primarily, the intelligible is the grasped unity; and it is only by their relations to that unity that other instances of the intelligible are intelligible ... common matter is intelligible by information ... essence is intelligible by inclusion ... individual matter is intelligible tangentially ... contingent existence is intelligible again tangentially' (1988: 102, in 'A Note on Geometrical Possibility'). *Insight*, in the context of proving God's existence, distinguishes 'the intelligibility of the merely conceived ... of material reality ... of inquiring and developing intelligence,' and complete intelligibility (1957a: 676). The present volume also treats the question in that context; see discussion 4 below, §2, Probability Theory and the Existence of God.

Related ideas: the various forms of intelligibility *in se*, note *e* to discussion 4 below; the unintelligibility of sin, note *h* to lecture 10 below (the false fact), and note *a* to discussion 5 (the surd of sin).

e [208] **Socrates ... understands something:** see *Insight* (1957a: 506–507) for a related analysis of Socrates. The pattern established in these analyses is found passim in Lonergan's theological works; see, for example, *De constitutione Christi* (1956: 27, 31–33), and *Divinarum personarum* (1957b: 206). It recurs later in this lecture, §1.6, Canons of Metaphysical Analysis. See also note *h*, discussion 4 below.

f [209] *intellectus agens:* our editorial change seems justified by Lonergan's regular usage in his Thomist studies, where he makes wonder a function of agent intellect; see, for example, 'agent intellect as spirit of wonder and inquiry' (1967a: 47), 'let active intelligence intervene ... there is wonder and inquiry' (ibid. 174), 'the light of intelligence within us, the drive to wonder' (ibid. 185); that seems to be his view still in *Insight* (1957a: 370 – the only reference in that book to agent intellect). It is true, however, that, in the intentionality analysis which *Insight* implicitly offers, the stress is on the dynamic orientation, the pure desire to know, and the metaphysical distinction between agent and possible intellect is not taken up (see, for example, 349, 370, and passim).

g [217] **cases where something has gone wrong:** wider reading enabled Lonergan later to differentiate Freud and Jung more accurately than he does here; see *Method* on Baudouin using 'Freud in reverting to causal objects and Jung in attending to subjective development,' also on Ricoeur seeing in Freud 'an archeology of the subject' without an explicit 'forward-moving teleology' (1972: 68); Jung comes up again in discussion 5 below, §3, Archetypes.

h [217] **For Eliade, the image is a transcultural language:** but not, for Lonergan, an unambiguous language, for in applying this a little later to the meaning of the death and resurrection of Christ (§ 2.2, Mystery and

Myth), he goes on to say the meaning is one 'that can develop with the whole religious development of the person,' indeed, 'the image is not tied down to one meaning' (218). Language, then, remains important as 'the vehicle in which meaning becomes most fully articulated' (1972: 112). 'Man's response to transcendent mystery is adoration. But adoration does not exclude words' (ibid. 344), and so there is a role for both linguistic and incarnate meaning (1974: 175, in 'The Response of the Jesuit as Priest and Apostle in the Modern World').

i [220] **Modernism:** Lonergan would soon give religious experience a more important role in his theology, briefly in 'Openness and Religious Experience' (1988: chapter 12), more fully in *Method* (1972: chapter 4, Religion); but even then he maintained the permanence of dogma (see chapter 12, §9) along with its historicity (§10). – To be distinguished from his position on modernism are his views on modernity (1988: 307, note *u* to chapter 15).

j [222] **derive categories:** the reference here is probably to the opening paragraph of chapter 17 of *Insight*, 'there is available a general theorem to the effect that any philosophy ... will rest upon the dynamic structure of cognitional activity either as correctly conceived or as distorted ... ' (1957a: 530); but readers of the later Lonergan will think of *Method* (1972: 281–91, on categories and their derivation).

k [222] **cultures:** in his education lectures the following year, Lonergan has parallel derivations from the invariant structure of the human good; in one of them too he sees the three levels of the human good as isomorphic with Sorokin's three types of society or culture or civilization (1959b: 49–50, in lecture 2). – Lonergan's views on culture developed slowly: reading Dawson in the early 1930s had started him thinking (1974: 264, in '*Insight* Revisited'); a position has developed by the time of *Insight*: 'Man can pause and ... ask what the drama, what he himself is about. His culture is his capacity to ask, to reflect, to reach an answer that at once satisfies his intelligence and speaks to his heart' (1957a: 236); *Method* puts it succinctly: 'A culture is a set of meanings and values informing a common way of life' (1972: 301). This could clarify the notoriously slippery current notion in which cultural studies are an amalgam of literature, history, sociology, anthropology, and communication studies (*The Chronicle of Higher Education*, January 18, 1989, p. A4).

l [224] **the categories of a scientific hermeneutics:** it might seem that Lonergan here excludes emergent probability from the human level ('on the less than human level ... emergent probability ... on the human level ... hermeneutics'), but he speaks, the scholastics would say, *sensu aiente*, not *negante*; see *Insight*: 'if human affairs fall under the dominion of emergent probability, they do so in their own way' (1957a: 210);

there is a 'generalized emergent probability,' and it is relevant to 'the threefold development in man' (462); 'the structural unification of the methods [is achieved] by generalized emergent probability' (486; see also 481–82).

Lecture 10

a [228] **fourth level of consciousness:** but, a little earlier (§ 1.1, Levels of the Good: 226), Lonergan had said, 'Value lies upon the level of judgment' – further evidence that his usage on 'levels' of consciousness is in transition. See note *h* to lecture 1, and note *b* to this lecture, below. See also 1988: notes *b* and *e* to chapter 7 (276); note *h* to chapter 11 (292); notes *g* and *p* to chapter 14 (301, 303); note *c* to chapter 16 (309). – On the related question of distinguishing self-knowledge and self-consciousness: note *f* to chapter 14 (ibid. 301); also lecture 6 above, § 1.3, Self-affirmation.

b [228] **what is at issue is fundamentally myself:** Lonergan has two stages of self-involvement: judgment and decision. *Insight* had said (1957a: 272), and these lectures repeat (lecture 5, § 4, Judgment and the Person Judging), that judgment 'involves a personal commitment ... is the responsibility of the one that judges.' But then freedom has 'the positive aspect of responsibility,' and this goes beyond judgment: 'Knowing cannot necessitate the decision ... The decision ... is ... a new emergence ... realizes an effectively rational self-consciousness' (1957a: 619).

Lonergan is quite definite on the difference of the two steps: 'there is a radical difference between the rationality of judgment and the rationality of decision' (ibid. 613), but he does not seem to have worked out the relation of the self-involvement in one to the self-involvement in the other, though the general topic had come up early in this seminar (see discussion 1, § 7, Self-appropriation and Self-involvement).

Perhaps there is an analogy and a clue in the relations among the functional specialties of his *Method*: 'one operates on all four levels to achieve the end proper to some particular level' (1972: 134). This indicates that the self may be involved even on the level of data, for we choose to be attentive, and judge what we should attend to, even though the proper end of attending is assembly of the data; similarly, the proper end of the second level is understanding, and when ideas occur they occur 'suddenly and unexpectedly' (1957a: 4) but again we choose to try to understand, and judge what means may help.

On that analogy, we may say the proper end of the third level is not self-involvement but the truth, and I have not the freedom in regard to the truth that I have in regard to my conduct; but because the act of judgment involves commitment on a high level (there is a choice between Yes and No, and even a third option: I don't know, 1957a: 272), my rationality is involved (Halifax lecture 5, §4, Judgment and the Person Judging), and to that extent I myself. The proper end of the fourth level, however, is closely related to the existential decision by which we make ourselves what we are to be: 'By his own acts the human subject makes himself what he is to be, and he does so freely and responsibly; indeed, he does so precisely because his acts are the free and responsible expressions of himself' (1974: 79, in 'The Subject'). See also 1985b: 127, 141, and passim, in the 'Lectures on Religious Studies and Theology,' on man as the self-completing animal.

This concept of 'man's making of man,' that was to become so important in *The Subject* (1968), was already a topic ten years earlier in these Halifax lectures: 'By my free acts I am making myself' (lecture 10, §1.4, Choice as a Determinant of Development: 229). No doubt the thematizing here owed something to the 1957 lectures on existentialism, but chapter 7 of *Insight* had the materials for Lonergan's own existentialist thought, even to the phrase 'man's ... making of man' (1957a: 233). Indeed, there are student papers in the Archives (one is dated precisely 'Dominica in Albis 1935' – File 713: History) which speak repeatedly of the making of man by man, though more in the context of human solidarity than of individual development.

c [229] **distinct individuals:** this question was an early preoccupation of Lonergan; there is in the Archives (File 713 – see preceding note) a paper, apparently from his student days, entitled *Pantôn Anakephalaiôsis*, which takes up this very question of the individuation of persons (1935: 11–12).

d [231] **perfect indifference:** see Lonergan's work on grace: 'The human will does not swing back to a perfect equilibrium of indifference with every tick of the clock' (1971a: 53); a note (ibid. 51) refers to this as 'the law of psychological continuity'; the indifference of the Ignatian *Spiritual Exercises*, which Lonergan made annually, would not eliminate this psychological continuity, but would control it on a higher ascetical level.

e [232] **cannot be rational:** the language here is that of *Insight*, where the exigence is 'for self-consistency in knowing and doing' (1957a: 599, and see 627–30); *Method* would speak rather of being 'responsible' (1972: 9–13, and passim) – a usage that focuses more on the 'morally self-conscious subject' of *Insight* (1957a: 599, and passim in chapter 18). See note h to lecture 1 above, notes a and b to the present lecture.

f [235] **approximations to the course of human history:** the paper of 1973, 'Insight Revisited,' dates these approximations twenty years before the Halifax seminar. 'It was about 1937–38 that I became interested in a

theoretical analysis of history' (1974: 271–72, with an account immediately of the three approximations). They appeared earlier in *De ratione
convenientiae* (1953: 6–9), and later in 'The Transition from a Classicist
World-view to Historical-mindedness' (1974: 7–8), with references there
to *Insight* and to *De Verbo incarnato*; also in 'Mission and the Spirit'
(1985b: 31–32).

The topic here is the history that happens, that is written about. It
was only slowly that the counterpart of this, the history that is written
(chapters 8 and 9 of *Method in Theology*), became thematic for Lonergan.
That is strange, since the distinction is already clear in the student
papers of File 713 (see note *b* above), more than twenty years before the
thematic treatment of the two as a related pair occurs in a lecture at
Thomas More Institute, Montreal: Notes from the Introductory Lecture
in the Philosophy of History (1960). On history see also note *e* to lecture
4 above, note *h* to discussion 3 below, and note *b* to discussion 5.

g [235] **situation, insight, policy, counsel, consent, course of action:** the
structure here builds on that of Thomas Aquinas, *Summa theologiae* 1-2, qq.
12–15 (*intentio, consilium, electio, consensus*); what follows ('new situation ...
new insights') is more Lonergan's own.

h [236] **false fact:** the objective *falsitas* Thomas Aquinas found in sin, a
concept that entered deeply into Lonergan's theology of grace. 'In this
passage [Thomas Aquinas, *De malo*, q. 16, a. 4, ad 22m] an assertion of
absolute objective falsity appears as an afterthought; it begins hesitantly
with a *nisi forte*; but it gains momentum as it proceeds, and it ends on the
level of the Johannine antithesis of Light and Darkness' (1971a: 111;
see 109–15, 144). – For the full force of the oxymoron 'false fact' see
Lonergan's phrase, 'that clear, precise, definitive, irrevocable, dominant something that we name fact' (1957a: 331; see note *m* to lecture 1
above; also note *a* to discussion 5 below, on the surd of sin). Another
clue is the scholastic doctrine *ens, verum, bonum convertuntur*; if truth (fact)
is convertible with being, what is convertible with the false fact?

i [236] **Realpolitik:** related to what Lonergan had said in 'Finality, Love,
Marriage' on the 'pseudorealist' (1988: 28); see note *o* to chapter 2 (ibid.
262) on the distinction between pseudorealism and naive realism; the
latter is an epistemological category.

j [237] **mystical body:** a pervasive idea in Lonergan's early theology (1988:
see the Index). There is an early paper entitled 'The Mystical Body and
the Sacraments' (1941); this antedated by two years the encyclical of Pope
Pius XII (*Mystici Corporis*, 1943). Also in the Archives is a 'domestic
exhortation' entitled The Mystical Body of Christ, given at Regis College,
November 1951. Possibly an influence here was Sebastian Tromp, who
in 1932 had produced a collection of texts under the title *De Spiritu Sancto*

anima corporis mystici (Rome: Gregorian University Press), was one of
Lonergan's theology professors, and was said to have had a hand in
drafting *Mystici Corporis*; the term and idea are, in fact, prominent in
the papers of File 713 (note *b* above), written shortly after Lonergan
came under Tromp's influence.

k [238] **transposition:** a term used regularly for the movement forward in
history, from scripture to dogma, but having a second application in
the movement from dogma to communication – see note *k* to chapter 8
of *Collection* (1988: 281; also note *o*, ibid.); now we have a third type,
transposition backwards in history, from the present to Aristotle.

l [243] **extrinsic causality ... universally valid and relevant:** the premise
we find here, the identity of the real with being, is exactly the same as in
the paper of 1967, The General Character of the Natural Theology of
Insight; there we read that to affirm this identity is to recapitulate the
Greek breakthrough from *mythos* to *logos*, and to fail to affirm it is to
find ourselves without any valid proof for the existence of God (1967c:
§6).

If Lonergan's own breakthrough was to identify the real with being,
and thus remove an antecedent block to any proof, his actual proof
can be related to traditional procedures. His general question, Why
should there be anything at all? recalls Leibniz's question, Why is there
something and not nothing? His single arguments can be related to
some of Aquinas's five ways: the argument from events to the argument
ex parte motus, that from laws to the Thomist *ex gubernatione rerum*,
that from the hierarchy of beings to the Thomist *ex gradibus ... in rebus*
(*Summa theologiae*, 1, q. 2, a. 3). But we should not look for exact correspondence with Thomas; see *Insight* (1957a: 678): 'besides Aquinas'
five ways, there are as many other proofs of the existence of God as there
are aspects of incomplete intelligibility in the universe of proportionate
being.'

m [245] **the real is intelligible ... God exists:** regularly in *Insight* Lonergan
insists that the real is 'completely' intelligible (1957a: 672–73), while in
this lecture he regularly omits the adverb; it may be that in this last
lecture of the seminar he was hurrying, to accommodate those with an
early departure schedule, but at least he provided useful evidence that
'the real is intelligibie' is shorthand for 'the real is completely intelligible.'

Discussion 1

a [271] **Fr Dhanis:** Edouard Dhanis, s.j. (1902–78), was professor of theology in the Louvain college of his North Belgian Province, 1933–49,
Rector of Bellarmine College, Rome, 1949–55, and Rector of the Gregorian University, 1963–66; at the time of these lectures he was professor

of fundamental theology there, as he had been since going to Rome.

b [279] **modernist:** see note *i* to lecture 9 above.

Discussion 2

a [285] **process ... insight and conception ... grasp of the sufficiency of
the evidence and judgment:** the first process, from insight to conception, is studied in chapter 1 of *Verbum*, the second, from grasp of evidence
to judgment, in chapter 2 (1967a: 47); each process issues in a word,
the first in a simple word, *verbum incomplexum*, the other in a compound,
verbum complexum (ibid. 2 [note 7], 4). In contrast to this twofold word
in us, in God there is only one divine Word, 'but what is uttered in the
one Word is all that God knows' (ibid. 196); either of the two processions
in the human mind is an analogy for the one procession of the divine
Word. (There is a second difference here between human mind and
divine: 'In us there are two acts ... an act of understanding ... a really
distinct act of defining or judging. In God there is but one act' [ibid.
198; see 191, 196].)

b [286] **actual intelligibility:** used here for the more accurate term 'actually
understood' (at 'the moment of insight'); see note *d* to lecture 7 above.

c [294] **what is not intelligent cannot be labeled intellectual:** dictionary
meanings fail to show the point of this; it goes back to the *verbum* articles,
where intelligence is identical with understanding, and understanding
means insight into phantasm, something quite different from the 'intellec-
tion' of the conceptualists; to refuse the label 'intellectual' to the latter is
the broom that sweeps so effectively. See the topic Intellect as Intelligence that came up twice in the evening periods: discussion 2, §5, and
discussion 4, §7; also discussion 4, §10, Intelligence in Contemporary
Thomism. Elsewhere in lectures and discussions, see pp. 19, 216, 349.

d [296] **a more schematic diagram:** on the role of the diagram in understanding, see note *k* to lecture 1 above.

e [301] **a Hungarian ... in Japan:** Fr Edmund [Odon] Nemes, student in
theology at Regis College, 1952–56, with Lonergan as professor during
one of those years; after his studies in theology he returned to Japan,
where he is now stationed with the Tokyo community for the sociopastoral
apostolate.

Discussion 3

a [308] **the community ... hands on:** later Lonergan would relate this
traditional pair (achieving development and handing it on) to his intentionality structure; achieving development is an upward movement from
experience, through understanding and judgment, to values and responsi-

bility; handing on development uses the same structure, but the movement is from above downward – see especially 1958b: 180–81, in the paper 'Natural Right and Historical Mindedness.'

b [310] **Marcel ... approaches being through the good:** in his existentialism lectures, Lonergan gave high marks to Marcel; he 'is a penetrating thinker and an extremely effective writer' (1957d: 2). On Lonergan's own development on the notion of the good, see notes *a* and *b* to chapter 7 of *Collection* (1988: 276); relevant to this question is that on the levels of consciousness: references are listed in note *a* to lecture 10 above (see also note *k* to lecture 9).

c [315] **never ... any success in teaching language to an animal:** Lonergan later in life referred to differences among animals in the span of attention they could give to a 'problem'; see *The Question as Commitment* (1977: 8–9). But 'attention' belongs to the level of empirical consciousness, and something more is required for language in the proper sense; for Lonergan this is not a matter of a Pavlovian reaction to a stimulus; it involves a *scientia nominis*, and so a genuine understanding; the *verbum* articles speak of defining as 'a fruit of intelligence, the *quid rei* of understanding the thing, and the *quid nominis* of understanding the language' (1967a: 42); see also *Collection* (1988: 94, in the paper 'A Note on Geometrical Possibility') and note *i* to lecture 5 above.

d [316] **shifted to 'explanatory' in the course of the book:** another development on this point appears when we compare the book with the lectures Intelligence and Reality. In these Lonergan distinguished 'descriptive, heuristic, terminal, and dialectical categories' (1951a: 23), divided the terminal into the regular potency-form-act, but had three sets of each of these: there were conjugate, substantial, group forms; substantial, conjugate, group acts; and group, conjugate, substantial potencies (24). The category of group potency, form, and act has been omitted from the book, but the reality it designated is there in chapter 15, in the long section on genetic method; see especially the discussion of field and generalized emergent probability (1957a: 462). The summary of the chapter lists the six familiar metaphysical elements, and then, instead of adding the three 'group' elements, goes on to say: 'From the structural unification of the methods by generalized emergent probability, there follow the structural account of the explanatory genera and species and the immanent order of the universe of proportionate being' (ibid. 486).

e [317] **intelligence and will:** the point of the example is that these two faculties are not reducible to one; when later Lonergan moved explicitly into intentionality analysis, he would insist more on the unity of the subject who both wills and understands, but he would not, I think, deny the metaphysical distinction of the faculties. See *Caring*: 'Although in

Insight I am still talking as if it were faculty psychology, what I am doing is not faculty psychology ... I still talked about intellect and will. I don't anymore. Potencies are not data of consciousness; operations and dynamisms are' (1982: 43) The main point is that they are not 'data of consciousness' – which does not deny that they are real.

f [318] **orbit around the earth every day:** the spinning of the earth suggests its turning on its own axis, but Lonergan may have used the term indeliberately for orbiting; incidentally, the expressions 'the sun goes round the earth, the earth goes round the sun' were those of the questioner; Lonergan's pair had been 'the planets move in elliptical orbits with the sun at their focus' and 'the earth is at rest and the sun rises and sets' (1957a: 294–95).

g [323] **direct realism:** Lonergan's normal usage is to speak of 'naive realism.' If 'direct' is not a slip of the tongue, it may refer to the absence of advertence to intervening questions, and especially the question for reflection (Is it so?), in naive realism's account of how we arrive at truth.

h [323] **history:** there is the history that happens on the grand scale (see note *f* to lecture 10 above); there is the history that is written (note *e* to lecture 4 above); under the latter heading there is the distinction between historical experience and historical knowledge (note *b* to discussion 5 below); but the present question does not seem to regard any of those exactly, referring rather to a particular development in history.

i [324] **mythic consciousness:** there has been criticism of the way *Insight* deals with myth, and Lonergan later acknowledges that his use of the word was 'out of line with current usage ... is not going to be understood outside [the context of that book], so another mode of expression is desirable' (1974: 275, in the paper '*Insight* Revisited'). It is not clear that he would revise his substantive position, especially in regard to the mythic differentiation of consciousness.

j [334] **philosophy and theology:** their distinction and relation preoccupied Lonergan from the beginning; late in life he was still pondering the problem – see especially the 1970 paper 'Philosophy and Theology' (1974: 193–208), the 1972 lectures *Philosophy of God, and Theology* (1973b), and the 1976 'Questionnaire' (1984: 6–14 and passim).

Discussion 4

a [339] **the Aristotelian theory:** extensively studied in Lonergan's dissertation; see especially chapter 4 of *Grace and Freedom* (1971a).

b [339] **intelligible in the other:** see note *d* to lecture 9 above; the special interest of the present discussion is in the application to the proof of God's existence.

c [350] **double problem:** another of Lonergan's 'afterthoughts' on the structure of *Insight* (see note *a* to lecture 2 above).

d [350] **came first to understand St Thomas:** it is an error to see Lonergan's route as going from St Thomas to modernity; see 1974: 38, in the paper 'Theories of Inquiry,' where he politely refutes that view: 'I know I owe a great deal to him. I just add, however, that my interest in Aquinas came late' – in part, at least, through Fr Stephanou.

e [356] **total intelligibility in itself:** note *d* to lecture 9 above lists the various ways a thing is intelligible in another, but there is also a short list of ways in which a thing (or component of a thing) is intelligible in itself; see 1988: the intelligible component of material things, the pure forms (angels), the 'simply intelligible existent [God], and in it pure form and existence will coincide' (102).

f [359] **a very complex question:** Lonergan's position on vital act was worked out during his doctoral studies; the term does not appear in the Index of *Grace and Freedom*, but the loci can be found there under *passio* (1971a); similarly, in *Verbum*, see the Index under *pati* (1967a; see especially 109: whether the 'I' in 'I see' is the efficient cause of the seeing, or may simply receive the 'seeing' as a *pati*). Fully thematic treatment is given in *De ente supernaturali* (1973a: 42–49); again, in *De Deo trino* (1964a: vol. 2, 267–70). There is in the Archives a collection of relevant data, in the Guide to Terms of Lonergan's Early Latin Works, compiled by Giovanni Sala.

g [365] **You eliminate ... disputed questions with that technique:** on the scandal of disputed questions, see *Insight* (1957a: xxvii), *De constitutione Christi* (1956: 19), the lectures on existentialism (1957d: 17), *Collection* (1988: 145, in the paper '*Insight:* Preface to a Discussion'), *De intellectu et methodo* (1959a: 11), *Method in Theology* (1972: 20–21, 158, 343). On the technique of eliminating many of them through the isomorphism of the cognitional and the ontological, besides the present discussion, see also lecture 9 above, §1.5, An Illustration of Metaphysical Analysis.

h [365] **one isn't to think of ... metaphysical analysis in terms of concrete problems:** verbally this is in conflict with the first canon of metaphysical analysis (213 above), 'one applies metaphysical analysis, first of all, concretely.' There is, however, no contradiction in the intended meaning: metaphysical analysis deals with the concrete, Socrates, but does so in order to speak of the metaphysical elements, central and conjugate potency, form, and act; and this consideration is concrete the way intentionality, the dynamism operative in the human subject, deals with the concrete. But if 'concrete' is understood in the sense of specific forms (as is the case here), metaphysical analysis leaves that to science. See *Insight*: 'If one wants to know just what forms are, the proper procedure is to

give up metaphysics and turn to the sciences' (1957a: 498). Perhaps, therefore, a better term than 'concrete problems' would be '*specific* problems';
but it is remarkable that in so many hours of impromptu answers to
questions, there is so little to correct in Lonergan's choice of terms. See
also note *e*, lecture 9 above, and on a related question (concrete reality vs.
possible worlds) note *f*, lecture 1.

i [366] **science ... within the descriptive field:** for Lonergan's position on
Aristotelian science, see note *d* to lecture 1 above, and note *h* to lecture
4; also note *e* to chapter 2 of *Collection* (1988: 260); for a brief note on
the present point, see *Insight*: 'the ten categories commonly ascribed to
Aristotle ... are descriptive' (1957a: 395). Lonergan, of course, besides
studying changing ideals of science in the past, went through his own
development, especially on what theological science is; compare the
1954 paper 'Theology and Understanding' (1988: 114–32) with *Method in
Theology* some years later.

Discussion 5

a [375] **the surd of sin:** a term that goes back to Lonergan's student papers
(Archives: File 713) and to his doctoral dissertation; see *Grace and Freedom*,
'the metaphysical surd of sin cannot be related explanatorily or causally
with the integers that are objective truth' (1971a: 113); the context here
was the individual sinner, and though the word does occur in that context
in *Insight* (1957a: 669), there is the more frequent category of the social
surd (229–32, 237, 628–29, 689–90). Later the social surd becomes the
social 'dump' (1985b: 105–106, in 'Healing and Creating in History'),
though 'objective surd' of the 'social situation' still occurs (ibid. 214–15,
in 'A Post-Hegelian Philosophy of Religion,' and see 1984: 15–16, in
'Questionnaire'). Though sin is totally unintelligible in Lonergan's doctrine, he makes the remark in 'Consciousness and the Trinity' that as
matter is intelligible only in form, so the social surd is intelligible only in
the dialectic (1963: 7). Interestingly, 'surd' does not occur in *Method in
Theology*. (See also note *h* to lecture 10 above, on the false fact.)
b [383] **Historical Knowledge:** Lonergan's *Method* will distinguish sharply
between historical experience and historical knowledge (1972: 181),
but that distinction is not operative here. (See also note *e* to lecture 4
above, note *f* to lecture 10, note *h* to discussion 3.)
c [386] **the cart before the horse:** earlier in the same year Lonergan saw
the objection in another image, 'If Aquinas had things right side up ...
then I have turned everything upside down' (1988: 142, in the 1958
paper '*Insight*: Preface to a Discussion'); in his philosophic language,

the difference is between knowing through intelligent grasp and reasonable affirmation, and knowing prior to all questions for understanding
and reflection, by 'taking a look' (see note *i* to lecture 1 above). – The
phrase 'people who know by taking a look' is of course ironic; they
think that is the way they know, for there is a difference between knowing
and knowing what our knowing is: 'it is difficult to know what our
knowing is ... But ... our knowing is prior to an analysis of knowledge
and far easier than it' (1957a: 683).

Works of Lonergan Referred to in Editorial Notes

We list here only those works of Lonergan that are referred to in the Editorial Notes above. Some of them are published, some are in the semipublished state of notes issued for students (in italics here), some are not published in any sense (in roman type here), but all are available in the Library and/or Archives of the Lonergan Research Institute, Toronto. We have indicated the number (anticipated or actual) for volumes appearing in the Collected Works (CWL).

1928a 'The Form of Mathematical Inference.' *Blandyke Papers*, No. 283 (January), 126–37 (CWL 17).

1928b 'The Syllogism.' Ibid. No. 285 (March), 33–64 (CWL 17).

1935 Pantôn Anakephalaiôsis: A Theory of Human Solidarity, A Metaphysic for the Interpretation of St Paul, A Theology for the Social Order, Catholic Action, And the Kingship of Christ, in incipient outline. Lonergan Archives paper (in 'File 713 History') dated 'Dominica in Albis' [= April 28].

1940 *'GRATIA OPERANS: A Study of the Speculative Development in the Writings of St. Thomas of Aquin.'* S.T.D. thesis, Gregorian University, Rome (CWL volume not determined). Rewritten form: see 1971a.

1941 'The Mystical Body and the Sacraments.' *The Canadian League* (The Catholic Women's League of Canada), March, 8–10, 32 (CWL 17).

1943a 'The Form of Inference.' *Thought* 18, 277–92 (CWL 4).

1943b Review of Harry M. Cassidy, *Social Security and Reconstruction, in Canada. The Canadian Register* (Quebec edition), April 10, 1943, p. 5 (CWL 17).

1944 An Essay in Circulation Analysis. Collège de l'Immaculée-Conception, Montreal. Unpublished typescript, 129 p. Title added from later 'editions.' Place and date of writing presumed (CWL 15).

1946 *De ente supernaturali: Supplementum schematicum.* Notes for students, Collège de l'Immaculée-Conception, Montreal (CWL 16).

1947a 'The Concept of *Verbum* in the Writings of St. Thomas Aquinas' (second of five articles). *Theological Studies* 8, 35–79 (CWL 2).

1947b 'The Concept of *Verbum* in the Writings of St. Thomas Aquinas' (third of five articles). Ibid. 404–44 (CWL 2).

1951a Intelligence and Reality. Notes for lectures at the Thomas More Institute, Montreal, March–May (dates given in CWL 4, 314 are to be corrected [CWL 21]).

1951b The Mystical Body of Christ. Unpublished typescript of conference to the religious community of Christ the King (Regis) College, Toronto, November (CWL 17).

1952a De conscientia Christi. Notes for students, Christ the King (Regis) College, Toronto, fall semester (CWL 16).

1952b Insight. Lectures at Christ the King (Regis) College, Toronto, November 1952 to April 1953. (On the book then in preparation; the Archives have notes taken by Thomas O'D. Hanley.)

1953 *De ratione convenientiae eiusque radice, de excellentia ordinis, de signis rationis systematice et universaliter ordinatis, denique de convenientia, contingentia, et fine incarnationis: Supplementum schematicum.* Notes for students, Gregorian University (CWL 6).

1956 *De constitutione Christi ontologica et psychologica supplementum confecit Bernardus Lonergan, s.i.* Rome: Gregorian University Press (CWL 7).

1957a *Insight: A Study of Human Understanding.* London: Longmans, Green and Co. (CWL 3).

1957b *Divinarum personarum conceptionem analogicam evolvit Bernardus Lonergan, s.i.* Rome: Gregorian University Press (CWL 9).

1957c Mathematical Logic. Notes for lectures, Boston College (CWL 18).

1957d Existentialism. Notes for lectures, Boston College (our references from counting pages in typescript made at Thomas More Institute, Montreal [CWL 18]).

1958 The Nature of Knowledge in the Natural Sciences. Notes for a lecture at Marquette University, Milwaukee, July 7.

1959a *De intellectu et methodo.* Notes taken by students and corrected by Lonergan of theology course, Gregorian University (CWL 19).

1959b The Philosophy of Education. Lectures at Xavier University, Cincinnati, August 3–14. There is an edited transcription, made by James Quinn and John Quinn (1979), of the tape-recording. A new edition of the lectures will appear under the title *Topics in Education* (CWL 10).

1960 The Philosophy of History. Lecture at Thomas More Institute, Montreal, September 23. Transcription of tape-recording (CWL 6).

1963 Consciousness and the Trinity. Lecture at the North American College, Rome, January 20. Transcription of tape-recording (CWL 6).

1964a *De Deo trino*. Vols. 1 (2nd ed.), 2 (3rd ed.). Rome: Gregorian University Press (CWL 9).

1964b *De Verbo incarnato* (3rd ed.). Rome: Gregorian University Press (CWL 8).

1967a *Verbum: Word and Idea in Aquinas* (ed. David B. Burrell). Notre Dame: University of Notre Dame Press (CWL 2).

1967b 'Theories of Inquiry: Responses to a Symposium.' American Catholic Philosophical Association convention, March 28–29, published in the *Proceedings*; reprint: see 1974 below (CWL 11).

1967c The General Character of the Natural Theology of *Insight*. Lecture at the University of Chicago Divinity School, March (CWL 14).

1968 *The Subject*. The Aquinas Lecture, Marquette University, March 3. Reprint: see 1974 below (CWL 11).

1971a *Grace and Freedom: Operative Grace in the Thought of St. Thomas Aquinas* (ed. J. Patout Burns). London: Darton, Longman & Todd. Rewritten form of 1940 above (CWL 1).

1971b Method in Theology. Lectures on the book of that title. Milltown Park, Dublin, August 2–14. Transcript of tape-recording.

1972 *Method in Theology*. London: Darton, Longman & Todd (CWL 12).

1973a *De ente supernaturali: Supplementum schematicum*. Revised edition of 1946 above. Toronto: Regis College (CWL 16).

1973b *Philosophy of God, and Theology: The Relationship between Philosophy of God and the Functional Specialty, Systematics*. London: Darton, Longman & Todd (CWL 14).

1973c Insight. Notes for a lecture on the book of that title, University of Guelph, November 27.

1974 *A Second Collection: Papers by Bernard J.F. Lonergan, S.J.* (ed. William F.J. Ryan and Bernard J. Tyrrell). London: Darton, Longman & Todd (CWL 11).

1976 *The Way to Nicea: The Dialectical Development of Trinitarian Theology* (A translation by Conn O'Donovan from the first part of *De Deo trino*). London: Darton, Longman & Todd (CWL 9).

1977 *The Question as Commitment: A Symposium*. Ed. Elaine Cahn and Cathleen Going. Montreal: Thomas More Institute Papers/77.

1982 *Caring about Meaning: patterns in the life of Bernard Lonergan*. Ed. Pierrot Lambert, Charlote Tansey, Cathleen Going. Montreal: Thomas More Institute Papers/82.

1984 'Questionnaire on Philosophy.' *METHOD: Journal of Lonergan Studies* 2/2, 1–35 (CWL 14).

1985a 'The *Gratia Operans* Dissertation: Preface and Introduction.' Ibid. 3/2, 9–49. Excerpt from 1940 above (CWL volume not determined).

1985b *A Third Collection: Papers by Bernard J.F. Lonergan, S.J.* (ed. Frederick E. Crowe). New York: Paulist (CWL 13).

1985c 'The Original Preface of *INSIGHT.*' *METHOD: Journal of Lonergan Studies* 3/1, 3–7 (CWL 3).

1988 *Collection* (2nd ed.). Ed. Frederick E. Crowe and Robert M. Doran. Toronto: University of Toronto Press (CWL 4).

Index of Lectures and Discussions

and agent intellect, 209; and cognitional process, 133, 134, 137, 150, 163, 164, 167, 271, 295; and concept, 62; free, 109 n. 4, 136, 174–75, 219, 314–15; and geometry, 23, 24, 55–56, 61, 62, 296; and the given, 174–76; and insight, 24, 25, 26, 27 & n. 23, 30–31, 34, 36, 42, 61, 62, 136, 165–68, 174–75, 216, 296, 314–15; as object, 165–68; significance of, 216–19; symbolic, 83. *See also* Diagram; Phantasm; Symbolism

Imagination, 25, 36, 61, 62, 92, 137, 140, 145, 146, 147, 148, 189, 191–92, 202–203, 212, 286, 342, 345, 352, 358 & n. 20; and concepts, 62

Immanent, 63, 89, 145, 148, 170, 175, 225, 228, 233, 345; intelligibility, 60, 61, 74 n. 17 (immanent/projected, 335–37); norms, 174; structure, 120

Immanentism, 180 n. 24

Immortality, 183

Imperative, 232–33

Implicit/Explicit: *see* Definition, nominal ... ; Ideal of knowledge, implicit; Metaphysics, as explicit/implicit

Incarnation, 210–11, 267, 279, 375, 377, 380–81

Individualism, 267, 378, 379

Induction, 7, 289–90

Infallible, 174, 194, 261, 351

Inferences, 157, 164. *See also* Conclusions

Infinity, 74, 82, 120, 130, 255–56, 275, 295, 311, 332, 338, 375, 390

Innate, 5, 13, 14, 189, 266

Inquiry, 35, 134, 135, 137, 139, 142, 145, 151, 154, 156, 162, 167, 166–69, 171, 173–74, 181, 189, 192, 196, 365; and cognitional process, 36, 47,

53–54, 59–60, 62–69, 80, 83, 109 & n. 4, 111, 131, 134, 151, 167, 169, 170, 196, 206, 274; and empirical presentations, 35, 36, 47, 109, 137, 142, 163–64, 165, 169, 176; and heuristic structure, 64–65, 196; as *intentio entis*, 166; as intellectual alertness, 36, 299–300; paradox of, 64 n. 5; and related terms, 47–48, 59, 109 & n. 4, 111, 131, 299–300. *See also* Heuristic; Questions; Reflection; Wonder

Insight(s), 14, 17–19, 21–32, 35, 36, 44–45, 48–56, 57–58, 60–72, 76, 89, 90–93, 97 n. 8, 103, 105, 108, 115, 119, 122, 123, 125, 131, 133, 134, 136, 137–38, 142, 143, 145, 150, 165–66, 169–70, 174, 198, 199 n. 25, 203–206, 213, 214, 235, 236, 238, 239, 240, 257–61, 265, 268, 269–70, 272 n. 30, 274, 275, 276, 278, 282, 283, 284–85, 287, 290, 296, 303, 313–15, 322, 327 n. 25, 351, 353, 354, 357–60, 378, 393; act of, 21–32, 257–59, 393; advertence to, 17, 19, 27, 32, 274, 289; analogy of, to data, 202–203, 204; anticipation of, 65–69, 80; apes and 'insight', 313–15; and Aristotle, 18, 29–30, 31, 48–52, 119, 199 n. 25, 213, 238, 268, 290; in art, 290–93; artistic expression of, 38–39, 283, 290–93; and being, 152, 154, 167–70, 303; casual, 25–26, 26 n. 21, 31, 49, 281; cluster of, 52–54, 55, 89, 90, 122, 178, 235, 275, 308, 379, 380, 384; and cognitional process, 53, 59–60, 62–69, 80, 83, 109 & n. 4, 133, 151, 163–64, 169–70, 274, 302; and common sense, 39–40, 88–93, 97 n. 8, 274–75, 304–306, 313–15, 322; communicating, 44–45, 48–52, 49 n. 25, 119; and computer, 25 n. 19, 26 n.

Considering; Inquiry; Insight;
Judgment; Supposition;
Understanding
Thomas Aquinas, St, 9–10, 18–19, 27 &
n. 23, 31, 33, 53–54, 57–58, 95–96,
113, 114, 123, 146 n. 9, 148, 155,
160–63, 165 & n. 11, 168, 184, 203 n.
6, 208, 209, 210, 213, 214, 219, 223,
230, 239, 240–41, 265–66, 268, 276,
277, 280–81, 282, 283, 293–94, 302,
312 & n. 9, 313 & nn. 12–13, 326,
330–31, 332–33, 350, 351–52 & n. 16,
357–359 & n. 30, 366–67, 383, 389–90
- Works cited: *Commentary on the Sentences*, 210; *De veritate*, 332, 333 n.
33; *In xii metaph.*, 238; *Quaestio
disputata De anima*, 165 & n. 11;
Sententia libri metaphysicae, 203 n. 6;
Summa contra Gentiles, 53 & n. 33,
162 & n. 9, 210; *Summa theologiae*, 9
& n. 6, 10, 18 n. 11, 27 n. 23, 53 &
n. 33, 146 n. 9, 148 n. 10, 162 & n. 9,
209 n. 12, 210, 230 n. 5, 241 nn.
15–17, 312 n. 9, 313 nn. 12–13, 326
n. 24, 330 n. 27, 332 & n. 32, 375 n.
7, 377 n. 12, 390 n. 23
Thomism, intelligence in contemporary, 19 n. 3, 357–59
Thucydides, 100
Time, 58, 104, 191–92, 204, 206, 217
To ti en einai, 51, 64, 213, 358
To ti estin, 51, 64
de Tonquédec, Josef, 177, 179
Topp, George, 327 n. 25
Tradition, 184, 261
Transcendental: being as, 148–49; ego,
138, 139; method of Kant, 30–31,
264; self, 271
Trent, Council of, 364
Trinitarian theory, 9–10, 113, 134 n. 3,
237, 282, 294, 333 n. 34, 358 & n. 30,
375, 376. *See also* God

Trobriand Islanders, 99–101
Truth, 14, 34 n.4, 74, 75, 84, 86, 92, 97,
102, 127, 136, 140, 148, 184, 207,
213–14, 219, 220, 241–42, 263–65,
271, 273, 279, 301, 318, 321, 327,
376–77; and absolute, 116–17, 118,
119; and definitions, 111; and fact,
319; and history, 237, 384–86; and
interpretation, 265–66; and judgment, 36, 107, 115, 117, 120, 126,
153, 171–72, 173, 176, 179, 182, 186,
187, 195, 242, 276–79, 336–37, 351,
362, 385; level of, 277–78, 291, 385;
metaphysics of a, 213; and object of
thought, 111; and objectivity,
171–72, 180; and similitude between
knowing and known, 240

Unconditioned, 120–21, 144–45; formally, 118, 134, 155, 208, 239, 242,
246; grasping the, 134, 135, 136, 137,
138, 140, 143, 150, 151, 159, 164,
168–69, 171, 172, 173, 179, 193, 206,
207, 209, 232–33, 239, 340, 346, 351;
virtually, 118–20, 121, 125, 126–31,
134, 150, 155, 169, 171, 172–73, 174,
176, 206, 207, 208, 209, 239, 244, 264,
340, 346, 351, 355, 391
Unconscious, 4, 15, 135, 149–51
Understanding, 5, 17, 29, 53–54, 70,
72, 75, 103, 110, 134–41, 144, 150–51,
154, 161, 171, 178, 179, 180 n. 24,
184, 193, 205–206, 207, 213, 215, 218,
219–21, 222–24, 262–63, 273, 294–97,
332, 333, 351–52, 362; and
abstraction, 41–43; acts of, 34, 43,
93, 159, 162, 165 n. 12, 196, 198, 208,
209, 210, 238, 239, 240, 246, 329,
330–33, 345, 358, 359, 366; actually,
34, 165, 208, 241, 348; analogous,
201–203; anticipating, 80, 196, 198,
214, 217; and being, 148, 151, 153,

van der Waals, J.D., 129
de Waelhens, Alphonse, 289 n. 10
Welt, 182, 183, 184, 185
Western culture and the scientific
  ideal, 301–302
What/Why?, 29, 32, 50–52, 64–65, 88,
  111, 133
White, Victor, 373 & n. 6
Whitehead, Alfred North, 10 & n. 27,
  65, 254, 255 & n. 6, 262, 301 & n. 17,
  302, 343
Whole: greater than part, 168; 'I' as,
  211 & n. 16; and metaphysics, 191,
  216; proportionate being as, 224;
  unity in, 211, 212. *See also* Unity-
  Identity-Whole
Will, willing, 9, 212, 219, 227, 228,
  229–30, 231–32, 317, 359, 366, 376,
  380; and freedom, 226–29, 230–32,
  366, 380; God's, 374–77; and image,
  217–19; potency, form, and act in,
  229–32, 380
Willingness, 227, 229–31

Wisdom, 91, 155, 161, 209, 223, 309,
  313; God's, 374–77, 383
Wolff, Christian, 11, 20, 35, 187, 264
Wonder, 142, 164, 189, 303; of agent
  intellect, 209, 295–96, 300; and final-
  ity, 150–54, 167; and seeking
  knowledge, 5, 36, 47, 163, 297,
  299–300, 302
Word(s), 14, 32, 36, 45, 110, 114, 127,
  134 n. 3, 214–15, 217, 218, 268, 284.
  See also Language
World: evil in, 333–34, 374–76; not
  completely intelligible, 242–46; 'this'
  vs. possible w., 383. *See also*
  Concern; Horizon; 'I' and my w.;
  Order; Real; *Sorge*, w. of; Universe;
  Welt
Wren-Lewis, John, 258 n. 13
Wulftange, Joseph, 254 & n. 5

'X' and heuristic structure, 63–65, 196,
  197, 202

The *Collected Works of*

Bernard Lonergan

was designed by

ANTJE LINGNER

University of

Toronto Press